P9-DDU-214

A Quiet Revolution

A Quiet Revolution

The Veil's Resurgence, from the Middle East to America

• LEILA AHMED •

Yale UNIVERSITY PRESS New Haven and London

Published with assistance from the foundation established in memory of Philip Hamilton McMillan of the Class of 1894, Yale College.

Yale University Press books may be purchased in quantity for educational, business, or promotional use. For information, please e-mail sales.press@yale.edu (U.S. office) or sales@yaleup.co.uk (U.K. office).

Set in Minion type by Vonda's Comp Services.
Printed in the United States of America.

Library of Congress Cataloging-in-Publication Data
Ahmed, Leila.
A quiet revolution : the veil's resurgence, from the Middle East to America / Leila Ahmed.
p. cm.
Includes bibliographical references and index.
ISBN 978-0-300-17095-5 (cloth : alk. paper) 1. Hijab (Islamic clothing)—Middle East. 2. Hijab (Islamic clothing)—United States. 3. Veils—Middle East. 4. Veils—United States. 5. Muslim women—Clothing—Middle East. 6. Muslim women—Clothing—United States. I. Title.
BP190.5.H44A46 2011
297.5′76—dc22 2010049535

A catalogue record for this book is available from the British Library.

This paper meets the requirements of ANSI/NISO Z39.48-1992 (Permanence of Paper).

10 9 8 7 6 5 4 3 2 1

Contents

Acknowledgments

First of all, I would like to thank the Ford Foundation for a generous grant in support of my research for this book, and particular thanks are due Constance H. Buchanan for her steadfast support and patience. My thanks also to Ike Williams and to the always cheery Katherine Flynn at Kneerim and Williams Agency for their enthusiastic efforts on my behalf. Thanks also to the anonymous readers at Yale University Press, and also at Columbia University Press, for their generous readings of my manuscript and for their invaluable comments and suggestions. Many thanks, too, to the entire production team at Yale University Press, with special thanks to Heidi Downey, senior manuscript editor, for her wonderfully precise and exacting copyediting, which greatly improved my manuscript. I had the good fortune of having Jennifer Banks, senior editor at Yale University Press, as my editor. Jennifer took a keen interest in the project from early on, and her reading of the completed manuscript, at once enthusiastic and incisive, proved enormously helpful in enabling me to bring my arguments into sharper focus in the final reworking of the text. I owe her very special thanks.

I have worked on this book for many years, and thanks are due many, many others, far more than I can name, among them the women, many of them students, who kindly gave of their time in agreeing to be interviewed, and the women and men whose writings and activism I have had the privilege of observing, following, and describing in these pages. My enormous indebtedness to other scholars in the field—predecessors, contemporaries, and colleagues—is evident throughout the book. I am very grateful also to students and colleagues here at Harvard, where I have had the extraordinary privilege of participating in conversations both in the classroom and beyond that have stimulated and enriched my thinking beyond measure. Numerous conversations, exchanges, and consultations through the years with colleagues both at Harvard and in the wider Boston community have been illuminating and helpful. I would like to mention Kecia Ali, Ali Asani, Dorothy Austin, Ann Braude, Bernadette Brooten, David Carrasco, Nancy Cott, Maria-Pia Di Bella, Diana Eck, Janet Gyatso, Shahla Haeri, Charlie Hallisey, Karen King, Michael Jackson, Baber Johansen, Roy Mottahedeh, Afsaneh Najmabadi, Jacob Olupona, Diana Rowan Rockfeller, Elizabeth Schussler Fiorenza, Jane Smith, and Malika Zeghal. Throughout, Karen Armstrong, a frequent visitor, has been a cherished friend and an extraordinary and wonderful interlocutor.

I am very grateful also for the leaves that enabled me to complete this book, and to William A. Graham, dean of the Harvard Divinity School, for his supportiveness throughout.

Finally, I am enormously grateful to family and friends for their support and patience through the years of my work on this project.

Introduction

I recall a particular evening a few months after I moved to Cambridge as one of those moments that was at the genesis of this book. After an early dinner with a friend who was visiting from the Arab world—a well-known feminist of Muslim background whom I will call Aisha—we were taking a leisurely stroll back to her hotel. Rounding a corner, we came to a spontaneous halt at the sight of a crowd gathered on the Cambridge Common, evidently enjoying a private event or celebration. What was arresting was that all the women were in hijab—the veil or head covering that some Muslim women wear. This was in the late 1990s, when the hijab was much less common than it is today in America. Seeing a public gathering of forty to fifty people, among whom all the women were in hijab, was still exceedingly rare. In fact, this may have been the first time I had seen such a gathering in America.

"To them," said Aisha as we stood observing the scene, "*we* are the enemy. That's how they see us, all of us, people like us, feminists, progressives. That's just how it is." She spoke ruminatively, as if resuming a conversation, which in a way she was. I understood at once of course whom she meant by "them": Muslims who wore or required the wearing of hijab. "We can't ignore that," she continued, "or simply pretend it isn't so. And anyway they *are* our enemies. They threaten us, ban our books or try to, oppose everything we stand for. That's just how it is."

It was one of those lovely, long summer evenings, a perfect sliver of moon in the deep sky. The Islamic calendar being a lunar one, I wondered for a moment whether the group had gathered in connection with a significant date or feast, but I couldn't think of anything, nor could Aisha. In the Muslim-majority countries in which we had both grown up, one didn't have to make a special effort to know where we were exactly in the Islamic calendar since its significant dates and feast days were ordinarily marked and celebrated by the broader society. But here we lived our lives by other times and other calendars, and special dates and feasts typically slipped by unremarked and unremembered. Even discovering when Ramadan was (in those pre-internet days) required special effort and research. Today, astonishingly to some of us, the Empire State Building is lit green to mark the month of Ramadan.

"And now," said Aisha, as we resumed our walk, the twilight now perceptibly closing in, "our own friends defend them. And what's worse," she went on, "as we were saying, they're right to do so. This is what they have to do in this country, defend minorities, defend people's right to be different. That's why we love their societies. That's why we want to be like them."

We had gone back and forth many times on this subject through the past few days, over coffee and tea and the meals we had shared. This was a new and different time for us, posing new questions in the field of women and Islam, in which we both worked. When we began working on the subject in the 1970s there had been neither a Muslim immigrant "problem" in Europe, as was brewing now, nor was fear of Islam and Muslims in connection with terrorism even an issue. Both of these had begun to become issues mostly in the 1990s. In France the subject of women and Islam and the veil in particular were emerging as highly politicized issues in the fierce national debates under way around immigration policies, and they were topics that were often invoked in particular by the Right, who were in favor of restricting immigration. How, we wondered, would these winds of change complicate our subject even further, and how would this affect our work?

I have not seen Aisha since that time. She used to visit the United States quite often but now no longer does so. When she was invited to a conference here some years back, soon after we had embarked on our wars with Afghanistan and Iraq, she wrote to say that she and many other intellectuals in her country had decided to suspend their visits to the United States so long as the wars continued.

She has not published anything on women and Islam since.

Many Americans and Europeans, in the 1990s and today, assume that some Muslim women wear hijab simply because they are observant Muslims. Wearing hijab, they assume, is just what devout, observant Muslims do. But for Aisha and myself, the hijab's presence meant not just piety—for we both knew many women in our home societies who were deeply devout yet never wore hijab. Rather, to us it plainly signaled the presence of Islamism: a particular and very political form of Islam that had been gaining ground in Muslim societies since the Islamic Resurgence of the 1970s, a resurgence significantly fueled by the activities of the Muslim Brotherhood.

Thus for us the hijab had meanings that it did not have for most Americans and even perhaps for many among the younger generations in our home societies—essentially because of the history we had ourselves directly lived and witnessed. This was history that we knew viscerally, in our memory and in the pulse of our being. For myself, for example, having grown up in Cairo in the 1940s, the hijab that I was seeing now in America, in its looks and style, powerfully evoked the hijab I recalled seeing in childhood worn by the women of the Muslim Brotherhood—and only by the women of the Muslim Brotherhood. It was a different kind of hijab from the traditional sorts that one might occasionally see at that time, albeit by the forties and fifties quite rarely, on the streets of Cairo.

So for me the sight of women in hijab now in America—in styles directly reminiscent of the hijabs of the Muslim Brotherhood—was an arresting and, frankly, given my memories of the Brotherhood, a disturbing sight: disturbing in any case if it was part of a growing trend, which, by the late nineties, it distinctly appeared to be.

My memories of the Muslim Brotherhood also dated back to childhood. They included a strong if vague impression of them as people who bombed places, including cinemas—a memorable detail for me since I enjoyed going to the movies. But most particularly I remember the

Brotherhood for the assassination of Nuqrashi Pasha, prime minister of Egypt. His death cast a tremendous pall over our home, as he was also a friend of my father's. Needless to say, this was not a home in which the Brotherhood and its goals and actions were viewed with even the slightest sympathy. The Brotherhood women's style of veil remained for me forever charged with these negative associations and memories. Its style was distinctive enough to cause me to ask, as a child, "Why are they dressed like that?" Because, was the answer, they are women of the Muslim Brotherhood.

I left Egypt in the late 1960s, by which time the Muslim Brotherhood had almost disappeared, many members having gone into hiding or fled the country because of the Nasser regime's systematic attempt to eradicate the group. In the late 1960s hardly anyone in such cities as Cairo or Alexandria wore hijab.

By the later 1990s other events were fueling my sense of wariness and unease with respect to the hijab's spread—and its incipient spread seemingly now even to the West. By this time the Islamic Resurgence had made extraordinary gains across Egyptian society. Even by the early 1990s, seemingly in direct correlation with the gains of the Resurgence, an escalating number of acts of militant Islamic violence were occurring in the country in a growing atmosphere of intellectual repression.

Just following the news coming out of Egypt was disturbing. In 1992 a well-known journalist, Farah Foda, a critic of Islamism, was murdered. The following year Nasr Hamid Abu Zayd, a professor at Cairo University, was tried on the grounds that he was an apostate. He was declared guilty and had to flee the country with his wife. In 1994 Naguib Mahfouz, the Egyptian novelist and Nobel laureate, was stabbed, and, although he survived, he was seriously injured. Mahfouz was in his eighties at the time, and his novels had been appearing freely in Egypt since the 1940s. The attack—by an Islamist on the grounds that Mahfouz's works were blasphemous—seemed a shocking gauge of the country's drastic descent into intolerance with the spread of Islamism and always, along with it, its signature dress, the hijab.

Through the 1990s the life of my colleague Nawal el-Saadawi, an Egyptian feminist, was repeatedly threatened by Islamists. Then, in 1997, an Islamist group perpetrated a horrific massacre at the temple of Hatshepsut (the only woman in ancient Egypt to rule as pharaoh) in Luxor, killing fifty-eight tourists. I was not at the time making a study of the veil's resurgence or of these events, but cumulatively such news seemed reason enough to make one exceedingly wary about the spread of the hijab as part of a trend now also growing in the West.

All of this then, and the possibilities, fears, and questions that these associations opened up for me, were instantly brought to mind by the sight of this distinctively modern-looking hijab. At some point in the ensuing months, as I continued to think over the questions that the hijab's presence inevitably raised for me (and always paying attention now when I saw women in hijab in the street or in the malls or in Harvard Yard—women who were, strikingly, almost always young), I found my questions growing more and more compelling. What history was this that I was living through and witness to? Was some kind of extremist, militant Islam taking root in the West, including in the United States? Was that what the presence of the hijab signified? Could the Muslim Brotherhood have somehow managed to establish a foothold here and in other Western countries? Where were these young women getting their ideas that they should wear hijab? And, most intriguingly, since they lived in a free country where it was quite ordinary for women to challenge patriarchal ideas, why on earth did they feel bound to accept whatever it was that they were being told?

I soon learned from my readings of various studies of Muslims in America, among them Jane Smith's book *Islam in America,* that the Muslim Brotherhood and other Islamist groups had indeed played key roles in the founding of many prominent Muslim American organizations, among them the Muslim Student Association (MSA) and the Islamic Society of North America (ISNA).[1] To get a sense of what was happening as this evidently Islamist form of Islam gained dominance in America and elsewhere in the West, I began visiting mosques and listening to sermons, I interviewed women who wore hijab, and I began to attend the open meetings of major Muslim American organizations, including ISNA.

My on-the-ground research confirmed what I had learned from my readings, but it also opened up new questions. The first time I attended Friday congregational prayers at a local mosque I found myself listening to an impassioned sermon delivered in praise of "the Martyr" (al-shaheed) Hasan al-Banna. Al-Banna, founder of the Muslim Brotherhood, had been killed ("martyred"), probably by Egyptian government agents in 1949 in retaliation for the murder of Nuqrashi Pasha. Praising al-Banna in particular for his stand against Western imperialism, the preacher delivered his address in the vehement Arabic anti-imperialist rhetoric familiar to me from my youth. I had not heard such speech since I left Egypt. I could not help wondering as I listened—we had already had, after all, the 1993 bombing of the World Trade Center—whether the CIA was paying attention to such mosques and sermons.

At the same time, my experiences at the mosque that day also led to new conundrums. I had listened to the sermon in the basement room assigned to the women members of the congregation, while the men occupied the main hall upstairs. The majority of the women were almost certainly not Arabic-speakers: many were dressed in the styles of South Asia, and some, as I could tell from their greetings and exchanges, were African American. One or two were Caucasian American, and three or four or so appeared to be Arab. During the sermon, which was in Arabic, most of the women had sat seemingly lost in thought—a natural enough response if they did not know the language. Others were keeping a watchful eye on their children, who ran in and out of the adjoining playroom or came to sit beside their mothers on the somewhat dingy beige-carpeted floor.

Since I seemed to be one of the very few people in the room who actually understood what the preacher was saying, it clearly was not the sermon that drew these women to attend mosque. Nor could one assume that the women attending this mosque—or any mosque—necessarily shared the political interests or even the broad general and presumably Islamist goals and commitments of the mosque's officials. Understanding what brought women to this mosque, and what *their* goals and interests were in attending mosque, would clearly entail careful observation well beyond just listening to sermons.

Besides specific questions such as these that were posed for me by what I was observing, there was always also the nagging question of why Islamism and veiling were apparently continuing to gain ground. Was that a sign of growing anti-Western feelings among Western Muslims?

What kind of Islam was this, exactly, that was gaining ground here, and how had it gained institutional dominance? And how would it evolve and develop in American society? Would it move toward blending and accommodation, or were we heading toward clash and collision?[2]

My first impressions of ISNA's conventions similarly confirmed my worst expectations even as they opened up new questions. Even though I knew of the Islamist foundations of the organization, I was still startled to see, as I arrived at the Convention Center amid a vast sea of people, that apparently every single female head was covered. It was hard to believe that I was in Chicago and not, say, in Saudi Arabia or Iran, although the scene was too colorful for either of those places, in particular because of the wonderfully vivid dress of the South Asian women. I think that I had expected, since we were, after all, in America, that there would be some women defying the hijab rule. But as far as I could see, mine was the sole uncovered female head in sight—a situation I quickly remedied with the scarf I had brought along "just in case." As an outsider and observer I obviously did not want to stand out.

Everything else about ISNA and the entire spectacle of the convention confirmed what the veil seemed to imply: that male dominance and gender hierarchy and separation were the ground rules here. Seating was gender segregated, and doorways, wherever possible, were gender segregated as well: one set of the double doors into the main auditorium was marked "women only," and the other was left unmarked. Young people manned the doors and firmly redirected one to the appropriate door should one approach the wrong one, even if no one else was passing through and there was no chance whatsoever of breaking the taboo of improper contact—that is, any physical contact—between the sexes. Overwhelmingly, too, it was men who were the speakers at most of the panels and plenary sessions. But there were some women speakers, and there were even a couple of heavily covered women—clad in long, loose robes and strictly concealing hijabs—who appeared on the podium as members of ISNA's predominantly male board. There were also panels—often made up of female speakers addressing "women's" issues, among them divorce and domestic violence—which presented viewpoints that sometimes seemed "feminist," or as much so as those I had heard voiced by conservative women of other religious traditions, Christian and Jewish, for example.[3] There was evidently ground here for further observation.

Even my interviews with young women who wore hijab prompted more questions. For example, one young woman, an African American, told me that she wore hijab as a way of calling for gender justice. "When people stare at me when I am on the T," she said (the T is the Boston underground transport system), "I find myself thinking that if there's just one woman out there who begins to wonder when she looks at me why she dresses the way she does and begins to notice the sexism of our society—if I've raised just one person's consciousness, that's good enough for me." Another interviewee told me that she wore it as a way of calling for justice for minorities. Of Arab-Caucasian descent and a convert to Islam, she explained that she wore hijab "for the same reason as some of my Jewish friends wear a yarmulke: as a way of openly identifying with a group that people have prejudices about and as a way of saying 'yes, we're here, and we have the right to be here and to be treated equally.'"[4]

By what means, I wondered, had this emblem supposedly of Islamic patriarchy and oppression of women emerged today in America as an emblem of a call for justice, and even for gender-justice, no less? I would eventually find an answer to this question—most directly in the details around the reemergence of the veil in the first place in the Middle East, and in the new meanings of the veil that began to be hammered out there, specifically in Egypt, in the 1970s and 1980s.

For, as I pursued my research on what was happening with Islamism and women and the veil in America (while also always following developments around the veil and Islam in Europe) I had simultaneously begun researching the story of the veil's resurgence, from the time of its emergence in the Middle East to its spread to the West. Why, after nearly disappearing from many Middle Eastern and Muslim-majority societies, had the veil made a comeback, and how had it spread with such remarkable swiftness?

The veil had reappeared during the Islamic Resurgence, a resurgence spurred into being in the 1970s by a variety of forces, among them, most importantly, the Muslim Brotherhood, an organization today considered a major force in the history of Islam globally. As Fawaz Gerges, a prominent expert on Islamic movements, wrote, the Brotherhood is today the "most powerfully organized movement in the world of Islam."[5]

Often referred to in Arabic as "al-Sawha al-Islamiyya," the Islamic Awakening, or simply as al-Sawha, the Awakening, the Islamic Resurgence brought into being the form of Islam now most commonly referred to in English as "Islamism." In the early 1990s this term began to replace other terms—among them "fundamentalism," "radical" Islam, "political" Islam, and Salafism—which had all been used to refer to various aspects of the Islamic Resurgence and the spectrum, or "continuum of movements" it comprehended, some radically militant while others, by far the majority, moderate and nonmilitant.[6] The attribute all Islamists share, as Azza Karam wrote in her work on Islamism, is the commitment to the "quintessentially political agenda" of Islamizing society. The "sine qua non of being an Islamist," she notes, is that of being actively engaged in the work of bringing about social and political change in society—people and structures of government. To be an Islamist, she continues, "it is by no means sufficient to be a Muslim." Rather, "an Islamist must be committed to active engagement in the quest for a more Islamic and just society. All Islamists will share this ultimate aim."[7]

How and why had women come to be drawn to this movement, and how and why had they been persuaded to adopt the veil, first in the Middle East and then globally? What was in it for women? What exactly *was* Islamism from the point of view of women? There were a host of further questions, too. For example, what role, if any, had women themselves played in the Islamist movement and in spreading the resurgence of Islamism and the veil? As I would discover—and as I describe in the following pages—women had in fact been and continued to be key participants in the movement. Indeed, one woman, Zainab al-Ghazali, had been of such importance to the Muslim Brotherhood and the Islamic Resurgence that she is viewed by some today as the "unsung mother" of the Muslim Brotherhood.[8] Other questions that I pursued included men's views of women's roles in the movement, and what men's roles had been in strategizing around women's involvement, as well as around methods of spreading the veil. All of these and more were key questions for which we had no answers. There had been a number of studies on the veil's resurgence, primarily in Egypt and Turkey, but there was no work that I knew of bringing such findings together and piecing together and filling out the story of the veil's resurgence and onward spread in the Middle East and now in the West, and that also explored the subject's complexity and its local and global implications.[9]

Telling the story of the veil's resurgence, along with that of Islamism, takes up Part 1 of this book. Specifically, I follow here the story of the emergence of the Islamist Resurgence and, along with it, of the veil, beginning in Egypt in the 1970s. Egypt, home of the Muslim Brotherhood, the model for and mother institution of Islamist organizations worldwide, was at the epicenter of the Resurgence. America, of course, where I pursue the story of the veil, is one of the most important Western societies to which Islamism has spread. Although I study Egypt and America specifically, the patterns and processes of the rise and spread of Islamism and the veil constitute, I believe, patterns that could be traced and replicated in relation to other Islamic and Western societies.

There is today of course a vast literature on Islamism and, in particular, on militant Islamism—a form of Islamism that, according to the experts, makes up no more than a "tiny minority" of the broad Islamist movement.[10] The narrative that I follow here in relation to Islamism differs from others in that it is focused specifically on women and Islamism and on the veil's return. If even among men it is only a "tiny minority" who are involved in militancy, overwhelmingly women's involvement in Islamism is of the nonmilitant variety.

Chapter 1 takes the 1950s as its starting point—the era when being unveiled and bareheaded had become the norm in the cities of Egypt, as well as in those of other Muslim-majority societies. Looking back from that vantage point, I recapitulate the debates around veiling that arose in the late nineteenth century in the era of British imperialism, debates that would give rise to the unveiling movement of the early twentieth century. This movement would sweep across Muslim societies through the first decades of that century almost as spectacularly as the veiling movement would spread in the closing decades of the same century. It is in these contentious debates of the imperial era and the unveiling movement they gave rise to that the seeds were sown for the veil's repeated reemergence since, often as a quintessential sign (among other things) of irresolvable tension and confrontation between Islam and the West. Understanding the dynamics and meanings with which these debates over the veil were charged is important to our understanding of why this garment continues to be such a volatile, sensitive, and politically fraught symbol today.

Chapter 2 presents an overview of the major developments in Egypt between the 1920s and the end of the 1960s, developments that would set the stage for the Islamic Resurgence. The following two chapters focus on the 1970s: the decade in which Islamism and the veil first made their forceful appearance. Drawing on contemporary accounts, these chapters reconstruct the story of the veil's reemergence as they recapitulate the explanations that women offered to interviewers as to why they had decided to veil. These chapters also describe the forces that came together in this decade—including the Muslim Brotherhood and forces supported by Saudi Arabia—to galvanize and bring into being the Islamic Resurgence and the return of the veil. The following two chapters continue to explore the veil's spread from the 1970s through the 1990s. Chapter 6 closes with an account of Islamism's and the veil's acceptance across the majority of Egyptian society—for by the end of the 1990s, Egypt had become a society in which the overwhelming majority of women were veiled.

Chapters 7 and 8 take up the story of the expansion and spread of Islamism and the veil to America. I describe the history of the founding of Muslim American organizations and follow the steady rise of Islamist-influenced organizations and their emergence in the 1990s to positions of dominance on the American Muslim landscape.

The 1960s marked the beginning of an era of growth in the Muslim population of America, the consequence of two key processes. One was the growing numbers of Muslim immigrants who began arriving in the United States following changes in immigration laws in 1965, changes that opened the doors to non-European immigrants. The other process was a suddenly rising rate of conversion to Islam among Americans and particularly African Americans, beginning in the 1960s. African Americans today make up it is thought about 40 percent of American Muslims, a population estimated at 4 million to 6 million. (Estimates suggest that Asian and Arab American Muslims, the two other largest groups, make up about 30 percent and 15 percent, respectively.) Islamism, as I describe in Chapter 7, began to take root in America through immigrant activism and also by way of international connections between Islamists and African American Muslims. I pursue the story of the development of Islamist organizations through the changing climate of the 1990s, following the 1993 bombing of the World Trade Center, and close Chapter 8 with the debates that began about Islam in America at the end of the 1990s, thus bringing us to the eve of the twenty-first century—and of the attacks of 9/11.

Over the course of the chapters making up Part I, I explore the objectives and motivations of Islamists, and the methods and strategies they deployed in their pursuit; Islamist notions about women and their proper roles; women's importance to the Islamist movement; and women's extensive and lively activism. Many of the questions that I posed earlier—how and why the veil has spread, why women had accepted it, why women were drawn to Islamism and came to serve among its footsoldiers and activists—steadily come to be answered.

The history of the rise and spread of Islamism and the veil in Egypt that I follow out in Part 1 often evokes and foreshadows—even down to the Egyptian government's attempt to ban the veil in schools as it sought to halt the spread of Islamism—events and happenings that a decade or two later also would begin to occur in the West. Consequently, this history of a state's attempt to control the spread of veiling and Islamism, played out in a Muslim-majority country, is potentially instructive also with respect to developments around Islamism and veiling that are under way today in the West.

Most importantly though, understanding what happened in Egypt, the country at the epicenter of the Islamist movement, and how in less than three decades Egyptian society was transformed from a majority unveiled, non-Islamist society to a majority veiled Islamist society, are essential to our informed analysis of what is happening today with women, Islamism, and the veil in the West. To attempt to understand developments under way today in the West in relation to women and the veil without knowledge of the legacies, commitments, and ideologies with which Islamism arrived in the West—commitments and ideologies hammered out in other countries with quite different social and political histories—would be like setting out to understand the first fifty years of Puritan history in America with little knowledge of who the Puritans were and how they differed, say, from Catholics and other Christians, and without knowledge of the social and political conditions that shaped the broad package of beliefs, commitments, and ideologies with which the Puritans arrived in the New World.

These legacies of the Islamic Resurgence and the beliefs, practices, and commitments of Islamism are fully and vibrantly alive today in America and elsewhere in the West. Islamism, a special and powerful form of Islam, is today inextricably part of the DNA of the dominant form of Islam in America—and indeed in the West. Consequently too, Islamism has already begun to become part of the very fabric and DNA of the West itself.

How would Islamism adapt to its new democratic environment, and how would it evolve and develop in relation to women in particular? Or would it perhaps fail to adapt, or even actively resist adapting to its new environment? Were we embarked on a course that would inevitably lead to clash and collision? Those questions are at the heart of Part II of this book, which is based on my ongoing observations of the issue of women and Islam and Islamism, specifically in America through the first decade of the twenty-first century.[11]

As it proved, this decade, inaugurated by the tragedy of 9/11—an act of violence committed in the name of Islam against America—would be one of the most eventful and volatile decades in modern history as regards relations between Islam and the West and specifically Islam and America. We plunged at once into wars with Afghanistan and Iraq, both Muslim-majority countries. In the United States, 9/11 set in motion a variety of responses, ranging from sporadic attacks on American Muslims —including attacks on women in hijab—to government actions and regulations subjecting Muslims to new levels of scrutiny and resulting in, among other things, the arrest of many Muslims and the closure of a number of Muslim charities.

All of these events directly or indirectly affected the lives of Muslims in America. In addition, in the aftermath of 9/11 the very subject of women in Islam would become a topic of intense public interest and even come to be regarded as a matter of national import. First Lady Laura Bush, for instance, broadcast a radio address presenting the issue of women in Afghanistan as one of integral importance to American security. "Civilized people throughout the world," she said, "are speaking out in horror—not only because our hearts break for the women and children of Afghanistan, but also because in Afghanistan we see the world the terrorists would like to impose on the rest of us. . . . The fight against terrorism is also a fight for the rights and dignity of women."[12] Two days later Cherie Blair, wife of the British prime minister Tony Blair, issued a similar statement, and these views were echoed and disseminated by the media, which were filled now with images of veils and particularly of the burkas of Afghanistan.[13] Taking their cue from the two first ladies, the media began to portray the war in Afghanistan as a righteous war by virtue of our concern to save the women. As the British journalist Polly Toynbee wrote, the burka became the "battle flag" and "shorthand moral justification" for the war in Afghanistan.[14]

In the context of this sudden public interest in the subject of women and Islam, a flurry of books on the topic appeared in Europe and America, among them Azar Nafisi's *Reading Lolita in Tehran* (2003), Irshad Manji's *The Trouble with Islam* (2004), and Ayaan Hirsi Ali's *Caged Virgin* (2006). These books captured a huge readership in Europe and America but they also triggered sharply critical analyses from academics.

It is still even today a rare week when some issue or other relating to women, Islam, and/or the hijab or burka does not make headlines in Western media. This broad public interest in the subject seems in turn to have energized religiously committed Muslim American women, precipitating them into active engagement with the topic of Islam and women's rights. In consequence, Islamic feminism in America is more lively today than at any other time in my own lifetime.

All of these conditions and developments collectively—be it the wave of anti-Muslim sentiments, the wars into which we plunged, and the emergence of the subject of women in Islam as a topic of national and public import—directly and indirectly affected the lives of Muslims in America and also critically shaped the trajectory of American Muslim feminist activism through this decade. Each of the three final chapters explores aspects of this lively and evolving scene. Chapter 9 focuses primarily on the changes under way in the broader society, on the issue of the hijab, and on the public conversation on women and Islam. Chapter 10 describes the developments I observed at ISNA, today the most prominent and influential organization on the Muslim American landscape, as I continued to attend its conventions. I present here too brief biographical sketches of some of ISNA's most prominent women.

In the final chapter I describe the lively activism that has been taking place among American Muslims around issues of women and gender. I conclude by drawing together my findings about women, Islam, and Islamism, and the new and unexpected trajectory that Islamism appears to be taking in the new democratic environment in which it is evolving.

The process of research and writing itself seems to quietly work almost always to dissolve one's most settled assumptions and to challenge and unravel no less entrenched presuppositions. Once more I found this to be the case as I worked on this book, even more sharply, perhaps, in this instance than in the past. My search for answers to the particular questions I set out with propelled me in the first place into investigating the history of the veil in Egypt, including through the decades when I had lived there myself. Setting out to revisit, as I assumed, a familiar history and one that was redolent with memories, I found myself instead exploring this history through narratives that were quite different from and even oppositional to the narrative of Egypt's history in which I had myself been embedded and which had largely shaped my personal and intellectual trajectory. Similarly in Part Two of the book, as I followed out how Islamism was evolving in America in our times, and in particular the new directions in which Islamist-influenced women appear to be taking Islam, I would find myself gathering evidence—which I set forth in the following pages—that would lead me to conclusions which would fundamentally challenge and even reverse my initial expectations.

O•N•E

The Islamic Resurgence and the Veil

From Emergence to Migration

·1·

Unveiling

In 1956, Albert Hourani, the Oxford historian and best-selling author of *The History of the Arabs,* published a short article in the *UNESCO Courier* entitled "The Vanishing Veil a Challenge to the Old Order." Pointing out that veiling was a fast-disappearing practice in most Arab societies, Hourani gives a brief history of how and why the practice was disappearing and why, as he believed, veiling would soon become a thing of the past.

The trend to unveil, Hourani explains, had begun in Egypt in the early twentieth century, set in motion by the writer Qasim Amin. Amin had argued in his book *The Liberation of Woman* that "gradual and careful change in the status of women" was now an essential step in the advancement of Muslim societies. The changes he recommended, which included women's casting off their veils, were, Amin emphasized, "not contrary to the principles of Islam." While Amin's ideas had been met with great resistance, Hourani writes, they gradually gained acceptance and spread first in Egypt and then to the "more advanced Arab countries," among them "Syria, Jordan, Lebanon and Iraq."[1]

Hourani's article is illuminating not only for its reporting about veiling in the 1950s but also for what it reveals about the views and assumptions about veiling that were common among intellectuals of the era. Hourani notes that the spread of education had been enormously important to unveiling. Educated women would not accept veiling and seclusion, and educated men, who wanted "their wives to be companions," were similarly in favor of unveiling. As Hourani observed with respect to the 1950s, "In all except the most backward regions polygamy has practically disappeared and the veil is rapidly going."

By this decade, Hourani wrote, the veil had virtually disappeared in Egypt, although, he admitted, veiling lingered among the "lower middle class, the most conservative of all classes." Similarly, he reported, the veil was disappearing from most other "advanced" Arab countries. It was only in the Arab world's "most backward regions," he continued, and specifically "in the countries of the Arabian peninsula—Saudi Arabia and Yemen," that the "old order"—and along with it such practices as veiling and polygamy—"still persist[s] unaltered."

Clearly Hourani's narrative is grounded in a worldview that assumed that the way forward for Arab societies lay in following the path of progress forged by the West. Within this narrative framework, the way forward for such societies entailed leaving behind their "backward" practices and adopting the "advanced" norms and practices of modernity and the West.

Today, in our postmodern era, it would be almost unthinkable that an Oxford academic would casually use such terms as "advanced" or "backward" to describe cultural practices, but for Hourani, writing at midcentury and at the height of the modern age, these were simply the terms that were in common use for expressing the assumptions of the day, assumptions that, at midcentury, were in fact common to the dominant classes of both the Middle East and the West. As the British-born son of well-to-do Lebanese Christian parents who had settled in England, Hourani belonged by heritage and location to both groups. A rising young academic at the time he penned those words, Hourani also would be one of the first individuals of Arab heritage—maybe even the very first—to gain acceptance at the professorial level into the elite academic world of Oxbridge.

The notion that the presence or absence of the veil was a mark of the level of advancement or backwardness in a society—a notion that is assumed to be true in Hourani's text—was an idea that first appeared in Arab societies in the late nineteenth century, in the very book, *The Liberation of Woman,* that Hourani cites as having launched the unveiling trend in Egypt and other Arab countries. In fact, the entire thesis underpinning Hourani's assumptions in "The Vanishing Veil"—that Muslim societies are to be counted as advanced or backward by the extent to which they have abandoned their native practices, symbolized by the veil, in emulation of those of the West—is exactly the thesis that Amin puts forward in *Liberation of Woman.*

Amin's text is grounded in the idea of the self-evident and comprehensive superiority of Europe and its societies and civilization. This idea is present not simply as the implied and underlying framework (as in Hourani's text), but as the book's explicit thesis. It is this thesis, in fact, that forms the basis of Amin's argument for abandoning veiling and changing the status of women in Islam.

Amin's admiration for European civilization and European man is evident throughout his book, as is his dislike and even contempt for native ways. Arguing, for example, for the unveiling of Muslim women, Amin asserts that veiling had once been practiced in European societies, too, but as they had advanced they had left the practice behind. "Do Egyptians imagine," Amin continues,

> that the men of Europe, who have attained such completeness of intellect and feeling that they were able to discover the force of steam and electricity . . . these souls that daily risk their lives in the pursuit of knowledge and honor above the pleasures of life . . . these intellects and these souls that we so much admire, could possibly fail to know the means of safeguarding woman and preserving her purity? Do they think that such a people would have abandoned veiling after it had been in use among them if they had seen any good in it?[2]

Praising European civilization as one that had "advanced with the speed of steam and electricity" to conquer "every part of the globe," Amin notes admiringly that wherever European man goes "he takes control of its resources . . . and turns them into profit . . . and if he does harm to the original inhabitants, it is only that he pursues happiness in this world and seeks it wherever he may find it." When the European colonizers encountered "savages," Amin writes, "they eliminate them or drive them from the land, as happened in America . . . and is happening now in Africa. . . . When they encounter a nation like ours, with a degree of civilization, with a past, and a religion . . . and customs and . . . institutions . . . they deal with the inhabitants kindly. But they do soon acquire its most valuable resources, because they have greater wealth and intellect and knowledge and force."

It was from within this framework of understanding—a framework that obviously saw European civilization as representing the pinnacle of human achievement in the hierarchy of civilizations—that Amin set forth his argument that Muslim societies urgently needed to pursue reforms that would enable them to emulate Europe and follow in its footsteps.

Among the most important of these essential reforms, Amin went on to argue, were changing the status of Muslim women and abandoning the practice of veiling. For what Muslim society needed above all, Amin insisted, was a profound transformation—not simply of outward practices, such as veiling, but of the very character of its men. "The grown man," Amin explained, "is none other than his mother shaped him in childhood." This fact, Amin stressed, was the very "essence" of his call for the liberation of women. For, he wrote, "*It is impossible to breed successful men if they do not have mothers capable of raising them to be successful*" (emphasis in original).

The publication of Amin's book would provoke a furor in the press in Egypt, a furor that would resonate widely elsewhere in the Muslim world. In addition, *The Liberation of Woman* (Tahrir al-Mar'a) would come to be seen, as it is in Hourani's article, as having introduced important new ideas, ideas that marked the beginning of the spread of unveiling and, along with it, the advancement of women across the Arab Middle East. In fact, though, as I argue later in this chapter, the current of unveiling was already under way at a grass-roots level among women who were themselves carrying the movement forward.

Certainly, though, the publication of Amin's book was an important event, introducing novel and provocative ideas to the world of Arabic debate and letters. Most importantly and influentially, the book brought together two quite different strands of thought, both of which were in wide currency at the time—but in different societies.

The first set of ideas had its provenance in ideas that were current in Europe in Amin's day. As European imperial expansion—particularly British and French—reached new heights, so also did Europeans' ideas about the inherent racial and civilizational superiority of Europeans. This was the era (as many historians have noted) when the notion that human history consisted of a hierarchy of races and civilizations, at the pinnacle of which stood European man and his civilization, had become widely diffused in European and North American thought. Anthropology along with other fields of study of that era provided "scientific" evidence—such as that offered by the measurement of skulls—which established the "truth" of the idea of European racial superiority. The measurement of skulls, as feminist scholars have pointed out, similarly served to "prove" the intellectual inferiority of women. In England in particular, proving the inferiority of women, as well as of the British Empire's non-European subjects, was an important goal for the Victorian establishment of the day. British women were beginning to agitate against the government, just as were "the subject races" abroad, demanding such things as equality and suffrage.

Belief in the superiority of European man and his civilization and in the inferiority of Others—which encompassed all non-European peoples and civilizations—were the commonplaces of the day. In addition to the broad and overarching narrative of the West's overall superiority, there were also stock narratives that defined the particular inferiority of each different group—Hindus, for example, or Muslims or "Orientals" or sub-Saharan Africans. And dress in some cases (too much covering, for instance, with respect to Muslim women, and too little in relation to some sub-Saharan African societies) came to epitomize, to European eyes, the differentness, Otherness, and inferiority of those groups and societies. In the last decades of the nineteenth century these narratives of racial, religious, and civilizational inferiority came to focus specifically on the issue of women and the ways that men of Other societies oppressed and degraded women. This narrative was useful in this era of European imperialism in that it cast European man in his role as colonizer as someone who, by virtue of his imperialist rule, was not only bringing civilization to backward peoples but also saving local women from the oppression and degradation imposed on them by native men. Gayatri

Spivak would famously call this the trope of "white men saving brown women from brown men."[3]

Thus Hinduism was seen as essentially inferior for many reasons, but the evidence of its inferiority in the European narrative was succinctly and vividly encapsulated in its practices regarding women, and most particularly in the practice of suttee—a widow's self-immolation following her husband's death, a practice which, though never in common use, was focused on by the British as exemplifying Hindu attitudes to women. Similarly, veiling and segregation were seen as reflecting Islam's depraved attitudes toward sexuality (exemplified by the fact that Islam permitted polygamy and divorce—both practices considered anathema in nineteenth-century Europe). These ideas became centerpieces in the European narrative of Islam and its "degradation" of women, and the visually arresting sign of the veil became a symbol both of Islam's degradation of women and of the religion's fundamental inferiority. These views about the veil as emblem of Islam's inferiority and its treatment of women became prevalent in the late nineteenth century, most particularly in France and Britain, as both nations were extending and deepening their dominion over Muslim lands.

Qasim Amin, an Egyptian lawyer from the upper-middle class, had studied in France, where he had certainly encountered such ideas. We know, in fact, that he felt so strongly about one book in which a French author had set forth precisely such ideas regarding Islam's inferiority and its degradation of women, citing the practices of veiling and segregation as evidence of that degradation, that he wrote an impassioned response to it entitled *Les Egyptiens: Reponse a M. le duc D'Harcourt.* In it Amin rebuts many of D'Harcourt's critiques and staunchly defends Islamic practices, including veiling and segregation. Moreover, Amin (particularly affronted, apparently, by D'Harcourt's assertion that Islam encouraged sexual license and "lust, obscenity and degeneration") even went on to criticize European societies for their depravity, a result of their easy mixing of the sexes.[4]

A few years later, however, Amin would entirely reverse his views. Princess Nazli (a niece of Khedive Ismail, ruler of Egypt in 1863–79) reportedly had had a hand in bringing about this change. Nazli Fazil, who spoke several languages fluently, including French and English, and was described as a "determined champion of female emancipation," had not been pleased with Amin's defense of Islamic practices.[5] She therefore invited him to the salons she held in her home in Cairo, frequented by leading liberals and intellectuals, to expose him to their views on the subject. (Nazli was unique in Egypt in her era as a woman who hosted salons in which she mingled "unveiled with male guests." Being a member of the royal family, she had "special leeway."[6]) Evelyn Baring (later Lord Cromer), Britain's consul general in Egypt from 1883 to 1907, was occasionally among Nazli's guests, and the princess, in the words of Ronald Storrs, a member of the British administration, was "embarrassingly pro-British."[7]

A few years later, as Amin evidently continued to ponder and discuss these issues, along with other Egyptian intellectuals of his day, he would put forward in *The Liberation of Woman* the thesis and positions already described. The book was in fact written in Europe in 1897 when Amin was spending the summer with three other Egyptian intellectuals in Geneva. All were men who, like Amin, had spent time in Europe and were at home with European thought.

Amin's generation was probably the first generation of Arabs and Muslims to live the experience of biculturality—of double or divided consciousness. It was an experience that W. E. B. DuBois was just beginning to give voice to in America. In those same years Amin was struggling first to respond to European views of Islam and Muslims such as those set forth by the Duc D'Harcourt—views that he and other Europeanized Egyptians were now encountering for the first time—and subsequently coming to rethink his initial response to those views.

The very fact that Amin occupied this liminal, in-between space enabled him to import into Arabic thought and letters ideas that at the time were the commonplaces of European thought. Translating and importing these ideas, he intertwined them with another set of ideas, ideas in this case that were already under lively discussion in Muslim societies. This was the already well-developed argument that Muslim societies must "catch up" with Europe and emulate and import, in particular, European scientific and technological advances. It would thus be, above all, this fusion of European views on Islam and women in Islam with the local desire to catch up with Europe that would give his book its force, causing it to provoke intense debate on its publication in 1899.

Ideas about the importance of emulating the scientific advances and technological know-how of Europe, especially in their military applications, first emerged as goals of major importance in Muslim societies following Napoleon's invasion of Egypt in 1799. Subsequently, in 1801, it would be only with the aid of a British force that the French were ousted from Egypt. The Napoleonic invasion, representing Europe's first conquest of Muslim lands forming part of the Ottoman Empire and marking the beginning of Europe's steadily growing imperial domination over those lands, remains to this day an iconic moment in Muslim and in particular in Islamist narratives of history. The inability of the forces of the Ottoman Empire (of which Egypt was part) to repel the French vividly brought home to both Ottomans and local rulers how far the Ottoman Empire and the Islamic world had fallen behind Europe in military might.

In the wake of these events, both Turkey and Egypt launched themselves on the path of catching up with Europe. In Egypt, Muhammad Ali, an officer who rose to be commander in chief of the Ottoman force sent to Egypt to expel the French, was appointed governor of the country. He quickly set about the task of importing European technologies and military and scientific know-how. He sent student missions to Europe and established military and medical academies in Egypt, academies that were often staffed by Europeans. He also founded translation schools with the object of spearheading a project of translating European scientific knowledge and literature into Arabic.

Muhammad Ali, who became khedive of Egypt, pursued other changes, too, including agricultural reforms to increase productivity, and he established factories to produce textiles from locally grown cotton. The latter project did not prosper, however, as the British were determined to stifle local competition for textiles produced in their own mills. Through a treaty with the Ottomans—who resented the advances made by Muhammad Ali—they succeeded in undermining Egypt's nascent cotton industry.

Through the first half of the nineteenth century and beyond, Muhammad Ali and his successors continued to make advances by importing European know-how. Rail lines, for example, constructed in the 1850s, were an innovation that tremendously improved traveling conditions for, among others, the Westerners who were coming to Egypt in increasing numbers as tourists. In addition, Egypt was part of the Overland Route to India, the route taken by British officials and their families and others working in the service of the British Empire in India. Missionaries were also coming to Egypt and beginning to set up schools there.

All of this meant that Europeans and other Westerners—and their dress and ways—were increasingly becoming a familiar part of the Egyptian landscape. And as the decades passed, Egyptians too—students, the wealthy classes—were visiting Europe in rising numbers and becoming acquainted with the West. And some of the wealthier Egyptians were adopting Western ways: following European clothing and furniture styles, and hiring European governesses to instruct their children.

A study of the Europeanization of dress and fashion that occurred in Turkey over the nineteenth century (an arduous task entailing close study of paintings and manuscript illustrations) observed that changes in Turkish dress and fashion through this period were directly related to the growing numbers of Europeans in the country, along with the growing availability of European goods.[8]

Such a study has yet to be undertaken in relation to Egypt. A letter written in the 1840s by a traveler who had returned several times to the country over the preceding couple of decades captures a sense of the palpable and rapid and yet also intrinsically ephemeral changes that contemporaries felt themselves to be witnessing. Lamenting in his letter that Cairo was becoming altogether too Europeanized, the Orientalist Edward W. Lane wrote that officials in Egypt were now abandoning native dress ("just as they had done in Istanbul") and were taking to wearing European clothing. Lane (who himself always abandoned what he considered uncomfortable Western dress the moment he arrived in Egypt in favor of the loose and comfortable robes of that country) found this change in local dress ridiculous. Now, he wrote, these officers were wearing "frock-coat, waistcoat, and trousers, the last as narrow as ours." All of this was part of a trend, Lane went on to note, in which a "rapid march" toward the adoption of European ways in general had now become a "gallop." People, especially the well-to-do, were even changing the furniture of their houses. Divans were being bundled out of doors, replaced by chairs and tables. Some people in Egypt, Lane further noted, were "very angry" at these changes, rightly (in his opinion) regarding them to be signs of deeper and more important changes that were now inexorably under way.[9]

This passion for emulating European ways was given lively and ostentatious expression in the plans and activities ordered by Khedive Ismail for the lavish celebrations to mark the opening of the Suez Canal in 1869. The preparations included the reconstruction and redesign of entire areas of Cairo, where an opera house—the first such construction in Egypt—was to be built, and they included the widening of some of Cairo's streets, which would now feature lampposts so that they would resemble the boulevards of Paris. European royalty were invited to attend, and Verdi was commissioned to compose the opera *Aida* in honor of the occasion.

But Ismail's extravagance and debts would soon set in motion a train of events that would lead to the landing of British forces in Egypt and, thereafter, to the beginning of the British Occupation of Egypt in 1882. When Ismail proved unable to repay his debts to European banks, British and French financial controllers were appointed to oversee their repayment. When Ismail failed to comply with their recommendations, the British arranged to have him deposed in favor of his son Tewfik. In 1881, unhappy with Tewfik's rule and his compliance with the European Powers, a group of Egyptian officers rebelled, demanding change and a constitution that would limit the ruler's autocratic powers. Tewfik appealed to the European Powers for assistance against the rebellion. The French refused. The British, however, bombarded Alexandria and landed their troops in the country. Thus began their Occupation of Egypt, which would endure until 1954.

The British appointed Evelyn Baring, later Lord Cromer, as their consul general and agent in Egypt. Cromer was a member of the powerful Baring banking family (rivals of the Rothschilds) to whom Ismail had owed large debts. He had first come to Egypt as the British controller overseeing Ismail's debt repayments. Following the British Occupation, Cromer would return to Egypt in 1883, now as Britain's consul general, a post he would retain for twenty-four years. Despite his innocuous-sounding title, Cromer in fact would rule the country essentially as its "uncrowned king" throughout his tenure. Nevertheless, the khedive would be the country's nominal ruler.

The system of rule the British established in Egypt would come to be known as the Veiled Protectorate. Under this system, as Afaf Lutfi al-Sayyid Marsot explains it, "the British in Egypt were to be the real rulers, but were not to be responsible to anyone but the British government. They were to rule from behind a façade of Egyptian ministers who had little authority, and were rubber stamps for the British manipulators."[10]

During his first decade in Egypt, Cromer would work to restore Egypt's finances. But he would also take a strong stand against ending the Occupation within a short period, which the British had initially promised to do. Cromer maintained that Egyptians were incapable of self-government without European assistance.[11]

These positions were naturally resented by many in Egypt. In addition, Cromer, as well as his advisor on education, Douglas Dunlop, would provoke intense resentment with their inflexibility and biases on education. Even Egyptians who favored working with the British administration toward eventual independence were critical of Cromer's refusal to invest the country's resources in improving education—even though, as Cromer himself admitted, there was strong demand for educational opportunities for their children, girls as well as boys.[12] Prior to British rule, free education had begun to be available at some government primary schools. But the British administration not only refused to expand education in response to demand, it even cut back on free education. By the time Cromer left Egypt in 1907, free education in government primary schools, he would proudly note, had been "practically abolished."[13]

Also fueling popular resentment against the British were the practices of racial bias and discrimination that they introduced into the country. There were bitter complaints, for example, about the administration's practice of passing over qualified Egyptian applicants for government posts in favor of novices freshly arrived from Britain.[14]

In 1906 an incident occurred between villagers and British soldiers in the delta village of Dinshawai, and the outcome would be a court case that contemporary Egyptians and their allies in Britain would see as epitomizing British racism and injustice. The situation was a complicated one, involving British soldiers out pigeon-shooting and accidentally wounding several villagers, following which the soldiers were chased and beaten by some villagers. One of the soldiers, ordered by his officer to run back to camp for help, died that evening of sunstroke and a blow to the head. The verdict following the trial included the execution by hanging of four villagers for intentional murder, penal servitude for life for two men, including the husband of a woman who had been wounded by British gunfire, and the public flogging of eight men. The hangings and floggings were to be carried out in front of the villagers. The pronouncement of the verdict plunged the country into a mood of gloom and outrage.[15] In the aftermath of this event Cromer resigned on grounds of health.

Soon after leaving the country Cromer published his book *Modern Egypt*. In it Cromer (who had earlier served in India as secretary to Lord Northbrook, viceroy to India and Cromer's cousin) freely expressed his views about race and his beliefs regarding the inferiority of the "dark-skinned Eastern as compared to the fair-skinned Western." In addition, Cromer made clear his strong belief in the inferiority of Islam to Christianity and of Muslims to Christians.[16] Such views were not of course unique. Rather, as Cromer's biographer Roger Owen observes, Cromer's views on these matters "were probably held by the vast majority of Europeans and North Americans at this time."[17] Cromer's book quickly became a success, selling very well in England and America. Owen speculates that among the chief reasons for its success was that it "reflected the spirit of the age: a pride not only in empire but also in the management of subject races."[18]

Similarly, Cromer repeated in his book the typical views of the day about Islam's "degradation" of women as exemplified in the practice of veiling. While Christianity "elevated" women, Cromer wrote, Islam "degraded" them, a fact that was evidenced, he declared, by "radical" differences, among them particularly the fact that "the face of the Moslem woman is veiled when she appears in public. She lives a life of seclusion." In contrast, "the face of the European woman is exposed to view in public. The only restraints placed on her movement are those dictated by her own sense of propriety."[19]

Cromer, it should be made clear, was most emphatically not a supporter of the movement for women's rights—in fact, he was its formidable opponent, serving for a time as the president of the Society Opposed to Women's Suffrage. In a speech against votes for women, for example, Cromer asked whether it was acceptable for an imperial nation to "dethrone woman from that position of gentle yet commanding influence she now occupies . . . and substitute in her place the unsexed woman voting at the polling booth?" This "battle of the sexes" must be staunchly resisted, Cromer wrote, for it would sow "discord and confusion in every family in the country." Men needed to be "manly" and women "womanly." Any "endeavour to invert the natural role of the sexes," Cromer argued, would be disastrous for England and Empire.[20]

In relation to Muslim women, however, Cromer firmly maintained the key importance of ending the Islamic practices of veiling and segregation. This was essential, he wrote, because of the "great influence" that women exercised as wives and mothers over "the characters of their husbands and sons." The position of women in Islam and the practices of veiling and segregation self-evidently, Cromer declared, "produced a deteriorating effect on the male population." Consequently, the "position of women in Egypt, and in Mohammedan countries generally," he further asserted, was itself the "fatal obstacle" obstructing the attainment of "that elevation of thought and character which should accompany the introduction of European civilization."[21]

Changing the position of women in Egypt was thus the prerequisite to the country's advancement and thus also to Egypt's gaining independence from Britain. It was necessary, first, to breed Egyptian men who were capable of taking over the reins of power from the British. Achieving this and other necessary conditions for independence, according to Cromer, could be the "work of years or 'possibly' generations."[22]

While this was Cromer's rhetorical stance regarding women and Islam, on the practical level his rule contributed little to improving the condition of women in Egypt. As we saw earlier, he chose not to invest government revenue in education despite the growing demand from Egyptians for schools, including schools for girls. Furthermore, he refused to fund a school for female doctors that had been functioning since the 1830s, agreeing only to continue to fund the training of women as midwives. When told of the local preference among women to be treated by women doctors, Cromer replied, "I am aware that in exceptional cases women like to be attended by female doctors, but I conceive that in the civilized world, attendance by medical men is still the rule."[23]

One further aspect of the contemporary scene must be taken into account, as it sheds light on the debate around the veil, and on the intense and ferocious discussions Amin's book provoked.

Through the Cromer era, and particularly in the 1890s and early 1900s, there were political divisions in Egypt between, on one side, a group of intellectuals and politicians who in some ways welcomed and supported the British presence as preferable to the autocratic government of local rulers, who governed under the overall suzerainty of the Ottoman Sultanate in Turkey. Their hope was to work collaboratively with the British administration toward establishing Egypt as an independent, democratically governed nation free of both British control and Ottoman rule. This group (often referred to as the liberals), which included Amin, were on cordial terms with Cromer, with whom they were willing to work toward the goal of eventual independence. Consequently, this group was on poor terms with the Khedive Abbas Hilmi, who had succeeded his father Tewfik as ruler of Egypt and who, unlike his father, did his best to resist the British, whose dominion he bitterly resented.

On the other side from these "liberals" were nationalist and pan-Islamist politicians and intellectuals who were deeply opposed to the British Occupation and who called for Islamic unity and solidarity in the face of European imperialism, as well as for the restoration of ties with Istanbul and the Ottoman Empire. This faction, hated by Cromer, was often befriended and secretly supported by the khedive. The views of the liberals—whose careers Cromer backed in various ways—would gain in influence through the Cromer era and come to gain dominance for the following two or three decades. Saad Zaghloul, for example, who was appointed minister of education by Cromer, would become the country's first elected prime minister in 1923. Cromer also helped advance the career of Muhammad Abduh, an Islamic thinker and reformer who was critical of local autocratic forms of government. Cromer, as he noted in *Modern Egypt,* assisted in bringing about Abduh's appointment to the important post of chief mufti of Egypt in 1899.[24]

Abduh, who studied at al-Azhar and spent a period of exile in France, became prominent for his call for the reform of Islam and the reinterpretation of the Islamic heritage, including the reinterpretation of key Quranic verses directly affecting women, such as those referring to polygamy. Correctly interpreted, Abduh argued, this verse would be seen to be indicating that polygamy was permissible only in exceptional circumstances.[25] Cromer appreciated the positions Abduh took and described him as someone who "admitted the abuses which have sprung up under Oriental Governments" and who "recognized the necessity of European assistance in the work of reform." Muslims such as Abduh, Cromer further wrote, were the "natural allies of the European reformer" and thus deserved "all the encouragement and support which can be given them."[26]

The reformist positions Abduh took, as well as, perhaps, his cordial relations with Cromer, would earn him the enmity of many in the religious classes of Egypt, as well as that of the khedive. Describing Abduh as "in reality an Agnostic," Cromer wrote that he was on "bad terms" with the khedive, that he faced strong opposition from "conservative Muslims," and that he was able to retain his post as mufti of Egypt only by virtue of "strong British support."[27] However, in fairness to Abduh it should be noted that scholars have long debated Cromer's motivation in including these remarks on Abduh in his book, as well as his motivation in characterizing him as an agnostic. Similarly, some debate the significance of the fact that Abduh, like his mentor al-Afghani, were members of Masonic Lodges.[28]

According to a noted Abduh scholar, Muhammad ʻAmara, the book *The Liberation of Woman* was not written by Amin alone. Rather, it was the product of collaborative efforts by Amin and other members of the group of liberal Egyptian intellectuals who gathered that summer in Geneva. According to ʻAmara, Abduh in particular contributed significant portions of the book. At the time of its publication there were rumors that the book had been written at Cromer's urging.[29] And certainly the views that Amin and his collaborators gave voice to in this book, and those that Cromer would later publish in his *Modern Egypt*, seem to directly echo one another. To be sure, both books expressed views on Islam and women that were in wide circulation in European societies in that era. However, their close resemblances may also have been reinforced by conversations that Amin and Abduh and others of their circle may have had with Cromer.

The Liberation of Woman received enthusiastic praise from the British-backed paper *al-Muqattam,* which hailed it as the best book to appear in years. It triggered the first major controversy to erupt in the Arabic press: more than thirty books and articles were published in response to it, the majority of them critical. In particular, the book drew angry responses from nationalists and pan-Islamists, people who above all were opposed to the British Occupation. They argued, among other things, that what was needed was not the hasty imitation of the West in all things, which *The Liberation of Woman* seemed to advocate, but rather a return to Islamic values accompanied by the judicious adoption of certain Western practices.[30]

Some of Amin's nationalist critics, for example, were not opposed to the idea of women's education; on the contrary, some called for their education well beyond the primary level, which was all that Amin had called for. On the other hand, however, they objected to Amin's call for unveiling and to his unqualified and undiscriminating enthusiasm for everything European. Some of those opposed to unveiling included, to be sure, women who were allied to nationalist pan-Islamist figures, but they also included women who were evidently speaking or writing from what we would call today a feminist position. One woman, for example, objected to the fact that men were yet again telling women what they should or should not wear. Man, this writer lamented, was once more "being as despotic about liberating us as he has been about our enslavement. We are weary," she concluded, "of his despotism."[31]

The divide between Amin and his supporters, on the one hand, and his critics, on the other, was not in reality a divide between feminists and anti-feminists but rather between those who were strongly anti-British and opposed to the Occupation and those who, like Amin, took a more sanguine view of Cromer and the British presence.

Such, then, were the origins of the notions informing Hourani's assumption in the 1950s that the presence or absence of the veil in a given Muslim society was a sign of whether that society was "advanced" or "backward," marching forward on the path of progress or remaining mired in the old order. Thus by the mid-twentieth century, when Hourani was writing, the European views and narrative of the veil that had been imported and launched into circulation in Arabic at the end of the nineteenth century had become the commonplaces of the day, not only for Hourani and most Westerners but also, by and large, for many middle- and upper-class people living in Muslim-majority cities around the world.

These ideas, emerging in Egypt at the level of intellectual and political debate, proved tremendously influential in the history of the unveiling movement. They were particularly influential in terms of fostering and promoting a particular ideological framework and way of understanding the meaning of the veil's presence or absence, a framework that would gain widespread acceptance in Egypt and also (as Hourani indicated) in due course in many other Arab societies.

The most prominent proponents and opponents of unveiling were men who had the privileges of class and status and carried political clout in the social and cultural domains. But at least one elite woman, Princess Nazli, also was a strong proponent of unveiling and an influential member of these high-level intellectual and political circles. Another important female figure in the history of early twentieth-century feminism was Huda Sha'rawi, also a woman of the upper classes, whose life and activities have been extensively chronicled by Margot Badran. As a young woman in the 1900s, Sha'rawi organized lectures for women and helped establish a philanthropic society. In 1923 she founded the Egyptian Feminist Union (al-Ittihad al-Nisa'i al-Misri), and she remained the spokesperson for feminism in Egypt until her death in 1947. Zainab al-Ghazali, the future Islamic leader, would briefly join the Egyptian Feminist Union at the age of sixteen, but she would leave it within the year to found her own women's organization.[32]

In fact, though, the unveiling movement that would sweep across much of the Muslim world over the course of the first half of the twentieth century took place above all at the level of ordinary people. On the level of day-to-day experience it was, after all, women who unveiled, essentially for their own reasons—reasons that were expressive of their individual desires and hopes about how to live, and of their own views on fashion and as to proper and attractive dress.

Perhaps their decisions in the matter of the veil also were informed by the ongoing debates among men and members of the upper classes—European and Egyptian. But it is quite likely that the kinds of arguments that Cromer and Amin were making—that the veil denoted some sort of inherent inferiority of a given religion, race, or civilization—were by no means the most significant factors in women's decisions about whether to veil. It is possible, too, that such discussions going on in the rarefied world of the elites, would have been perceived by many women as abstruse and irrelevant debates that were scarcely even on their radar screens.

Whether to wear the veil was, for the women of the day, a matter of fashion and of wearing proper and appropriate dress. In Muslim-majority societies up to that era, wearing the veil had not been confined to Muslims. Rather, until the colonial era, the veil (in the sense of head-covering) was considered proper dress for all women, regardless of religion. Jewish, Christian, and Muslim women covered their heads and wore some version of what we today call the veil. As the wave of unveiling began to quietly gather force at the turn of the century, Christian and Jewish women seemed to be unveiling just slightly ahead of their Muslim sisters. Evidently, though, most at this point considered the custom to be a "cultural norm rather than a religious imperative."[33] At any rate, the practice of wearing the veil was not confined to or (among Egyptians) associated specifically with Islam and Muslim women. Salama Musa, for example, a noted Coptic intellectual and journalist of the era, mentioned in his memoir that his mother and sisters unveiled in 1907 and 1908.[34] It was in these years, as the European understanding of veiling as a practice only of Muslim women began to gain ground in Egyptian society, that veiling would become identified as a uniquely Islamic practice.

As we have seen, the currents of fashion and the desire for things European had been flowing with their own force and speed through the preceding decades. Those who could afford to replaced their old furniture with European-style tables and chairs and so on. The new furniture implied and often inevitably required different ways of daily living. Many people now sat on chairs instead of cross-legged on cushions or with their legs drawn up beside them on ottomans, and they ate at tables instead of perhaps sitting around trays on the floor.

As European ways and people became a more familiar part of the mental and physical landscape for Egyptians, and as the dazzling and extraordinary technologies of Europe—from trains to telephones, electricity, street lights, tramways, and motorcars—increasingly became part of their world, the desire to live, dress, and *be* like Europeans, to have and enjoy the amenities that Europeans enjoyed, gathered pace.

In these last decades of the nineteenth century and in the opening years of the twentieth, the political ideas of Europe—democracy, equality, meritocracy—were proving to be as seductive and winning as were the dazzling products of technology. To people living in societies where autocracy, class stratification, and gender and ethnic and racial privilege (of Turks over Egyptians, as well as of British over Egyptians) had been the fixed rules of existence, the very ideas of democracy, equality, and meritocracy were tremendously exciting, exhilaratingly opening up new horizons and possibilities. The desire that Egypt become a society in which democracy, equality, and meritocracy were realities was intense and widespread, as memoirs from the era, such as Salama Musa's, make clear.

The liberals who were on cordial terms with Cromer were already busy, as we saw earlier, devising a program that they hoped would lead Egypt to independence as a democracy free of both colonialism and autocratic government—whether of the local khedive or of the more distant Turkish sultan. Egypt, their hope was, would be a democracy that, while not perhaps granting women equal status with men, nevertheless would encourage and nurture women's capacities—both for their own sake and so that they might produce and raise better men.

That was the dream. This dream, encapsulating the desires for comprehensive social and political change on multiple levels—in matters of governance, class and gender, ethnicity and race, and opportunity—came to be epitomized for many by the act of unveiling.

By the last years of the nineteenth and the opening years of the twentieth centuries, the sight of unveiled Western women going about their business—tourists traveling up the Nile to the temples of Luxor, European wives residing in Cairo, independent Western women earning their living as teachers and governesses—were becoming familiar sights in Egypt.

Cities, too, were changing. Department stores opened in Cairo and Alexandria in the 1890s, and women of the upper classes now went out to shop instead of having goods sent to their homes to select from. The presence of European women in the streets also changed the possibilities for local women. In earlier decades only poor women peddling food or vegetables would be commonly seen in the streets, and men would shop for their female relatives. At the turn of the century an American visitor reported that groups of women were now commonly seen shopping in the bazaars, in contrast to what she had observed on a visit in the 1860s.[35]

Egyptian women increasingly appeared in the streets with ever lighter veils, and soon with no veils at all. Upper-class women traveling to Europe frequently chose not to wear veils while in Europe, and soon they were casting them off as soon as they boarded ship. One visitor in the early 1900s described how women "shrouded up to the eyes" would arrive at the Cairo railway station and, at Alexandria, would board the steamer in such dress. Then they would appear the next morning "unveiled, bareheaded, clad in the latest Parisian traveling fashion."

Tramways had begun running by the late 1890s, and schoolgirls, sometimes without veils, could be seen waiting at tram stops to board the "women only" compartments on their way to or from school. There was a growing number of schools for girls, including missionary schools, and some forbade veiling. One teacher at the American missionary girls' school in Luxor, which initially had mostly Christian students, recalled that the end-of-year exam, which required girls to appear in public without veils, had at first been an ordeal for the (presumably Christian) girls, who found themselves having to appear in public "for the first time in their lives with their faces uncovered."

Whether to veil or not became a burning subject among women —Jewish, Muslim, and Christian. They wrote to the many women's journals that began appearing in this era, asking for advice. One woman wrote to say that she had a "dear friend" who "thinks as I do that the veil has no meaning in this age and she wants to unveil as I have, but timidity and respect for custom prevents her from doing this." The writer had "tried very hard," she explained, "to help her overcome her feelings," but was unsuccessful. She was now writing for advice on how to persuade her friend. Women were thus experimenting with dress and fashion for their own reasons, deciding for themselves what meaning the veil held, and whether, indeed, the veil had "no meaning in this age."

Unveiling would become ever more clearly the emblem of an era of new hopes and desires, and of aspirations for modernity: of the possibility of education and the right to work for both women and men, and of equal opportunity and advancement based on effort and merit instead of inherited privileges be it of class or race.

Increasingly, too, unveiling became a metaphor for all of these hopes, on both the public and personal levels. A newspaper founded in 1914, for example, took the name *al-Sufur* (Unveiling), because, explained its editor, "women are not the only ones who are veiled in Egypt . . . we are a veiled nation." By taking the name *al-Sufur,* he continued, the newspaper was declaring its endorsement of "complete unveiling, progress and reform in all domains." As the nation moved in 1919 toward hoped-for independence from the British, a young Egyptian artist produced a sculpture that he entitled *The Awakening of Egypt.* It showed Egypt as a young peasant woman lifting her veil. The sculpture would subsequently be reproduced and prominently installed as a monument in front of the Cairo rail station.[36]

The hopes and longings of the young women of the day who boldly took the step of setting aside their veils are encapsulated in the story of one young woman of that era, Nabawiya Musa.

Musa, born in 1886, was the daughter of an Egyptian army captain who died before she was born. Musa's mother, surviving on her husband's military pension, chose not to remarry in order to devote herself to her two children. Musa had to battle her mother (which she did with her brother's assistance) to continue her education beyond primary school. She graduated in 1906 from the Teacher Training Program at the Saniyah School and began teaching at the girls section of the Abbas School. Here she discovered that male teachers received almost twice the pay as females. She asked why and was told that it was because they had secondary school certificates in addition to teaching diplomas.[37]

Musa therefore decided to sit for the secondary school certificate exam. Since no schools were available to train women for this exam, she had to prepare for it on her own. This she did even though she learned that the Ministry of Education (controlled, as were all government departments, by the British) did not allow women to sit for this exam. Nevertheless, and in defiance of Douglas Dunlop, the British advisor on education, she presented herself for the exam and passed with flying colors. Her success was widely reported in the press, which was jubilant that an Egyptian woman had acquitted herself well in the exam and had triumphed in the face of unjust British rules.[38]

Musa would receive a salary raise, thereby becoming the first "woman teacher to receive a salary equal to male teachers." She would go on to become a prominent educator, activist, and writer, taking on throughout her life issues relating to women, education, and work. She continued to take political stands against British and local government injustices, including stands that would land her in prison.

Musa, who was twenty-one when she sat for the exam, stopped wearing the veil two years later. She described a spirited exchange she had one day on the tram with a woman who criticized her for not wearing the veil. Musa's own garb, she pointed out in her response to the woman, was discreet, modest, and unrevealing, whereas the "ornaments" and attributes of the woman criticizing her were entirely in plain view, even though she wore an evidently flimsy veil.[39]

All of Musa's stances and actions would not have been possible in the premodern and precolonial eras. Standing up for her rights, challenging the government, taking exams that placed her on a par with men, and demanding equal pay became possible only with the coming of modernity. And all of these issues are part of the meaning of unveiling in this era. For men as well as for women, unveiling—as the editor of *al-Sufur* suggested—was emblematic of the desire and hope for a new social and political order, for the promise of modernity. It was emblematic of the will to stand up to injustice in all its forms—British colonialism and racism, autocratic rule, a rigid class system, a restrictive gender system. It was emblematic, too, of the will and commitment to work for a new political and social order: for a world remade.

Anbara Khalidi, a young Palestinian woman who would become a prominent activist, traveled to Egypt in 1910 and was exhilarated to see how many women were unveiled. She was "delighted" she wrote, at the appearance of Egyptian women, who were "more emancipated than us" and saw the world "with unveiled eyes."[40]

But women themselves were divided on the question of veiling. One woman, for example—Fatima Rashid, the wife of Muhammad Farid Wajdi, owner of a noted nationalist newspaper—supported women's education but opposed unveiling. She wrote in 1908, "This veil is not a disease that holds us back. Rather it is the cause of our happiness . . . and we shall guard it carefully. . . . [It] is our symbol and the symbol of our Muslim grandmothers."[41]

Another woman, a journalist writing in 1910, noted with surprise the ever-increasing numbers of women who were now to be seen in the streets without veils. Where had all these women come from, she asked. "Did they fall from the sky?" This rapidly spreading phenomenon of unveiling was evidently as astonishing and alarming to her as the appearance of women in veils here in America would be for some of us more than eighty years later.[42]

Members of the ulama—the class of religious scholars—were emphatically not pleased with the unveiling trend. In 1914 they published a recommendation that the government discourage the trend by imposing a prison sentence or at least a fine on women who appeared without veils. But the desire for unveiling and all that unveiling stood for was already sweeping onward.

At the start of World War I, the British deposed the Khedive Abbas Hilmi because of his pro-Ottoman sympathies, installing Khedive Hussein Kamel in his place. Using Egypt as a base during the war, the British requisitioned food and farm animals for their armies and compelled the peasantry into forced labor—digging ditches in Palestine, for example. It was a time of great hardship for many Egyptians, and a time during which resentment against the British presence intensified. "Whatever friendly feelings the fallahin [peasantry] might have harbored for the British presence in Egypt," wrote al-Sayyid Marsot in her history of Egypt, those feelings now had "totally evaporated."[43]

Nationalist fervor and calls for an end to the British Occupation continued to grow throughout the early twentieth century. The British now implied that Egypt's cooperation during the war would result in independence at the end of it. But when the war ended, independence was not granted. Riots and demonstrations then broke out across the country, and the British agreed to abolish the Protectorate and declare Egypt independent. However, that independence was hedged with conditions that would allow the British to continue to exercise control over key areas of the country's government, conditions that in effect rendered Egypt's independence essentially "well nigh void."

Still, political parties were formed and the apparatus of electoral democracy put in place; elections were held, and the Umma Party, led by Saad Zaghloul—who had been part of Cromer's Egyptian circle—won, and Zaghloul became prime minister. A constitution was drawn up guaranteeing freedom of speech. The new government of this newly "independent" country had "all the trappings," as al-Sayyid Marsot put it, of a "modern, democratic, representative government."

The ensuing decades would be times of tremendous turbulence in the Middle East. Following World War I, the European Powers drew new maps of the region, essentially creating a new Middle East comprising several new states out of the Ottoman Empire's former territories in the region: Lebanon, Syria, Iraq, Palestine, and Saudi Arabia. In addition, the British government laid the groundwork, with the Balfour Declaration of 1917, for the establishment of Israel.

With the installation of the new "democratic" government of Egypt, the surviving members of the circle of modernizing politicians and intellectuals and their supporters and protégés held positions of great social and political power—much as they had under the British, especially when compared with their pan-Islamist opponents. The ideas they had embraced and promoted as to the proper (and Westernizing) direction in which the country should move, including with respect to unveiling, were now unambiguously the ideas of the government and ruling elite.

In reality, unveiling was by now steadily becoming the norm, particularly among the younger generation of urban middle- and upper-class women. By 1928 women had begun attending the country's main university in Cairo after a government decree issued in 1927 permitted them to do so. Thus the ideas that had been daring and innovative at the end of the nineteenth century were rapidly becoming the reigning norms and assumptions of the middle classes.

All of the baggage that had come in with these ideas—as to the "backwardness" of veiling, and of unveiling as sign of advancement—was by the time of my own childhood, the 1940s, simply part of the normal assumptions and self-evident "truths" of the day. Pious as well less religious women typically wore no veil. For us, as Hourani's article correctly captures, not wearing hijab was simply the "modern" and "advanced" way of being Muslim. Islam sans veil was essentially to us "true" Islam—Islam stripped (as we saw it) of centuries' worth of false and backward cultural accretions.

There was no suggestion whatsoever in that era that women's unveiling signified their rejection of Islam or their secularism. Notably, there is no such suggestion in Hourani's essay either: on the contrary, Hourani emphasized that Amin had made a point of asserting that the changes he was recommending were in no way "contrary to the principles of Islam."[44]

The idea that women who did not veil were secular, a common view today, was simply not among the meanings of unveiling in that era, at least not among the dominant middle classes in Egypt or among people of Hourani's background and education. Perhaps such ideas were coming into circulation in other populations—in Saudi Arabia, for example, and among the Muslim Brotherhood. In the ensuing decades, as both the Saudis and the Brotherhood steadily gained power, so did the view that women who did not veil, and Muslim-majority nations whose women did not veil, were secular—or at best were people who had fallen away from the practices of "true" Islam.

Thus the ideas and practices that had articulated the desires and beliefs of an earlier era became, in Egypt by the 1940s, the hackneyed assumptions of the socially and politically dominant groups in the country's cities. Grounded in an earlier generation's acceptance of the beliefs and prejudices of European imperialist societies, these assumptions and the practices associated with them were also expressions of an inner landscape that was charged and layered with the longings of that earlier generation.

The story of how these ideas would become the assumptions of much of society, accepted by the vast majority of the population, only to be undermined and reversed in the ensuing decades, forms the subject of the ensuing chapters.

One noteworthy fact about the unveiling movement is how it originated not in precolonialist Middle Eastern notions of the meaning of the veil, notions rooted in Islamic, Christian, and Jewish local meanings, but rather in Western nineteenth-century ideas about the veil's meaning.

With the rise of the West to global dominance, Western views of the world would come to supersede local meanings in a vast range of matters, including the veil. For even in such countries as Turkey, which never experienced direct colonial domination but which was nonetheless powerfully affected by the spread of Western ideas, the local meanings of the veil came to be superseded by Westerners' view of the veil as a sign of the inferiority of Islam and Muslim societies and peoples, as well as of Islam's "degradation" of women.

This, one could say, was at root the reason that Amin (reproducing ideas such as Cromer's) advocated the casting off of the veil in Egypt in 1899: to erase from Egypt and Islam this blot of inferiority. Similarly, it was in order to eradicate this sign of inferiority from his society that Kamal Ataturk, the leader and modernizer of Turkey, would declare in a speech in 1925: "In some places I have seen women who put a piece of cloth or a towel or something like that over their heads to hide their faces, and who turn their backs or huddle themselves on the ground when a man passes by. What is the meaning and sense of this behaviour?" Ataturk went on, "Gentlemen, can the mothers and daughters of a civilized nation adopt this strange manner, this barbarous posture? It is a spectacle that makes the nation an object of ridicule. It must be remedied at once."[45] By this time such opinions were becoming the norm among the middle and upper classes in the Muslim world. In the 1930s the shah of Iran banned the veil, and police were required to remove it from women who did not comply.

In much of the Arab world, the process, as Hourani described it, happened gradually and without enforcement. Women in the region (with the exception of the Arabian Peninsula) unveiled through the first half of the twentieth century for a plethora of reasons, among them as expression of their longing for the goods, opportunities, and amenities of modernity. All of these meanings, along with others, were simultaneously present and in the air in that era. But it is noteworthy that the process of unveiling occurred initially because the Western meaning of the veil—as a sign of the inferiority of Islam as religion, culture, and civilization—trumped and came to profoundly overlay the veil's prior indigenous meanings (common to all three monotheistic religions in the region) of proper and God-given gender hierarchy and separation.

·2·

The Veil's Vanishing Past

The world that Hourani evokes and the assumptions that underlie his essay were, then, entirely those that shaped my own consciousness growing up in Egypt in the 1940s and 1950s. Besides offering a snapshot of where the different countries of the region stood with regard to veiling, Hourani's article also perfectly captures the middle- and upper-class ethos of that era around veiling.

Through those decades and until the end of the Nasser era in Egypt in the late 1960s, the hijab became ever more rare. By the late fifties, even the class that Hourani had written of a few years earlier as tenaciously holding on to the practice—the lower middle classes, the "most conservative of all classes"—were now joining the broad tide of women who wore no veils. If the era of the 1900s to the 1920s was the Age of Unveiling, the 1920s to the 1960s was the era when going bareheaded and unveiled became the norm. A good proportion of the women coming of age during these decades (women of my mother's generation, for example—she was born in 1908—as well as, of course, women of my own generation) never unveiled because, in fact, they had never veiled.

But in about the mid-seventies, the veil began to reappear, first among small groups of female university students, and then—taking contemporaries completely by surprise—in society at large. Within a couple of decades, women who had never worn hijab began to do so.

And young girls were soon growing up unaware that there had been a time when Muslim women—devout, mainstream Muslim women, and not merely secular women—had not worn hijab. The entire era of Muslim women going bareheaded was being quietly erased from Muslim memory, and even Muslim history. For through these and the ensuing years, and as Islamists steadily gained ascendency, that era would be recast as a secular age, a time when women had given up veiling because they were no longer devout or even believing Muslims and had given up on Islam.

How and by virtue of what forces was this extraordinary transformation accomplished? In this and the following chapters I pursue this question, piecing together the available facts of the emergence and spread of the veil and the forces that brought about the veil's resurgence—critical among these being the Muslim Brotherhood and the powerful Islamist currents backed by Saudi Arabia.

In this chapter, covering the 1920s to the end of the 1960s, I review the events that set the stage for the dynamic Islamic Resurgence of the 1970s. I describe the founding of the Muslim Brotherhood and some of its commitments and activities until it fell afoul of the Nasser regime in the 1950s. I also describe other important developments in the Nasser era, including the fierce rivalry (dubbed the Arab Cold War) between Saudi Arabia and Egypt, a rivalry in which the Muslim Brothers would side with Saudi Arabia. I end with Egypt's and the Arabs' military defeat by Israel. That defeat is seen as marking the end of Nasserism, even though Nasser himself lived for another couple of years, and as ushering in the new mood of religiosity that would sweep across the country.

Drawing on my own memories I can supplement and slightly adjust Hourani's overview with respect to Egypt. While it was true that it was rare by the late 1940s and early fifties to see anyone in a veil in the city centers and modern neighborhoods of Cairo or Alexandria, where the middle and upper classes lived, the veil was still an ordinary part of life in other segments of society. In the villages, for instance, women typically wore a head veil. While working in the fields they wore loose, full-length gowns, often black but sometimes in colorful floral patterns, along with a loosely flowing black head covering in a fairly light fabric. It was common, in the area in which we lived, on the outer edges of Cairo, to see women from the nearby village dressed in this way—but always wearing a black outer garment over the colored robes—walking past our house on their way to shop or to run errands or pursue work in the city.

Through the forties and early fifties women who lived in Old Cairo and in the poorer districts bordering modern Cairo (Hourani's "most conservative of all classes") might also be seen wearing a veil or covering. The style of their covering was quite different from that of village women. The city form of covering at this class level, called a *milaya laff* ("wrapping sheet"), consisted of a black enveloping wrap, covering both head and body, that women wore over their clothing when they went outdoors. Sometimes they would draw the garment across the lower half of their faces, particularly if they found themselves in a direct exchange with a man. Sometimes a woman dressed in this way might also wear a heavy (rather than flimsy) black veil over the lower half of her face. This would be held in place by a cordlike thread, sometimes adorned with a decorative gold ring that rested on the nose. The hijab worn by middle- and upper-class city women of my grandmother's generation (she was born in 1885) also differed from either of these styles. In their case the head covering was made of very light material that was closely and complexly wrapped around the head, so that it looked opaque. When they ventured outdoors (my grandmother even covered her head indoors after her son died) they might additionally wear a flimsy white veil over the lower half of the face.

The only times I saw my mother in a veil was when she attended funerals. A covering of black see-through material wrapped closely around the head was routine formal wear for funerals (among the deceased's close relatives, in any case) for women of my mother's generation well into the 1950s.

Another type of covering was also occasionally to be seen: a scarf—and often an expensive-looking European-style scarf—that covered the head and was tied under the chin. This was a style in favor among "very conservative" middle- and upper-class families who had cast off traditional hijabs but evidently considered covering to be an essential requirement. I personally knew no one in our city community who dressed in this way, but we did have distant relatives whose main residence was in the countryside who followed this style when they came into the city

—women both of my mother's and my own generation. And certainly it was a style that even I, as a youngster, recognized as one of the ways people might dress. Along with the scarf, such women wore "conservative-style" Western dress: long sleeves and skirts (never pants—none of us wore pants) that were about mid-calf in length. This was how most of the rest of us dressed, too; the only difference I recall was that in our family our sleeves were not always full length, although they were never shorter than just above the elbow.

There also were, as mentioned earlier, the coverings of the women of the Muslim Brotherhood. Like the coverings of the women who wore European-type headscarves, these too were not like any traditional veils. Unlike the headscarfed women, though, these women wore, along with their modern-style head coverings in mainly solid neutral colors (and which covered their heads and necks more fully than a headscarf would), not conservative versions of Western-style dress but modern-looking Islamic style robes that, like their head coverings, differed from traditional styles of dress.

While the attire of the women wearing European-style scarves seemed to signal that the women were "like us" but more conservative—that they too were going with the flow of Western dress and ways while also adapting them to what they considered to be Islamic requirements—the dress of the women of the Muslim Brotherhood seemed to distinctly signal that they were definitely not "like us" and perhaps were even opposed to "us" and the Westernizing current that we—the dominant in society—were part of. Although I cannot be certain of this today, I believe that even as a youngster I sensed that this was what their dress meant and what they wanted us to understand by it: that they were both different from and opposed to us.

Certainly the Brotherhood affirmed the veil as a foundational Islamic requirement. The universal importance of this rule was manifest on the practical and visible level: the women of the Brotherhood invariably wore hijab. The Brotherhood was generally deeply critical of the Egyptian government and opposed to the broadly Westernizing trend being set and followed by the governing middle and upper classes. The veil of the Brotherhood women was a visual emblem of the Brotherhood's commitment to a form of Islam requiring hijab, and at the same time it signaled their opposition to the dominant classes and the direction in which they were taking society.

Founded in 1928 by al-Banna, the Muslim Brotherhood quickly gained grassroots support among young men of the urban working classes and first-generation rural immigrants, groups that formed the core of al-Banna's following. Gradually the organization would gain followers in the middle classes.[1]

As Egypt staggered through the depression era, the series of governments that came after Egypt's partial independence in the early 1920s proved for the most part incompetent and/or corrupt, as well as incapable of either ending British control or addressing the economic needs of the people.

The Brotherhood, responding to these conditions, preached a message of hope and renewal through a return to Islamic values, and it increasingly took a strongly anti-imperialist stand against the British Occupation—the stand that the government was failing to take. It became active in providing social services. It set up schools and clinics and provided a network of support for the poor, among them the rural immigrants who in these difficult economic times were moving to the cities in large numbers. It was not enough, however, al-Banna argued, for the Brotherhood to offer services and education to the poor, as other Islamic groups were doing. To reach the "desired goal[s]" of ending imperialism, establishing a nation based in Islam, and achieving social justice, another kind of educational undertaking was required. A "renascent nation," al-Banna wrote, required the "education and moulding of the souls of the nation." It required an education that would create a "strong moral immunity, firm and superior principles, and a strong and steadfast ideology. This is the best and fastest way to achieve the nation's goals and aspirations, and it is therefore our aim and the reason for our existence. It goes beyond the mere founding of schools, factories and institutions, it is the 'founding' of souls [insha' al-nufus]."[2]

At the time he established his organization, al-Banna was a twenty-two-year-old college graduate in Cairo who had chosen to attend the secular Dar al-Ulum rather than al-Azhar, which his father favored. He was appointed to a position in the school system in Ismailia, a town in the Suez Canal Zone, an area where the British army presence was most in evidence and where, "equally hateful to Banna," the Suez Canal Company was an obvious presence. Here the "conspicuously luxurious homes of the foreigners overlooking the 'miserable' homes of their workers" were starkly noticeable. Here even the street signs, as al-Banna noted, were "in the language of economic occupation."[3]

Dedicated from early in his college career to the idea of work "in the service of humanity," al-Banna supported the founding of the Young Men's Muslim Association in Cairo in 1927. In Suez, pursuing his goal of service, he began teaching adults in the evenings at mosques and coffeehouses. According to the Muslim Brotherhood's accounts, he would found the organization in response to a request from a group of Egyptian men who worked in the British camps and who heard his teachings. Telling him that they were "weary of this life of humiliation and restrictions," and saying that they saw that "the Arabs and the Muslims have no status . . . and no dignity . . . they are not more than mere hirelings belonging to foreigners," the men asked al-Banna to lead them on the path to "service of the fatherland . . . the religion, and the nation."[4]

The Brotherhood rapidly gained followers through the thirties and forties. It built mosques and schools, as other Islamic groups were doing, but the Brotherhood outstripped them by building and developing an expanding network of clinics, health-care centers and hospitals, and ambulance services that they made available not only to their members but also to the needy in the general population.

In the thirties, as Jewish immigration to Palestine began to pick up in the face of growing anti-Semitism in Europe, people in Arab countries, including Egypt, who had hitherto paid little attention to the Palestine issue, began to sympathize with the Palestinians.[5] When the Palestinians launched a strike in 1936 against the British and the Zionists, the Egyptian government took no position, having been given secret orders by the British to neither raise money nor show sympathy for the Palestinians. The government also had been ordered not to permit Palestinians to speak publicly in Egypt in support of their cause. In contrast, the Brotherhood now raised funds in support of the Palestinian strike, and in general it took a firm stand in support of the Palestinian cause, a cause now increasingly popular among the broader population. This position further added to the society's appeal.[6]

After gaining followers from the middle class as well as from rural immigrants and the urban working class, by the 1940s the Brotherhood had amassed a large enough following to rival al-Wafd, the country's dominant political party. By this time the Brotherhood had also developed a military branch. Of all the organizations and parties founded in this era, the Muslim Brotherhood alone would grow to become a formidable force in history, first in Egypt and eventually globally.

On the political level, the Brotherhood's goals included, first, freeing Egypt and other Islamic countries from imperialism. Their objectives were also to reinstitute Islamic laws and to work for Islamic revival and unity, and ideally for the return eventually of the caliphate abolished in 1924 by Ataturk. Their ultimate goal in this domain was the "universal Brotherhood of mankind and the global hegemony of the Islamic nation."[7]

This meant that they rejected the notion of an Egyptian nationalism defined by geography—the notion embraced by the reigning government of the day. Instead, they were committed to the idea of the larger Islamic umma, or community, "linked together by bonds of creed and Brotherhood which extended far beyond the borders of Egypt." They conceived of Arab unity in support of the Palestinian cause as a necessary first step toward Islamic unity.

On a social level, their goals included working to purify society and restore it to Islamic values and laws. From early on they called for the prohibition of prostitution, alcohol, nightclubs, and gambling, as well as for government action to curb Christian missionary activities. For a while in the late thirties a radical element among the Brotherhood tried also to push forward its agenda with regard to the veil and what it viewed as proper dress for women by smearing mud on the clothes of unveiled women. The Brotherhood leaders, however, insisted that the organization's message be spread through persuasion, not force, and they expelled the radicals behind these tactics.[8]

Of particular importance was the Brotherhood's increasingly pronounced commitment to the ideal of social justice. Criticizing the upper classes for squandering the resources of the people, the Brotherhood emphasized its own stance of activist social responsibility and its work in the service of promoting a just social and economic order grounded in

Islamic principles. From the thirties on, pursuing the goals of social justice and of reducing the gap between rich and poor became key elements of their ideology. These commitments and actions, which the Brotherhood both articulated and visibly and energetically worked for, were deeply resonant with the popular understanding of Islam as a religion committed above all to social justice, and they naturally gained the Brotherhood the support of many.[9]

At the heart of the entire project of bringing about a "renascent nation" was al-Banna's notion of the education and "founding" of souls. Educating souls and "imbuing them with love for the Islamic cause" was of importance because, among other reasons, once this love is sufficiently strong, "it generates the will to sacrifice . . . and makes the members contribute whenever necessary to make the projects of the Muslim Brothers successful." Quoting the Quranic verse "Verily God will never change the condition of a people until they change it themselves," the Muslim Brotherhood made it a goal to energize Muslims to throw off attitudes of fatalism and apathy and take charge of their own destiny.

Al-Banna conceived of the Muslim masses as a "dormant force" that needed to be awakened and activated by the Muslim Brothers. He described the difference between the Muslim masses and the Brothers in the following way: among the masses, Islam was an "anaesthetized faith, dormant within their souls . . . according to whose dictates they do not wish to act; whereas it is burning, blazing intense faith fully awakened in the souls of the Brothers."

The goal and mission of these awakened souls ablaze with faith was that of awakening other Muslims and persuading them to accept the Brotherhood's understanding of Islam. Thus the Brothers saw themselves as a "distinct group separated from the Muslim masses" and as an "avant-garde" that was ahead of and even above the ordinary masses. Some scholars believe that these attitudes nurtured a sense of self-righteousness and "intolerant arrogance" among the Brotherhood that would result in acts of violence made possible by their sense of superiority and difference. Others, however, note that the Brotherhood would not be involved in violence until the 1940s, and that when acts of violence were committed by the organization's military wing, their actions were strongly condemned by the leadership.[10]

Within this overall framework, the idea of "jihad"—to strive or struggle in the service of Islam—came to hold enormous importance for the Brotherhood, who now elaborated a distinctive and complex understanding of the meaning of "jihad." Besides referring to the duty to wage war against the occupying imperial power, "jihad" also meant, in Brotherhood terminology, the obligation to work to "eradicate the deeply ingrained resignation of the souls and minds of their co-religionists and remove their inferiority complexes." It meant, further, commitment to productive work; activism dedicated to improving the condition of the Muslim community; and the obligation to speak out against unjust rulers and to demand justice. The definition, elaborated by the classical Muslim jurist Abu Sa'id al-Khidri, of speaking "truth in the presence of a tyrannical ruler" became a guiding principle for the Brotherhood—as indeed, according to Brynjar Lia, "it still is."

During the war years Egypt again became a base for the British army. This created conditions of hardship, particularly for the poor, who did not have enough to eat and who rioted against the British, whose army they saw as the cause of their troubles. The common sight of British soldiers in the streets and the suddenly growing numbers of bars and brothels shocked many. The Muslim Brothers in particular were "outraged that their poorer women were opting for a life of sin through the lure of British gold," and they redoubled their efforts to convey to the people that the British were trampling on Islamic mores and ethics even simply by their presence.[11]

In 1942 the British surrounded the king's palace with tanks and ordered him to appoint the prime minister they favored. This flagrant display of brute British power would rankle deeply among Egyptians—including the group of officers who, in 1952, would seize power in a coup that drove King Farouk into exile.

The United Nations in 1947 voted to partition Palestine into an Arab and a Jewish state, a decision that distressed and affronted Arabs and Muslims everywhere. Following Britain's departure from Palestine and Israel's declaration of independence in May 1948, the Arab states, including Egypt, declared war on Israel. The Egyptian government had been opposed to such a war. The prime minister met with the king to inform him of the government's position and notify him that Egypt had neither adequate arms nor enough trained men to go to war with Israel. But the king, fearing that other Arab leaders would go to war and steal a march on him and gain victory, determined otherwise. The following morning the country's prime minister read in the papers that Egypt had declared war on Israel.[12]

The Muslim Brothers, who had started recruiting volunteers even before the British withdrawal from Palestine, sent a contingent of volunteers from their wing of armed and trained men. In the ensuing battles, which proved disastrous for the Arabs, only the Brotherhood's volunteer forces acquitted themselves well. Their effectiveness alarmed the prime minister, Mahmud Nuqrashi, alerting him of the potential threat that such a force posed to the Egyptian state. The Brotherhood's military wing had already carried out acts of political assassination and violence in the country, beginning early in the forties, including the assassination of a judge who had sentenced a Muslim Brother to prison for his attack on British soldiers. Such attacks by members of the organization's military wing reportedly occurred without the knowledge or support of al-Banna, who was said to have reacted with revulsion to such activities. With attacks now occurring on the properties of Egyptian Jews and Jewish businesses, as well as on British interests, this was a time of deep tension in the country.

On December 8, 1948, Nuqrashi issued an order dissolving the Muslim Brotherhood in Egypt. Commenting on this order, a pro-government newspaper observed that the Brotherhood was the government's strongest opponent. The Brotherhood, it noted, was not just a party; rather, it "resembled a state with its armies, hospitals, schools, factories, and companies." On December 28, Nuqrashi was assassinated by a third-year veterinary student who was a member of the Brotherhood.[13]

In February 1949, Hasan al-Banna was himself assassinated, presumably by government agents. During the following years the Brotherhood, which by now had branches all across the country and a following of more than half a million men, would continue to be banned, and some of its members would be pursued and imprisoned. In 1949 there were over four thousand Brotherhood members in prison.[14]

In July 1952, a group of military officers who included the future presidents of Egypt Gamal Abdel Nasser and Anwar Sadat, toppled the government, sent King Farouk into exile, and took power. Calling themselves the Free Officers, they consisted of a band of officers who had secretly pledged to drive the British out of Egypt. The impetus for their formation had come in 1942, when the British surrounded the king's palace with tanks and ordered him to appoint the man they wanted as prime minister. This, Sadat would later write, was an incident "that our generation cannot forget." Sadat and Nasser and others among the Free Officers also had served in the war with Israel in 1948. The Arabs' humiliating defeat by Israel, along with the deaths of comrades, which they blamed on government incompetence and negligence, further strengthened the Free Officers' resolve.[15] On July 23, 1952, as Farouk sailed in his yacht from Alexandria and into exile, the officers announced to the Egyptians that they were under new government.

When they first came to power the Free Officers had the support of the Brotherhood, for among the officers were men, most notably Sadat and Nasser, who had had close connections with the Brotherhood in the 1940s. The Brotherhood had even been expecting to share in the Free Officers' powers after the coup.[16] However, this did not come to pass, and when the new government failed, under Nasser's leadership, to move toward instituting an Islamic state, Brotherhood members grew vocally critical. In 1954, as Nasser was delivering a speech celebrating the withdrawal of the last British troops from Egypt, he was the target of an assassination attempt—an attempt that the government said had been carried out by the Brotherhood.

The Nasser government banned the organization (as the previous government had done) and arrested its leaders, as well as many thousands of its members. It would continue this policy, with growing ferocity, through the 1950s and 1960s, culminating in the imprisonment and torture of some of the Brotherhood's leading figures. These included two figures of major importance to the Muslim Brotherhood. One was Zainab al-Ghazali, who, although she never held any official position in the organization, is commonly viewed as a major figure in the history of the Brotherhood. Ghada Talhami, in her study of the Islamic mobilization of women, notes that some consider al-Ghazali to be one of the three most important leaders of the Brotherhood, and Roxanne Euben and Muhammad Qasim Zaman even assert that "if Hasan al-Banna is the father of the contemporary Islamist movement," al-Ghazali can be characterized as "its largely unsung mother."[17]

The other important figure in the history of the Brotherhood arrested in the Nasser era was Sayyid Qutb, the organization's leading intellectual and ideologue. He would be imprisoned and tortured twice over the course of the fifties and sixties, and was executed in 1966. Qutb is most widely known as a thinker and philosopher and as the author of books that have inspired Islamist militants. Al-Ghazali admired his work and taught it in the seminars she ran. Nevertheless, in her own activism she espoused and committed herself to advancing the Islamist cause through outreach and education, and she typically represented herself as opposed to the use of violence.

Through these years of persecution by the Nasser government, many among the Brotherhood's leadership, as well as among its rank and file, fled into exile. A significant number among them went to Saudi Arabia and other Arab Gulf countries, where they were generally welcomed. The Brotherhood's socially conservative outlook and deep commitment to Islam was in consonance with the Wahhabi perspective on Islam that was dominant in Saudi Arabia, as well as with the less strictly conservative forms of Islam that were prevalent elsewhere in the Arabian Peninsula. Brotherhood members were additionally welcome because they typically were well-educated people—engineers, chemists, doctors, scientists, and teachers. Saudi Arabia and the Arab Gulf countries in the fifties and sixties had recently begun to develop their oil fields, and with their accumulating wealth they were seeking to invest in, among other things, the social development of their societies, including the establishment of schools and colleges. So this influx of educated manpower was a valuable resource in the Arabian oil states' pursuit of these goals.

The Nasser era (1954–69) was a politically turbulent time, as well as a period of social transformation in Egypt and in the region. In the fifties Nasser participated, alongside Nehru of India, Sukarno of Indonesia, and Tito of Yugoslavia, in the Bandung Conference and in other meetings of the "non-aligned nations," as they called themselves. Such meetings were often accompanied by and concluded with deep criticisms of Western colonialism—statements that, along with their accompanying attitudes, were not welcomed by the Western powers.

In addition, Nasser now believed that he needed to arm his country in the face of Israel's growing military capacities. When Western nations placed conditions he considered unacceptable on the sale of arms to Egypt (France, for example, demanded that he cease supporting the Algerian revolution), Nasser turned to the Soviet Union. In 1955 he signed an arms deal with Czechoslovakia.

This move angered the United States, which responded by abruptly withdrawing, on July 19, 1956, the funding it had promised for the construction of Egypt's Aswan High Dam. Nasser reacted swiftly, nationalizing the Suez Canal on July 26. The canal's revenues would now be used, he proclaimed, to build the High Dam. Loudly condemning the canal's nationalization, Britain and France joined with Israel in an attack on Egypt in October. The city of Port Said was bombarded, and Egyptian casualties were high. Both the United States and the Soviet Union condemned the attack, and the U.S. called for an immediate ceasefire.

The attack brought worldwide condemnation of the attackers, as well as sympathy and admiration, particularly in the colonized and formerly colonized Third World, for Egypt's valiant stand against this brazen imperial aggression. Furthermore, it precipitated Nasser onto the world stage as a leading figure in the struggle against imperialism. In the Arab world in particular, writes historian Afaf Lutfi al-Sayyid Marsot, he became an adulated figure who stood for "unity among Arab peoples, pride in self, an end to colonial influence, independence." After the Suez War, she continues, Nasser's picture "was to be found in every shop and bazaar in all Arab countries."[18]

Arab nationalism, as embodied in the anti-imperialist and anti-Israeli positions and rhetoric espoused by Nasser, became a powerful force across many Arab countries throughout the fifties and into the mid-sixties. Several such countries had just emerged or were in the process of emerging from British or French domination. The French army had left Syria in 1946, and France declared Algeria independent in 1962. Iraq, under British control and of compelling interest to them because of its vast oil reserves (British and American oil companies already held huge stakes there), remained under British control through a series of coups and uprisings until—and indeed beyond—the army coup of 1958, which overthrew the Iraqi monarchy installed by the British. Egypt's monarch and its government, viewed as both corrupt and unable to free themselves of the shackles of British control, had been overthrown in the Revolution of 1952.

Also among the political and ideological currents sweeping across much of the Arab region was a commitment by the new wave of rulers to socialism and to sweeping away classist attitudes, as well as to pan-Arab nationalism. In Egypt this would result in land reforms which allowed the confiscation of the agricultural properties of large landowners (over a certain acreage) and the redistribution of the land to agricultural workers. It also resulted in the nationalization of factories and in policy changes that introduced new opportunities for the working classes. For instance, the government now made education, from primary school through university level, free for all who qualified.

The trend toward socialism in Egypt was not, however, accompanied by a Soviet-style rejection of religion. On the contrary, the Nasser regime was well aware of the importance of religion and of laying claim to and acquiring legitimacy and authority through appeals to religion. From early on, for example, the Free Officers would sometimes preach the Friday sermon, and Nasser and other members of the government were often photographed in mosques at prayer. Similarly, in 1954 Nasser made a pilgrimage to Mecca, an event that was widely reported on in the media. In addition, Nasser also frequently delivered important speeches in mosques, including the mosque of al-Azhar. It was from here, for example, during the Suez crisis, that he delivered a powerful and memorable speech that galvanized the country in resistance to the tripartite attack.[19]

The Nasser regime took measures to exert its influence over the country's religious institutions to bring them into line with its ideologies. New laws were enacted to give the government greater control over the prestigious and internationally renowned Islamic al-Azhar University, for example—an imposition of government control that prompted some officials and professors at al-Azhar to resign in protest. Many did not, though, and some Islamic scholars began publishing books and articles supporting and justifying government policies in Islamic terms.[20] Socialism, for example, some Islamic scholars now maintained, was deeply grounded in Islamic ideals, ideals that exhorted Muslims to create a society in which the poor were free from hunger and need and exploitation and injustice.

Nevertheless, the drift toward socialism was in part a sign of growing Soviet interest and influence in the region. Naturally growing Soviet influence was a matter of concern to Britain and the United States in relation to the Middle East in general, but most specifically in relation to the oil-rich countries of Iraq and Saudi Arabia. The political currents of the day had already swept away two Arab monarchies and replaced them with regimes that were fiercely anti-imperialist. Moreover, the Arab nationalist rhetoric of the time, and in particular that emanating from Egypt, was specifically targeting the monarchy and ruling powers of Saudi Arabia. Nasser denounced Saudi Arabia's rulers as allies of imperialism and, in particular, of the United States. He described the government as supporting "imperialist causes" and as "impeding the liberation of the struggling Islamic nations." He went on also to assert that the form of Islam that they were enforcing in their country was a "feudalistic," nonegalitarian form of Islam that was "reactionary and stifling" and would lead only to "retardation and decline."[21]

Nor did Nasser confine his attacks on Saudi Arabia to rhetoric. By the early sixties he was sending contingents of the Egyptian army to support a revolutionary, socialist, and anti-royalist war in Yemen, a country on Saudi Arabia's southern border. To counter Nasser's support for the revolutionaries, Saudi Arabia now vigorously supported the Yemeni monarchy.

These were not matters that Saudi Arabia and its allies took lightly. Other monarchies in the region had toppled and been replaced by governments whose ideologies were pan-Arabist, anti-imperialist, and inclined toward socialism. Saudi royalty feared that such winds might sweep through their own country.

Through the fifties Saudi Arabia was beginning to emerge as a new economic force in the region. Drawing on their gathering wealth, the Saudi regime now began its efforts to counter the wave of Arab nationalism and socialism sweeping the region, and to respond to and undermine the Nasserite ideology that was making such gains in the Arab world. The objective was to spread instead its own ideological commitments, including to the form of Islam, Wahhabi Islam, that prevailed in the Saudi kingdom. The struggle between these two blocs, the royalist Saudis on the one hand and the Arab nationalists and socialists on the other, most starkly epitomized and represented by the struggle for power between Saudi Arabia and Egypt, would later come to be dubbed (by Malcolm Kerr and others) the Arab Cold War.[22] These local struggles also directly involved obviously the two sides of the global Cold War who, in these years, were contending for power and influence here and elsewhere across the world.

Saudi Arabia's moves to counter pan-Arabism and Nasserite ideology with its own religious and ideological commitments would prove to be of momentous importance to the rise and spread of the Islamic Resurgence and of course, therefore, of the veil. Consequently, Saudi Arabia and the religious and ideological commitments it now set about promoting and propagating play key roles in the story that I tell in this book.

Saudi Arabia pursued its goals in part through the founding of organizations and institutions that would prove to be of key importance to the work of spreading Saudi ideology. Thus in 1961 the Saudis instituted a new university in Medina whose objective was the training of Muslim missionaries. And in 1962 they began to pursue the goal of establishing a new transnational organization, the Muslim World League (Rabitat al-'Alam al-Islami).

The first meeting took place in Mecca after the completion of that year's pilgrimage. This meeting brought together scholars, intellectuals, and politicians from across the Muslim world. It was convened to "discuss the affairs of the Islamic Ummah in view of the threats posed to it by 'communism' in general and the 'irreligious' Egyptian president Nasser in particular." A council made up of twenty-one members was appointed, and it convened in December. The council members made clear that the League was trying to "bring together mainstreams of contemporary Islamic ideology and theology" and that it was seeking to represent "within itself some contemporary mainstreams of Islamic thought."[23]

The grand mufti of Saudi Arabia headed the council, and Saudi Arabian Wahhabism naturally was well represented at the meeting. Also on the council were Said Ramadan, the son-in-law of Hasan al-Banna and claimant to the leadership of the Muslim Brotherhood, and Maulana Abu'l 'Ala Mawdudi, the founder and leader of the Jamaat-i Islami, an organization similar to the Muslim Brotherhood and founded in India in 1940. Like the Brotherhood, this organization had been running into difficulties in its home country—now Pakistan.

The League stated its intention to "promote the message of Islam" and to "fight conspiracies against Islam." In addition, it committed itself to working for Islamic solidarity and for the "cooperation of all Islamic states." It also argued for an "Islamic bloc" to take a stand "against Baathist [Arab socialist] regimes."[24]

Backed with almost limitless funds, the League set about its goals of countering Nasserite ideology and of combining the forces it had gathered in order to disseminate and promote to Muslims worldwide the socially conservative Islam that they espoused.

As Nasser used his powerful propaganda apparatus, including the radio station Voice of the Arabs, to disseminate his views and launch his rhetorical attacks on Saudi Arabia, the Saudis responded with a barrage of rhetoric and criticism directed at the Nasser regime. Condemning socialism and Arab nationalism as "un-Islamic," they accused Nasser of misleading the people into putting their faith in the secular ideologies of socialism and Arab nationalism instead of in Islam. Stressing Saudi Arabia's centrality for Muslims as the custodian of the holy cities of Mecca and Medina, and the authority of its pronouncements by virtue of that position, Saudi Arabian rhetoric emphasized that religious and not national or ethnic bonds must form the ground of identity among Muslims. Muslims must anchor their identities and the goals of their struggles and political activism in Islam alone, and they must turn away from such delusory and un-Islamic secular ideologies as Arab nationalism and socialism.[25]

The League distributed books and pamphlets, sent out missionaries, and supported the work of Islamist activists. It also supported the building of mosques in Egypt, the Arab world, and worldwide. To an important extent the League was able to pursue its goal by drawing on the skills and manpower of the Muslim Brothers who had come to Saudi Arabia to escape persecution in Egypt. As mentioned above, many among the Brotherhood who had fled into exile were educated, and held positions in Saudi colleges and other institutions.

The League now drew on the skills of Brotherhood members to organize their projects and to write, edit, and produce books and pamphlets and, in general, to do the work of promoting and disseminating in Egypt and across the Muslim world the League's understanding of Islam. Similarly the task also of mounting a rhetorical and ideological attack on Nasserism and Nasser's ideologies and of blasting them as false and empty rhetoric when set alongside the power and truth of Islam and obedience to Islam, now fell largely to members of the Brotherhood.

It was thus often members of the Brotherhood who, backed by the League's vast resources, now manned and oversaw the League's publications and publishing houses, and who directed and ran its projects, media, and missions. Nasser's intimate enemies and the very people who had fled into exile from his persecutions were now disseminating through pamphlets, publications, radio broadcasts, and other media a barrage of rhetoric whose broad objective was that of undermining and discrediting Egypt's "irreligious" president: the president whose "secular" ideologies (as these were dubbed in the new rhetorical wars) of Arab nationalism and socialism were leading the Muslim peoples away from the ways of God and Islam. Muslims must reject these irreligious ideologies and return to placing their faith in Islam and God alone. Only Islam—and not Arab nationalism or Arab unity or unity in the name of any one or other ethnicity—offered the true and proper ground of faith, identity, and unity for Muslims.

During the Nasser era much of the Arab world, just as Hourani reported from his own direct observations, had marched inexorably forward into the Age of No Veiling—an age that was to reach its peak in the late sixties and would persist well into the seventies and even on into the early nineties. Although already widespread in the cities by the forties, being unveiled increasingly became the norm during the Nasser era, spreading even to Hourani's "conservative lower classes" and also into the countryside.

The women of the Brotherhood of course continued to wear their covering. But in the Nasser era and during the government crackdown on the Brotherhood, the Brotherhood constituted a group that was distinctly marginal to the larger society. Even when they had been a powerful movement they still constituted no more than a small minority of the population.[26] Accordingly, in the 1950s the Brotherhood simply did not figure as a force at all in Hourani's admittedly brief overview of the veil.

The government's commitment to breaking down class barriers and erasing class difference in part contributed to the spread of the practice of not wearing veils. By the forties veiling was most notably a marker of class difference—whether in relation to Hourani's conservative "lower middle class" or with respect to village women.

The government actively promoted, in education, salaries, and other ways, the concept of women's equality and their right to work. Women received the vote in the constitution of 1956. By 1962 women had been appointed to senior government positions, and all the women holding such positions were bareheaded—like the majority of women in mainstream society. All of this doubtless contributed to the growing ordinariness of women going about their lives without veils. Among other things, the absence of the veil implicitly proclaimed and affirmed the national ideal of women as equal citizens. Not wearing any sort of hijab had become so common for women by the end of the fifties that on one occasion, when Nasser was making a speech in 1962, a citizen called out to him asking him to require women to veil. Nasser brushed aside the request, saying that he did not wish to "engage in battle with 25 million people [Egypt's estimated population at that time] or at least half of them."[27] This response obviously indicates that Nasser took for granted that the vast majority of Egyptian women wore no hijab and that most Egyptian men supported this. Of course myriad media images from that era fully bear out his assumption that uncovered heads for women were now entirely the norm.

The tide would begin to turn following Nasser's and the Arab world's devastating defeat by Israel in the war of 1967. Nasser had himself of course come to power when a group of military officers had been spurred by Israel's defeat of the Arabs in 1948 into taking action to overthrow the government. Opposition to Zionism as well as to imperialism had been staples of Nasser's political rhetoric, along with the often-repeated promise that never again would Egypt be defeated by Israel. Lavishing funds on armaments and on the army, whose officers became the privileged classes of Nasser's regime, he had boasted that in any war with Israel, Egypt would achieve a swift and decisive victory.

Instead, the Egyptian air force was wiped out in minutes and Egypt soundly defeated—losing twelve thousand men. The defeat would mark the end of Nasserism.[28]

Just as the defeat of '48 had led officers to conclude that the values, methods, goals, and ideals of the old regime were bankrupt and useless and must be swept away, this defeat was read in the same way by the officers of the day. One such officer would later write:

> The Egyptian officers and soldiers saw their colleagues burned by napalm. We saw the army of our country destroyed in hours. We thought that we would conquer Israel in hours. . . .
>
> I discovered that it wasn't Israel that defeated us, but it was the [Egyptian] regime that defeated us and I started to be against the regime. . . . there was an earthquake in the Arab-Islamic personality[,] not only in Egypt but in the entire Arab world.

In later years the author of these words, Essam Deraz, would volunteer his services to other Muslims under attack—serving in the war in Afghanistan against the Soviets. Here, in the 1980s, he would serve on the front lines along with Osama bin Laden.[29]

Like the defeat of 1948 and arguably even more profoundly, the

1967 defeat would have an earthquake-like effect on the Arab world, setting in motion enormous changes.

Historians write that a mood of religiosity swept across the country in the wake of the 1967 defeat. That defeat profoundly shook people's confidence in the government, and they began to see its promises as false and its "secular" ideologies as empty. For answers, people now turned to Islam and to religion, as indeed over the preceding few years a stream of rhetoric emanating from Saudi Arabia and the Brotherhood had exhorted them to do.

Soon after the defeat an apparition of the Virgin Mary was seen beside a small church on the outskirts of Cairo. Muslims as well as Christians flocked by the thousands to see it, camping out overnight to watch for her appearance. Miracles and cures were reported. Some interpreted the Virgin's appearance as a sign intended to draw Muslims and Christians together into unified opposition against the Zionist enemy.[30] Others saw it as a divine sign offering comfort to Egyptians, as if to say that despite their defeat God was on their side. The mood of religiosity had palpable and tangible consequences too. Quranic reading groups now multiplied, and monasteries, which had been closing for lack of applicants, were deluged with applications.[31]

The defeat allowed the government's conservative Muslim critics to say that the defeat was a vindication of what they had said all along, that "the ways of 'Islamic socialism' were not the ways of God." It was a clear sign, they declared, of God's punishment of Egypt and the Arabs for putting their faith in Arab nationalism and turning away from Islam. The only way to recapture ascendancy and victory, they argued, was "by a total renunciation of man-made ideologies and a reorientation towards an unwavering commitment to the realization of Islam in the world. Israel did not get the victory because it represented a better system or a truer religion or a more perfect response to God's revelation; rather, God used Israel to punish His errant nation and allowed the forces of evil to conquer the Muslims because they had strayed from the Straight Path."[32] Similarly, the Saudis described the defeat as a "divine punishment for forgetting religion."[33]

As the mood and language of religiousness gained force, the government also took to invoking religion and the symbolism of religion in ever more public and formal ways. Soon after the defeat, for example, the top government figures attended mosque together. And in July of that year, in a speech marking the anniversary of the revolution, Nasser himself suggested that perhaps the reason for the defeat was that "Allah was trying to teach Egypt a lesson, to purify it in order to build up a new society." And in a further gesture of conciliation Nasser released a number of Muslim Brothers from prison.[34]

This turn to religiosity would set the stage for the rapid return of the Muslim Brotherhood and the growing powers of Islamist groups generally in the ensuing era of Sadat.

·3·

The 1970s

Seeds of the Resurgence

Following Nasser's death in 1970, Anwar Sadat, then vice president, became president of Egypt. Although regarded at first as a temporary figurehead, Sadat moved quickly to consolidate his power and to veer away from the political and ideological course that Nasser had set. In particular, he began to distance the country from the Soviet Union and to turn away from Nasser's proclaimed commitment to egalitarianism and socialism. Declaring his intention to pursue a pro-capitalist stance and economy, Sadat began to seek alignment with the West, and in particular with the United States.

As he had anticipated, these ideological shifts provoked fierce criticism from the Left. To silence his critics and gain allies among religious conservatives, Sadat completed the process that Nasser had begun, releasing Muslim Brothers from prison and inviting back to the country Brotherhood members who had fled to Saudi Arabia and elsewhere. A fair number of those who had gone into exile to the Arab oil states had acquired considerable wealth there, so the prospect of their investing in Egypt would have been an additional reason for courting their return.[1]

Sadat now explicitly swathed himself in the language of religion—for example, he described himself as the Believer President (*al-rais al-mu'min*). He encouraged and even gave secret support to Islamist groups, particularly on university campuses, where Leftist students had had a dominant role in running student organizations.[2]

This was the Cold War era. Sadat's rapprochement with the Brotherhood—a religiously based organization that had been persecuted by the Soviet-leaning Nasser—along with his broad support for Islamist organizations in general as he steered the country away from the Soviet Union and socialism toward closer ties with the United States, were all moves that were viewed positively by Washington.

Washington in those days had no quarrel with the Muslim Brothers or with Islamists. When the Saudi-based League had begun funding Islamist groups in the 1960s in Egypt and elsewhere, the United States had viewed that development approvingly, as it was eager to encourage trends that undermined the "godless empire" of the Soviet Union and its allies.[3]

The Sadat government allowed the Brotherhood to resume its social activism on the condition that it confine its activities to the nonpolitical domains of *da'wa* (religious outreach), education, charity, and religious teaching. Committed as ever to the goal of Islamizing society, the Brotherhood accepted those terms, which enabled it to operate as a legitimate organization, and the Brothers poured their energies into providing alternative educational, medical, and social services.[4] Thus, reemerging after the Nasser era as an organization that was now on cordial terms with the government, the Brotherhood would also become a changed organization in outlook and approach. Most importantly, its leadership would now explicitly renounce violence, committing the organization to using only legal means to express its opposition.[5] This decision would alienate the more radical members and bring about breakaway militant groups.[6]

The leadership's position against violence was the result, in part, of a debate that had developed within the Brotherhood and other Islamist groups during the years of Nasser's persecutions, during which Brothers had undergone imprisonment and torture while members of its leadership had been executed, among them the Brotherhood's leading intellectual, Sayyid Qutb. In his books, and in particular in *Milestones,* a book written mainly in prison, Qutb asserted that the societies of the so-called Muslim world were not in fact Islamic but rather were *jahiliyya* societies: societies that were no longer observing the laws of Islam or living in ways that acknowledged the sovereignty of God.

Jahiliyya was an important term to Qutb, and it remains important in the Islamist vocabulary. It was a term that Qutb himself had borrowed, as he acknowledged, from Mawdudi, founder of the Jamaat-i Islami of Pakistan, a parallel organization to the Muslim Brotherhood founded in India in 1940. From the root word *jahl* (ignorance), jahiliyya is a term that occurs in the Quran with reference to the condition of "ignorance" that characterized Arabian society prior to the Islamic revelations.[7] Before Qutb's adoption of the word, *jahiliyya* was in common usage as a term simply denoting the pre-Islamic era in Arabia. Through Qutb's work, however, and applied to contemporary times, the word would come to connote a condition more "sinister" than the "naïve" ignorance of ancient Arabia, for today jahiliyya was a condition that had been "willfully created by men who usurp the role of God."[8] "Today we are in a similar or darker jahiliyyah," as Qutb wrote, "than that contemporaneous to early Islam." All that surrounds us, he continued, "is jahiliyyah": "People's visions, beliefs, their habits and customs, their sources of knowledge, art, literature, rules and laws, even what we consider as Islamic education, Islamic sources, Islamic philosophy and Islamic thought—all of it is the product of the jahiliyyah."[9]

Because of these conditions, "true Islamic values," Qutb maintained, are unknown in the so-called Muslim World (let alone elsewhere), and consequently they "never enter our hearts," nor are our minds "illuminated by Islamic concepts."[10]

In such times it was essential, Qutb wrote, for a Muslim "vanguard" consisting of a "coalition of committed individuals" whose "total existence" was "focused on the mission" of reviving Islam to set forth on this momentous and essential task. *Milestones*, written in the early 1960s—the height of the Cold War—was a book that Qutb wrote specifically to counter and rebut both communism and capitalism, and to promote the revival of Islam as the only viable third way. Islam alone, according to Qutb, was capable of addressing man's needs for both bread and spiritual meaning, and of anchoring man in the reality of God and in the moral universe that God had decreed. The Islamic system, grounded in social justice and binding Muslims to obedience only to God, simultaneously liberated them, Qutb argued, from subservience to any human being. Islam "provides us," wrote Qutb, "with the bread that communism provides, and frees us from economic and social disparity, realizing a balanced society while sustaining us spiritually."[11]

The Muslim confession of faith, "La illaha illa Allah" (there is no God but God), as Qutb understood it, was a revolutionary teaching, a teaching against all human sovereignty and usurpation of powers, whether by princes, governments, or priests. It was a teaching that was altogether against the oppression of one individual by another. "There is no governance except for God," Qutb wrote. "No legislation but from God, no sovereignty of one [person] over another because all sovereignty belongs to God."

Because Islam alone—not socialism or capitalism—was capable of providing for all of man's basic needs, the revival of Islam was essential. Indeed, Qutb maintained, Islam's eventual hegemony over the entire world was inevitable, because Islam alone was grounded in the truth of God's revelation. However, he said, the revival and eventual world hegemony of Islam could be realized only through the dedicated and selfless labor and struggle—jihad—of the vanguard of committed Muslims.

The term jihad is from the root word *jahada,* meaning to strive or exert oneself. In the sense of engaging in exertion or jihad to further Islam, the term was defined by classical Islamic jurists as referring to four types of religious obligation. First was the jihad of the heart, which was "concerned with combating the devil and evil things." This form of jihad was regarded by the prophet as the "greater jihad." Second and third were the jihad of the tongue and hand, which pertained to the obligation of "enjoining the right and forbidding the wrong" in society. The fourth meaning of jihad, the jihad of the sword, was that of "fighting unbelievers and enemies of the faith."[12]

Jihad of the sword was not considered by classical jurists to be one of the five pillars—that is, one of the five fundamental obligations—required of all Muslims. The jurists did, however, consider it to be a duty of all Muslims when the Muslim community and faith were under attack. Qutb and militant Islamists would depart from this understanding, however, and define jihad as one of the foundational pillars of Islam and thus an obligation of all Muslims. Over the decades since Qutb's death, radical Islamists have read Qutb's books, particularly *Milestones,* as advocating jihad in the sense of armed and violent struggle. They believe that it constitutes a legitimate strategy against unbelievers of all stripes, including those "heathen," jahiliyya peoples, and most particularly their illegitimate and heathen rulers in the so-called Muslim lands.

While some of Qutb's ideas clearly had their antecedents in ideas that al-Banna had enunciated and that had emerged in the early years of the Brotherhood—such as the notion of the Muslim Brothers as a band of "awakened" souls and as a vanguard—he took such ideas much further, in a dramatically more radical direction.

In the 1960s, the more militant younger members of the Brotherhood embraced Qutb's ideas and argued for the use of violence to bring down the Nasser regime. Qutb, who had been released from prison in 1964, was again arrested in 1965, along with other Brotherhood members, on charges of plotting to assassinate Nasser. On the almost exclusive evidence of his writings, and in particular of *Milestones,* passages of which were quoted at his trial, Qutb was convicted and sentenced to death. He was executed on August 29, 1966.

Qutb's execution elevated him to the rank of martyr in the eyes of many Islamists, a fact that made it difficult for those in the Islamist leadership who opposed his views, especially in relation to the legitimacy of violence, to openly criticize him. Nevertheless, the Brotherhood leader Hasan al-Hudaybi in 1969 published *Du'a,la Qudah* (Preachers, Not Judges). Arguing in this book that the proper role of Islamists was that of teaching and preaching true Islam, and not that of judging or condemning the Islam of others, al-Hudaybi was implicitly refuting Qutb's ideas.[13]

In the 1970s the leadership explicitly repudiated the idea of using violence to achieve the Islamist goal of establishing an Islamic state ruled by a government grounded in the laws of sharia. In repudiating violence altogether the Brotherhood leadership was now committed to pursuing its objectives through peaceful means and a gradualist approach.[14]

Not everyone in the organization embraced these commitments made by the Brotherhood leadership, however. Although the broad majority and mainstream membership accepted them, some members on the more militant fringes wholly rejected them, and some among these broke away to found alternative Islamist groups.[15]

The leadership's commitment to a gradualist approach entailed, above all, a commitment to transforming society from the ground up, through steadfast collective efforts of outreach and charity work and, most important, education. The gradualist approach was seen as essential to bringing about an Islamic society governed by sharia, in that the first step was to undertake the work of the Islamic education or reeducation of the population. It was necessary, they maintained, to educate the general population before people would abandon the forms of belief and practice that the majority society now followed—forms and practices that the Brotherhood regarded as those of lapsed and passive or "dormant" Muslims. Simultaneously, the population needed to be persuaded to replace their beliefs and practices with the committed, activist form of Islam and its accompanying prescriptions and rituals (among them the hijab for women) as preached and practiced by the Brotherhood.

By means of this process of Islamic reeducation, society would be made ready for the eventual institution of Islamic government ruled by the laws of sharia. For, as the Brotherhood leadership reasoned, once people had become Islamically educated they would readily accept Islamic government and sharia out of their own convictions. The key, therefore, was to work steadily to build up and educate the population, generation by generation, until the Brotherhood's views and teachings had become the beliefs and norms of the broad majority and of wider society. Once more the project of the education of souls and the work of daʿwa, of calling people to the Brotherhood understanding of Islam, became a central mission for the organization.

According to Zainab al-Ghazali, the "unsung mother" of the Brotherhood, the decision to pursue this nonviolent, educational approach was arrived at by a core group of the Brotherhood's leadership—a group that included al-Ghazali herself, as well as Sayyid Qutb, whom al-Ghazali consulted during his imprisonment through regular contact with his sisters. Other prominent Brotherhood figures whom al-Ghazali consulted with included al-Hudaybi, who had succeeded al-Banna as the Brotherhood's Supreme Guide, and Abdel-Fattah Ismail, a prominent figure in the Brotherhood whom she met during a pilgrimage to Mecca in the mid-fifties. As al-Ghazali wrote in her memoir, it was during those critical years of Nasserite persecution that this core group concluded that "preparing our youth for da'wa" was the one strategically essential task. "It was of paramount importance," she wrote, "that we prepare future generations in the persons of these youth who would hopefully become teachers of education and training in their own right for subsequent generations."[16] This core group decided, al-Ghazali wrote, that they would keep at the task of the Islamic training of "youth, elders, women and children" for thirteen years—thirteen being the number of years that the first Muslim community, under the leadership of the Prophet Muhammad, had practiced da'wa and endeavored to convert the heathen in Mecca. After thirteen years the leadership would survey the situation. If by then 75 percent of the people believed that "Islam was a complete way of life" they would call for the establishment of an Islamic state. If the percentage was less, she continued, they would continue their efforts "for another thirteen years, and so on, until the ummah [community] is ripe to accept Islamic rule."[17]

Put simply, as one activist explained to a researcher, "I won't go to the government now and say this is wrong and this is right. I will go to those around me and build them up, teach them. Then when we are 90 percent of society, then those who I have brought up will go to the government, not me."[18]

During the mid-1960s, the years of Nasser's worst persecutions, according to Gilles Kepel, a noted student of Islamist movements, young activists favored the use of violence to bring down Nasser; al-Ghazali, on the other hand, held fast to the idea that the only path forward for the Brotherhood lay in the commitment to tirelessly working for the education of one generation after another.[19]

Among the Brotherhood leadership the emphasis remained on education and on a gradualist approach including with regard to the matter of the imposition of sharia. Omar Tilmesani, for instance, who took the leadership of the Brotherhood in 1973, maintained that social and economic justice must first of all be established in society before sharia could be instituted. In the absence of such conditions, he argued, imposing sharia could lead to its being put to "illegal use," resulting in injustice. Furthermore, he declared, prior to imposing sharia, careful studies needed to be undertaken with the object of "unifying and synthesizing" past and present legal opinions. In addition, he said, studies of the laws of other societies should also be undertaken, laws that, if they were not in conflict with sharia, could also be drawn on to formulate laws "suitable to the needs of Egyptian society." No model as yet existed, he pointed out, as to how sharia should be implemented in the contemporary world. Therefore, when Egypt produced the first model of a sharia-based system of laws, "that model should be flawless so as not to disillusion those in other countries who wished to do the same."[20]

Banned from political activities, the Brotherhood poured all its energies and resources into offering a broad range of charitable services. These included not only schools for the poor, which the Brotherhood had long offered, but also private Islamic schools for the well-to-do. In addition, they set up nurseries and day-care centers for young children, as well as clinics and hospitals, legal aid units, and youth centers.[21] Often such services would be provided at facilities attached to the rapidly growing numbers of mosques that the Muslim Brothers, along with other Islamist groups, were funding and building.

Providing for the needs of the poor and donating skills, services, and financial support in the interests of working for justice and for the greater good of society as a whole were always key parts of the Brotherhood's broad ethos, strategies, and methodologies. Offering services to the poor and to others in times of crisis—earthquakes, floods, fires—has been a mainstay and hallmark of Brotherhood activism, and typical of the work of Islamist groups modeled on the Brotherhood that began to multiply in the 1970s. Islamist charities and relief agencies working in Egypt and around the world also began to multiply. Typically these organizations provided (and still provide) for the needs of poor, distressed, and dispossessed Muslims wherever they are—Palestine, Bosnia, Kashmir, Afghanistan, and elsewhere. In many such countries, as in Egypt, the services that the Brotherhood and other Islamist groups offered, generally at nominal cost, usually were far better than anything the government offered, if such services were even available.[22]

Such work significantly improved the quality of life and alleviated real material hardships for countless people. It was also a highly effective form of da'wa; as the members carried out their service to society they exemplified the genuineness of their ethical commitments and their dedication to serving those in need. Their example doubtless drew people to their cause, beliefs, and ways of practicing Islam.

The 1970s, the decade in which the Muslim Brothers and other Islamist organizations began to flourish, was also the decade in which the Sadat government abandoned the Nasserite principles of socialism, and along with this the socialist policies that Nasser's government had pursued. Such policies had provided at least a modicum of relief for the poorest and most needy in society, relief that was now withdrawn even as economic problems were worsening and hardships were growing for many Egyptians.

In place of socialism Sadat initiated what he called an "open-door" policy toward Western capitalism. This had brought in, among other things, Kentucky Fried Chicken and McDonald's, along with lavish consumer goods—all of these beyond the means of most Egyptians.[23] Only a tiny percentage of the population, some of whom had become immensely wealthy through their connections to the government and foreign agencies, was able to enjoy such luxuries.[24]

Scandals and stories of corruption, greed, and profiteering at the upper levels of society were rife. These topics were commonly taken up in the Islamist leaflets and pamphlets, including the Brotherhood's journal *al-Da'wa,* which was now available at newsstands on every street corner and at bus and tram stops. As one commentator noted in an issue of *al-Da'wa,* in a time of corruption and economic crisis, government policies seemed focused on importing "trivial goods like false eyelashes" while neglecting the necessities.[25]

Other Islamist organizations likewise expanded through the seventies, among them organizations on university campuses that received the covert support of the Sadat government.[26] These organizations were particularly strong in the most competitive and prestigious faculties, such as engineering, medicine, and pharmacy, which in the Nasser era had been the bastions of left-wing student activism. By 1975, Islamists had gained control of important campus committees, among them the Committee for Publications. This allowed them to produce and distribute Islamist pamphlets at low cost. Within another couple of years Islamists had taken over all of the important student leadership committees and positions.[27]

Enrollments at Egyptian universities had risen rapidly through the sixties with the availability of free education. They continued to rise at an even faster rate through the 1970s, creating ever greater pressures on the resources—housing, transport, lecture halls—of cities and of campuses. By 1977 the student population had swelled from two hundred thousand in 1970 to over half a million. The numbers were rising faster—at almost twice the rate—among women than among men.[28]

These overcrowded conditions were particularly hard for women. Young female students, often from rural backgrounds, who found it culturally uncomfortable and inappropriate to be in close quarters with strange men, now had to join them in crowded lecture halls and in congested public transport. All of this was occurring, moreover, during a time of worsening economic conditions, and when lavish consumerism was practiced only by the wealthy few and when many of the goods filling the markets, including clothes and Western fashions, were well beyond the means of most young women.[29]

This was the time that the new veil and Islamic dress—a distinctive and arrestingly different form of dress that always included a head covering or hijab—began to make its appearance on the streets of Cairo and other Egyptian cities. Women in this new style of dress suddenly became a very noticeable presence, particularly, according to a contemporary observer, Fadwa El Guindi, immediately following the 1973 October war with Israel.

The '73 war had been launched by Egypt and Syria with the object of recapturing the territories taken by Israel in the '67 war. It was a surprise attack by the Arabs, and the Arab armies were successful at first. Subsequently, the Israeli forces would rally. Still, the Arabs had been successful enough to shock Israel and the world into realizing that Israel was not, after all, invincible.

In Egypt, this war, launched during Ramadan, the holy month of fasting, and also on Yom Kippur—became viewed as a victory, and Sadat was regarded as hero. Islamists would say that the Egyptians had been successful on this occasion, in contrast to their defeat in 1967, because this time they had gone to war not for Arab nationalism or some other secular cause but in the cause of religion. This time, it was said, they had gone to war shouting "Allah Akbar!" (God is Greater).[30]

Sadat and his supporters also would use religious language and symbolism to describe the war: even the name by which the war would be known in Egypt, the Ramadan War, foregrounded its religious dimension. Sadat would use the term jihad in referring to this war—a term which again connoted that it was a struggle or battle undertaken in the service of Islam. In addition, Sadat would now begin to refer to himself as al-rais al-mu'min the "Believer President."[31]

El Guindi, who had reported that Islamic dress had suddenly become noticeable after the Ramadan War, would be one of a number of scholars to address this phenomenon, as well as other aspects of Islamism, that now, along with the veil, began their rapid spread.

Initially, and through the 1970s, these developments took everyone by surprise—it was a turn of events that no historian or student of society had predicted. Contemporaries making up the Egyptian mainstream were also bewildered and sometimes shocked and disturbed by the appearance of the hijab and the new and formidably concealing styles of dress.

By a stroke of fortune, we now have a wealth of material and studies available on this era of dramatic transition in Egypt (and soon also across the Muslim world) out of the Age of No Veiling and into the era of hijab and Islamic dress. The seventies and eighties in the United States saw the rise of women's studies and feminist scholarship in the American academy. The developments that were under way in Egypt regarding the returning veil and Muslim women's seeming "return" to patriarchy became an attractive topic for doctoral students in these fields and an apt testing ground, so it seemed, for the latest American feminist theories and research methods.

Consequently, we have today a series of studies, on which I draw in the following pages, that collectively richly document how women were persuaded to change their dress, whether because they joined the Islamist movement or because they were going along with the current for a variety of reasons. Such studies also document the stages and process by which this transformation in dress and in the practices of Islam took place in Egypt in that pivotal era. A profound social and religious transformation under way in these decades would momentously shape the direction that Islam, Islamic activism, and the veil would take, not only in Egypt but also globally.

Among the first on the scene and keenly observing these developments in the late seventies was El Guindi, who found that the appearance of the hijab was linked to an emergent movement of Islamic religiosity that was at that point essentially confined to student and university life. Women who participated in this movement and took up the hijab, El Guindi found, reported undergoing an "internal transformation." The experience of this transformation had the effect of making such women feel, El Guindi wrote, separated "psychologically and intellectually from mainstream society." As they became participants in and affiliated with the movement, the women would now take on not only head covering but also Islamic dress, and they would begin to scrupulously follow the specific "ritual, behavioral and verbal prescriptions" required by the movement. Among the most important of these behavioral prescriptions was a strict adherence to the foundational taboo against the mixing of the sexes—a taboo of course signaled by hijab and Islamic dress.[32]

The women's different dress and their observance of required rituals and prescriptions created a sense among them that they constituted a separate community from the broader society. Their dress enabled them to easily recognize each other as members of this separate, special community, a community living dispersed among the mainstream and committed to its own quite different mores, values, and ideals.[33]

Affiliation or membership in the movement was informal, El Guindi reported. The movement comprehended sororal/fraternal collectivities, which offered separate and parallel opportunities for involvement and leadership among both men and women. The goals of these groups were broadly reflective of the goals and ideals articulated in the Islamist pamphlets and periodicals that were in wide circulation during this period. Their aim was to bring about the ideal Islamic society based on the Quran and the Sunna (the literature of the early Islamic period reporting the sayings and practices of the Prophet Muhammad). They opposed "Communism, Zionism, and Feminism," and they understood

Islam as they practiced it to be distinctly different from Islam as followed and practiced by mainstream society, and as different from the Islam of the Establishment.[34]

More specifically, they saw Islam as they followed it to be different both from Islam as practiced in mainstream society and from Islam as followed and practiced by al-Azhar—even though this institution was widely regarded at the time by many Sunni Muslims across the world as perhaps the major center of Sunni learning as to the correct beliefs and practices of Islam. This tendency, however, of seeing their Islam as different from that of al-Azhar was in sync with the Brotherhood's perspective. The Brotherhood did not for the most part share mainstream society's general respect for al-Azhar. Even early on al-Banna had favored modern interpretations of Islam that addressed the modern needs of Muslims over the scholastic readings that focused on ancient texts emanating from al-Azhar and its ulama (men of learning). And during the Nasser era, when al-Azhar was brought under government control, tensions between al-Azhar and the Brotherhood grew more intense.

Women's involvement in the hierarchical structures of Islamist organizations represented a new development for Islamic organizations. In the Muslim Brotherhood, the dominant Islamist organization prior to the 1970s, women had not held organizational roles that entailed responsibility paralleling those assigned to men. The Brotherhood's main interest in relation to women had been that of educating them in the principles of Islam and in practices to be cultivated within their own homes. The ideal Muslim woman was seen as a "homebound but religiously enlightened woman who left the home only to carry out the task of educating other women."[35] Now, however, female students were participating "side by side with men" in the movement's activities and responsibilities. The Sisters' hierarchy paralleled that of the Brothers, El Guindi noted, and a sister leader could even serve as a vital link to university authorities or in relation to the Brothers' hierarchy.[36]

The seventies would witness the emergence of militant Islamist groups, some of them established by former Muslim Brothers who had suffered torture in Nasser's prisons and who now refused to accept the Brotherhood's position against violence. Even these militant Islamist organizations could include women, as government investigations of some of the groups would show. The practices of one militant Islamist group in particular, Jamaat al-Takfir wal-Hijra (Society of Repentance and Flight, a name given to it by its opponents), would scandalize many Egyptians when details of their practices became known following the arrest in 1977 of some of its members, who were charged with kidnapping and murdering a cleric from al-Azhar.

Jamaat al-Takfir wal-Hijra was founded by Shukri Mustapha, an agricultural engineer and a Muslim Brother who had been imprisoned by Nasser in 1965 and released by Sadat in 1971. Like a number of others on the militant edge of the Brotherhood, Mustapha regarded the Brotherhood leadership as too weak and accommodationist vis-à-vis the government, as well as mistaken in renouncing violence.

Mustapha maintained that most Muslim societies were in a state of jahiliyya. Only his own followers were true Muslims; most people, and in particular the political leaders of Muslim (or so-called Muslim) societies, were *kafirs* (heathens). True Muslims, he believed, must flee from these corrupt societies, just as the Prophet Muhammad had fled when he had undertaken hijra (migration) to Medina from the corrupt jahiliyya society that had persecuted him. Today such groups, according to Mustapha, should form alternative societies in the wilderness from whence they could fight the heathens and their corrupt leaders and infidel practices.

Mustapha's group did in fact withdraw from society and live in communes in the hills, following rules that were broadly Islamic but modified by Mustapha. Members, women and men, were required to sever their ties with the rest of society and to regard their own family members as infidels to whom they owed neither obedience nor responsibility. The group practiced unconventional and unorthodox marriages, with Mustapha having the power to dissolve or arrange marriages at will. The group was accused of enticing young women away from their families.[37]

Saleh Siriyyah, the leader of another jihadi group, also similarly preached that Muslims who did not follow pure Islam were kafirs, and that armed struggle—armed jihad—against the political leaders of so-called Islamic societies whose populations were in reality kafirs was a necessity. Siriyyah considered that jihad in the sense of armed struggle (jihad can also refer to inner struggle or endeavor) was obligatory for Muslim women as well as for men.

In the later seventies, as violent incidents from such groups escalated, government investigations brought to light the fact that in practice women were excluded from most militant organizations. The exception to this was the organization founded by Mustapha. However, such groups are exceedingly secretive, and only scant information is available about them. Siriyyah and Mustapha were executed by the Egyptian government for their part in acts of murder and violence, Siriyyah in 1975 and Mustapha in 1978.

The students and organizations that El Guindi studied all belonged to the broad spectrum of mainstream, nonviolent Islamist organizations. (She remains our most important source on women in Islamist organizations in that era.) It is these organizations, among them the Muslim Brotherhood, that make up the vast majority of the Islamist movement.

Just as the hijab served to signal to like-minded others (and to society at large) the presence of members of this different, alternative community living in the mainstream, the ways in which women and men of this movement formally referred to each other as "brother" and "sister" similarly served, as El Guindi noted, to reinforce a sense of community and belonging.[38]

The hijab was only one of the distinctive features of the new Islamic dress being adopted by women. Abandoning the Western-style fashions of women in the mainstream—dress which they themselves had worn prior to undergoing their personal religious transformation—women who took up hijab also took to wearing what they referred to as *ziyy* or *zia Islami,* or shar'i (Islamic dress or legal dress).

The zia came in a variety of styles that typically corresponded to different degrees of religious understanding and commitment, as well as to different levels of leadership in the hierarchy of sisters. Dress progressed in terms of strictness from maxi-length skirt or pant-suit with long-sleeved shirt and headscarf to a *khimar,* a "head-cover which covers all the hair down below the neck and in front goes below the chin while still exposing the entire face." This was worn with a *gilbab,* a long, loose robe with wide long sleeves. These garments were essentially standardized and were typically in sober solid colors, such as navy blue, brown, or beige. Typically they were made of "thick opaque material."[39]

This standardization in material and color had the effect of erasing social and economic differences between wearers. In this way Islamic dress powerfully modeled and embodied (as El Guindi noted) two key ideas that were foundational to the Islamic movement. They visually embodied and proclaimed the central importance of a society committed to gender segregation, and they embodied and modeled egalitarian principles and notions of social equality and justice across classes, another foundational commitment for the Islamist movement. As noted earlier, social justice had from the start been a key commitment of the Muslim Brotherhood.

The zia islami, in its telling and significant variations for insiders as well as in its overall uniformity, was something new to Egypt. These were not styles that the women's mothers or grandmothers had ever donned. The zia was thus unmistakably *modern* Islamic dress, devised in styles and materials that signaled at once both the modernity of its wearers and their Islamic commitment. The dress also clearly indicated to the mainstream Muslim majority that the wearers were in some way affirming and embracing a different way of practicing and living Islam. Consequently, the wearers of this dress conveyed or at least seemed to convey an implicit rejection of the ways and dress of the mainstream, as they seemed also to be conveying the message that the dress of Muslim women who did not dress as they did was not properly or adequately Islamic. (In the debates under way today in some Western countries—in France, for example—Islamic dress is indeed being read as implying a rejection not only of mainstream dress but also of the values and commitments of mainstream society.)

By the end of the seventies this form of dress was still essentially a campus phenomenon, and even on campuses it was confined to a small minority. The number of women wearing zia, wrote El Guindi in 1981, was insignificant in terms of Egypt's total population. And yet the visual presence of this "new woman," as El Guindi called her, was quite dramatic, as well as mysteriously arresting and compelling. The dress somehow conveyed, El Guindi reported, strength and power.

For the larger mainstream society the steady increase in Islamic dress that was evidently under way around them was a clear and visible sign of the growing strength of a minority in Egyptian society who lived by and were committed to different rules and a different understanding of Islam from that of mainstream society. Moreover, this was an understanding of Islam that seemed distinctly at odds not only in matters of dress but also implicitly in terms of goals and ideology, with the ways, goals, and commitments of the larger society.[40]

This new dress was not something that observers could easily understand or make sense of. It was not a return to traditional or old-fashioned and vaguely familiar form of dress. Members of the broader society, El Guindi reported, observed these developments with puzzlement and a growing sense of unease. Why was this happening, they wondered? Was this some sort of identity crisis? Was this, as one interviewee remarked to El Guindi, "our version of America's hippie movement, a fad, a youth protest or ideological vacuum"?[41]

Parents of the women in zia tended to be particularly distressed, El Guindi found. "Where did we go wrong?" they wondered. If their daughter was unmarried, they anguished over who would marry her now that she was "hidden under a 'tent'"? Some people were not only baffled but also offended and angered by the dress. As one woman said, "That a young woman goes on pilgrimage to Mecca two or three times this is not a phenomenon, this is good, it is being a good Muslim." But, she continued, "to dress like these college girls and cover with a veil, now that is a phenomenon. It is not even Islamic."[42]

Feminists of the day also denounced the new veil. Among these was Amina al-Said, a prominent journalist and one of the first generation of Egyptian women to benefit from the early twentieth-century movement to both cast aside the veil and open up educational and professional opportunities to women. In 1932, al-Said had been a member of the first group of women to graduate from Cairo University (then King Fuad University). Almost at the first appearance of the new hijab in the early 1970s, al-Said wrote an editorial in the feminist journal *Hawwa* (Eve) to decry the new dress as a garment that resembled the "shrouds of the dead." In words that echo Hourani's essay (and before that, Amin's work and Cromer's pronouncements), al-Said declared that the veil was "truly the greatest enemy of civilization and progress."[43]

It was not only feminists who would take a stand against the veil or Islamic dress. As the phenomenon gained ground in university lecture halls, some professors would summarily dismiss from their classes students who dressed in this way.

In mainstream society there was speculation that some women were wearing this dress because they were being paid to wear it by the Muslim Brothers or by agents of Saudi Arabia.[44] Another researcher, John Alden Williams, reported that when he asked people why they thought Islamic dress was on the rise, they were likely to "shrug their shoulders, roll their eyes and reply that they can't imagine." Pressed, they often elaborated by saying that "it's all because of the Saudis." The Saudis, they say, "give a lot of money to writers and *shaykhs* to further their fundamentalist vision of Islam."[45]

In response to questions about the resurgence of "fundamentalist" Islamic groups, such as "the old Muslim Brotherhood," that was evidently under way, people would assert, Williams reported, that they were subsidized by Saudi or Libyan money. Other findings that Williams reported in fact appear to lend some credence to such reports. Williams notes, for example, that among the people he interviewed, one student at Cairo University stated that she received a "small sum of money to hand out head-kerchiefs to her classmates and more money for every woman she converted to the wearing of shar'i dress; money that came from a Saudi source." In addition, Williams noted, men who joined the resurgent Muslim groups had been known "to threaten to divorce their wives if they do not adopt shar'i costume."

Williams interviewed nonveiled women as well as veiled women about what they believed constituted proper "Islamic" dress, and he described the Cairo scene with regard to women's dress in the late seventies. He provides us with a wonderfully detailed glimpse into how people thought about Islamic dress in these very early days of the transition to veiling.

It had become rare in the seventies, wrote Williams, "to see a veil, and common to see Egyptian imitations of most recent Western dress, including the mini-skirt." Even in small provincial towns, Williams continues, "women advertised their attachment to modernity by adopting forms of dress regarded as contemporary, international and modern." In contrast, "women who continued to go out in the black milaya . . . were pityingly or contemptuously referred to as *baladi giddan* (very provinicial) and were looked upon as backward anomalies, or as mere peasants with quaint, disappearing manners."

While the few women who continued to cover were regarded as backward, women who did not cover and who wore Western-style dress (without veil) were not seen as any "less Muslim" than others. Certainly, Williams writes, "they were viewed as pious and observant." When questioned on their views on dress, "orthodox women in 'modern dress' denied that there was anything un-Islamic about this, provided the dress was not gaudy and/or abbreviated. They argued that early Islam had not segregated or veiled women—except perhaps in the case of the Prophet's wives," who, the women explained, were living right by the main mosque where there was constant coming and going and where the Prophet's wives hardly got any privacy at all. It was "generally assumed," Williams noted, that the way women dressed "was the way it should be." Egyptian women with their modern dress and no veil, Williams's interviewees assumed (echoing the views of Hourani and those of others before him), "were demonstrating how the Arab woman of the future would behave and dress."

Williams also notes that in recent decades conservative women who had been concerned to identify themselves as observant Muslims had worn simple modern dresses with long sleeves, along with a scarf over their hair—and that some women still dressed like that. While such dress was on the conservative side, it was not conspicuously different from the modern Western-style dress, noted Williams, in the way that the zia shar'i was. Thus women adopting the latter appeared to be "evincing an aspiration to dress counter to recent norms of clothing, and claiming to be more observant of the Law than other women." By their choice of dress the women in the zia appeared to be "sitting in judgment" on their society and "critical of the way it appears to be going."[46]

Both El Guindi and Williams maintained that, at least to begin with, the spread of the hijab and Islamic dress represented, above all, a women's movement: a movement that both favored and advanced women's interests. Explaining her reasons for coming to this conclusion, El Guindi pointed out that Islamic dress was clearly being adopted specifically by university students. Moreover, the largest proportion of women adopting this dress were students in sciences and in such fields as medicine and engineering. It was being adopted by students in the liberal arts, too, but in smaller numbers. The women who were preponderantly adopting it, therefore, were those intending to become professionals, not stay-at-home wives.

Given the conditions in which they lived and worked and the crowded conditions in lecture rooms and on public transport, where harassment of women was routine, El Guindi further argued, Islamic dress imbued women with a kind of moral and religious authority that might discourage such harassment. In El Guindi's words, a woman in public space had a choice "between being secular, modern, feminine, and frustratingly passive (hence very vulnerable), or becoming *mitadayyina* . . . (religieuse) hence formidable, untouchable, and silently threatening."[47]

The young women who are out in public in the zia Islami, El Guindi concluded, had made the choice, "and the choice . . . became a movement." By invoking Islam and declaring herself to be grounded in Muslim ethics, "this new Egyptian woman," El Guindi wrote, "is liberating herself . . . by choosing to veil and not to be molested or stopped" as she assertively enters public space.

Williams (who, like El Guindi, was a U.S.-based scholar) was also convinced by his research that, initially at least, the Islamic dress trend represented a women's movement. While Williams was clearly aware from the start that there were a variety of factors besides women's own desires influencing the trend toward Islamic dress—as his reports of rumors on the role of Saudi money and other pressures indicated—he nevertheless also believed that Egyptian women were "no sheep," and that no one was likely to "persuade them to exchange the cooler, more comfortable modern dress for zia shar'i unless they wish to do so."[48]

Furthermore, the responses Williams received when he asked women why they had adopted Islamic dress convinced him that they had taken it up at their own initiative. Women also indicated that this dress solved the problems they were confronting on a personal level. One young woman, for instance, explained that now that she had taken on this dress she felt "very happy and had a real sense of peace with herself." Previously she had felt "pulled this way and that" in her effort to be like others, but now "she had taken her stand; she knew who she was, a Muslim woman, [and] men would not now mistake her for an easy mark." In this instance, Islamic dress had evidently both solved the problem of harassment and resolved, as Williams put it, "some sort of personal identity crisis."

Williams gives other examples of how women's adoption of Islamic dress had led to the resolution of problems. One woman, for instance, explained that the events of 1967 had been a "rude awakening." Then, she went on, "in 1973, it seemed that God was answering our prayers. We had become too careless. Now we want to respond to God with faith." Another woman similarly stated that until 1967 she had accepted the "way our country was going," believing that Nasser "would lead us all to progress. Then the war showed that we had been lied to; nothing was the way it had been represented. I started to question everything we were told. I wanted to do something and to find my own way. I prayed more and I tried to see what was expected of me as a Muslim woman. Then I put on shar'i dress." Another woman suggests that taking on Islamic dress represented a fundamental shift in her understanding of the direction her society had taken and of the new direction that it now needed to take: "Once we thought that Western society had all the answers for successful, fruitful living," she said, and that "if we followed the lead of the West we would have progress. . . . Now we see that this isn't true: they (the West) are sick societies; even their material prosperity is breaking down. America is full of crime and promiscuity. Russia is worse. Who wants to be like that? We have to remember God. Look how God has blessed Saudi Arabia. That's because they have tried to follow the law. And America, with its loose society, is all problems."

These responses suggest that adopting hijab sometimes at least connoted a turning away from and even an outright rejection of the West and its ways. Such responses clearly mark a dramatic shift that had occurred by the 1970s from the views that had prevailed in the early century and the hopes and aspirations that the idea of emulating the West had engendered among the forebears of these women. Casting aside their veils had been a symbol for that generation of their longing for the day when Egypt would be an unveiled society pursuing the exhilaratingly hopeful ideas and ideals—equality, democracy, the right to work for equal pay—of modernity and the West.

Williams concluded, as El Guindi had done, that what was afoot in Egypt with the spread of Islamic dress was in some important way a "women's movement." And yet in the very last paragraph of his article he also observes—without offering any further evidence or explanation—that just as his article is going to press (in early 1979), there were clear signs that "what had been a women's movement was now being exploited by men for their own purposes."

A study that appeared a couple of years later confirmed some of Williams's findings. In this case the study was undertaken by Zainab Radwan, an Egyptian academic based at the National Research Center in Cairo. Radwan's research, comprising questionnaires for university students, was also conducted with the object of understanding why the hijab was gaining ground among university women. Radwan's research found that the response Williams cited from one of his interviewees, that donning the hijab had brought her inner peace, was the commonest response given by women who wore hijab: 50 percent of the hijabi women chose this response from multiple possible responses. Other reasons attested to by Williams's research also figured in the responses to the Radwan questionnaire: 19 percent of hijabi women responding to the questionnaire reported that they wore hijab to avoid being harassed in public, and 20 percent said that people treated them with new respect after they put it on.[49]

The occurrence of similar responses in Williams's and Radwan's research suggests that there were by then a number of stock responses in circulation—responses perhaps specifically intended to be offered to enquiring scholars, anthropologists, and others—explaining women's feelings and motivations as to their decision to don the hijab. Indeed, the very fact that a questionnaire asking women why they had chosen to don hijab featured "inner peace" or "decrease in sexual harassment" as possible responses suggests that the questionnaire had been devised to include responses that the researchers had identified as being already in circulation.

The accounts and analyses cited thus far regarding the spread of the practice of veiling through the 1970s are those of contemporary observers and scholars, American and Egyptian, who were studying the phenomenon. I will complement these accounts with one from the perspective of a woman of that era—Ekram Beshir—who took up the hijab and Islamic dress in the 1970s. The narrative of experiences that Beshir offers both resonates with and weaves together themes that had emerged in the findings of El Guindi, Williams, and Radwan. But it weaves these together into a new kind of coherence, the coherence that these trends and facts take on when viewed and experienced from the other side of the great cultural divide of that era—the divide between mainstream society and Islamists.

Beshir was a medical student at Alexandria University in 1971, an era, she tells us, when the miniskirt was at the height of fashion. "The university," writes Beshir, "was flooded with Egyptian women wearing painted faces and western-style hair—and then there was me, I wore hijab. I wasn't the only one in Alexandria wearing hijab at the time, but out of several million people, it was a very rare sight."[50]

Besides disapproval from an aunt who would often ask her why she was "acting so silly," and an uncle who wondered how she would ever find a husband dressed like that, Beshir notes that one of her professors regularly commented on her dress. On one occasion, on a particularly hot day, he asked her why she wore "that thing" on her head. As she began to respond, "Because I am a Muslim and Allah asks Muslim women to . . ." the professor interrupted her furiously saying, "I'm Muslim, my wife's Muslim, they're Muslim!" He motioned to people in the busy campus. "So you're questioning how faithful we are too?" Almost reduced to tears, Beshir returned home and found consolation in the Quran.

Soon after, Beshir met and married her husband and immigrated to Canada. There her husband became heavily involved in founding the first Muslim Student Association chapter at Carlton University in Ottawa. Both she and her husband would become involved in organizing Islamic children's camps and *halaqa* circles and youth conferences, and

Beshir would go on to become a founding member of the first full-time Islamic school in their district in Ottawa.

Beshir gives an account of how she found herself awakening to Islam and to a new sense of obligation to awaken others to Islam (that is, to perform da'wa). Her account affords invaluable insight into the process of inner transformation that, as El Guindi surmised, young people who were drawn to the movement found themselves undergoing.

A medical student at the time, Beshir experienced family illnesses and was living in a time of political turbulence in Egypt—a time, she writes, when "Israel kept declaring war on Egypt and other surrounding countries." She found herself feeling "confused and scared" and felt that she "couldn't go on living with this feeling that something pivotal was missing in my existence." Searching for meaning, she attended a Thursday-evening class on Islamic education taught by a professor who was the father of one of her close friends. From that day forward the class, she wrote, became a "basic necessity for me":

> It nourished and fostered me, but most of all it enlightened me. It was as if I had woken up one day with my mouth parched, my body dehydrated and my heart yearning. Yearning for what I didn't know. Until I sat in the lecture hall full of curious students that first Thursday evening and the aching began to disappear. I had found it. Every Thursday after that I took a sip and I kept taking sips until my lips were no longer dry and my body was no longer drained. I began to learn the real meaning of life.

This experience critically informs Beshir's subsequent sense of commitment to working for Islam. "There's a lot more to Islam," she writes,

> than locking yourself up in the local mosque and praying 24/7. Prayers and pure rituals are not ends in themselves, but they are prescribed to train and prepare us to fulfill our responsibilities in life. Islam is about community, cooperation, and support. . . . I believe that da'wa is a big component of worshipping in Islam. For if all the knowledgeable Muslims out

> there isolated themselves for worship, how could they ever pass on their knowledge? How would I have ever discovered the true Islam? . . . My thirst was quenched after a rigorous sequence of trial and error. Now it seems undoubtedly clear to me that I had to help others find what they are looking for, help show them what they are missing out on. In my mind, it was simple really—if everyone passes on the message, everyone will be happy. It was then that I adopted a new lifestyle: that of a Muslim committed to action.

Beshir also considered the hijab to be an important part of the work of daʿwa. The hijab, she wrote, is "a great form of daʿwa, whether in Egypt or in Canada: when you wear the hijab, you're no longer just representing yourself, you're representing Islam. No matter where you live in the world, people will always question what is different. Wearing hijab definitely makes me different. I learned not to get offended when asked about my way of dressing: people are just trying to understand, and it's every Muslim's job to help them understand."

Besides exemplifying how the elements of Islamism and veiling identified by academics come together in the life lived, Beshir's story is also illuminating concerning how the Islamist movement would begin to seed itself in North America and elsewhere in the Western world, developments that I discuss in subsequent chapters. I return to Beshir's life story in the final chapter of this book when I examine how Islamist ideas and commitments, whether brought over by immigrants or as they emerge among American- and Canadian-born children of Islamists or among converts, are coming to blend in with quintessentially North American ideals of activism in pursuit of the goal of a just society.

Over the next three chapters, I trace the process, means, and methods by which the Resurgence, and with it the veil, spread in the seventies and ensuing decades in Egypt, the country which first underwent this process and forged the methods, strategies, and ideas that the Resurgence would take across the world.

First, though, I continue my exploration of this critical decade of the 1970s, the decade when a variety of galvanizing forces came together to propel the rise and spread of Islamism.

·4·

The New Veil

Converging Influences

The 1970s was a critical decade with respect to the emergence and spread of the Resurgence. In this chapter I continue my exploration of the 1970s and of the forces and elements at work in Egypt that were important to this movement. I consider, for example, Saudi Arabia's contributions to fostering in a variety of ways, some quite unexpected, a climate that would nurture and galvanize the Resurgence, and I explore how Saudi Arabian interests intersected and combined with those of the Muslim Brotherhood.

This decade in Egypt would prove to be the crucible of the first experimentation with and forceful practical expressions of Qutb's explosive ideas, which were interpreted as legitimizing violence and endorsing a religious obligation on Islamists to free nominally Muslim societies from their "illegitimate" and "heathen" rulers—rulers who claimed to be Muslim but who were not viewed as Muslim under Qutb's and other Islamists' definition of Islam. Sadat would be assassinated in 1981 by a young man who was a member of Islamic Jihad, a group that espoused these views. Another member of this same group, Ayman al-Zawahiri, is today well known as Osama bin Laden's second in command.

I conclude this chapter with a brief recapitulation of aspects of Qutb's life and thought, and I summarize his views on women and their place in his ideal Muslim society. I pair this sketch of Qutb with one of Zainab al-Ghazali, the "unsung mother" of the Muslim Brotherhood.

A number of factors converged in Egypt in the 1970s to create the conditions that would bring into being and dynamically energize the Islamic Resurgence.

Toward the end of the war of 1973, as the tide had begun to turn against the Arabs, the oil-producing states imposed an oil embargo on countries supplying Israel with military equipment, a move that would send oil prices soaring and that consequently proved very profitable for the oil-producing states. Prices would remain high, ensuring that Saudi Arabia would henceforth have vast means for pursuing its "ancient ambition" of establishing hegemony over the Muslim world and of spreading its Wahhabi Islam to the world.[1]

After 1973 the activities of the Muslim World League grew exponentially. Founded in the early sixties to counter Nasser's Arab nationalism and promote Islam in its place as ground of identity and community, in the 1970s the League was opening offices across the Muslim world and indeed across the globe—wherever Muslims lived. Managed by members of the Saudi religious establishment and their coworkers and supporters, the League financed the building of mosques and supported their religious staff and workers across the world. It also established Islamic publishing houses and oversaw the widespread distribution of free Qurans, as well as of books and tapes promoting the Wahhabi doctrine, including the writings of the twelfth-century scholar Ibn Taymiya, as well as the writings of Muhammad Ibn Abd al-Wahhab. The League also supported Islamist associations in the West as well as in the Muslim world. As already noted, the people manning and directing many of the League's projects and missions often were members of the Muslim Brotherhood or were members of other Islamist organizations, particularly the Jamaat-i Islami of Pakistan.

Wahhabi Islam follows a school of belief and practice founded by Ibn Abd al-Wahhab, who lived in Najd, in central Arabia, in the eighteenth century. Ibn Abd al-Wahhab (1703–92) was a zealous religious reformer who sought to cleanse Islam from what he called blasphemous "innovations," practices that had crept into Islamic usage over the centuries and needed to be purged in order to bring about a return to Islam's pure, original beliefs and practices. Three well-known incidents, one relating to the felling of a sacred tree, another to the destruction of the tomb of a revered Muslim, and the third relating to the stoning of an adulteress, are described as encapsulating Ibn Abd al-Wahhab's positions.

The first incident occurred in relation to a number of trees that people in the town of al-Uyaynah in Najd regarded as sacred and on which they hung objects, offering prayers and petitions for relief and for cures or blessings. This practice, seemingly indicating that people believed that there were forces with the power to bless or intercede with God, represented to Ibn Abd al-Wahhab a profound violation of the Muslim affirmation of *tawhid*, the oneness of God—an affirmation that implied that God alone had power to bless and respond to prayers. To Ibn Abd al-Wahhab, such practices were blasphemy. When his warnings to people to desist from them were ignored, Ibn Abd al-Wahhab instructed his supporters to cut down the trees. He himself took on the task of cutting down the most revered of the trees.[2]

Similarly, Ibn Abd al-Wahhab destroyed a popular monument over the tomb of Zayd Ibn al-Khattab, a Companion of the Prophet, because it venerated a human being. According to Ibn Abd al-Wahhab, in the "true" form of Islam, only God was to be venerated. To Ibn Abd al-Wahhab, all of these actions smacked of *shirk*—polytheism—which was not tolerated in Islam.

The third incident, the stoning of the adulteress, occurred when a woman informed Ibn Abd al-Wahhab that she was committing adultery, then refused to obey his instructions to desist. She returned repeatedly, so the narrative goes, to inform him that she was not desisting. The stoning penalty for adultery is not in the Quran, which, in fact, specifies a different punishment—fifty lashes. However, it does figure in the *hadith*, or sayings of the Prophet. Ordinarily in Islamic law the Quran, the word of God, trumps the sayings of the Prophet, but not in this case for Ibn Abd al-Wahhab and for some other Islamic jurists.

Ibn Abd al-Wahhab's views and actions won him the enmity of some tribal leaders in Arabia and the support of others. In 1744, Ibn Abd al-Wahhab forged an alliance with one of these diverse tribal leaders,

Muhammad Ibn Saud. Ibn Saud adopted Ibn Abd al-Wahhab's teachings and committed himself to cleansing Arabia of blasphemous "innovations" and returning it to the practice of a "purified" Islam freed of such distortions. He set out to become the dominant tribal leader in Arabia, a goal he achieved. In 1802, Ibn Saud's descendants captured the cities of Mecca and Medina, the holy cities of Islam, from the Ottomans —who at this point were the masters of the Islamic Ottoman Empire, whose territories included much of the Middle East and land beyond. Mecca and Medina were recaptured by the Ottomans in 1818. Eventually, following the fall of the Ottoman Empire and the European Powers' establishment of new nations in the Middle East out of the Ottoman Empire's former territories, the Kingdom of Saudi Arabia would be established in 1932 as an independent kingdom under the rule of the Saud dynasty.

Mecca and Medina were now in the territory of the newly established Saudi Arabia. Among the first acts carried out by King Abdel Aziz Ibn Saud was the destruction of the tombs of the imams and other revered figures of early Islam in Mecca and Medina. He wanted to cleanse Islam of idolatry and "false superstitions" in accordance with Wahhabi doctrine.

Wahhabis considered both Sufis and Shi'is to be heretics and zealously opposed their beliefs and practices and strove to eradicate them. Among the first tombs to be smashed in Medina following the establishment of the state of Saudi Arabia had been the tomb of Fatima, daughter of the Prophet Muhammad and an especially revered figure among Shi'is.

Prior to the 1960s, Wahhabi Islam had been confined to Saudi Arabia. Religious piety and practice across the Muslim world were rooted in Muslim traditions of learning and practice and at the same time they were rooted to some extent in local traditions and practices. Within the enormously diverse area where Islam was practiced, extending from China and Indonesia through India, Africa, and Europe, forms of folk piety and practice differed. Even at the level of the theological positions espoused by the ulama, the scholars of Islam (whose understandings of Islam may differ from those of the common people), there were differences within the Muslim world—different schools of Islamic law were followed in different regions, for instance. Until Saudi Arabia's rise to economic power, Wahhabi Islam had not been particularly well regarded in any of the world's major centers of Islamic learning, such as those in Turkey, Egypt, Morocco, India, and Indonesia.

After 1973, as Gilles Kepel, an expert on contemporary Islamist movements writes, Saudi zeal "now embraced the entire world." Saudi goals were to reach out and spread Wahhabism across the Muslim world and into the "heart of the West where Muslim immigrant populations were the special target." The Saudi objective, Kepel observes, was to "Wahhabize" Islam, thereby reducing the "multitude of voices within the religion" to the "single creed" of Saudi Arabia. Simultaneously, they promoted the ideal of Islam as transcending national divisions. "All Muslims," wrote Kepel, "were offered a new identity that emphasized their religious commonality while downplaying differences of language, ethnicity, and nationality."[3]

As a result of the Saudis' energetic and well-funded activities, for the first time since the rise of Islam the "same books (as well as cassettes) could be found from one end of the Umma [the community of Muslims] to the other"—whether in Africa, Asia, Europe, or the United States. All emanated from the "same Saudi distribution circuits . . . [and] all hewed to the same doctrinal line and excluded other currents of thought that had formerly been part of a pluralist Islam."[4]

Across the world there now were clear and visible signs—the growing number of mosques, the changing architecture on the skyline, the increasing commonness of the hijab—of the gains that Wahhabi Islamism was making, thanks in important degree to the vast economic resources of Saudi Arabia.

And everywhere the building of mosques was accompanied by the distribution of texts and teachings promoting Wahhabi Islam. At the same time, though, the Wahhabi Islam that was being disseminated across the world was significantly inflected with the teachings, ideals, and ideologies of the Islamist movement more broadly, and most particularly with the ideas and ideals of the Muslim Brotherhood, whose members were essential to the spread and advancement of Saudi Arabia's global projects. It was, above all, through the Muslim Brotherhood and its personnel, know-how, networks, and organizations, as well as those of other Islamist organizations such as the Jamaat-i Islami, that the League was able to pursue and implement its projects.

As Kepel describes it, "The Muslim Brothers grafted their political interests onto the Saudi oil pipeline. . . . Muslim Brothers, residing in Saudi Arabia, rose to international influence alongside the dynasty by adding intellectual value to Islamist thought at a time when Wahhabism was not exportable. Through the international organizations they ran for the dynasty and those they controlled directly, the Brothers quietly carried out their own program of global expansion." Their programs and outreach efforts were directed both at Muslims within the Muslim world, whom they hoped to influence and win over to their form of religious belief, practice, and commitments, and at Muslims in the West, as they were eager to "win the hearts of young Muslim immigrants who had settled there."[5]

There were certainly differences between the teachings, outlook, and doctrines of Wahhabism and those of the Brotherhood. For example, the Brotherhood, at least initially, had not shared the Wahhabis' relentless opposition to Sufism. Al-Banna had himself been initiated into a Sufi order, and he regarded Sufism as a genuine expression of popular piety, a piety that he trusted and honored as embodying essential elements of Islam. Furthermore, the Brothers' message of social justice and their commitment to working for social justice were not shared by the Wahhabis. Consequently, despite their close alliance with the Saudis, the Muslim Brothers agreed not to operate and proselytize within Saudi Arabia.[6]

Furthermore, while Wahhabism was anchored in Ibn Abd al-Wahhab's eighteenth-century interpretations of earlier theological texts, the Brotherhood's ideology tended to favor and advocate contemporary interpretations of sacred texts—interpretations that directly addressed the needs of contemporary Muslims. Al-Banna himself stressed that "interpretations and meanings of the Glorious Quran must be linked 'scientifically, socially and morally' to aspects of modern life," and that "modern theories and ways of thinking" must be employed in response to the needs of the modern age and its specific problems. Similarly, al-Banna had early on rejected the idea that it was important to meticulously study and follow the enormous literary legacy of Islamic thought and tradition, and had even questioned the usefulness of the Islamic legal schools.[7]

Al-Banna had been educated in the modern secular institutions of Egypt, institutions that had been set up in the late nineteenth and early twentieth centuries to rival and supersede the country's traditional religious educational establishments. His father had hoped that he would attend the al-Azhar, the center of religious training, but al-Banna chose to attend a primary teacher-training school in Damanhour, going on to attend Dar al-Ulum, the premier secular modern teacher-training college in Cairo.

Many Muslim Brothers also were graduates of the secular educational system. Often they majored in the sciences, with many of them becoming engineers, chemists, pharmacists, and doctors. Brotherhood members typically were not trained in traditional Islamic learning and scholarship—a fact which in the early days earned them the opposition of the traditionally trained religious elite and religious scholars, such as the ulama of al-Azhar.

This lack of traditional religious training was not viewed within Islamist circles as a drawback. On the contrary, secular and scientific training was viewed as particularly apt in that it equipped leaders to draw on the tools of modernity to interpret Islam in ways that addressed the "practical and mundane problems of modern Muslims" as it propelled the Islamist movement in its goal of widespread Islamic activism and renewal.

In fact, leadership emanating from secularly trained intellectuals rather than from traditionally and Islamically trained scholars has been the hallmark, as Olivier Roy has observed, of twentieth-century Islamist movements. This fact is recognized among Islamists and is endorsed by a variety of Islamist intellectuals and religious leaders. Ismail al-Faruqi, for example, a leading Islamist thinker based in America, observed that "Muslim social science researchers are the ulema of today." Similarly, Hasan Turabi commented that "because all knowledge is divine and religious, a chemist, an engineer, an economist or a jurist are all 'ulemas.'" And Mawdudi, founder of the Jamaat-i Islami, remarked that "whoever devotes his time and energy to the study of the Quran and the Sunna and becomes well versed in Islamic learning is entitled to speak as an expert on matters pertaining to Islam."[8]

Modernity and the ideas of the West are inextricably part of the Islamist movement of today, as Roy goes on to emphasize. With the exception of Iran, the Islamist movements of the twentieth century have everywhere been led, as Roy notes, not by clerics but by secularly trained intellectuals steeped in a "Westernized environment" who subsequently took on the task of working and writing as religious thinkers. Such thinkers typically insist in their writings, Roy further notes, on the "rationality of religious prescriptions." Their very insistence on rationalism, and on rationality as a vital category, is itself a "sign that modernity has worked its way into the very heart of Islamist discourse."[9]

From early on al-Banna himself had deliberately sought to minimize and set aside doctrinal and theological differences among Muslims, and he had applied himself to working to bring about consensus in the interests of pan-Islamic unity. This continued to be a feature of Islamist thought and Brotherhood activism as the Brothers worked with Wahhabis and across their differences for common goals, among them the renewal of Islam worldwide, the establishment of Islam as a primary ground of identity transcending all national borders, and the promotion and dissemination of the socially conservative forms of Islam to which Wahhabis, the Muslim Brothers, and other Islamists were committed. Most notable and visible was their signature commitment to gender segregation and thus also to the presence of the hijab as mandatory for women: dress that proclaimed that foundational commitment.

In Egypt, the Brotherhood and other Islamists set out to win over the mainstream Muslim majority, encouraging them to leave aside their beliefs, habits, practices, and ways of dress and to adopt in their place those of the Islamists. This entailed the double task of persuading people both that Islam as they, their parents, and grandparents had practiced it was flawed, faulty, inadequate, and incorrect, and that only Islamic beliefs and practice as taught by Islamists represented those of "true" Islam. The task for activists was to work through da'wa to awaken the Muslim majority from their "anaesthetized faith" and convert them to the engaged, activist Islam preached and practiced by Islamists, along with all its specific commitments of practice, lifestyle, and dress. Their goal was to transform the "somnolent" masses into people with "blazing . . . fully awakened" souls who would be imbued with "love for the Islamic cause" and thus willing to devote themselves to working and making sacrifices for the good of the community.

And in Egypt the Islamist cause would, within a few short years, prove spectacularly successful.

The soaring oil prices after the war of 1973 and the enormous wealth the Arab oil states commanded thereafter would give rise to other conditions—aside from vastly increased resources for funding Islamist outreach—that would further contribute to the spread of Islamism and that would promote the spread of Saudi Arabian and Gulf forms of religious practice to Egyptians and other Arabs and Muslims.

First, Saudi and Arab Gulf wealth opened the door to immigrant labor from many parts of the world, particularly from the neighboring and linguistically compatible Arab world. Graduates of Egyptian universities (the beneficiaries of Nasser's policies, which had made university education free and available to all who qualified) now eagerly competed for the opportunity to work in the Arabian Peninsula, where salaries were far higher than those of Egypt. The figures for Egyptians, both men and women, employed in the Arabian Peninsula rose through the seventies and early eighties from 10,000 in 1968 to 1.2 million by 1985.[10]

After a stint in the Arabian Peninsula, returnees to Egypt had acquired the funds to buy properties and goods that had previously been out of reach. They were very well to do compared to Egyptians who had not had the opportunity to work in the Peninsula. Many retained the styles of dress they had adopted there, and these styles, including hijab, now became among the fashions of the wealthy. Just as in earlier decades wearing European-style dress and adopting Western languages had been signs of wealth and chic, so now it was the hijab and dress and practices in the style of Saudi Arabia that were the signs of wealth, chic, and prestige.[11]

The wealth of the oil-producing countries was itself regarded as a sign of God's favor to Muslims, and in particular to Muslims who followed the strictest forms of Islam, including wearing hijab. Other Muslims would do well to adopt those conservative practices, many thought, so that they too could receive God's bounty and blessings.[12]

Moreover, returnees contributed to Islamist causes, charities, and voluntary associations, and made donations for the building of mosques and other Islamic institutions. The numbers of privately funded mosques (as distinct from state-funded mosques staffed by government-appointed imams) now rose rapidly—increasing from twenty thousand in 1970, according to one study, to forty-six thousand by 1981. Mosques, in turn, often offered, besides the daily and Friday prayers and sermons, varieties of services and religious instruction, including day-care centers and kindergartens and health-clinics and lending libraries of books and tapes.[13]

In 1973, too, Islamist associations began to organize summer camps similar to those that the Muslim Brothers had organized prior to Nasser's dissolution of the Brotherhood in 1954. Those attending those camps, noted Kepel, would be "initiated into the 'pure Islamic life.'" This involved "regular daily prayers, ideological training, an apprenticeship in the skills of the preacher and the tactics of proselytism, socializing within the group and more." These summer camps served as schools and training camps, Kepel continues, "for the cadres and future cadres of the Islamist movement." Within a few years its graduates would be among the activists in the vanguard engaging in da'wa and promoting the spread of Islamism.[14]

As the power and influence of Islamism grew, the government also continued to try to gain support and authority by promoting religion and religious themes. Ever larger numbers of mosques had become centers of Islamist preaching and activism, much of it often implicitly critical of and oppositional to the government. As private, Islamist-funded mosques grew in number, mosques were clearly venues that no state could afford to ignore. Thus government-built mosques also began to multiply; they were staffed by imams appointed by the government and delivered government-approved sermons.[15]

Seeking to gain legitimacy among the steadily more religiously inclined populace, the government increased religious curricula in schools and universities and increased religious programming on radio and television. It was probably in these years that the terms secular and secularist—language initially promoted most likely by the Muslim Brothers and the League to discredit Nasser's Arab nationalism and socialism—began to be liberally applied retrospectively and of course pejoratively to the Nasser era, including to the norm of bare heads that many Muslim women of that era, the pious as well as the less pious, had widely adopted.[16]

By the later seventies the Islamist currents that Sadat had encouraged were now on a collision course with his government. From 1977 onward, after members of the militant Islamist group Takfir wal-Hijra murdered a former minister and were captured and brought to trial, the fissures between Islamists and the government, moderates as well as radicals, grew clearer. Sadat's trip to Jerusalem in November 1977 and his subsequent Camp David negotiations, both of which were opposed by Islamists, moderates and militants alike, exacerbated tensions.

On his return to Egypt after signing the Camp David accords in March 1979, Sadat began to launch verbal attacks on Islamists. He was critical not only of militants but also of those who "cloaked" their criticism of him in religion, specifically the leadership of the Muslim Brotherhood. Soon Sadat began taking action against Islamist organizations—moderate as well as militant—freezing the assets of those on university campuses and eventually, in September 1981, even ordering their dissolution. Meanwhile, Sadat was also arresting many of his nonreligious critics, imprisoning many intellectuals in 1981.[17]

On October 6, 1981, Sadat was shot on the stand where he was reviewing the military parade commemorating the launch of the 1973 Ramadan War. A military truck had come to a halt before the stand and four men jumped out, firing automatic weapons. Sadat and a number of dignitaries were instantly killed. One of the men, who would become known as the group's leader, had shouted as he opened fire: "I am Khalid al-Islambuli. I have killed Pharaoh, and I do not fear death."

The four were part of the militant organization Islamic Jihad, whose leader and theoretician was Abdel Salam Faraj. Faraj was an electrician who had written a book called *Al-Farida al-Ghaiba* (The Neglected Duty, sometimes translated as The Hidden Imperative), a book informed and inspired, as were so many Islamist writings, by Qutb's ideas. "The neglected duty" was jihad. The book strongly affirmed the notion that righteous, committed Muslims had a duty to struggle against God's enemies and rise up against and remove illegitimate un-Islamic regimes and rulers.

Khalid al-Islambuli, a twenty-four-year-old officer in the army at the time, was the one who had hatched the idea of assassinating Sadat on the occasion of the military parade. He had joined the army because he dreamed of becoming a pilot, but he had been appointed instead to the artillery corps. On September 3, 1981, he had returned home to learn that his brother, the leader of a nonmilitant Islamist organization on the campus of Asyut University, had been arrested with others in Sadat's crackdown on all Islamists. Khalid, filled with grief and anger and intent on vengeance, devised the assassination plot, which he took to Faraj, who approved and facilitated it. Khalid and his three accomplices, as well as Faraj, would be executed in 1982.

Another member of Islamic Jihad was Ayman al-Zawahiri, Osama bin Laden's second-in-command. Following Sadat's assassination, al-Zawahiri was arrested for and convicted of dealing in weapons. He received a three-year sentence.

For al-Zawahiri, as for so many others, Qutb's philosophy had been a critical influence. Al-Zawahiri would declare in 2001 that "Sayyid Qutb's call for loyalty to God's oneness and to acknowledge God's sole authority and sovereignty" had been the "spark that ignited the Islamic revolution against the enemies of Islam at home and abroad. The bloody chapters of this revolution continue to unfold day after day."[18]

*

> Mankind today is on the brink of a precipice, not because of the danger of complete annihilation which is hanging over its head—this being just a symptom and not the real disease—but because humanity is devoid of those vital values which are necessary not only for its healthy development but also for its real progress. Even the Western world realizes that Western civilization is unable to present any healthy values for the guidance of mankind. It knows that it does not possess anything which will satisfy its own conscience . . .
>
> The leadership of mankind by Western man is now on the decline, not because Western culture has become poor

> materially or because its economic or military power has become weak. The period of the Western system has come to an end primarily because it is deprived of those life-giving values which enabled it to be the leader of mankind . . .
>
> It is necessary to revive that Muslim community which is buried under the debris of the man-made traditions of several generations, and crushed under the weight of those false laws and customs which are not even remotely related to Islamic teachings, and which, in spite of all this, calls itself "the world of Islam."[19]

Qutb's writings remain the key works of the Islamic Revival, which has been steadily unfolding throughout the forty-plus years since his death. While *Milestones* is regarded as the "ideological foundation of radical political Islam"[20] and has been reprinted many times and translated into many languages, all of Qutb's books continue to be widely read and studied and his theories and scholarship discussed and debated—and occasionally also criticized and repudiated, including by learned conservative scholars of Islam. Qutb can be justly described, in the words of Roxanne Euben and Muhammad Zaman, as among the "most influential architects of contemporary Sunni Islamist political thought" and as a thinker whose works have "provided several generations of Sunni Islamists with a moral map of history and politics in which Muslim experiences of impotence and suffering are simultaneously explained and offered redress."[21]

Qutb's influence indeed has been so profound and pervasive that, as another Qutb scholar, Yvonne Haddad, remarked, "In a certain sense, a great deal of what is being published at present is either inspired by his writings, plagiarized from his books, or is commentary on his ideas." Writing in the 1980s and noting that Qutb's influence knew no borders, Haddad went on to list just some of the developments under way around the world that marked the trail of Qutb's pervasive influence. In Iran, for example, she notes, Qutb's writings not only inspired such prominent intellectuals as Ali Shariati but they inspired the student revolutionaries who in 1979 brought down the shah. In Kuwait, the International Islamic Federation of Student Organizations translated and published his books in English. And in the United States his works would find readers among both immigrant and African American Muslim audiences. Thus in the U.S. his books were "highly recommended to members of the Muslim Student Association," a group whose members were preponderantly immigrant, and they would also be popular "among members of the American Muslim Mission (popularly known as Black Muslims)" who, Haddad explains, found Qutb's "'evangelical' rhetoric and Quranic centeredness strongly supportive of their worldview as they [sought] to transform American society and to convert others to the faith of Islam."[22]

Born in a village in southern Egypt in 1906, Qutb pursued his college education in Cairo, where he attended not the religious institution of al-Azhar but the secular teacher-training college, Dar al-Ulum. Here he came under the influence of Abbas Mahmud al-Aqqad, a prominent Egyptian intellectual and literary figure noted for his openness to the strongly pro-Westernizing currents in Egypt of that era. Al-Aqqad fled to the Sudan in the early nineteen-forties when the Germans appeared to be advancing on Egypt, fearing that he would suffer reprisals at their hands because of his forthright criticism of Adolf Hitler.[23] During Qutb's years as a student he would become deeply interested in English literature, and he was a voracious reader of English writings in translation.

After graduating, Qutb worked for the Ministry of Education. Like his mentor al-Aqqad, he would become known through the first decades of his life as a literary figure, the author of books of poetry, criticism, and novellas. Among his works was an autobiographical book, *A Child from the Village.* The book, a moving evocation of village life, is also a passionate plea for Egyptians to remedy the gross inequalities and injustices rampant in their society and which the book vividly portrays. The work is dedicated to Taha Husain, author of the classic autobiography *Al-Ayam* (The Days) and a writer who had been severely criticized by some in Egypt for what they perceived to be his overly pro-Westernizing views.

Appearing in 1946, *A Child from the Village* was among the last books Qutb published that were primarily literary and non-Islamist. His book *Social Justice in Islam,* one of his weightiest and now most studied works, published in 1949, marked the beginning of his turn toward Islam as the ground of his thought. It also marked the start of his steadily more emphatic turn toward Islamism. During the forties, according to Haddad, Qutb, "like other Egyptian intellectuals who had been enamoured with the West," underwent a profound transformation. This came about, she wrote, "as a result of British war policies during World War II and as an aftermath of the creation of the state of Israel. The latter he perceived as a rejection of the rights of Arabs to self-determination and a rejection of their equality to Western man."[24]

Through the forties Qutb grew increasingly more outspoken in his criticism of the ruling establishment in Egypt, including King Farouk, and he also began to be deeply critical of the United States, particularly, as the Qutb scholar Adnan Musallam explains, as a result of President Truman's support for Jewish immigration to Palestine. "At last," Qutb wrote in response to Truman's position, "the conscience of the United States" had been uncovered. The Palestinian problem had shown "that this 'conscience' gambles with the fate and rights of humans in order to buy a few votes in the election." Americans, Qutb continued, like other Westerners, suffered from a "rotten conscience" (*damir muta'affin*). "Their conscience is all derived from the same source—namely, the materialistic civilization that has no heart or conscience, and which hears nothing but the sounds of machines." Declaring that "I hate and despise" all Westerners—"the British, the French, the Dutch and now the Americans who were at one time trusted by many"—Qutb adds, "I hate and despise just as much those Egyptians and Arabs who continue to trust Western conscience."[25]

In 1948, sent on a study mission abroad by the Ministry of Education, Qutb left for America—some now speculating that he had been deliberately dispatched on this trip in the hope that exposure to the West would moderate his views.[26] Qutb attended the Colorado College of Education, graduating with an M.A. degree in 1951. He then returned to Egypt, his American experience evidently having entrenched rather than dissipated his deeply negative views of the United States.

Qutb's book *Social Justice in Islam* was published in Egypt while he was abroad, and it had been well received, particularly by the Muslim Brothers, who initiated cordial relations with him on his return. Qutb had dedicated the book to "the youngsters whom I see in my fantasy coming to restore this religion anew as it began fighting . . . for the cause of Allah by killing and getting killed, believing in the bottom of their hearts that the glory belongs to Allah, to his Prophet and to the believers." The Brotherhood took this dedication—mistakenly, according to Qutb—to be a reference to themselves.[27]

Thus began Qutb's relationship with the Brotherhood. Through the early fifties Qutb continued to write prolifically, publishing several books as well as numerous articles, some of which were published in the Brotherhood's journals. One article denounced the religious establishment of al-Azhar, which, he maintained, was failing in its task of reviving the "Islamic idea" and developing it through studies and research and, in this way, preparing for the "practical application" of this Islamic idea "in the light of present realities." Qutb was, to begin with, on good terms with Nasser and the officers of the coup of 1952, and he even served as consultant to them for some six months. By this point, though, he was already beginning to distance himself from them, and in 1954, following the Brotherhood's attempt (according to the government) to assassinate Nasser, Qutb was among the Brotherhood members arrested and imprisoned. Thus began the years of imprisonment and persecution under Nasser that would culminate, as already described, in Qutb's execution.

Scholars who have combed through Qutb's writings for passages about women's rights and roles concur that Qutb adamantly advocated policies that were systematically restrictive and confining to women. He maintained, as Roxanne Euben describes in her study of Qutb, that women's responsibility to society was "synonymous with her biological function in life." Being the caretakers of the family and children, according to Qutb, defined woman's "identity, importance, and dignity."[28]

Similarly, Lamia Shehadeh points out that although Qutb undoubtedly revolutionized Islamic thought by incorporating into his views ideas of individual liberty and freedom from servitude as fundamental elements of the ideal Islamic society and thus of the society that the Muslim vanguard must struggle to achieve, when it came to women he evidently had no hesitation in confining them to "permanent servitude to their husbands and families." Qutb declared that all human beings "are equally God's slaves, no one has the right to exercise authority over another." Nevertheless, Qutb categorically affirmed the "wife's subjugation to her husband."[29]

Moreover, like al-Banna, as Shehadeh also points out, Qutb called for new and comprehensive rereadings and reinterpretations of Islam, rereadings that would be responsive to the needs of the day. And, again like al-Banna, Qutb maintained that individuals were capable of interpreting the texts "without any authoritative human guide, albeit after having mastered the disciplines of linguistics and grammar among others." These views, and Qutb's call for the reinterpretation of the Quran, reflected both his position that "Islam is eternally valid" and consequently capable of accommodating changing times and societies, and his concomitantly flexible approach to issues of tradition and jurisprudence, which he viewed as open to reinterpretation and redefinition. But regarding women, Shehadeh points out, Qutb was content to keep them—indeed, even committed to keeping them—"chained to their past."

Qutb's views of women and their roles were not characteristic of the positions that would be taken by many of the Brotherhood's leaders as the Brotherhood's position on women evolved through the seventies and after, as I discuss in Chapter 6.

Qutb never married, which was unusual for men in Egyptian society in that era. Nevertheless, women in various capacities—and in particular his mother and sisters—were undoubtedly important in his life. Qutb's account of his mother and of the women in the village in which he grew up, in his autobiography, is informed by a deep sense of empathy and a clear sensitivity to the difficulties of life that fall particularly heavily on women—to the point that his later rigidity regarding women's status seems surprising and suggests that he had become distinctly less empathetic and more extreme in his views of women over time. In Qutb's adult life, his sisters, Amina and Hamida, no less than his brother, Muhammad, worked as his assistants, and they too were activists alongside him in his Islamist work. Amina and Hamida were both also arrested, as was Muhammad, within days of Qutb's second arrest in 1965. Muhammad Qutb, released from prison by Sadat in 1972, settled in Saudi Arabia, where he taught at a university and edited and published his brother's books, seeking in his own work to reconcile differences between the views of the Brotherhood and those of the Wahhabism of his adopted country.[30]

Also arrested in 1965 was Zainab al-Ghazali, the "unsung mother" of the Brotherhood. Al-Ghazali in every sense and at every point in her life might be said to have blazed her own path to power and influence. Born in 1917 in a village in the Egyptian delta, she came from a well-to-do family which traced its lineage to Umar Ibn al-Khattab, one of the four caliphs of early Islam revered by Sunnis. Her father was a cotton merchant who had studied at al-Azhar and who devoted his spare time to touring the country and preaching in mosques and teaching the "Islamic call and religion."[31] Al-Ghazali's father encouraged her to become a Muslim leader. "He always used to say to me that, God willing, I would be an Islamic leader," al-Ghazali wrote. In particular, he held up for her the example of Nusaybah bint Kaʿb al-Mazini, a woman known for her prowess as warrior, famed for wielding her sword to devastating effect in a number of the battles of early Islam.

While al-Banna and Qutb had continued with their studies through college, al-Ghazali's formal schooling ended with secondary school. At the age of sixteen she joined the Egyptian Feminist Union, an organization founded in the 1920s by Huda Shaʿrawi, the upper-class Egyptian woman who was the most prominent feminist figure of the first decades of the twentieth century. Shortly afterward, however, al-Ghazali withdrew from the organization. "With my Islamic upbringing," she explained years later to an interviewer, Shaʿrawi's call for the "liberation of women" had not seemed to her to be the "right way for Muslim women." Women needed to be "called to Islam," al-Ghazali felt. Consequently, Shaʿrawi's organization seemed to her "misguided" because it failed to recognize that, "as all rights derived from Islam, there is no 'woman question' distinct from the emancipation of humanity, which is possible only through the restoration of Islamic law as sovereign." To put into effect her own perspective, al-Ghazali shortly afterward, aged eighteen, founded her own organization, the Muslim Women's Association (Jamaat al-Sayyidat al-Muslimat).

A few months later, after delivering a lecture in 1939 for the Muslim Sisters at the headquarters of the Brotherhood in ʿAtaba Square, in Cairo, Hasan al-Banna invited her to take charge of the Sisters division of his organization. This would have entailed incorporating her association ("the newborn of which I was so proud") into the Brotherhood. After briefly discussing the matter with the General Assembly of the association she had founded, al-Ghazali declined the invitation. Al-Banna, who was known for a style of leadership that "brooked little dissent," was angered by her response, and to appease him al-Ghazali informed him that although the group insisted on retaining its independence it would always support the Brotherhood. This failed to satisfy him. Time passed, al-Ghazali writes, continuing her account, and the events of 1948 took place: that is, the government issued orders to dissolve the Brotherhood, and many Brothers were thrown into prison. On the morning following the order to dissolve the Brotherhood, she continues, "I found myself sitting at my desk with my head in my hands, weeping bitterly. I felt that Hasan al-Banna was right, and that he was the leader to whom allegiance is due from all Muslims." She then sent a message with her brother to al-Banna which read, in part: "My Lord, Imam Hasan al-Banna: Zainab al-Ghazali al-Jabili approaches you today as a slave who has nothing but her worship of God and her total devotion to the service of God's call. . . . Waiting for your orders and instructions, my lord the imam."

Shortly afterward they met at the Association of Muslim Youth, where al-Ghazali was to deliver a lecture.[32] As they went up the stairs together she said, "By God, I pledge allegiance to you, to work to establish the state of Islam. The least I can offer you to achieve it is my blood, and the Muslim Women's Association with its name." He said, "I accept your pledge of allegiance. The Muslim Women's Association may remain as it is."[33]

Soon after, even as al-Ghazali was striving to mediate between al-Banna and Mustafa Pasha al-Nahhas, Egypt's former prime minister, al-Banna was assassinated. Besides grieving over this al-Ghazali was soon contending with the government's order to dissolve her association, an order she successfully contested.

In the immediate aftermath of the 1952 revolution all seemed well. Only days before al-Ghazali had received a visit from Major General Muhammad Naguib, one of the leaders of the revolution. He had been accompanied by Prince Abdallah al-Faisal of Saudi Arabia.

Then, in the wake of the alleged assassination attempt on Nasser by the Brotherhood, began the wave of imprisonments and executions of Brotherhood members, including many of its leaders. Al-Ghazali now felt that she had been "drafted into the service of the Islamic call" in response to the devastated families—children, wives, widows, elderly, now homeless parents—of the men who had been rounded up and were suffering imprisonment, torture, and execution. People needed food, clothing, shelter, and there were rents to be paid, school supplies to be provided. Organizing donations and distributions, mobilizing networks of support and communication and connecting with the leadership whether in prison or outside it, al-Ghazali's work was key to the sustenance of the organization through these times.

Through this period al-Ghazali played a key role in the discussions among the Brotherhood's leadership. She was in close touch with Qutb, even when he was in prison, through his sisters. In the seminars and Islamic study groups that she led through this period, made up of young men who met at her home, the readings were often Qutb's writings, including *In the Shade of the Quran* and drafts of *Milestones,* which Qutb was completing in prison and which his sister Hamida brought to them. "When we had finished reading what she brought us, she would bring more," wrote al-Ghazali. These were "sweet glorious days," she wrote, "and Allah's bounties passed by while we studied and taught ourselves, as well as prepared our youth for da'wah."[34]

Al-Ghazali also was collaborating with Hasan al-Hudaybi, who had succeeded al-Banna as Supreme Guide of the Brotherhood, and with Abdel Fattah Ismail, a major figure in the Brotherhood who would be her close collaborator until his execution, along with Qutb's, in 1966.

It was in these years that al-Ghazali and the Brotherhood leadership would devise their plan to pursue the program of Islamic education. All of their meetings had to be carried out in secret because of the government's ban on the organization. But, as al-Ghazali wrote—evidently rebutting the accusation that they had been plotting violence and the overthrow of the government—"I call on God as my witness that our program consisted of nothing but the education of the Muslim individual so he would know his duty towards his Lord, and the creation of Muslim society, which will of necessity be separate from pagan society."[35]

In 1964 the government ordered al-Ghazali to dissolve her organization, which, she said, had a countrywide membership of 3 million women.[36] Shortly before this she had been the target of an assassination attempt, and in 1965 she was arrested and charged with complicity in a plot to overthrow the government. Qutb and Ismail, also arrested, were sentenced to death and would be executed. Al-Ghazali was sentenced to twenty-five years of hard labor. After enduring "six brutal years," during which she was subjected to horrifying tortures, al-Ghazali was released as a result of an amnesty issued by Sadat.[37]

Al-Ghazali would describe some of her prison experiences in her memoir, *Ayam min Hayati* (literally "days of my life"), titled *Return of the Pharaoh: Memoir in Nasir's Prison* in the English translation. In this book, more reflexive hagiography (as the memoir was aptly dubbed by Euben and Zaman) than autobiography, al-Ghazali describes the torture and suffering she endured during her interrogations in ways that establish "her insight, endurance, authority and stature as unique among women and superior even to that of most men." She also describes the mystical visions she experienced, visions that affirm her closeness to the Prophet as well as her importance to the Brotherhood as equal to that of al-Hudaybi, Supreme Guide of the Brotherhood.

After her release al-Ghazali resumed her work as an Islamic activist and educator. Interviewed in 1985 by Kristin Helmore of the *Christian Science Monitor,* in "her fashionable Cairo apartment," al-Ghazali appeared dressed in white robes, "with only her face, hands, and sandal-clad feet uncovered." She had clearly specified the subjects she was willing to speak about and those that she was not, and she displayed, according to her interviewer, the "iron determination of one who has given her every waking moment to a cause, and the inner stillness of one who is wholly convinced that she is right."[38]

In answer to one of Helmore's questions—concerning the differences between a "devout Muslim woman and one who is more modern" —al-Ghazali eyed Helmore's "pink, short-sleeved dress sternly" and said that modern women, "like you, for example: If you don't go back to your religion and dress as I do, you'll go to hell. Even if you're a good Muslim and you pray and do what is right, if you dress the way you do all your good deeds will be canceled out."

When asked about her activities and about Islam and women she replied, "Islam is best, because it makes women and men equal. Since I was 18 years old I have had the role of making people understand what Islam means to women and what women are in relation to Islam. I am now 68 and I am still doing the same thing." Al-Ghazali said that a woman had the right to decide whether she wanted to marry, and that she had the right to practice birth control—"It's up to her," al-Ghazali said, "but the husband and wife have to agree." She also said that a woman had the right to work in any field she chose: "in politics, in agriculture, commerce, anything. But her main role is to be a wife and mother. As long as she maintains both roles, she can also work."

Al-Ghazali's view on a woman's right to work provided she fulfills her duties as wife and mother represented the common Islamist position on the subject in the 1980s and beyond. Still, al-Ghazali's complex viewpoints, positions, and commentary, as well as her own actions, on this general subject are worthy of full and extended study—study which they have not yet received. Nor indeed have al-Ghazali's life and work been the subjects of the substantial and exhaustive study that a figure of her importance—to the history of the Muslim Brotherhood, the history of Egypt, the history of the Islamic Resurgence, and the history of Islam worldwide—should receive.

Only a comprehensive study of this nature might fully cast light on, among other things, the questions and debates that have surfaced around her positions regarding women. For, while formally espousing the common Islamist position (as of the 1980s) as to women's rights to pursue careers, provided they fulfill their obligations to husband and family, al-Ghazali herself divorced her first husband (having first ensured that her Islamic marriage contract specified her right to divorce) because marriage "took up all my time and kept me from my mission" and because her husband disapproved of her Islamist activities. When marrying a second time, al-Ghazali stipulated to her future husband that she would leave him if marriage prevented her from "continuing in my struggle in the path of God . . . the struggle to which [I] have devoted [myself] from the age of eighteen."[39]

Al-Ghazali also describes in her memoirs how, in the fifties and thereafter, her husband would admit male callers at all hours, then call her or wake her up to meet with them before himself retiring. She recounts a conversation with him in which she explained at the outset of their marriage that she was a woman who, "at the age of 18, gave her whole life to Allah and dawah. In the event of any clash between the marriage contract's interests and that of dawah, our marriage will end, but dawah will always remain rooted in me." She accepted, she explained to her husband, "that ordering me to listen to you is amongst your rights." However, she went on, "Allah is greater than ourselves and His dawah is dearer to us than ourselves. Besides we are living in a dangerous phase of dawah."[40]

In this "dangerous" phase for the Islamist cause, the work of da'wa and of establishing Islam, for women who constituted the Islamist leadership or vanguard, clearly took precedence over duties to husband and children that pertained in more normal times. Once Islamic rule was established, al-Ghazali also explained in her book, "women's position will be at its proper place, whereby they can educate the men of this Ummah."[41] In line with this thinking, al-Ghazali considered the fact that she had no children a "great blessing."[42]

Ghada Talhami, whose research regarding Islamist views of women's roles in the movement I discuss in chapter 6, points out that the notion that the obligation to work in the service of Islam took priority over other obligations for women as well as men who were part of the Islamist vanguard was among the views espoused by some Islamists. And as Talhami noted, al-Ghazali refers to herself in her memoir as part of the vanguard.[43]

Al-Ghazali's second husband died while she was in prison after having been compelled to divorce her following her arrest or face imprisonment himself. She died in 2005 at eighty-eight. Throughout she had continued to work for the cause of Islam, as speaker, writer, and always as teacher.[44]

The 1970s would close with an event that would dramatically mark the emergence of Islam as a political force in the modern world: the Iranian Revolution, led by Ayatollah Khomeini, which toppled the shah and instituted the Islamic Republic of Iran. This would be one of those moments when the veil's meaning as emblem of challenge and confrontation between Islam and the West seemed to vividly and forcefully break into the foreground. The Iranian Revolution was not only anti-shah but also anti-Western and particularly anti-American. Through the early days of the revolution, and especially through the American hostage crisis, images of the chadors of Iranian women (the enveloping covering that became widespread after the new Islamic government imposed the requirement of veiling) and images of burning American flags became globally familiar signs of the new Iranian Islamic order.

Despite the real divide between the Shi'i Islam of Iran and the Sunni Islam that was dominant in the Arab world and across much of the world, the success of the Islamic Revolution in Iran delivered an exhilarating boost of hope to Islamists everywhere. (Nor was it only Islamists for whom the Revolution spelled new hope: the French philosopher Michel Foucault also welcomed it and flew to Iran to interview its leaders.)[45] The Revolution's success was read by Islamists as a sign that powerful authoritarian governments and unjust rulers such as the shah of Iran—even those allied, as he had been, with great world powers such as the United States—could be brought down by a popular uprising and by people united in their opposition to tyranny. Soon after, of course, Anwar Sadat—viewed as a "pharaoh" and an unjust ruler by his assassin—would be killed.

Zainab al-Ghazali, in 1981, was among those who supported the Iranian Revolution, as she stated in an interview. Interviewed again a few years later, however, she was now opposed to it because of its violence, declaring that the regime the revolutionaries had instituted "was not really an Islamic state."

In contrast to the Iranian regime, which imposed veiling, the quiet revolution that the Sunni Islamists were setting in motion in Egypt was seemingly rather implanting in women the will and desire to wear hijab. In the following two chapters I explore the ongoing spread of the veil and the apparent willingness and even active desire of an ever-growing number of women to wear it.

·5·

The 1980s

Exploring Women's Motivations

By the mid-1980s it was clear that deep changes were under way and that the Islamist trend was not destined to fade away. Signs that a "quiet conversion to a new way of life" was in progress were in evidence everywhere. The numbers of mosques multiplied—by the early eighties as many as four thousand new mosques were estimated to have been built in Egypt.[1] As the architectural landscapes of cities changed, so did their auditory landscapes. In many Cairo neighborhoods the call to prayer now came from several minarets at once and typically through loudspeakers. As many have noted (and as I heard for myself), gone were the days of *adans* (calls to prayer) chanted simply by the unamplified human voice blending with the sounds of the city or quietly marking the dawn.[2]

The look of the streets was changing, too, as dress and fashion changed. Some men took to wearing beards as well as baggier, looser clothes and long shirts, sometimes even *djellabas.* But changes in men's dress were less common and certainly less eye-catching than in women's dress, as more and more women adopted hijab and/or Islamic attire. The changes for women seemed to be more symbolically charged and to be unambiguously signaling the steady gains that Islamism was making.

For Islamists, the hijab's growing presence was doubtless an encouraging sign of their spreading influence. For women of the Egyptian mainstream, however, who still made up the unveiled majority, and for men opposed to the Islamist trend, the hijab was seen as a sign of the growing strength of people opposed, or seemingly opposed, to their own way of life, and an augury of possibly unwelcome and even menacing changes to come.

Egypt was the first country in which the new hijab and Islamic dress had begun to appear, along with other signs of an evidently rapidly rising Islamist movement. These trends attracted the interest of many scholars, among them academics interested in political and militant Islam (in the 1970s and 1980s the term Islamism had not yet come into use) and also—thanks to the rise of feminist scholarship in America—academics interested in focusing on the veiling trend and on issues of women's motivations and agency, topics that were gaining theoretical importance in American feminist scholarship.

These researchers, studying the rise and spread of Islamism and the veiling trend from various perspectives, would come up with quite different and sometimes seemingly contradictory findings. There would be those, as I will describe, who would see the conclusions of those studying these phenomena from different perspectives from their own as categorically incorrect. The dividing line fell between those who saw veiling as essentially a trend being driven forward by women for their own specific reasons and those who saw it as emanating from male Islamist leaders for whom the veil was critical to their overall strategy of spreading Islamism.

In this and the following chapter I review and draw together the findings of these researchers who, through different lenses and perspectives, set out to understand the spread of Islamism and the veil during the critically transformative decades of the 1970s to the 1990s. I endeavor to create an overview of the various and multiple forces that gave rise to this dynamic Islamist movement, a movement that would become a force in global history and that would carry along with it wherever it took root its imprint and emblem, the hijab.

I begin by describing in this chapter the findings of two scholars who set out to study women's consciousness, agency, and motivations around the issue of the hijab. Both researchers would interview women who wore hijab, as well as women who did not. The first of these is Arlene Elowe Macleod, who began her research in 1983, and the second is Sherifa Zuhur, who conducted her research in 1988, the year Macleod brought hers to a close. Macleod studied a group of eighty-five working women, twenty-nine of whom wore hijab when she began. By the time she completed her research—and indicative of the rapid march of the trend—sixty-nine of the women wore hijab. Without exception, all of the women in Macleod's study who wore hijab had begun to do so as adults, typically after leaving college and upon entering the workplace. For all of them, therefore, taking on hijab and/or Islamic dress marked, as Macleod put it, a "dramatic" as well as recent change in their lives.

Both Macleod's and Zuhur's findings are illuminating regarding these crucially important years in Egypt, when the Islamist movement and veiling were at a point of dynamic growth and change. In addition, their studies are also illuminating by virtue of the intimate details they provide. The women relate a variety of reasonings, rationales, and individual circumstances as influencing and shaping their decisions to veil, and their stories notably foreshadow some of the explanations and meanings of the veil that are emerging today in Western societies. It was in these decades, and as the veil began to be explained as dress that was freely chosen and whose meanings could be rationally articulated, that the veil would begin to break free of its historically bounded meanings.

Among the questions Macleod posed to the women she studied was why it was, in their opinion, that some women were beginning to wear hijab, and why, "after wearing western dress their whole lives, women would suddenly decide to alter their dress so radically?"[3]

Some said they thought that there was a "general sense that people in their culture were turning back to a more authentic and culturally true way of life." Others said that in the past people had been "thoughtless and misled" and now realized that their behavior had been wrong. As one woman put it, "in the past people didn't understand that these values are so important, but now everyone has come to see that they are good and strong. So we know now we have to act like Muslim women, that it is important." One woman who had adopted the hijab explained, "Before I did not know what I was wearing was wrong, but now I realize and know, thanks be to God." A number noted that Muslim women in general held to certain beliefs and followed patterns of behavior that were different from those of Western women. In the words of one woman, "We Muslim women dress in a modest way, not like Western women, who wear anything . . . Muslim women are careful about their reputation. Egypt is not like America! In America women are too free in their behavior!"

Other responses (all of which offer a snapshot of the kinds of ideas and explanations that were in the air at the time) explained the trend in terms of hard economic times. "Everyone is more religious now," said one woman. Another opined that "everyone is realizing that life is difficult now and that we must return to the true values of our religion and way of life." Overall, these responses resonated with those reported by Williams and Radwan, as they resonated with the Islamist narrative (as Macleod noted) disseminated in Islamist pamphlets and other publications, which were widely available and which declared that a return to Islamic values was "necessary for times to get better." There was a widespread feeling among Macleod's interviewees that life was hard and needed answers "beyond the confusion and commercialism of the everyday grind."

Also informative about contemporaries' experience at this moment is the fact that the majority of the women in Macleod's group (60 percent) said that they "simply did not know" why things were changing and why the trend was happening—even as they recognized that they themselves were part of it. "I don't know why everyone wore modern dress before and now we do not," said one woman, "but this is the situation." Many of them (56 percent) suggested that it appeared to be a matter of fashion. As one woman put it, "I don't know why fashions change in this way, no-one knows why, one day everyone wears dresses and even pants. I even wore a bathing suit when I went to the beach . . . then suddenly we are all wearing this on our hair!"

When Macleod asked women who wore hijab why they had adopted it, the responses she received initially echoed the stock responses that Williams and Radwan had earlier reported. Some said, for example, that on donning it they had found "peace." One woman explained that she had felt "very troubled" before deciding to wear it and that afterward she felt "completely different" and that she now "knew who I was." Others noted that the hijab protected them from harassment. "When I wear this dress," one woman explained, "people on the street realize that I am a Muslim woman, a good woman. They leave me alone and respect me."

In following the women's lives, however, and continuing to interview them over five years—years through which more and more of the women began wearing hijab—Macleod was able to collect information on the specific circumstances in which they made the decision to wear hijab, as well as on other matters relating to veiling about which she had questions. Among these, for example, was the question of whether donning hijab correlated with an increase in religious observance—and on this point Macleod found essentially no correlation. Only a "tiny minority" of women, veiled or unveiled, prayed daily the five prescribed prayers or "concerned themselves with fulfilling their other religious duties." A few women (both veiled and unveiled, apparently) performed religious duties such as prayer about a "third of the time," while the remainder, whether veiled or unveiled (as Macleod this time specifies), "seldom performed any religious actions or indicated personal religious emotions, with the exception of fasting during Ramadan or celebrating the various holidays, such as the birthday of the Prophet."

This did not mean, though, that the women did not consider themselves to be practicing Muslims. On the contrary, Macleod found that among the largely lower-middle-class community she studied, Islam typically formed the "strong and unquestioned . . . foundation of their lives." Although there were variations in people's personal commitments, overall Islamic beliefs and rituals nevertheless formed a "foundation for society in a way perhaps difficult to understand in secularized, commercialized America."[4]

Nearly everyone prayed on Fridays. Generally they all observed the Ramadan fast and hoped one day to go on pilgrimage. There were differences, though, Macleod found, between the ways in which men and women typically practiced their faith. Men often attended mosque on Fridays, whereas women usually prayed at home. Women were also likely to offer prayers to "special saints" whose shrines they visited—particularly in times of stress and need. Sometimes a group of women would set forth together to visit a shrine, such as the ancient and revered shrine of Sayyida Zainab, our Lady Zainab. Zar ceremonies, practiced by some in Egypt, were often viewed as "lower class" and were not typically attended by women of this community.

Regarding the specific circumstances and reasons for which women decided to veil, Macleod found (once more in part echoing Williams) that the decision to veil typically resolved specific problems in their own lives, problems usually arising from tensions around issues of family and work or of being able to move freely in the public world.

Macleod substantiates this conclusion with many examples. One woman, for instance, explained that her husband "did not like the way men at the bus-stop would talk to me as I left for work. You know, they would ask me the time, or how are you or whatever. It is very innocent, but my husband is a jealous man. Well I guess he loves me and that is all that is important, and so I decided to put on the higab [Egyptian pronunciation] to prevent him from these strong feelings. Why should that come between us?" Another woman who loved her job broke off her first engagement because her fiancé wanted her to quit work. Becoming engaged a second time, she declared that she would wear hijab when she married. This would help "balance" matters between home and work, she said. A third woman decided to adopt Islamic dress a few months after the birth of her first child. "Many factors influenced the decision," Macleod reported, "her sense of increased family responsibilities and her husband's discomfort with the compliments men paid her at work and her feeling that her proper place was at home with the children . . . coupled with the realization that she probably could not afford to stop working." As the woman explained, "I want to quit my job but we need the money. When I wear this dress it says to everyone that I am trying to be a good wife and a good mother. The higab is the dress of Muslim women and it shows that I am a Muslim woman."

In effect, donning hijab allowed women to go about their lives and keep their jobs while affirming their identities as Muslim women and presenting themselves as women who were conforming to conservative Islamic notions of women's roles. Thus, concluded Macleod, women could affirm community belonging and respect for community values and make public by their dress their commitment to their families and their roles as wives and mothers. Hijab also allowed them to retain their jobs and move freely in public. In short, it had now become a "culturally available way" by which women could resolve tensions about their roles and make the statement that they were "good Muslim women." The hijab's popularity, Macleod argued, arose from its ability to offer a "symbolic reconciliation" between these areas of tension.

Macleod concluded that, among the women she studied, the "essence of the meaning of their veiling" was that it was a response to the local and specific circumstances and relationships in which the women were immersed, rather than a response to "larger questions of politics and international relations." Consequently, Macleod takes a position that is strongly opposed to any notion that the "new veils are . . . sign[s] of support of the Islamic resurgence." The evidence she had gathered simply did not support the idea that women adopting the hijab were joining a movement "directed against the West or against the state," or that they were linked to Islamist groups and their "oppositional politics." Quite the contrary, her observations indicated that for these women "the idea of being Muslim has more to do with their role as wife and mother in the family, rather than with expressions of nationalism or anti-Western feeling," and that "we should be most cautious about assuming such oppositional politics or religious militancy among the majority of veiling women," as well as about assuming that they were "part of some militant or political movement which has a settled program of behavior . . . such as fundamentalist groups or political organizations." Such interpretations were, said Macleod, simply "misguided."

To be sure, though, Macleod observed, the veiling trend was occurring in the context of a resurgence in "fundamentalist Islam," a resurgence that was undoubtedly creating a heightened preoccupation with religious matters. Men in particular, she found, were likely to "debate religious matters and sometimes follow the arguments in the newspapers by prominent religious thinkers." Women took less interest in the discussions and tended to "regard this religious interest as a public and political matter, one out of their realm of real interest, the family." Overall, men and women in the community she studied tended to regard "fundamentalist groups . . . as political organizations, better avoided." Often they characterized the militants as "crazy people," and many "emphatically point out that Islam does not countenance violence. Politics, not religion, is seen as the concern of such groups."[5]

Altogether, then, the veiling trend among the women she studied was under way, said Macleod, because the veil offered a way of symbolically reconciling tensions around, in particular, issues of work and gender roles. These findings also led Macleod to conclude that veiling was "primarily women's idea and women's decision," and that its spread was unrelated to militant or oppositional Islam. The spread of hijab was essentially a manifestation of a "voluntary movement," a movement that was clearly "initiated and perpetuated by women" and under the control of women.

And yet Macleod could not completely accept this conclusion. As the evidence she gathered toward the end of her research period shows, there were new pressures on women to adopt hijab, making it a matter not entirely of their own choice and volition. There was clear evidence, Macleod reported, of the growing influence of men on the trend. While in 1983 and 1984 Macleod's interviewees had confidently told her that "this movement was under their control and at their initiative," by 1988 several women now admitted to her "that they had put on the dress recently to avoid men's constant harangues." Women who had originally said they would not wear it now reported that they had "succumbed to the insistence of male family members "and growing conformity in the office."

Women reported that a variety of social pressures were making it ever more difficult to not veil. They reported feeling that veiled dress was steadily becoming "less one option among many and more the correct thing to do." Few women naturally felt able or willing to argue that their "religion or cultural traditions are in some way wrong." A number of the women in the group had privately conveyed to Macleod that they did not believe in wearing hijab. One older woman, for example (and older women were more likely, she found, to be openly opposed to it), had commented that "these girls can wear higab if they want, but I will never wear it. I worked very hard to be in the position I am in today . . . and these young girls do not know how hard it was in the past for women. Really it does not matter what people wear, but I will not wear it." Younger women confided that they did not believe that wearing hijab was necessary to being a good Muslim. But the young often found it very hard to take a stand against wearing it and typically deflected questions about it by declaring that they intended to wear it at a specific time—on marriage, say, or when the feeling and need to do so "strikes in her heart."

Part of the ethos of the day regarding the adoption of hijab was, Macleod reported, that taking on the hijab should come about not out of compulsion but rather as the result of a woman's personal choice. This is an ethos that is clearly a product of the late twentieth century and one that unmistakably postdates the cycle of history of the 1900s to the 1970s and from unveiling to veiling. Before the era of unveiling, covering was just normal dress for all women in Muslim majority societies, and choosing not to cover was not an option. As we will see in Chapter 9, the idea that women had to be personally convinced of the need to veil—an idea that first emerged, probably in Egypt, in the 1970s and 1980s—is now commonly accepted in twenty-first-century America.

In the context of the new veiling movement, this ethos, noted Macleod, enabled women at least to defer the decision for a while. Such was the tactic used, for example, by one young woman when she was teased by fellow workers about when she meant to begin wearing hijab. "I don't feel this need in my heart yet," she had said, unable to openly state her own conviction that the veil was not required at all: "God willing, I will feel it someday, and then of course I'll put on the higab."

The pressure for women to wear hijab was distinctly growing. There was evidence, Macleod found, that women were being pressured not only by the men in their families but also by male religious authorities. Several women now mentioned that they had decided to wear hijab because of their local religious leaders. Others mentioned that male relatives would cite the authority of religious men in their "attempts to persuade fiancés, wives or sisters to veil."

In the face of these findings, Macleod concluded that the hijab trend was initially a women-initiated movement controlled and driven forward by women's own needs, choices, and volition. But by the late eighties it was increasingly becoming co-opted by men.

While women who wore hijab in Macleod's group had all grown up wearing "modern" or "Western" dress, the veiled women in Zuhur's 1988 study, conducted just five years after Macleod had begun hers, had typically begun wearing hijab as schoolgirls, having been influenced by teachers and peers. Parents and siblings had at first hated their adoption of the hijab, they reported, but they had eventually accepted it. Some had even gone on to adopt it themselves.[6]

Through the eighties the Islamist current had continued to gain strength. Islamist schools multiplied, and Islamist notions of correct dress and proper religious practices were spread through these schools' curricula and teachings. Government schools joined the effort as well. For the government, eager to show itself as no less religiously committed than the Brotherhood and other Islamist groups, had continued to try to gain popular support by promoting religion and religious themes in schools, as well as by building more mosques and increasing religious programming on radio and television.

To meet their teaching needs, government schools hired instructors of religious education who most often were graduates of Islamist schools. Similarly, the increase in religious programming and the emphasis on religion in all departments also created more jobs, opportunities, and positions of influence for people who had had Islamist training and education.

By the late eighties the generation of university students who had been on the frontlines of Islamist groups in the seventies had graduated and joined the workforce and were advancing in their professions. Typically these graduates (and their successors) were people who had trained in such professions as engineering, medicine, law, chemistry—professions with considerable prestige and influence. By the early 1990s, Islamists had gained control of a number of the most important and powerful professional organizations of the country—among them engineering, medicine, and law.

Whereas in the seventies it had been veiled women who had been seen as different and who might find themselves, as we saw in the case of Beshir, the targets of hostility, by the late eighties it was unveiled women who could find themselves in this situation, as one of the stories told to Zuhur by an interviewee indicates. This woman, who had "light hair" and was "quite fair," was visiting a friend in the hospital and was waiting for the elevator. "I was dressed decently," she explained, wearing a mid-calf-length skirt and a short-sleeved blouse when "one of those religious types with a beard and long shirt, shouted at me, 'How dare you come to our country and insult our religion!' Well," the woman concluded her story, "it's my country and my religion too. How dare he talk to me as if I'm a foreigner!"[7]

Zuhur's study explores and compares the views and attitudes of the unveiled woman with those of the "new Islamic woman" on a number of issues, including women's rights. She found no differences between them on this matter. They held similar views as to the "nature" of men and women—both considering them to be "equally capable but complementary rather than identical." And both unveiled and veiled (including "even the more conservative respondents") believed that "women should be given equal opportunities with men, and equality under the law so long as the principles of sharia were upheld." Similarly, both groups found Islamist critiques of Western societies as "lax in their moral values" to be resonant and meaningful.[8]

Both were equally critical of the government and viewed the current social and moral condition of the country to be distressing. Differences emerged as to their attitudes, however, regarding the possibility of an Islamist government: unveiled women did not see the rule of Islamists as a desirable alternative to their current government, whereas veiled women emphatically did. Unveiled women were alarmed at the gains Islamists were making and feared that their continued gains would lead to the curtailment of their own civil rights. Veiled women hoped for the day when an Islamic state would be instituted and "all other women will wear higab."[9]

Echoing the findings of earlier researchers, Zuhur found that unveiled women did not believe that the veil was required by Islam. Many claimed that its use was spreading through society because women were being paid to wear it by the Brotherhood and other Islamist groups and by funds from Saudi Arabia and Libya.

Veiled women, on their side, considered unveiled women to be failing to practice a foundational Islamic requirement, and they saw their own adoption of the hijab to be a sign of their social and moral awakening. Among the elements that had made the Islamist message attractive to women (and more successful among them than had been "internationally anticipated"), Zuhur suggests, was "its association with cultural authenticity, nationalism, and the pursuit of *'adala*, or social justice."[10]

As veiled women's hope for an Islamist government indicated, Zuhur's veiled women, in contrast to Macleod's interviewees, seemed to be adopting the hijab not merely (or perhaps not at all, since Zuhur does not address this point) to resolve personal dilemmas but because they were self-consciously affiliating themselves with the goals of Islamism. However, the veiled women in her group were not themselves Islamist activists, Zuhur emphasized. (Aiming primarily to study "what takes place in the mind of the 'average' woman," and to portray the world of "ordinary women," Zuhur deliberately excluded activists from her study.)

Just as the fact that the veiled women in Zuhur's study were likely to have adopted hijab as schoolgirls—and thus at a far earlier age than those in Macleod's study—the differences between Macleod's and Zuhur's groups with regard to their attitudes toward Islamism perhaps similarly reflected the fact that Zuhur's research, conducted a few years after Macleod's, captures yet another and more advanced moment in the ongoing progress of Islamism.

Like Macleod, Zuhur also set out to investigate whether women who wore hijab were more religious than those who did not. Like Macleod, she concluded that they were not. Zuhur did find, though, that while veiled and unveiled women may be equally pious, the ways in which they conceived of and practiced their religion differed in subtle but palpable ways. The difference lay above all in the profoundly different emphasis they placed on the importance of the "inner" practices of religion, on the one hand, and on "outward" and "visible" practices on the other. For veiled women, the emphasis typically fell on the outward practices and on the public display of piety and religiousness. Often, in response to the question of whether they considered themselves religious, veiled women were likely to say, "Since I veil, I am religious."[11] They might also say that since they prayed regularly and fasted and read the Quran, they were religious.

Unveiled women, in contrast, were more likely to define religion in terms of the inner dimensions of religion, and in terms of good deeds and of dealing with people in the "right way." "The unveiled woman considers the *jawhar* [the jewel] or essence of her religion, to be more important than the *mazhar* [the appearance] or exterior practices, although most observe [also] the *mazhar* through regular prayer, fasting during Ramadan, reading of the Quran, and so on." As one unveiled woman explained, she considered herself religious "because I believe in God and I try to deal with people in the right way." While many unveiled women, Zuhur found, also performed the "outward" practices of religion, such as prayer and fasting during Ramadan, some did not—but they nevertheless considered themselves to be religious. One respondent, for instance, declared, in response to Zuhur's questioning, that she did not pray or fast, "and if that's what you mean, then I'm not religious." But, she went on, "Islam is a *din muamalah* (a religion of social association and reciprocity): religion is how you treat people, how you live your life, and in that sense I am religious."

Emphasizing that her findings showed above all that Muslim women "conceive of and practice their religion in diverse ways," and that some unveiled women considered themselves to be no less pious than veiled women, Zuhur notes that the nonveiled woman "may be equally pious,"and therefore cannot be termed "secular." The use of this term to refer to nonveiled women was evidently beginning to come into academic currency at the time that Zuhur was writing, and in the interest of accuracy Zuhur, as she is careful to point out, chose to refrain from using it.[12] (Notably the term does not occur as an appropriate description for the nonveiled in any of the prior academic writing in English on women and veiling reviewed here—from El Guindi to Macleod.)

Zuhur's attempt to pinpoint the different understandings of the meanings of religion and of what it meant to be a religious or pious person, brief and unelaborated though it is, nevertheless touches on a key matter: the redefinition of the very meanings and practices of piety, and of the very understanding of religion and what it meant to be religious, that the spread of Islamism was bringing about in these decades. Similarly, Zuhur's scrupulous refusal to adopt the term "secular" for nonveiled women on the grounds of its essential inaccuracy underscores the new descriptive force that the term "secular" was beginning to gain in these years, as it underscores also the transitions in meanings and dress that were now under way as new forces gained power and their vocabularies of dress, language, and religious practice steadily gained ascendancy.

As we saw earlier, the Muslim Brotherhood from its very founding had had the goal of persuading the general population to leave aside their traditional ways of living and practicing Islam, ways that the Brotherhood regarded as passive and "dormant," and of educating them into adopting in its place the engaged, activist ways of Islamism along with all its attendant requirements, rituals, and prescriptions, including veiling. Older, more traditional ways of living and practicing Islam, passed from one generation to the next, would come to be looked down on by Islamists as constituting incorrect ways of practicing the religion.[13]

I have described in this chapter the gist of the findings about the spread of veiling put forward by researchers whose focus lay in exploring and understanding women's own consciousness and subjective experience of veiling. In the following chapter I turn to the work of researchers whose primary interests lay in investigating and understanding other dimensions of the Islamist and veiling trend, including militant ones, as well as, more broadly, the movement's goals, strategies, and methods.

· 6 ·

Islamist Connections

In contrast to the findings of researchers focused on exploring women's motivations for veiling, quite a different set of factors emerges as of central importance to the spread of veiling in the works of researchers focused on studying the Islamist movement. While scholars exploring primarily women's personal motivations for veiling—from El Guindi through Williams to Macleod and Zuhur—typically concluded, albeit often with some reservations, that the decision to veil was the result of women's own choices, the findings of researchers studying the Islamist movement more broadly suggest rather that veiling spread because Islamist male leaders conceived of veiling as strategically important to their movement.

The study of Islamism has of course given rise to a vast literature in our time. Among the studies that I follow out and piece together in this chapter are those of three scholars who cast important light on the subjects of Islamism, women, and the hijab in the two critical decades of the mid-1970s to the mid-1990s. Gilles Kepel's important work *Muslim Extremism in Egypt,* published in 1984, was the first of these works to appear. Next was Ghada Talhami's *Mobilization of Muslim Women in Egypt,* published in 1996. Unlike Macleod and Zuhur, who approached their subject through the lenses of women's studies scholarship, focusing therefore primarily on women's agency and consciousness, Talhami focused on how Islamists mobilized women and conceptualized women's roles in the movement, as well as how they conceptualized the issue of the veil and its role in the Islamist movement. A third work, Carrie Rosefsky Wickham's *Mobilizing Islam,* published in 2002, richly details by what means Islamism succeeded in disseminating its norms of belief, practice, and dress throughout society in just two decades. Wickham's work does not focus on women, nor does the author approach her topic with a women's studies lens. Nevertheless, she pays close attention to women's as well as men's mobilization by the Islamist movement and thus provides important additional information about the Islamist movement and the veiling trend in this critical period.

These works were based on research conducted from the mid-1970s to the mid-1990s and thus capture different important moments over the course of those two transformative decades. Piecing together these researchers' findings alongside those offered by the scholars focusing specifically on women allows a complex and more complete portrait to emerge as to the dynamic, complicated, and multidimensional process—political, social, and religious—that brought about the spread of Islamism and its emblem, the veil.

Kepel's work, focused on Islamist developments in the seventies and early eighties, drew attention to the important role that Islamist organizations played in promoting the veil and Islamic dress on university campuses. He describes how the extreme overcrowding on public transport and in lecture halls prompted the publication of a number of articles in the proliferating Islamist journals of the day. Writers complained about the Islamically inappropriate gender-mixing occurring on campuses and called for the adoption of Islamic dress for women as a means of protecting their dignity.[1]

In response to the overcrowding, Islamist organizations in 1977 began offering a bus service exclusively for women. The service was immediately in very high demand among women, and, in response, the Islamists made Islamic dress a requirement for women who wanted to use the service.

Similarly, also to address the problem of overcrowding and of mixing of the sexes (a mixing that one writer in *al-Da'wa* described as a

"Western weapon of corruption designed to make us abandon our Islamic personality"), Islamist organizations introduced the requirement that men and women sit in different rows in lecture halls. Segregated seating, like the bus service, was very popular among women, who might find themselves in lecture halls where their neighbors were "virtually piled on top of them."[2]

In addition, in response to the difficulty that students, and in particular women, faced in buying clothing and keeping up with fashions (in times of lavish consumption for some and economic hardship for the majority), Islamist organizations began to offer Islamic dress for women at low or nominal cost.[3]

All of these measures for the most part significantly improved the quality of life for female students and were reportedly welcomed by them.[4]

Besides making life easier for women, these services and arrangements also of course helped disseminate Islamist notions and practices of correct dress and norms of gender segregation—notions that were foundational to the understanding of Islam that Islamists were promoting, and to the Islamic society that Islamists hoped to institute. To use Kepel's perhaps somewhat overdramatic words, "One begins by declining to sit next to a classmate of the opposite sex and then finds oneself, little by little, fighting for the establishment of the Muslim state."[5]

Clearly Kepel's findings cast a significantly different light on the veiling trend of the seventies that El Guindi and Williams had reported on and about which they had largely concluded, on the basis of the research they had conducted among women, that it was a trend signaling a new assertiveness among women and reflecting above all their own independent decisions to don the hijab. Both scholars thought that, overall, women were choosing to adopt hijab as a result of a personal decision rather than in response to external pressure or instigation.

I believe, however, that Kepel's findings neither negate nor invalidate the conclusions of those earlier observers. Rather, we must view the findings as reports arrived at from different angles of observation and through accessing different types of information relevant to the intertwined realities of the veiling trend and Islamism—both part of a vast and enormously complex, multidimensional, and worldwide movement.

Kepel's studies also show how both women's veiling and the matter of women's participation in the movement were topics that received careful attention from the male Islamist leadership. Both veiling and women's activist involvement in Islamism, his findings show, were considered strategically important to Islamism. In 1980, for example, 'Isam al-'Aryan, a young doctor and well-known Islamist leader, published an article in *Al-Da'wa* in which he listed women's veiling as among the first and most important of four signs of the Islamist movement's advances.

Al-'Aryan analyzes in his article the history and broad condition of contemporary Islam. He notes that Islam's recent history can be described as having gone through three distinct stages. First came Islamic civilizational decline, a condition that culminated in Western colonialism and in the domination of Muslim lands by infidels. In the wake of colonialism came the era of nationalism and so-called independence, an era in which, in Egypt, people believed that they had won independence. But this had been a mistaken belief, as the infidels in fact had continued their control, though now they worked behind the scenes, their Western perspectives and ideas having "penetrated the minds of the people." During this phase of history, Westernized scholars, including some of the country's most distinguished intellectuals, such as Taha Husain (said al-'Aryan), in effect were reproducing the colonial ideas they had imbibed, telling their Muslim compatriots that the "reason for their backwardness lies in religion," and then urging them to institute a "separation between religious sciences and the new sciences." Such advice led Muslims to misguidedly experiment with "Western-style democracy and Communist socialism: the fruits have been bitter."[6]

The third era was that of the Islamic Awakening, said al-'Aryan. In this era the Muslim world's "ten million" students, "from Casablanca to Jakarta," as well as the workers would become now the "cadres of the future Islamic states."

There were four important signs, al-'Aryan continued, that would signal the ongoing advancement of the Islamist movement. The first of these, he said, would be women's increased wearing of the veil. "When the number of women students wearing the veil rises, that is a sign of resistance to Western civilization and of the beginning of *iltizam* [pious commitment] towards Islam." Other signs included men wearing untrimmed beards and djellabas, and people's attendance at public prayers on the two great feast days.

This last point referred to another aspect of the strategy Islamists were pursuing for drawing ever larger numbers of people into their movement: involving them in public prayers. People participating in such activities, no matter how "irregular their normal religious observance," would be infused, Islamists believed, with a new and reenergized religious commitment.

Islamist associations began to organize public prayers on university campuses and at venues beyond the university. In 1976 they began holding huge gatherings in stadiums and major squares in Cairo and Alexandria, and soon also in cities throughout Egypt. *Al-Da'wa* claimed that their gatherings brought together as many forty thousand and one hundred thousand at specific venues in Cairo and Alexandria in 1976 and 1977. Women as well as men were present, separated by an opaque screen. Sermons and lectures were delivered by star preachers of the Islamist movement, such as Yusef al-Qaradawi and Muhammad al-Ghazali, who flew in for those events from their prestigious positions in Arab Gulf states.

Besides revitalizing people's religious commitments, mass gatherings also served to vividly signal to the government and to the larger society the substantial and growing reality of Islamist presence and strength. The growing commonness of the veil similarly served the same purpose: making visible to the dominant society the presence of people committed to an ethos and vision that was different from and indeed seemingly implicitly oppositional to that of mainstream society and the reigning political order.

Interviewed in 1988 on the subject of women and veiling, al-'Aryan observed that "we do not have to impose the higab in any case, women are adopting it of their own volition." Women, he further explained, had an "active role to play in the Islamic movement." He also said that the movement "must utilize the talents and skills of women in redesigning a society that requires the input and expertise of all its members."[7]

Conducting her research in the 1990s, Talhami explored the changes that had occurred among Islamists, beginning in the 1970s, with regard to the inclusion of women as activists in their movement, and with respect to their views and discussions of women's roles.

Prior to the seventies the Muslim Brotherhood had not set out to recruit women nor to involve them in their programs. In conducting its activities on university campuses through the 1930s and 1940s the Brotherhood had routinely targeted only males for recruitment into the student cells that it organized on university campuses and at high schools. By the late thirties the Brotherhood controlled many such cells.[8]

Early in the 1930s a project was set up for the establishment of a Muslim Sisterhood, which envisaged providing religious education to women through programs dedicated to explaining the "duties and rights" of Muslim women and the "means of raising good Muslim children and keeping a Muslim home."

In 1937 a Muslim Sisterhood was in fact established. It was this organization that al-Banna had sought to interest al-Ghazali to preside over, under his leadership. Made up essentially of the wives of Brothers, its first president was Labiba Ahmad, who was the editor of a journal, Al-Nahda al-Nisa'iyah (Women's Renaissance), as well as president of her own women's organization, Jam'iyyat Nahdat al-Sayyidat al-Misriyat (Society of the Renaissance of Egyptian Ladies). The Muslim Sisterhood did not participate in the Brotherhood's political debates or its advocacy work. Among other things, it undertook some charitable work, providing, for instance, health-care education for women in villages.

The positions that the Sisterhood took often were not particularly supportive of women's right to employment and education. When a ruckus arose at Cairo University because of the rising levels of male harassment of female students, Ahmad's journal published an appeal to the government to end coeducation because it "violated Islamic religious teachings." In the same vein, Brotherhood cells on campuses at this time typically strongly opposed women's right to education and work.[9]

This was of course far from the position that Islamists would take in the seventies when, in response to the perception that inappropriate gender-mixing was occurring, they set about finding solutions to enable women to continue their studies while also creating an acceptably segregated environment, both through women's dress and separate seating. (Through the fifties and sixties, as we saw, Zainab al-Ghazali was a prominent and exceedingly active figure with the Brotherhood. But this was evidence of al-Ghazali's own personal leadership, not of the Brotherhood having sought to encourage women's activism and leadership in the movement.)

Exploring Islamist literature of the era to understand these changes, Talhami found that there was now, as in the seventies, a "plethora of Islamist writings on women"—a subject which, she notes, had not been of particularly consuming interest to Islamists in earlier decades. Issues of women's roles and rights to education and to work were being extensively discussed now, as were issues of women's importance to, participation in, and responsibilities toward the Islamist movement. Even the question of whether women had a duty to participate in jihad, in the sense of armed struggle, was discussed.

There was little disagreement among the mainstream Brotherhood's leaders that women did meet the qualifications for armed jihad. There were differing views, however, on whether women had an obligation to undertake jihad only in defense of community, and also on whether women could abandon home and family to fulfill these obligations.[10]

There was also consensus as to women's right to education and to work, although all agreed that women's primary responsibility was to home and family, and that issues of rights could be discussed only in relation to the social good. There were shades of opinion on this matter, too, although there was general agreement with the opinion articulated by one Islamist ideologue, Hamid Suleiman, to the effect that women may work outside the home "if no social or moral damage accrued . . . and if their work did not interfere with their domestic duties." Suleiman also maintained that women could hold any position in society other than that of head of state or Grand Imam.[11]

Others also, and most notably Muhammad al-Ghazali, a leading Islamist thinker of this period, wrote in firm support of women's right to work. Al-Ghazali also strongly critiqued opponents of women's rights, even arguing against the evidence used to support the notion that women were unfit to serve as political leaders. With respect to the hadith in which the Prophet Muhammad reportedly commented, referring to a Persian queen, that "those who are governed by a woman are doomed to misery," al-Ghazali maintained that this was because the Persian queen had ruled incompetently and that she had "completely neglected shura [consultation]." Al-Ghazali continued: "Had there been shura in Persia or had the woman governed like the leader of the Jewish people, Golda Meir, there would have been a different comment."[12]

Indisputably, though, the consensus was that the Islamist foundational ideal was of women as members of families headed by men, devoting their primary energies to nurturing and educating children—a role "decreed by her special nature," as Muhammad al-Ghazali maintained.[13]

Working through this literature—and in the context now, by the early 1990s, when Talhami was pursuing her research—of women's evident activism in Islamism, Talhami goes on to argue that when the Brotherhood reemerged in the seventies as an organization that had renounced violence and committed itself to working through da‘wa and education to bring about the sharia-based Islamist society, it came to grasp the key contributions that women could make both by their dress and by their activism, to the project of the re-Islamization of society. Consequently, Islamists now deliberately set out, Talhami asserts, to mobilize women "as recruiters and advocates of the puritanical ideology."

This did not mean that Islamists were abandoning their commitment to the ideal of women as members of families headed by men and whose first duties were to the family. Rather, notes Talhami, the Brotherhood now saw its entire membership, including its "politicized female members," as part of the vanguard. The role of the vanguard was that of working through the gradualist nonviolent means of the jihad of education and da‘wa to bring about the transformation and re-Islamization of society. It did not matter, as Zainab al-Ghazali had stated, how long it took: this was the task that the vanguard, women and men, were called to in these extraordinary times. Women who were part of this vanguard were exempt, Talhami concluded, just as Zainab al-Ghazali was exempt, from "many of the rules of Islamic feminine orthodox behavior." Thus the vanguard, Talhami continues, "was an extraordinary formation for extraordinary times. Women, it was assumed, would resume their place in the Islamic utopia of the future, where men would carry the burden of managing the affairs of the family."

Women were offered a vision, Talhami wrote, "of future economic equality and plenty, where no one went hungry or unclothed. It was a vision moreover of a righteous society where dignity and humanity would be amply protected." And women themselves, particularly university women, were attracted and mobilized by this "revivalist social gospel of economic equality and authentic Islamic existence."

Altogether, Talhami concluded, also citing the themes and arguments that figured in the Islamist literature she analyzed, the mobilization of Islamic women in Egypt was a "careful and orchestrated endeavor to produce a breed of Islamic feminine activists. While university women were among the most susceptible to the message of Islamist regeneration and renewal, more traditional and homebound women were also targeted." Talhami also noted in the literature a preoccupation with issues of women and veiling, particularly in the work of writers advocating resistance to Western imperialism. Women were "reminded of the degradation heaped upon them as a result of the economic imperialism of the West" and were cast at once as "heroines and defenders of the fabric of Islamic society," and as at the center of a "regenerative effort to restore" the Muslim world.[14]

In rebuttals of the idea of Western superiority Talhami found the "veiling issue became the centerpiece of the Islamist debate," with the writers going to great lengths to explain and justify its practice. Critiques of imperialism and of the idea of Western superiority were accompanied by critiques of past and contemporary Egyptian intellectuals, including feminists, who, Islamists maintained, had been "dazzled by the glitter and the glory of European civilization," and who had promoted Western ideas and values in part because "orientalism had succeeded in sowing the spirit of defeatism in Muslim minds by emphasizing all that was negative in the Islamic heritage." The strategy they used to discredit feminists in particular was that of portraying them as un-Islamic and as culturally Westernized.

Talhami also draws attention to the extraordinary importance that some militant jihadists gave to the veil. Shukri Mustapha, leader of the radical militant group Takfir wal-Hijra, believed that the "true Muslim community" must follow a number of principles that rendered it distinctive, including the wearing of Islamic dress. Salah Siriyyah, founder of another radical group, went so far as to assert that those "who opposed Islamic dress for women and advocated indecent dress deserved to be killed."

The "Islamic veil," Talhami writes, "was therefore important because it defined the Islamic movement and gave it an identity distinguishable from the rest of society." She continues firmly: "Any other explanation of the spread of the veil—attributing this custom to hard economic times and general inability to purchase Western clothes—is far from valid. Neither is it accurate to claim that women cleverly assumed the veil to facilitate their freedom of movement." There is only one correct reading, Talhami maintains, of the spread of the veil. "The veil was conceived by the originators of the radical Jihad group as an assertion of the superiority of Islamic societal rules of the past, as well as an identity symbol to separate true believers from the quasi believers."

It is not clear why Talhami assumes that what the veil meant to the "originators of the radical jihad group" trumped its meanings across all groups. After all, those scholars who had suggested (and whose suggestions Talhami here categorically dismisses) that women had their own motivations for wearing hijab were writing of women who were not members of radical Islamist groups.

Talhami was writing her book in the mid-1990s, the era when incidents of violence and religious intolerance toward intellectuals had reached shocking levels in Egypt. This backdrop—seeming to suggest that radical militants were gaining influence and power—perhaps influenced Talhami to give more weight and centrality to militant extremist views of the veil than they in fact merited.

In any case, Talhami does appear to be rather too sharp in her criticism of previous researchers. The evidence presented collectively by the scholars reviewed so far suggests that many forces were synergistically driving forward the profound sartorial and religious transformation in Egypt over those decades, a transformation that already was beginning to spread globally.

*

Al-Islam hua al-hal
(Islam is the solution)

—Slogan of Muslim Brotherhood

By the early 1990s, Islamists had gained control of several of the most influential professional organizations, including those of engineering, medicine, pharmacy, and law. Their growing power and influence in the country was increasingly evident now in many institutions, including the media and schools and colleges. The products of earlier Islamists' educational efforts had now come of age and were themselves donating time and labor as volunteer doctors, lawyers, teachers, and other professionals to promote the Islamist cause.

By now Islamists had established private schools to serve the middle and upper classes, in addition to their many schools to serve the poor. The government through these years (in an attempt, as we saw earlier, to gain legitimacy by co-opting religion) had greatly increased religious teaching in schools, as well as religious programming in the media.[15] All of these contributed to the ever-growing dominance of the language of religious piety as the acceptable and normative language throughout society.

In the early 1990s, however, the government attempted to change course with respect to religion in education. Growing tensions around the issue of increasing Islamist influence in schools developed into a crisis that erupted in 1994 around, specifically, the issue of Islamic dress and the veil in schools. The early 1990s was a period of suddenly escalating Islamist violence after a time of quiescence through the eighties, following the government's crackdown on Islamist extremism after Sadat's murder in 1981.

In 1991 the minister of education, who had held the post since 1987 and who had been a strong advocate of a "return to conservative religious values," was removed from office and replaced by Kamal Baha Eddin, a man who had served as secretary general of a youth organization in the Nasser era. Baha Eddin immediately set about reorienting schools away from religion and Islamization. Declaring that education was a matter of critical importance to national security, Baha Eddin stressed that schools had the mandate in these times of "protecting the nation's youth from dangerous, or 'extremist' elements within society."[16]

In 1993 a senior official in Baha Eddin's ministry published a report stating that ninety state schools and three hundred teachers had been found to have links to illegal Islamist organizations. The report had indicated that most of these schools and teachers were located in southern Egypt, but in an interview Baha Eddin said that extremism was not in fact limited to any particular region but was now a "nationwide phenomenon." Government schools, Baha Eddin asserted, were filled with Islamist teachers "who were using their position to indoctrinate Egyptian youth." "The terrorists," the minister declared, "had been targeting schools for years. . . . We have found schools where students are told not to salute the flag, sing the national anthem or talk or study with Christian students." Gaining control of the schools, the minister wrote, was a matter of national security.[17]

Islamist extremism and terrorism were on the minds of many in Egypt in the early 1990s. Mainstream Islamists had been steadily gaining ground across society and in the professions through the 1970s and 1980s, and these were gains that continued apace. But now new factors, and in particular the Soviet withdrawal from Afghanistan in 1989, followed by the fall of Kabul, meant that jihadi warriors who had come to Afghanistan from all over the Muslim world to fight in the jihad against the Soviets would now be disbanded. Several hundred Egyptian "Afghans" trained and radicalized in Peshawar and knowing only the ways of war and violence now returned home—injecting a new level of violence and militancy into society. Militant extremist groups, reinvigorated by the return of these hardened jihadi fighters, now embarked on an unrelenting campaign of murder and acts of atrocity.[18]

Violent attacks now began occurring with increasing frequency against such targets as video stores and nightclubs—venues identified by militant Islamists as promoters of "moral decadence."[19] Attacks occurred too against government buildings, banks, and government officials. Similarly, Coptic (Egyptian Christian) churches and businesses were targeted.

Prominent intellectuals who were critical of Islamism or whose views extremists considered un-Islamic also became targets. Naguib Mahfouz, for example, the novelist and Nobel laureate, was stabbed—on the grounds that his books were blasphemous. He survived, though the attack left his writing hand crippled. This attack—which took place in 1994, when Mahfouz was in his eighties—seemed a shocking gauge of the country's sharp descent into intolerance, as well as a stark measure of how drastically it had changed through recent decades.

Such attacks on writers were perhaps inspired by the Ayatollah Khomeini's 1989 fatwa against Salman Rushdie. The turmoil it caused in Western societies, particularly Britain, possibly made the targeting of intellectuals seem an attractive strategy for militant Islamists whose anger was directed at Western powers, as well as at local governments and local writers.

In 1992 the journalist Farah Foda, a well-known critic of Islamism, had been assassinated. Foda, although reportedly personally religious, was a committed supporter of secular government.[20] Foda's murder and the ensuing trial caused consternation among many, for at the trial Muhammad al-Ghazali, the prominent Islamist, appeared on behalf of the defense.

Al-Ghazali had previously taken clear stands against violence, repeatedly rejecting it as un-Islamic. He had denounced the attempted murder of Mahfouz as a "crime against Islam."[21] On this occasion, however, al-Ghazali argued that "anyone who resisted the full imposition of Islamic law was an apostate who should be killed either by the government or by devout individuals,"[22] a statement that provoked strong criticism. The Egyptian High Court of State Security rejected the defense's argument, noting that people could not be allowed to accuse others of heresy and apply punishment to them "according to his own whims" or according to the "misguided" fatwas of those "who claim authority in religion." They sentenced one of the two accused to death, and the second to fifteen years' hard labor.[23]

As noted earlier, the Brotherhood and mainstream Islamists did not espouse or support violence.[24] On the other hand, the growing influence of the Brotherhood and of mainstream Islamists in society and in the professions did lead to a growing atmosphere of repression. In these years the legal system was used by Islamist lawyers to, in effect, harass and persecute people who did not share the views of Islamists. In 1991 the writer Ala Hamid was sentenced to eight years in prison for writing a book that was considered blasphemous.

Similarly, in 1993, Nasr Hamid Abu Zayd, a professor at Cairo University, was denied tenure and brought to trial on the grounds that he was an apostate. As there was no apostasy law in Egypt, an Islamist lawyer had filed suit demanding Abu Zayd's forcible divorce from his wife on the grounds that a Muslim may not be married to a non-Muslim. The court eventually ruled the marriage null and void—and Abu Zayd and his wife had to flee to Europe for asylum. This current of thought and legal action would continue in Egypt. In 1999 another such case was brought against the feminist Nawal el-Saadawi, also attempting to forcibly divorce her from her husband on grounds of her purported apostasy. Eventually the court would rule—in the summer of 2001—in favor of el-Saadawi.

The violence that began to tear at the country in the early 1990s would continue to escalate, culminating in the massacre at Luxor in 1997 when sixty people, most of them tourists, were gunned down. The attack had been carried out by Islamic Jihad, a group at this point headed by Ayman al-Zawahiri (a figure well-known today as Osama bin Laden's second in command). Intent on dealing a crippling blow to the Egyptian economy, of which tourism was a vital component, the attack provoked shock and revulsion in Egypt "at this completely unprecedented slaughter of foreign visitors." Many Egyptians who depended on tourism for their livelihood were directly affected by these murderous acts. The event proved to be a "turning point in the counter-terrorism campaign in Egypt" as the government cracked down on militants who were now loathed by the population.[25]

The changes and the powerful Islamist current that was under way, and most particularly the issue of Islamist militancy and violence, were now matters of public concern that were being addressed in the media. By the early 1990s, for example, critics had begun openly lamenting that the "influence of Wahhabi Islam (the ultra-conservative strand of Islam dominant in Saudi Arabia) had begun to erode the more flexible and permissive form of popular Islam that had evolved in Egypt."[26]

Others forthrightly took up the issue of Islamist militant violence. *Akhir Sa'a* (a "semi-official" journal, Wickham notes) published an article claiming that extremists were using mosques as recruiting grounds. "From inside the private mosques," the article declared, "the light of religious extremism beams forth."

Militant groups, the article continued, were using mosques to store weapons, and Islamists were "trapping" innocent youth: "The private mosques have become the biggest snare of the youth, who comes originally to pray, but who, upon being ready to leave, is seized by an extremist as his next victim, who sits him down and whispers at him, and his nice-sounding, honeyed words have an effect, who promises him a straight path to heaven if he obeys the ruling of God (and the extremist takes it upon himself to interpret what they are) and warning him of the sufferings of hell if he disobeys." In this way, "unsuspecting youth, who started out just wanting to pray, ends up a member of a Shawqiyya or Ikhwaniyya . . . or Salafiyya extremist group which are enemies of the state." The writers emphasized that they were not calling for "a halt to the building of new mosques" but "for a change in what is going on inside them, especially now that some of them have become laboratories for the incubation of extremism."[27]

It was against the backdrop of such events and public discussions that the fracas over schools and in particular over veiling in schools erupted. After the appearance of the ministry of education's report claiming that many government schools and teachers had links with illegal Islamist organizations, the weekly magazine *Ros al Yousef*, another semi-official publication, also conducted its own independent study of Islamist extremism in schools. It reported that the Muslim Brotherhood was "buying up preschools and elementary schools, and that Jihad [an extremist group] exerted control over teacher training institutes."[28]

Ros al Yousef also reported that teachers purportedly "preached to students about the apostate Egyptian government" and "played recorded sermons of the dissident Sheikh Omar Abdel Rahman." Sheikh Omar, a radical Egyptian cleric who would later be charged in the United States for his involvement in the 1993 bombing of the World Trade Center, had been advisor to militant jihadists groups in Egypt in the 1970s, including the group which assassinated Sadat. Through the 1980s he had been active in Pakistan and elsewhere, recruiting jihadists for the war in Afghanistan. On his return to Egypt after the end of the Afghan war he was under investigation for involvement in terrorist activities when he managed to flee to America.

Stories were now commonplace in the Egyptian press and also figured in complaints to the ministry about how "teachers were either forcing or scaring young girls into wearing the hijab." Reportedly cassette sermons on the theme of the Torture of the Grave (Azab al Qabr) were in wide circulation.

The new education minister, Baha Eddin, set out to change the curriculum and purge Islamists from government schools. Since, as government employees, they could not be fired, he transferred them instead to other employment in remote areas. Some contested their transfer in court, and in some instances they won. One such case, for example, involved the principal of the Mother of the Believers Secondary School for Girls, who had been transferred for allegedly compelling a girl to wear hijab. The court ruled that "inviting students to be conservative, respectable and wearing hijab is not in opposition to the constitution which draws on the sharia as the source of legislation."

The government tried also to impose restraints on school dress, introducing laws banning hijab for girls in grades one through five and requiring girls in middle school who wished to wear it to obtain written permission from guardians—thereby giving parents rather than teachers authority over children's attire. Government officials were deployed outside schools to enforce the regulation.

The consequence was a debacle for the government. Schoolgirls reacted with horror to seeing their friends and peers being barred from entering school, and children as well as teachers joined in the protest against such measures. As one student later recalled: "All of us students were involved in this and we encouraged each other. The teachers also got involved. Even the girls who didn't use to wear the hijab came to school wearing it. We wrote slogans on the walls and encouraged each other to wear hijab."

Parents also protested, stating, for example, as did one father: "I am a simple Muslim and I don't belong to any extremist organizations or even a political party. I just tried to follow the instructions of our religion, the first of which is to raise my children in the proper Islamic way." Furthermore, in addition to being vigorously contested in the press, the ruling on hijab led to lawsuits in which parents sued for the rights of their daughters to wear hijab in primary school—lawsuits which were defended and often won by Islamist lawyers.

Linda Herrera, a scholar who studied these events in detail, concluded that overall the government's attempt to ban the veil in schools showed quite clearly that, for girls and women, the hijab and the teachings of conservative forms of Islam (that is, the practices of Islamism) had become the normative, expected, and even desired practice for many. "Large numbers of Muslim parents and students," Herrara wrote, quite evidently now approved of "the Islamization of education—not for political but for cultural reasons. They consider it appropriate for educators to socialize Egyptian youth as pious and culturally conservative Muslims."

It was this profound and pervasive transformation in the norms and practices of Islam that Islamism had brought about—and in scarcely more than two decades—that was and is perhaps its most remarkable achievement. As another academic astutely observed, the Islamist trend's "most characteristic manifestations" in Egypt "are not unpredictable outbreaks of sectarian violence, bombing conspiracies or the angry denunciations of creative artists (whether Salman Rushdie or Naguib Mahfouz) but rather the manifold changes it [the Islamic trend] has created in the way educated Egyptians practice, apprehend, and represent their religious heritage."[29]

What had been, a mere twenty years earlier, the revolutionary religious practices and beliefs of Islamist activists on the margins of mainstream society had pervasively become, by the mid-1990s, the ordinary, normal practices of the majority of Egyptians.

The most recent of the three studies focusing on Islamism and casting important light on the spread of veiling and women's involvement with the Islamist movement—or with the Tayar al-Islamiy, the Islamic Trend—is by Carrie Rosefsky Wickham, entitled *Mobilizing Islam*. Wickham, who conducted her research mostly through the early 1990s, was interested above all in studying and understanding the mainstream Islamist movement, not its militant fringe. For, she writes, "despite the high profile of Egypt's Islamic militants, it should be recalled that (1) they represent only a tiny fraction of those Egyptians active in the Islamic movement as a whole and that (2) their use of violence is repudiated not only by the general Egyptian public but also by the majority of people in the Islamic movement itself." Thus Wickham sets out to study the mainstream Islamist movement and to explore and analyze the means and processes that enabled Islamists to succeed "in capturing the hearts and minds of educated youth."[30]

Drawing on a variety of materials, including interviews with graduates and young professionals—people who had been in college in the seventies and eighties—the book offers vivid examples of how and by what steps, on a concrete, practical level, Islamists set about persuading others to accept their beliefs and ways, including their styles of dress. At the same time, Wickham's material offers illuminating glimpses of the goals, motivations, methods, and strategies of Islamists.

The common thread among Wickham's interviewees was their commitment to Islamist activism and their shared understanding of Islam as fundamentally entailing and requiring activism and service for the improvement of society and state. Some of them held jobs in Islamic institutions, but the majority had their main job in unrelated areas and worked part time in the service of Islamism, often for very low pay or on a volunteer basis. Lawyers, engineers, doctors, and other professionals offered their services in Islamic health clinics, day-care centers, kindergartens, and after-school programs; or they taught religious lessons or (if they were men) preached at the mosque.

Activism and a sense of obligation and responsibility to work to reform and improve society were the defining features, Wickham found, of Islamists' "radically new and activist interpretation of the Islamic faith." Asserting that participating in the work of improving society and state was a religious obligation of every Muslim (a *fard*), Islamists rejected the "confinement of religion to matters of private faith and ritual," emphasizing rather that Islam was "*din wa dawla:* both a system of individual faith and conduct and a comprehensive guide for the organization of society and state."

Motivating them in their own work as activists was the desire to bring about change and build a new and just Islamic society. This broad goal and vision was shared, Wickham found, by Islamists across the spectrum, regardless of whether they were affiliated with the Muslim Brotherhood, say—which rejected violence—or with more militant Islamist organizations. Wickham found too that her interviewees, who belonged to a variety of organizations, including, in some cases, militant groups, were generally reluctant to admit a connection with any organization at all. The early 1990s was an era when the government was cracking down on Islamists and making sweeping arrests, often indiscriminately grouping together militant and mainstream Islamists.

This era is viewed by human rights activists and other observers as a period when the government's struggle to stamp out Islamist violence "degenerated into indiscriminate state repression," as John Esposito wrote. "More than twenty thousand Islamists were imprisoned . . . many of them having been detained without charges and subjected to torture. Extralegal military courts that exclude the right to appeal were created; laws were enacted to restrict freedom of the press, take control of mosques, and prevent elected Islamists from leading professional associations." Esposito's account goes on: "Like other authoritarian regimes in the Middle East, the Mubarak government seized the opportunity to use its war against terrorism to silence both extremists and mainstream legal opposition." It cracked down not only on groups that had "carried out violent attacks," but also on others, and most particularly on the Muslim Brotherhood, which "had become dominant in university faculties, labor and professional organizations and many municipalities."[31]

In this atmosphere, the threat of arrest for anyone admitting connection with any Islamist group, no matter how nonviolent, was ever present.

Islamists' shared activist conception of Islam, Wickham found, shaped and informed their relations with each other. It also defined their relations with the "ordinary Muslims, whose beliefs and conduct they sought to change."[32] Through da'wa these activists enthusiastically set out to "educate their uninformed peers" about the proper practice of Islam and their proper duties as Muslims.

The da'wa message they preached quite noticeably was not a message that appealed primarily to people's own self-interest. On the contrary, it stressed moral and ethical renewal and emphasized a "new ethic" of activism and responsibility that was religiously obligatory. The duty of working for the reform and renewal of society was, they taught, incumbent on every Muslim, "regardless of its benefits and costs."

In their daʿwa activism, notes Wickham, Islamists were drawing on a well-established Islamic tradition of daʿwa, which they transformed as they adapted it to their specific purposes. Daʿwa traditionally entailed outreach targeting non-Muslims for conversion to Islam. Among Islamists the targets of outreach and daʿwa were now the "ordinary" Muslims among whom they lived: people who, in the eighties and early nineties, still made up the mainstream Muslim majority. These "ordinary" Muslims regarded themselves as already observant Muslims. But to Islamist eyes they were people who had "grown up with a mistaken understanding of Islam" and who observed and practiced their religion in "faulty or incomplete" ways.

Their goal, quite simply, as Wickham also notes, was to "indoctrinat[e] their targets with a particular interpretation of Islam." Moreover, this interpretation of Islam was one that, as Wickham points out, "stood apart from and challenged the validity of mainstream forms of religious faith and practice."

Wickham's research offers direct information on how Islamists persuaded their peers and other "ordinary" Muslims in mainstream society to adopt their understanding of Islam and its proper duties and practices, including how they induced women to adopt a new style of dress.

Islamist associations, Wickham shows, served their members in a wide variety of ways, providing them, for example, with valuable social support networks. Many of Wickham's interviewees mentioned that Islamic networks had helped them secure jobs, obtain visas to work abroad, gain access to funds distributed by mosques, and even improve their marriage prospects. Islamist peers, for example, "could vouch for the morals of unmarried men and women and expand their range of eligible mates."[33]

Both men and women shared in these benefits. Being part of the Islamist network and wearing Islamic dress in fact empowered the young, Wickham found, giving them a sense of moral authority in relation to parents and neighbors, for instance. Thus, paradoxically, Wickham observed, adopting a strict Islamic code enabled women to be freer to flout traditional limits on their autonomy. This was particularly important to lower-middle-class women traditionally subject to confining conventional codes. By adopting Islamic codes and dress, such young women "gained an aura of respectability that enabled them to move more freely in public spaces without fear of social sanction." In addition, Wickham points out, "they were able to invoke their 'rights in Islam' as a means to mobilize social pressure against parents or spouses who mistreated them." Such findings of course are entirely in consonance with Macleod's findings.

But Wickham goes on to make quite clear that, practical and useful though the dress was for some women, hijab and Islamic attire were also being quite deliberately, actively, and systematically promoted by Islamists. Among the women who adopted the dress were young women who attended weekly religious classes taught by teachers who circulated from one neighborhood mosque to another. Several among them, including some who wore *niqab* (the veil covering the lower half of the face), said that they had first been persuaded to wear it through the sermons of a charismatic young preacher at their neighborhood mosque. In addition to persuading young women to wear Islamic dress, this imam would rebuke parents who objected to the niqab. "What's wrong with it? Isn't it proper, following the path of the Prophet?" In addition to attesting to the methods of persuasion being used, this account (along with those offered by researchers of the previous decade) attests to the growing commonness of women's attending mosques, a further change that Islamism was bringing about, and further evidence of the movement's ongoing successes.

Two of Wickham's descriptions illuminatingly capture Islamist outreach and da'wa methods and strategies. Simultaneously they vividly convey a sense of how Islamists thought about the da'wa work they engaged in. In the first of these vignettes, Wickham, interviewing a group of young male Islamists, asks if they distributed pamphlets outside private mosques after Friday prayers. The government does not permit this, they respond—and in any case, as one of them goes on to explain, handing out pamphlets is not an effective way of reaching people, for people simply take the pamphlet, read it, and throw it away. "What is needed is a change of heart," the speaker continued. For example, he said:

> A group of my committed friends and I will think of getting two or three other guys from our neighborhoods more involved. So we invite them to play soccer, but of course it's not only soccer; we also talk to them about right and wrong. They see that we play fair, that we don't cheat, that we set a good example, and gradually, gently, over time, we try to show them the right path. [34]

In the second account Wickham describes a number of interviews she conducted: one set with a woman who had been persuaded to wear Islamic dress, and then another set with the women who had persuaded her, as well as others, to wear it. The woman, Salma, had acted in high school, and in her junior year she was asked to play a "big role." One of her classmates, who wore *khimar* (a garment that, Wickham explains, was an "Islamically correct" dress covering hair, neck, and torso), invited her to come and talk with another young woman, Siyam, who in addition wore the niqab. Siyam explained to Salma that "acting was forbidden in Islam," and she suggested that Salma begin reading the Quran. When Salma did so, she found herself in tears. But how, she asked, could she leave acting? "They said, what's more important, to please God or to be an actress? I told them I will start wearing the khimar on the first day of Ramadan. So two weeks later, at the start of Ramadan, they brought me the khimar. The girls all helped with the cost; that's how they do it, they bring it to you as a gift."[35]

The second set of interviews included conversations with the women who had been involved in introducing Salma to "the movement." Thus one woman explained that she and others in her Islamist circle had identified Salma as someone "who would be receptive to the idea of veiling, given that she was serious and well-meaning. 'We saw in her the desire to be a good person and to obey God.'" Their actions obviously were among the strategies activists drew on to help women make the decision to veil. As another Islamist woman explained, "We buy the khimar for those who can't afford it, or one of us gets the material and another one sews it. When a woman is ready to make the decision, we try to get things ready very quickly, before she changes her mind." Peer pressure and gentle albeit insidiously powerful coercion toward social conformity and the acceptance of "correct" religious practice ("Isn't it proper, following the path of the Prophet?") clearly were all brought into play in the process of Islamist da'wa and outreach in regard to Islamic dress.

A sense of the motivations of Islamists and of the vision and commitments informing their work vividly emerges from Wickham's reports of her interviews. One woman who had been active in the movement since the 1970s explained that she fully identified with the goals of the Muslim Brotherhood as articulated by al-Banna. "Our goal in life is to promote the da'wa. I want to add a brick to the edifice of Islam in my society and in the world." In pursuit of this goal she explained, "I will raise my children in the correct way and, through my work, try to ensure that the people around me come closer to Islam." This woman's commitment had led her to establish an Islamic kindergarten. "'When mothers come to the mosque, I encourage them to send their children to our school; I tell them not to worry about the money.' She stressed that the earlier a child was imbued with the principles of Islam, the better. 'The new generation is in our hands,' she declared."

Activism also meant fully engaged participation in the political process. While non-Islamists typically withdrew from the political process, viewing it as hopeless and/or dangerous, the Muslim Brotherhood, for example, stressing every Muslim's duty to work for social and political reform, urged people to be fully involved in society and to vote. Wickham quotes one young activist saying to her: "The young person who is religious is the one who is interested in the affairs of society—Islam requires it." Another said: "An observant Muslim will not be quiet when she sees oppression or wrong-doing going on around her."

Mainstream Islamism, maintains Wickham, in contrast to militant Islamism, is not simply "against the status quo but also for a better alternative." Though couched in religious terms, their vision for a better society, she writes, "embodies many of the same hopes and aspirations—for freedom from dictatorship and for social justice and public accountability—that have inspired secular movements for democracy elsewhere around the globe." The hope it offers for a better future through the project of social and moral renewal is, she writes, a "constructive and life-affirming one," and it is the "main source of its appeal."[36]

This focus on the future and a passionate preoccupation with working to change and improve society also gave Islamists an optimistic outlook, which they evidently also cultivated. Wickham found that a sense of optimism about the future was widespread among Islamists. In the words of one young Islamist who worked in a bookstore selling Islamic books: "If you talk to ordinary youth, you will find that they are negativists . . . they are miserable and they complain a lot and they feel that nothing can be done. But Muslim youths are positive thinking."

Indeed, in interview after interview, Wickham notes, Islamists pointed out that while others despaired and complained, they were "positive thinkers." Despite the difficulties that Islamists were undergoing, they commonly believed that the "influence of Islam as a global force was destined to expand."

This faith in Islam's inevitable advance was prevalent among reformists and militants alike. Accompanying it, often, was the belief that the West was in decline, a fact evidenced, they argued, by the "high rates of crime, teen pregnancy, and drug use; the breakdown of the family, and the presence of homelessness and poverty amid great wealth." Only Islam, they believed, "could offer humankind the moral and spiritual framework it needed, and in time this would be obvious to all."[37] An Islamist journalist captured this common understanding of Islam's inevitable advance in the following words:

> First Islam will spread through the neighborhoods, and then to Egyptian society as a whole, and then to the Egyptian state, and then to other Muslim countries, and then to countries in which Muslims were formerly the rulers, and then to other parts of the world, including Europe and the United States.[38]

Such was the vision and the world that Islamists were tirelessly working to bring into being. This was the early 1990s, a time when Islamism was certainly a rising force in Egypt but when also its vision, commitments, and practices had not as yet become the norm for the overwhelming majority of society, as they would come to be by the close of the century.

Wickham describes a moment in 1991 that captures a sense of the vision, energy, and commitment that Islamists were bringing to their lives, at work and at play, in pursuit of their goals of steadily working to Islamize and profoundly transform society—first Egypt's, then those of other Muslim countries, and onward to other parts of the world, "including Europe and the United States."

On a spring evening that year, Wickham joined an audience of about three hundred to watch a play at the Engineers' Association Sporting club. The club, in Zamalek, an affluent Cairo suburb, in the past had been frequented by Westernized engineers and their families. Now, and since Islamists had taken over the Engineers' Association in the mid-eighties, it catered to a different clientele. The women in the audience all wore Islamic dress and sat on the right of the central aisle—the men sat on the left.

The play, performed by male engineers, consisted of three religious stories illustrating the oppression of believers and their courage and resoluteness—though not always their triumph—in the face of tyrannical rulers. The most striking moment, notes Wickham, came at the end of the performance when one of the actors placed a small child on his shoulders. "A Quran was placed in one of the child's hands and a sword in the other" as the actors invited the audience to join them in a song whose refrain was, "The Islamic Awakening it is coming, it is coming."

"Outside the walls of the club," Wickham writes, "on the wide boulevards that curve along the Nile, affluent Egyptians in Western clothes strolled in the twilight, oblivious of what was going on inside."

Today as the first decade of the twenty-first century draws to a close, the Islamist form of religious belief and practice—along with its visual accompaniment, the hijab and Islamic dress for women—has in fact become the form of belief and practice of mainstream Muslims in Egypt. Islamists seem indeed to have accomplished or to be very close to accomplishing their dream, at least in Egypt.[39]

Islamist forces, including the Muslim Brotherhood, the Muslim World League, and the Jamaat-i Islami, have played key roles in establishing mosques in Europe and America, as well as in establishing major and enormously influential Muslim organizations such as the American

Muslim Students' Association (MSA) and the Islamic Society of North America (ISNA), organizations that today are the most important and influential organizations in America.

In Chapters 7 and 8, I follow out the story of the migration of Islamism—of peoples and ideas—to North America and the story of the establishment and rise to dominance on the American Muslim landscape of the Islamist perspective embodied in such organizations as ISNA and MSA. In the 1990s, the period I focus on in Chapter 8, Islamist violence erupted in America—just as it did in Egypt in those years, and for the same reasons: the end of the Soviet war in Afghanistan and the return of jihadis to civil society. Indeed, even the very same men who were behind the violence in Egypt—among them Sheikh Omar Abdel Rahman and Ayman al-Zawahiri—would appear in America in the 1990s instigating and participating in acts of murderous violence. The response, particularly in the media, to the eruption of Islamic violence in the United States would not be dissimilar to the response that emerged in Egypt.

·7·
Migrations

In this and the next chapter I follow out the story of the migration of Islamism to North America, and of the establishment and rise to dominance on the American Muslim landscape of organizations embodying the Islamist perspective. The growing influence of Islamism in America came about as the result of the migrations of both people and ideas: the sixties was an era of rapidly expanding Muslim immigration to America at a time when international connections were leading to the growing influence of Islamism among African American Muslims, as well as among immigrants. Understanding this background is essential to understanding the forms that Islamism and the veil would take as they evolved in America.

Here in Chapter 7, I focus on Islamist activism and networking in America from the 1960s through the 1980s, the period during which Islamists established and consolidated the bases of a number of their organizations, among them today's most prominent and influential American Muslim organizations, such as ISNA and the MSA.

The teachings of the Muslim Brotherhood and of the Jamaat-i Islami of Pakistan were already beginning to be disseminated in America in the 1950s and 1960s, when Muslim Brothers and members of the Jamaat-i, undergoing repressions in their home countries, fled abroad. As described earlier, many among the Muslim Brotherhood went to Saudi Arabia and the Arab Gulf countries. Some, including many students, came to America.

After World War II the United States pursued a policy of encouraging foreign students to come to the U.S., including establishment of the Fulbright Program in 1946, partly to encourage mutual understanding between the United States and other countries in the hope of forestalling future wars. Students were exempt from the immigration quotas in force at the time, and pursuing higher education and graduate studies in the United States became a route by which Muslims hoping to immigrate could come to this country.[1]

In the wake of World War II and the demise of the European empires, people of these former colonies, as well as of regions dominated albeit not formally colonized by Europe, who had previously looked to Europe as the place to go to pursue higher education, began to look instead to America, now the dominant Western power. Between 1948 and 1965 the number of students coming to the U.S. from Muslim-majority countries increased almost fivefold, from nearly three thousand to nearly fourteen thousand.

Among the wave of Muslims arriving in the United States in this period to pursue their studies was, famously, Barack Hussein Obama, Sr.—father, obviously, of the U.S. president.

Furthermore, as the United States entered the civil rights era, policy changes would be enacted to redress the racial attitudes of the past, which would tremendously affect the rate of immigration from countries outside Europe, including from Muslim-majority countries and countries with significant Muslim populations. In 1965, President Johnson signed into law the Immigration and Nationality Act, abolishing the national origins quotas that had virtually excluded immigration from Asia and Africa and other places outside Europe. Indeed, previous regulations had favored northern and western Europeans, and even set strict limits on the number of immigrants to be allowed in from countries of southern and eastern Europe—such as Italy, Greece, Poland, and Portugal.[2]

The new law would set in motion by far the largest wave of Muslim immigration to America (as well as of people of other religions of

Asia and Africa) that had ever occurred in U.S. history. A much smaller wave of Muslim migration had occurred in the late nineteenth and early twentieth centuries of people, Muslim and Christian, from territories such as Greater Syria and the Balkans, which were part of the then disintegrating Ottoman Empire.

Today, as a result of this post-1965 immigration wave and also as a result of a growing trend of African American conversion to Islam already under way in the sixties, the United States now has a significant Muslim population, variously estimated as between 3 million and 8 million. The largest proportion, estimated at 40 to 42 percent, is African American. Indo-Pakistanis make up the next largest group, constituting about 29 percent. Arabs make up about 12 or 15 percent.[3] The remaining roughly 17 percent are drawn from almost every ethnicity in the world—Iran, Russia, Europe, China, Indonesia and Southeast Asia, sub-Saharan and southern Africa, and South America. Students of Islam in America commonly pointed out that only Mecca during the hajj brings together such a range and variety of Muslims as now reside in the United States.[4]

The new immigration laws favored skilled professionals, and while Muslim immigrants of the earlier wave had typically been younger male laborers, Muslim immigrants of the post-1965 era were generally "older professionals who came either with their families or to join family members already here."[5] This bias in favor of professionals established the basis for the relatively high levels of education and income that many Muslim Americans enjoy today.

The consensus is that the vast majority of Muslim immigrants of the post-1965 era were not Islamists. Rather, they had been part of the mainstream Muslim populations in their countries, which—as we saw was the case with the mainstream in Egypt through the sixties and seventies—typically practiced and understood Islam as a matter of personal practice and of ethical and spiritual sustenance. They did not see it as in any way involving the political or social activism that was part of the Islamist package of practices and prescriptions, among them the veil.[6] As had been the case in Egypt, the practice of veiling had ceased to be a norm in the majority of urban centers from which these immigrants came.

A few of these immigrants, however, as well as some who were here as students, were indeed Islamists. As we saw in the preceding chapters, activist Islamists were extraordinarily energetic and skilled at networking, organizing, building institutions, and pursuing da'wa to promote their vision and understanding of Islam among "ordinary" Muslims. Typically they brought to this country the same zest and commitment they displayed in Egypt, and they were evidently as unstintingly generous here as they had been at home, in donating their time and skills in the service of the goals and ideals of Islamism.

A handbook published in the 1980s, entitled "How to Establish an Islamic Center: A Step-by-Step Approach," noted that Muslim immigrants had begun arriving in the 1950s and 1960s. They had included "Islamically-trained individuals from Egypt who were fleeing the oppression of the Nasser regime." The text adds: "Most of them were members of the al-ikhwan al-muslimun [Muslim Brotherhood]."[7]

Even as early as 1963 a group of Islamist activist students gathered in Urbana, Illinois, for a meeting whose outcome would prove momentous in the history of Islam in America. The group consisted of students who had already been active, on their different campuses, in founding Muslim associations and in organizing activities for the growing numbers of Muslim students arriving to pursue higher studies. Aware of each other's work and realizing that instituting a national organization to coordinate their activities would greatly increase their effectiveness, they decided to meet in Urbana with a view to establishing such an organization.[8] The organization they established was the Muslim Students' Association. Today the MSA and the Islamic Society of North America, established by the MSA in 1981, are the largest and most important and influential Muslim organizations in North America.

Among those present at that initial meeting were Islamists from around the Muslim world, including at least three Muslim Brothers from Egypt.[9] The 1950s and 1960s, as Gutbi Ahmed pointed out in his brief history of Muslim American organizations, were decades when Islamists across the Muslim world were undergoing persecution and fleeing their homelands or being driven into exile.[10] In Egypt, of course, the Brotherhood was experiencing, under Nasser, the worst era in its history. Islamists were banned also in these years in Pakistan, Indonesia, and elsewhere, including Iran, from whence the Ayatollah Khomeini, among others, had been exiled.

Many (among the Sunnis) had fled to Saudi Arabia and the Arab Gulf, where, under the auspices of Saudi Arabian Islamic organizations in particular, international Islamist links were forged and networks intensively developed. The Muslim World League had just been established in Mecca in 1962. Bringing together at its founding meeting Said Ramadan, the heir to the mantle of al-Banna, founder of the Muslim Brotherhood of Egypt, as well as the founder of Jamaat-i Islami of Pakistan, Abu'l 'Ala Mawdudi, and representatives of other Islamist groups as well as Saudi authorities, the objective of this organization was unambiguously that of promoting and supporting Islamism worldwide.

The men assembled at that founding meeting of the MSA in Urbana, wrote Ahmed, all came from "these places" where Islamists were suffering persecution. The organization they now set up in America, Ahmed continued, "clearly reflected the experience of the Islamic movement in their respective countries."[11] Thus the founding membership, drawn from the Muslim Brotherhood and the Jamaat-i Islami and other international Islamist organizations, bonded in their shared commitment to the common vision and goals of Islamism.[12] For those gathered there, wrote Ahmed, "Islam was seen as an ideology, a way of life, and a mission, and the organization was not considered simply as a way to serve the community but as means to create the ideal community and serve Islam."[13] Unsurprisingly then, given the provenance and make-up of the founding members, MSA's goals and purpose were entirely resonant and on a direct continuum with those pursued by Islamists in Egypt.

Once established, the MSA grew quickly. Consisting of 10 affiliated associations in 1963, by 1964 it had 30 affiliated associations. By 1968 the number of affiliated associations based on campuses across the U.S. and Canada had risen to 105.

In those early years, the majority of the MSA's membership was male. Most members were students in the hard sciences and medicine and engineering. A women's committee was formed in 1966 consisting mainly of the wives, mothers, and daughters of students, as well as some "single girls," most of whom were also students.

Initially the MSA functioned on a small budget based on membership dues, but by 1968 it was receiving funds from Muslim-majority countries, among them Kuwait and Pakistan. In 1965 the MSA had sent a delegation to Saudi Arabia to attend the meeting of the Muslim World League to promote and garner support for the idea of establishing a World Organization of Muslim Students.[14]

By 1968 the MSA had begun publishing a newsletter, *Al-Itihhad*, as well as printing and distributing books and pamphlets and other materials promoting Islamist views. Among the books they distributed in 1968 was a short work by Sayyid Qutb, translated under the title *The Religion of Islam*. It was published by al-Manar press in Palo Alto, California, in 1967.[15] Altogether, and largely as a result of the MSA's activism, from the 1960s onward a "growing body of English-language literature" was becoming available in the United States presenting the works of Qutb and Mawdudi and the views of the Muslim Brotherhood and the Jamaat-i Islami as the correct and normative understanding of Islam.[16]

The MSA officers and members plunged into the work of outreach, teaching and preaching, setting up venues for congregational prayers, founding mosques and Islamic centers, establishing and running schools teaching Islam (Sunday schools and summer camps)—activities that had been honed by the Muslim Brotherhood in Egypt in earlier decades and through which they had powerfully spread their message. During the Nasser era such activities had of course ceased or gone underground in Egypt, only to resurface in the seventies with renewed dynamism. Introduced to American shores in the fifties and promoted with the founding of the MSA in the sixties, Islamism would begin to take root and spread in America.

The group would continue its dynamic expansion through the 1970s and beyond, an expansion in part spurred by the rapid rise in Muslim immigration beginning in the late 1960s and by the steadily growing demands being made on the facilities and services the MSA was offering. As Muslim families settled in America many of them began to turn, as Catholic and Jewish and other immigrants had done before them, to religious centers in search of community and assistance in raising their growing families.

The earlier wave of immigrants, which had consisted almost entirely of young men who had come to work in factories and had sent home their savings, had not resulted in the founding of many mosques or Islamic institutions to which the post-1965 immigrants could turn. Among the few mosques or Islamic centers established during the earlier migration was the first mosque in America, founded in Cedar Rapids, Iowa, in 1934. Now the oldest surviving mosque in the country, it is known as the Mother Mosque of America.[17] The impetus behind its founding had been the arrival of immigrant men's wives and families. Muslim men had settled in Cedar Rapids in the late 1890s and, by the 1920s, they were evidently occasionally gathering in one another's houses for congregational prayers. However, it was only when they were joined by their wives that the community began raising funds for a mosque. In 1933 the women founded a social club through which they "pushed the men" to raise funds for a mosque. It would serve as a social center as well as a place for congregational prayers; additionally, it offered classes in Islam and Arabic.[18]

By 1971, in response to growing demands on their services, the MSA's officers began studying the possibility of setting up a national headquarters and hiring a permanent secretariat of full-time workers. They would accomplish this goal by 1975, when the MSA opened its new headquarters in Plainfield, Indiana, built on land it had bought for this purpose for the price of $500,000.[19]

The association was organized into local, regional, and zonal structures across the United States and Canada. Its local chapters, responsible for the daily and ongoing work of "organizing juma [Friday] and Id prayers, seminars, conferences, Quranic study circles and social activities," were considered to be the backbone of the association.[20] The MSA also had departments overseeing its various activities and institutions, departments that might sometimes be headed by women, according to Ahmed. Each department director, Ahmed wrote, "held a doctorate in his or her respective field."

Simply listing the different departments' responsibilities vividly conveys the enormous scope of the work that the MSA was involved in carrying out. The North American Islamic Trust (NAIT), for example, established in 1975, served as the financial arm of the MSA. It oversaw and held title to MSA properties, such as "mosques, student houses, Islamic centers and service organizations." It also oversaw the Islamic Book Service, the agency responsible for the distribution of Islamic literature and other materials, such as tapes, in both English and Arabic, across North America.

Another important department was the Islamic Teaching Center, concerned with da'wa and outreach in general. Taking on the task of training people, particularly the young—"that key element of society" in the work of outreach and da'wa—it developed summer schools and camps to attract elementary-age as well as high school students. The Center also oversaw and arranged lectures, study groups, and correspondence courses focused on da'wa. It was responsible for outreach to non-Muslims as well as to Muslims, taking its project to American prisons. In 1981 the Center contacted "4,000 inmates in 310 prisons, enrolling more than 500 in an Islamic Correspondence Course." Da'wa to prisoners was also in these years evidently a matter of interest to the Muslim World League. A senior official of the League noted that in 1977 the League was involved in "carrying the message of Islam to our African-American brothers who are unfortunately in prisons."[21]

From the start the MSA had offered its energetic work of teaching, outreach, and service to the already settled American Muslim communities, descendants of the earlier wave of immigrants. The MSA encouraged members to volunteer as prayer leaders, lecturers, and purveyors of Islamic knowledge for these communities, and as Sunday school teachers for their children. Convinced that they themselves "had arrived at *the* proper understanding of Islam," writes Kambiz GhaneaBassiri in his history of the MSA's activism in relation to the settled Muslim Americans, the MSA members presented themselves as instructors and leaders in Islamic understanding, "quite undeterred" as GhaneaBassiri also notes, by the fact that scarcely any of the MSA's members had any formal training in Islamic scholarship.[22] Lack of such training in Islam was, as we saw earlier, overwhelmingly the norm rather than the exception among Islamists, who, like Hasan al-Banna himself, were typically educated in secular rather than religious institutions. Often, moreover, their academic training was in the hard sciences.

The Islam they taught and inculcated was, to be sure, their own committed, activist, and deeply modern understanding of Islam. This was a form of Islam that, emerging as it did in the twentieth century, was shaped by the assumptions of the supremacy of rationality and the irrelevance, for the most part, to a "true" understanding of the Quran, of the long Islamic tradition of what were, in the eyes of many Islamists, mere casuistry and interpretation. The Quran as they saw it was essentially a transparent text that any rationally trained person—a doctor, an engineer, a social scientist—working within the framework of Islamism could reasonably interpret for himself and others.

Some scholars maintain that the MSA had close links with the Muslim World League, and that through the 1960s and 1970s they were deeply influenced by Wahhabism. Hamid Algar writes that in those decades "no criticism of Saudi Arabia would be tolerated at the annual conventions of the MSA."[23] At Friday prayers, Algar also noted, the League's publications, both in English and Arabic, were made available at MSA venues. As noted earlier, the League did in fact typically make available materials—books, tapes, pamphlets, educational materials and literature—promoting Wahhabi thought to mosques and Muslim organizations across the world, in addition to providing support for the building of mosques and Islamic centers.

The MSA's intellectual mentor for some years, Algar further noted, was Ismail al-Faruqi, a scholar who had devoted substantial work to the study of Ibn Abd al-Wahhab, the founder of Wahhabism. In 1980 the MSA's publishing division brought out three works by al-Faruqi on Ibn Abd al-Wahhab entitled *Sources of Islamic Thought.*

Gradually, however, according to Algar, the MSA would diversify its relations with the Muslim world, though its connection with Wahhabism did remain strong for some time. In due course, he writes, in a book published in 2002, the hundreds of Muslim student groups that composed the Association would reflect a "diverse range of opinions" and thus would resist "any uniform characterization." By 1983 the MSA had 310 local affiliates across the campuses of North America, with a membership of some 45,000.[24]

By the late 1970s the MSA found itself once more considering expansion. Specifically, the group saw the need for establishing a separate organization dedicated to serving the broader community—rather than primarily attending to the needs of students, which had been the original mandate. By now a number of the organization's officers were no longer students and had themselves settled in America and begun raising families. In 1977, the MSA leaders held a series of meetings with prominent Muslim activist members from across the United States and Canada, and they appointed a taskforce to study the needs of the nonstudent Muslim American population and to put forward proposals for courses of action.[25]

In 1981, in response to the taskforce's recommendations, the MSA established the Islamic Society of North America (ISNA).[26] Once ISNA was established, the MSA withdrew to its original purpose of focusing on college and university campuses, passing on to ISNA the work of dealing with the larger Muslim community and many of the departments and institutions that had been under the MSA's purview, including NAIT and the Teaching Center. By the 1980s, NAIT, which held the titles to ISNA and MSA properties, included among its holdings 300 of the roughly 900 mosques that there were at that time in America.[27]

As was the case with the MSA, some of ISNA's founding members had belonged to or had had connections with the Muslim Brotherhood (in its Egyptian and other Arab branches) and/or with the Jamaat-i Islami.[28] Former MSA officers and people from these backgrounds would hold the leadership positions in the new organization.

By the late eighties ISNA also had acquired land in Plainfield, Indiana, costing $21 million. Here it would construct an Islamic center, which included a large mosque, a library for books and audiovisual materials, and a complex of buildings for training facilities and classrooms. It included a daycare center, dormitories, and recreational facilities.[29]

As Muslims settled down and raised families in North America, ISNA was also engaged in developing policies with respect to new issues that were arising. In the mid-eighties ISNA addressed itself to the role of Muslim Americans and Muslim American organizations in American political life. Following procedures instituted by the MSA, ISNA set up a Planning Committee to study the matter and establish plans for the ensuing years.

The Planning Committee held a public hearing to identify priorities for the forthcoming decade. It followed this with a report recommending that ISNA direct its attention to educating American Muslims on their voting rights in the United States, with the goal of mobilizing them to vote on issues affecting Muslims. Prior to this there had been some criticism of ISNA's leadership by ISNA members on the grounds that the leadership rested "primarily in the hands of individuals with Islamic movement backgrounds, that is the Ikhwan al-Muslimun [Muslim Brothers] and Jamaat-i Islami," who were seen as preoccupied with politics and the Islamic movement back in their homelands.[30] Perhaps in response, in part, to such criticism the ISNA leadership took a strong position in support of the report, and in support of educating Muslim American citizens to be full participants in mainstream American politics.[31] The position that ISNA adopted—of encouraging activism and engaged involvement in the political process among its membership—was, as we saw in the last chapter, a policy that Islamist groups had energetically pursued in Egypt.

Some other Muslim American organizations would take a different view of this matter. Throughout this time, it should be noted, other Muslim American organizations were also being founded, although the MSA and ISNA emerged as the most prominent. One other important, although still secondary, organization was the Islamic Circle of North America (ICNA), founded by South Asians who broke away from the MSA in 1971.[32]

The Tabligh-i Jamaat in particular, a group with roots in India and a long tradition of noninvolvement in politics in whatever country they found themselves, was among those critical of ISNA's position on voting. The Tabligh-i focus was primarily on promoting the correct ritual elements of Islam, and in particular on calling "lapsed" Muslim males back to worship in mosques. In the 1980s the annual conventions of this organization sometimes brought together as many as 10,000 people—all males. When ISNA announced its decision to actively pursue educating Muslim American and Canadian citizens for participation in mainstream American and Canadian politics, the Tabligh-i Jamaat published an article making clear that they, in contrast, "will have nothing to do with politics in Canada [where they were based] or even with Islamic movements in the Muslim world." A further article appearing in the newsletter of a Tabligh-i–controlled mosque in Cleveland also emphasized that a "*kufr* (unbelief) system (that is, the American government) cannot give rise to an Islamic state."[33]

ISNA was thus pursuing in America a course parallel to that pursued by the mainstream moderate Islamists in Egypt in the seventies and thereafter, a course consonant with its commitment to pursuing goals entirely within the legal political framework and through education, social activism, advocacy, and participation in the political process. They brought with them the goal of working always to improve society—whatever society they found themselves in—and of doing so by applying their Islamic ethics and values. A booklet entitled *In Fraternity: A Message to the Muslims of America*, published in 1989 by the Minaret Publishing house in Los Angeles, advised that "the best that Muslims may offer to America are their Islamic values and ethical norm." Written by three leadership members, among them the brothers Hassan and Maher Hathout, who had been members of the Muslim Brotherhood, the booklet went on to observe that "to be American . . . is not to blindly accept America as it is, but to strive to make it cleaner and better by using the available freedom, the constitutional rights and the democratic process persistently and relentlessly towards reaching that goal."[34]

In the eighties ISNA was beginning to emerge as the most prominent Muslim organization in America. By 1994 it had the largest number of mosques affiliated with it across America. In a survey conducted that year, 39 percent of mosques in America described themselves as affiliated with ISNA, 19 percent with W. D. Mohammed, 5 percent with the Tabligh-i Jamaat, and 4 percent with ICNA, while 24 percent described themselves as unaffiliated.[35]

Other organizations with similar Islamist roots were founded to serve different purposes—the Council on American-Islamic Relations (CAIR), for example, founded in 1994, focuses on pursuing civil rights issues on behalf of Muslims in America. CAIR would also come to public prominence in the 1990s. This organization also, like ISNA and the MSA, included among its founders former members of or people with connections to the Muslim Brotherhood and the Islamist movement. Seen as an agency devoted to particular causes and by no means a rival to ISNA, CAIR would come to be a prominent institution on the Muslim American landscape, further adding to the commanding public position that Islamist organizations would come to enjoy—and still enjoy—in America.

ISNA and, to a lesser degree, CAIR, would come to represent the dominant and authoritative voice of Sunni Islam in America. It is often to ISNA and CAIR, for example, that government agencies and journalists turn for information on the Islamic position and for guidance on Islam's beliefs and practices. The groups' views typically represent the Islamist understanding of Islam as reviewed in the preceding pages. The veil as a religious requirement is absolutely and undeviatingly present in Islam as they represent it. Both organizations, for example, typically refer to the hijab as the "religiously mandated covering for Muslim women," and in their publications—magazines, pamphlets, books—women invariably are shown wearing hijab. The importance of hijab was the message that ISNA taught to the young in their schools, kindergartens, summer camps, and training centers. Zainab al-Ghazali's response to the journalist cited earlier, to the effect that failure to dress in the Islamically required way, including in hijab, would cancel out all good deeds and lead to hell, encapsulates just how foundational women's dress and hijab are to the Islamist message.

The consensus in the scholarship on Islam in America (as already noted) is that the vast majority of Muslim immigrants to America had no connection with Islamism in their home countries. Typically there was a "wide gap," through the seventies and eighties and beyond, as Ghanea-Bassiri wrote, between Muslim activists and the "larger Muslim population."[36] This larger group of Muslim immigrants had no tradition of organizing or even, for many of them, of attending mosque, and no desire to proselytize. As had been the case among the mainstream in Egypt, Islam was above all, for many in this group, a matter of personal ethical and inner spiritual resources.

A poll taken in 2007 reported that 72 percent of American Muslims said that religion was "very important" to them, and 18 percent said that it was "somewhat important." Only 40 percent, however, reported attending mosque regularly or even occasionally.[37] Yet this figure represents an enormous increase in attendance over scholars' estimates of mosque attendance for the 1980s and 1990s, which ranged from 5 percent to 15 percent.[38] Evidently a dramatic increase in attendance occurred after 9/11 and in the wake of the problems that many Muslim Americans began to experience after that tragedy.

Preoccupied essentially with the exigencies of establishing themselves in their new lives, and lacking the resources that people had in their homelands for raising children within their faith—such as the support of community and extended family—many immigrants apparently were glad to send their children to Sunday schools and summer camps to learn about Islam. Only gradually, as children came home to declare that the Islam the family practiced was "wrong," would parents register that their children were learning different forms of religious belief and practice. Anecdotes abound of families who experienced this, as do stories of parents quarreling with daughters over their daughters' insistence on wearing hijab.

Even if parents had noticed differences earlier, the parents, for the most part not scholars of Islam but simply practitioners of the forms of Islamic piety that they had grown up with, were probably themselves intimidated by and came to accept the Islamist claim that "correct" Islam was only Islam as Islamists believed, taught, and practiced it.

Making up, as the scholarly consensus has it, the majority of American Muslims of immigrant background, these non-Islamist American Muslims nevertheless, having no organization or institution representing them, by and large also have no voice within the public conversation on Islam in America.[39]

Moreover, as GhaneaBassiri observes, the "overwhelming majority of Muslims who were not activists," and who had come to this country from many different parts of the world, did not readily "forgo their sectarian beliefs and cultural practices. Unlike Islamists," GhaneaBassiri continues:

> they did not reduce Islam to an ideology that could be separated from culture, work, family life, and community and then imposed them upon those aspects of life in order to conform them to some puritanical reading of the Quran and the hadith. It is thus not surprising that most American Muslims in the 1970s and 1980s did not relinquish their cultural heritage to participate in the agendas of national Muslim organizations.[40]

As GhaneaBassiri also observes, most Muslims "of varying national and sectarian backgrounds who came to the United States in this [post-1965] period did not participate in any organization or collectivity that left a historical footprint. This does not mean that they did not actively or collectively practice Islam. They just failed to leave us a verifiable record of their activities." This Muslim American majority consequently is essentially commonly left out of accounts of Islam in America. Not only is it the case that government agencies and journalists typically turn to ISNA and CAIR and the like for authoritative opinions on Islam, but even academics, as GhaneaBassiri observes, typically "merely nod to the multiplicity of Islamic beliefs and cultural practices" and then proceed to focus their narrative accounts of "Islam in America" entirely on "those Muslims who were involved in building national institutions like the Muslims Students' Association, the Islamic Society of North America, the Islamic Circle of North America, or the ministry of Warith Deen Mohammed."

Over these same decades, too—the sixties, seventies, and eighties—Islamists and Islamist organizations in the Middle East were forging connections not only with immigrant Muslims but also with African American Muslims, both individuals and organizations.

Some important features of the Islamist movements that were under way in the Middle East and Muslim world through the thirties and forties made their appearance in America as early as the forties through, in particular, the teachings of Sheikh Daoud Ahmed Faisal (d. 1980), who is said to have had a Moroccan father and a Jamaican mother. There is no clear indication that Faisal was directly connected with either the Muslim Brotherhood or the Jamaat-i. However, his publications, as Edward E. Curtis wrote, "often borrowed from other Muslim missionary tracts," and Faisal's intellectual life bore the clear influence of the "Islamic reform and renewal movements" then under way in the Muslim world.[41]

Faisal, who published a book called *Islam, the True Faith: The Religion of Humanity,* set up a mosque in Brooklyn and succeeded, according to Curtis, in converting "hundreds if not thousands of African

Americans" to Sunni Islam. In 1962 some of Faisal's followers, influenced by the writings and thinking of Mawdudi, as well as by a member of the Tabligh-i Jamaat, broke away to set up another Sunni mosque, which adhered to the Tabligh-i commitments of renouncing worldly and political engagement. The members of this movement, which became known as Darul Islam and which still has a significant following among African Americans, sought to live a life of "strict adherence with the ethical example of the Prophet Muhammad of Arabia." Some of the men were polygamous, and the women "covered themselves with both a head scarf and a face veil."[42]

With Malcolm X, however, and subsequently Warith Deen Mohammed, connections between the Islamists of the Middle East—including the Muslim Brotherhood, the Jamaat-i Islami, and the Muslim World League—would begin to be forged and to steadily develop, connections that would come to have an impact on African American Islam.

In 1959, PBS (New York's WNTA-TV) aired a five-part series hosted by Mike Wallace about the Nation of Islam. The series, *The Hate Which Hate Produced,* presented a generally negative portrait of the Nation, an organization then headed by Elijah Muhammad, portraying it as anti-American and black-supremacist. This coverage drew criticism of the Nation from many, including Muslims in the United States. In fact the Nation had already drawn criticism from a broad variety of Sunni Muslims for its "black separatist version of Islam."[43]

In the wake of this intense and mainly negative publicity, Malcolm X, Elijah Muhammad's chief spokesperson, would find himself besieged when he spoke on campuses by Muslim students who, considering themselves "the guardians of 'true' Islam," emphatically rejected the Nation and its teachings. These exchanges would have an impact on Malcolm X. In 1962, a student from Dartmouth came to question him at the Nation's mosque, and then followed up their exchange by sending Malcolm X literature on Islam. Malcolm X read the material he had been sent and asked him for more.

"These students and the larger trend of which they were part," writes Curtis, "had a profound influence on Malcolm's religious life."[44] In 1964, Malcolm X broke with the Nation. After his break he sought out, at the urging of the students, the Egyptian professor Dr. Mahmoud

Youssef Shawarbi, who was a Fulbright fellow at Fordham University. Shawarbi instructed Malcolm X in the fundamentals of Islam and advised him to make the hajj. He also gave him a book, *The Eternal Message of Muhammad* by Abdel Rahman Azzam, an Egyptian and a leading figure in the founding of the Arab League. After serving as its first secretary general (1945–52), and after falling out with Nasser, Azzam left Egypt for Saudi Arabia.

Malcolm X would be very graciously treated by Azzam and by Prince Faisal of Saudi Arabia when he went on hajj. Malcolm X witnessed during the hajj, as he famously recounted in his autobiography—the mingling of "tens of thousands of pilgrims from all over the world. They were of all colors, from blue-eyed blonds to black-skinned Africans. But we were all participating in the same ritual, displaying a spirit of unity and brotherhood that my experiences in America had led me to believe never could exist between the white and the non-white."[45]

Malcolm X would now issue a "strong endorsement" of Sunni Islam. He would return to Saudi Arabia later that year to meet Said Ramadan, son-in-law of Hasan al-Banna, with whom he would continue to have exchanges.[46] During this visit Malcolm X received training in daʿwa at the Muslim World League. In addition, the University of Medina made a number of scholarships available to him to distribute to Americans wishing to study there. Malcolm X would also continue to have relationships with "various Saudi-financed missionary groups" until his assassination in February 1965.[47]

The trend toward Sunni Islam—and Sunni Islam, moreover, as taught and practiced by the network of interconnected Islamist organizations comprising the Saudi-based Muslim World League, the Jamaat-i, and the Brotherhood—among African Americans grew steadily stronger in the ensuing years. Other notable African American Muslim leaders pursuing this path included the jazz musician Talib Dawud, who was introduced to Qutb's writings by an Egyptian immigrant of the Muslim Brotherhood, and Ahmad Tawfiq. Tawfiq had studied at al-Azhar in the 1960s. Returning to the United States in 1967 with English translations of Qutb's works and inspired by the Muslim Brotherhood, he founded the Mosque of Islamic Brotherhood on East 113th Street in New York.[48]

After the death of Elijah Muhammad in 1975, his son W. D. Mohammed succeeded him. The younger Mohammed converted to Sunni Islam and led the larger proportion of the followers of Nation of Islam away from the beliefs taught by his father. (Louis Farrakhan, who rejected this move, would become the leader of those who remained with the Nation of Islam.) After W. D. Mohammed made this move to Sunni Islam he became a "major beneficiary of funds from Muslim majority countries." In 1978 a number of such countries, among them Saudi Arabia and Qatar, designated Mohammed the "sole consultant and trustee for their distribution of funds to missionary organizations in the U.S."[49]

Through the seventies and eighties Sunni Islam continued making gains among African American Muslims for many reasons, among them the growing availability of funding from Saudi Arabia and the Gulf in support of missionary efforts, and as a result of the growing presence of immigrant activist Muslims.

Sherman Jackson notes that the Salafi movement among African Americans, a movement he describes as "genetically linked to the Wahhabi movement," also began to make gains among African Americans in the 1970s, a time in which, Jackson writes, "many [African Americans] went to Saudi Arabia to study, often on scholarships provided by the Saudi government." The Salafi movement's influence, Jackson observes, "goes far beyond its numbers," as its "staunchly 'protestant' approach resonates with the generality of Blackamerican Muslims."[50]

Beginning in the seventies, African American Sunni Muslim leaders now "mingled regularly with foreign and immigrant imams," Curtis noted. By the early 1980s, he continued, as many as twenty-six African American communities "were receiving the services of leaders provided by the Muslim World League."[51]

Through these times some African American leaders and communities were strongly influenced by the Islamist writings of Sayyid Qutb and Abu'l 'Ala Mawdudi, writings that organizations such as the MSA and ISNA disseminated. Despite this, however, and despite the "patronage [which] many African American organizations received from Muslim-majority countries (such as Saudi Arabia) and pan-Islamic organizations (such as the Muslim World League) they nevertheless did not 'blindly sign on' to other people's agendas." Rather, as GhaneaBassiri explains, they "continued to practice Islam within the context of the heritage of Islam in African America and focused on the problems of their own communities."[52]

GhaneaBassiri goes on to note that there is a general tendency among Muslims in America to group themselves in mosques "on the basis of ethnicity and nationality"—and one might add common language—with South Asian and Arab being strong examples of these, a tendency, he observes, that also applies to African American groups. Thus while some African American leaders such as W. D. Mohammed and Siraj Wahhaj of al-Taqwa mosque in Brooklyn serve on the executive boards of national Muslim organizations like ISNA, they remain "culturally and socially within the African American Muslim community."

Importantly, all of this meant that through the seventies and eighties Sunni Islam would increasingly be the dominant form of Islam followed in African American mosques. This Sunni Islam, emanating from the League, blended and braided together Wahhabi Islam, the Islam of the Muslim Brotherhood, and that of the Jamaat-i Islami.

As ISNA and CAIR and other organizations with Islamist roots (among them, for example, MAS—an organization with ICNA and Jamaat-i connections founded in 1992)[53] increasingly gained prominence over the ensuing years, the Islamist form of Islam steadily became the normative form of Islam, increasingly accepted now by many Muslims as well as non-Muslims as the one "true" and "correct" form of Islam.

As such organizations gained prominence, they and their leaders became the nation's authorities on Islam. The government and media both turned to them—naturally enough, given that they were the most visible Muslim American organizations on the landscape. The idea that wearing hijab was a "religiously mandatory requirement" for Muslim women was of course among the ideas that they taught—as it continues to be, as a glance through any of the journals and materials they publish today makes clear.

Thus in the mid- to late 1990s, as a new generation of American Muslims schooled in such schools and attending mosques began to come of age, the numbers of young women in hijab seemed suddenly to multiply. An ethnically diverse first generation of American-born Muslims, all raised within the framework of the Sunni Islam of the Islamic Revival or Islamic Awakening, were reaching adulthood.

The 1990s was also the decade in which America experienced its first terrorist attack at the hands of Islamic militants. Islamist organizations continuing to emerge in these years into positions of uncontested dominance on the American landscape would find themselves under attack, caught up in the fierce debates of the day and the palpably more hostile atmosphere that was now gathering force regarding Islam in America—topics I describe in the following chapter.

·8·

The 1990s

A Changing Climate in America

Following the Soviet Union's invasion of Afghanistan in 1979, the United States and Saudi Arabia joined forces, out of their shared hatred for the Soviet Union and its "godless empire," to defeat communism in Afghanistan.

Saudi Arabia encouraged its youth to go to Afghanistan to fight the jihad against the Soviet Union. In Washington, the Reagan administration had elevated Wahhabism "to the status of liberation theology—one that would free the region of communism."[1] The jihadists, dubbed "freedom fighters," were "trained and equipped by the CIA and supported by petro-dollars from the Arabian Peninsula."[2] Fighters were recruited elsewhere in the Arab and Muslim world. When Egypt, in the mid-eighties, released Islamists jailed in connection with Sadat's assassination, they were sent on pilgrimage to Mecca, and from there they boarded flights to Pakistan to fight the communists in Afghanistan.

Islamist activists traveled internationally to preach and recruit for the jihad. They became the "beneficiaries of America's tolerance for anti-communists of any stripe," and they circulated and recruited freely, including among Muslims in America. Altogether the U.S.'s pursuit of such policies would have the effect, wrote Gilles Kepel, of turning the United States into an "Islamist haven."[3] The United States had become "one of the main fund-raising destinations" for the recruitment of jihadis—or mujahedeen—for the war in Afghanistan.[4] Recruitment activities were under way now in Brooklyn and New Jersey, for instance, and indeed the Services Bureau, an organization supported by Osama bin Laden and Abdullah Azzam, opened branches in thirty-three cities across America, and recruitment centers for the Afghan jihad were opened even on American university campuses.[5] Islamic student associations, according to Kepel, now welcomed "preachers and activists" who were members of the Muslim Brotherhood in the Middle East, and these student associations would set up the Islamist movement's "first English language websites."[6]

Contemporary observers of ISNA's 1987 Annual Convention reported that new currents were making themselves felt at ISNA and that there was a noticeably larger presence that year of Brotherhood members from abroad than had been the case in previous years. One such observer—Larry Poston—reported that the keynote speaker at the convention that year was Khurram Murad, a very senior figure in the Jamaat-i Islami known for his activism in the work of da'wa. Poston found Murad's speech alarming in its forcefulness. Urging Muslims to hold on to their faith and to pursue the work of da'wa, Murad's address concluded, wrote Poston, with a "ringing challenge to the listeners to both maintain and refine their Islamicity in the midst of a secular environment. If this is done, he stated, America will soon become a Muslim continent."[7]

While Poston found Murad's projected vision for America alarming, this was evidently not a speech promoting militant jihad against America—or indeed against anyone. Rather, as reported by Poston, it seems to have been a speech that remained fully within the confines of mainstream Islamists' commitment to pursue and promote their vision through advocacy and activism as voters and citizens. Preachers recruiting for the jihad in Afghanistan were apparently not doing so—or were not reported to have been doing so—at ISNA's conventions.

Through the late 1980s and early 1990s Afghanistan had become a gathering place and training ground for militant Islamists from across the world. Coming together there to fight a common enemy, they also built up a network of jihadis across the globe.

The Soviet Union withdrew its troops from Afghanistan in 1989, and the regime they had installed finally fell in 1992, shortly after the demise of the Soviet Union. With the fighting over in Afghanistan, as Fawaz Gerges, an authority on radical Islamism, wrote, "tens of thousands of hardened fighters baptized into a culture of martyrdom" were free now to cause havoc within Afghanistan and wherever they dispersed to across the world. Gerges continued, "How could these warriors be demobilized and reintegrated into their societies as law-abiding citizens? Could the genie be put back in the bottle?"[8]

Egypt, as we saw in Chapter 6, now experienced an outbreak of unprecedented violence, much of it associated with two militant Islamist groups to which Sheikh Omar Abdel Rahman was a religious advisor, and one that was headed by Ayman al-Zawahiri.[9] Both Abdel Rahman and al-Zawahiri were major figures in the Egyptian and international militant Islamist movements, and both had been initially arrested in Egypt in connection with Sadat's assassination. Both, following their release, went on to work for the jihad in Afghanistan. As Kepel noted, Afghan veterans who had acquired military skills in the training camps of Afghanistan would now deploy these skills "against their own regimes and then against the West from the 1990s onwards."[10]

It would not be long before America also would find itself the target of violence as some of the most radical jihadists made their way to America where they would plot and execute violence and raise funds and recruit for jihadism. One of these radicals was Abdel Rahman—known as the blind sheikh. Abdel Rahman would be tried in 1995 in the United States for his role in the 1993 bombing of the World Trade Center. He was convicted and sent to prison for life.

An Egyptian and a graduate of al-Azhar, Abdel Rahman had embraced the teachings of Qutb and Mawdudi and had become a religious guide of the Islamic Jihad, the group that assassinated Sadat.[11] Imprisoned for a time under Nasser, Abdel Rahman had left Egypt in the 1970s when Sadat attempted to "rein in" the Islamists, spending a period in Saudi Arabia, where he found "wealthy sponsors for his cause."[12] He was detained and tortured in Egypt for his role in Sadat's assassination but was eventually acquitted and released in 1984. Abdel Rahman then became an active preacher and recruiter for the jihad in Afghanistan, and as such he was favorably viewed by both the Saudis and the Americans.[13]

Brought to trial again in Egypt (and eventually convicted in absentia) in 1990, Abdel Rahman fled to Sudan, where he obtained a visa for the United States.

In America Abdel Rahman was based in the New York area, where there were recruitment centers for the war in Afghanistan and where he was free to preach and recruit at local mosques.[14] He applied for permanent residence status in January 1991, and, despite his well-known history of involvement with violent groups in Egypt, he obtained a green card in April—obtaining it with "unusual rapidity," Kepel remarked. Throughout this period Abdel Rahman also traveled frequently to Europe and the Middle East to raise funds and recruit for the jihad in Afghanistan—engaging, that is, in the types of activities that, since the eighties, "had been gratefully assisted and subsidized by the CIA."[15]

Ayman al-Zawahiri also was in the United States in 1993, raising funds in Silicon Valley for the jihad against America. The FBI knew about his activities but did not arrest him. It must have been obvious to the U.S. officials, commented Kepel, that "radical Islamism was breeding international terrorism." However, well into the mid-1990s they clearly "did little to act on that knowledge. Whether through negligence, ignorance, the work of obscure forces, or an excessively complex game of manipulation that turned against its authors, the United States managed to let two leaders of the most extreme forms of Egyptian Islamism obtain visas to enter the United States without encountering a single obstacle."[16]

Kepel's forceful views on this subject are echoed by others knowledgeable in such matters. A CIA agent who had worked in the Afghanistan operation was reported by the *Boston Herald* to have said: "By giving these people the funding we did, a situation was created in which it could be safely argued that we bombed the World Trade Center."[17] Similarly, the historian Chalmers Johnson wrote in his book *Blowback: The Costs and Consequences of American Empire:* "The term 'blowback,' which officials of the Central Intelligence Agency first invented for their own use . . . refers to the unintended consequences of policies that were kept secret from the American people. What the daily press reports as the malign acts of 'terrorists' or 'drug lords' or 'rogue states' or 'illegal arms merchants' often turn out to be blowback from earlier American operations."[18]

In Egypt, the spate of terrorist attacks of the early 1990s generated panic and anger and gave rise to strident criticism of the growing numbers of mosques as well as grim warnings from the media and government against Islamists—warnings that failed to distinguish between the vast moderate majority and the radical extremists.[19] The responses in the U.S. that the 1993 bombing of the World Trade Center triggered were on the whole not dissimilar, with the difference perhaps that while these attacks elicited from the Egyptian media and authorities sweepingly negative views of all Islamists, here in America the tendency was toward a negative perception of all Muslims. American responses would be further complicated and exacerbated by the complexities of U.S. relations with the Middle East—over its critical oil reserves, and with Israel, and also, by the 1990s, regarding American military intervention in the first Gulf War in Iraq.

There were other factors in the early nineties, beyond the first eruptions of Islamic terrorism on American soil, that would begin to tilt the ground toward an exacerbation of negative perceptions of Muslims in America. For of course a vein of prejudice toward Muslims has been an element—at times muted and at times more intense—of American as well as European society in the past, as such works as Edward Said's *Orientalism* and Jack Shaheen's *Reel Bad Arabs* explore in some detail. This negativity palpably began to increase in the 1990s. With the fall of the Soviet Union, as Zachary Lockman writes, observers began "to seek new ways of understanding the fault lines and potential sources of conflict in the post–Cold War world, and one of these involved a reversion to the old but still powerful notion that the world was divided into fundamentally different and clashing civilizations."[20]

Bernard Lewis, the influential public intellectual and longtime opponent of Edward Said (whose works Said had fiercely criticized for their anti-Muslim bias), published an article in 1990 entitled "Roots of Muslim Rage" in which he rearticulated the notion of a fundamental fault line and "clash of civilizations" between the Islamic world and the West.

Lewis's thesis was taken up and developed in an article (and subsequently a book) by Samuel Huntington. The article, "Clash of Civilizations?" appeared in 1993 in *Foreign Affairs*, the politically influential journal published by the Council on Foreign Relations. Mingling scholarship and policymaking was well-trod ground for Huntington, a Harvard professor who had been (as Lockman notes) a "leading advocate" in the 1960s of the U.S. war in Vietnam and of the "massive bombardment of the Vietnamese countryside."[21] Taking his title from a phrase in Lewis's article, Huntington wrote that the "fault lines of civilizations will be the battle lines of the future." One such major fault line, Huntington maintained, was that between Islam and the West. Another was that between "Confucian civilization"—by which Huntington meant China—and the West.[22]

Huntington's thesis was rebutted by many, among them Saad Eddin Ibrahim and Harvard's Roy Mottahedeh, a professor who was also a scholar of Islam.[23] Nevertheless, in the world of politics and in the broader political culture in the United States, Huntington's ideas proved tremendously influential. As GhaneaBassiri noted, they would come to have a "significant influence on the way in which U.S. relations with the Muslim-majority world" would be framed in the political arena and in the media and public conversation on Islam and the Muslim world.[24]

The "clash of civilizations" thesis was particularly popular, as GhaneaBassiri also notes, among people who were primarily concerned about U.S.-Israeli relations and the risks that "constructive relations" between the U.S. and Islamist organizations might pose to these. In addition, he continues, "militant pro-Israelis like Daniel Pipes and Steve Emerson . . . launched an anti-Islamism propaganda campaign of their own in the 1990s."

Pipes is the founder and director of the Middle East Forum, a small think tank whose goals he described as those of promoting American interests in the Middle East, specifically "strong ties with Israel, Turkey, and other democracies as they emerge," and "a stable supply and a low price of oil." According to Lockman, whose book *Contending Visions of the Middle East* provides a detailed account of the struggle over knowledge and politics in relation to the Middle East, a struggle that has been under way in America for some decades and that has resurfaced with particular intensity in recent years, Pipes has "carved out a small but moderately successful niche for himself in the world of right-wing punditry."[25]

A supporter of the Israeli Right who favors the use of military force over negotiation, Pipes published an article in 1990 called "The Muslims Are Coming! The Muslims Are Coming!"—an article that he developed into the book *Militant Islam Reaches America* (2002). Both article and book make clear, as GhaneaBassiri pointed out, that Pipes considers all Islamists to be militant Islamists. Thus Pipes evidently considered the MSA and ISNA to be "proponents of militant Islam," even though, as GhaneaBassiri observes, "they have never carried out or advocated any militant actions."[26]

After 9/11 Pipes would launch a website called Campus Watch, which listed professors at American institutions who did not share Pipes's views on Islam, Israel, and the Palestinians, defining their views as unacceptable, and describing at least one among them—John Esposito of Georgetown University—as an "apologist for Islamic and Palestinian terrorism." Campus Watch also invited students to monitor their professors and to report statements "which they deemed anti-Israel or anti-American." These actions provoked widespread anger among academics, and more than a hundred professors wrote in to criticize Campus Watch "for its crude attempt to silence debate about the Middle East."[27]

Pipes was nominated by President Bush in 2003 to the board of directors of the U.S. Institute of Peace, a federally funded institution "dedicated to preventing, managing and peacefully resolving international conflicts." The nomination astonished many, given Pipes's position in favor of "resolving conflict through superior military force." Muslim-American groups in particular were appalled, as they considered Pipes to be an Islamophobe whose writings and pronouncements "deliberately sought to spread fear and suspicion" of Muslims and Islam. Others too, notes Lockman, were outraged, including "moderate scholars who regarded Pipes as extreme in his views as well as in how he expressed them," and thus as not suitable for such a position. The *Washington Post,* reports Lockman, described the nomination as "salt in the wound" and a "cruel joke" for U.S. Muslims. When Democratic senators expressed their opposition and held up the nomination in Congress, the following month President Bush "bypassed Congress" and appointed Pipes to the position.

Another prominent voice on Islam in the 1990s and subsequently is Steven Emerson, a journalist with whom Pipes sometimes collaborated. Following the attack on the World Trade Center in 1993, Emerson produced a documentary called *Jihad in America* which aired on PBS stations nationwide in December 1994. The documentary in part follows the trail of U.S. involvement in and support for jihadism in Afghanistan, as well as the spread of jihadism to the United States. It also claimed that Islamist organizations, including organizations involved in violence in Israel, such as Hamas and Hezbollah, were also now operating in the United States.

Emerson's documentary both won awards and drew fierce criticism.[28] Some critics maintained that Emerson had made unsubstantiated accusations and also that the film contained a "fundamental deceit" —as an investigative reporter put it in *The Nation*—in that it showed clips of speakers calling for jihad without clarifying that they were "not referring to America but to Afghanistan and Israel."[29]

Following the bombings in Oklahoma in 1995, Emerson—according to this same reporter, Robert I. Friedman—"was a fixture on radio and TV, waging jihad on Islam," his assertions playing a role in "creating mass hysteria against American Arabs." Emerson, for example, appeared on *CBS News* on the evening of the Oklahoma bombings, reported Friedman, saying, "This was done with the intent to inflict as many casualties as possible. That is a Middle Eastern trait." The bombers were likely Hamas, Emerson had also said, as Friedman's account continues: "They hate democracy. They hate America."

And, indeed, following the Oklahoma bombing (a bombing for which Timothy McVeigh and his co-conspirators were convicted; McVeigh was executed in 2001) there was a backlash and a distinct rise in incidents of harassment against Muslims, as Nihad Awad, cofounder of the Council on American-Islamic Relations (CAIR), today the most prominent Muslim civil rights advocacy group in America, would later note. CAIR had been a fledgling organization (formed in 1994) when, Awad said, he received a call from the president of the Islamic Society of

Greater Oklahoma City, urging him to come to Oklahoma. Before the bombing and the "anti-Muslim backlash that followed," Awad would later explain, CAIR had been "asked to review a few incidents" relating to Muslim-American civil rights issues, but after the bombing "harassment and harmful acts increased." In Oklahoma in particular, Muslims, "particularly those of Arab descent[,] were viewed with suspicion." In fact, recounted Awad, "a Muslim family's home had been attacked, presumably by vigilantes who believed the rumors swirling about the bombing being the handiwork of Middle Eastern terrorists." Awad recalled speaking with the man whose home had been attacked, and also with his wife, "who miscarried her first child soon after the attack."[30]

In September 1995, CAIR would publish its first report on the status of Muslim civil rights in America, chronicling "more than 200 documented incidents of harassment of Muslims." Henceforth CAIR would publish such a report annually, giving the figures for and documenting the number of anti-Muslim incidents occurring in that year.

In the 1990s strong criticism and even fierce attacks on Islamist American organizations were voiced also by Muslims—Muslims who did not belong to the Islamist organizations that had risen to dominance in America and who disliked the kind of Islam preached and embraced by Islamists, their comments indicating that they evidently also resented the way in which the dominant Muslim American organizations were laying claim to be speaking for all Muslims when in fact they were not.

Khaled Abou El Fadl, professor of Islamic studies at UCLA at the time, had been a longtime critic of the "science-trained new spokespeople" who were essentially ignorant of the Islamic scholarly legacy of debate, discussion, and interpretation.[31] In the nineties El Fadl had written a book strongly critiquing the "Wahhabi puritan" strain that he saw as exerting a dominant influence in Muslim American organizations. He would follow this in 2005 with a book whose title, *The Great Theft: Wrestling Islam from the Extremists,* made clear his position. He fiercely denounced Wahhabi Islam and asserted that there was a deep schism in contemporary Islam between Muslim moderates—the camp in which he placed himself—and, as he puts it, "what I will call the Muslim puritans." Both groups, he wrote,

> claim to represent the true authentic Islam. Both believe that they represent the Divine message as God intended it to be, and both believe that their convictions are thoroughly rooted in the Holy Book. . . . Puritans, however, accuse the moderates of having changed and reformed Islam to the point of diluting and corrupting it. And moderates accuse the puritans of miscomprehending and misapplying Islam to the point of undermining and even defiling the religion.[32]

El Fadl's books certainly deepened the rift between him and the dominant Muslim organizations of America, but they did not draw the strong public response from American Muslim organizations that Sheikh Hisham Kabbani's attack would provoke. Kabbani was the representative in America of a Sufi order based in Cyprus, the Naqshbandi-Haqqani. He headed, at the time, a relatively small organization based in Flint, Michigan.

Testifying at an Open Forum at the State Department in 1999, Kabbani complained that there were Muslim organizations that had "hijacked the mike" and were claiming to be speaking on behalf of the Muslim community. Those organizations, he said (not naming any but implying a reference to ISNA and the MSA), were not the moderates but the extremists. Those "advising the media or advising the government are not the moderate Muslims," he said. He continued: "Those whose opinion the government asks are the extremists themselves. Those that have been quoted in newspapers, in the magazines, [on] the television, in the media, are the extremists themselves. You are not hearing the authentic voice of Muslims, of moderate Muslims, but you are hearing the extremist voice of Muslims."[33]

Attributing the rise of extremism to the spread of Wahhabism, an ideology that, as Kabbani noted, was fiercely opposed to Sufism, Kabbani went on to say that this extremist ideology was spreading fast in the universities through the national organizations and associations that had been established. Extremists had taken over, he said, "more than 80 percent of the mosques." Moreover, their organizations commonly raised funds ostensibly for charitable activities but in reality much of the money was used, said Kabbani, for other purposes, including "buying weapon arsenals."

Kabbani's comments drew swift response from a number of Muslim American organizations, among them ISNA and the MSA and CAIR, who issued a joint statement pointing out that Kabbani's congressional testimony had "put the entire American Muslim community under unjustified suspicion. In effect Mr. Kabbani is telling government officials that the majority of American Muslims pose a danger to our society."[34] Others would be critical of Kabbani as well, among them Robert Seiple, ambassador at large for religious liberty in the Clinton administration, who observed that Kabbani's comments "about 80 percent of the leadership of Islam in America being extremists are irresponsible and terribly unfortunate," and that such a viewpoint "just plays into the hands of those who would demonize and create division, and those knee-jerk types who see Islam as a monolith."[35]

The criticisms and denunciations of Muslims and Islamists launched by pundits and journalists such as Pipes and Emerson and others, as well as the attacks that came from Muslims who did not share the views, goals, and understandings of Islam of Islamists and their organizations, and who resented their dominance in the American Muslim landscape, would of course only grow fiercer and more intense in the wake of 9/11, as the American administration launched its war on terror.

Among the events that would have the greatest impact on the history of Islam in America in the 1990s, according to GhaneaBassiri, was the Persian Gulf War of 1990–91. Following Saddam Hussein's invasion of Kuwait in August 1990, an invasion universally condemned, the U.S. immediately deployed its forces in the region to protect its allies. After attempting to bring about Iraq's withdrawal from Kuwait through diplomatic channels, the United States, along with a coalition of Muslim-majority countries, launched an attack on Iraq known as Desert Storm.

In an attempt to give his conduct an aura of legitimacy and to appeal to Arabs and Muslims, Saddam Hussein now added the phrase "Allahu Akbar" (God is greater) to the Iraqi flag, and, linking his cause to that of the Palestinians, he fired Scud missiles at Israel in the course of his war against the U.S.-led coalition. Most American Muslims, wrote GhaneaBassiri, "were not fooled" by Saddam's manipulative tactics. Many were aware that Saddam had been an ally of the U.S., which had supplied Iraq's arsenal of war during the Iraq-Iran war of 1980–88, and they viewed Desert Storm as "a U.S. attempt to tame a rogue ally and to control the oil supply in the region."

Nevertheless, the overall sentiment among Muslim American organizations and the Muslims who participated in them was one of deep opposition to the war. A statement issued by ISNA just before the U.S. attack began noted that "World Muslim sentiment rejects in principle the presence of foreign military forces in the birthplace of Islam"—with reference obviously to the presence of U.S. troops in Saudi Arabia. ISNA's statement is worth quoting in full for the connections it makes and the vision that it brings to bear on the impending American attack. Such an attack set a dangerous precedent, ISNA asserted,

> sparking memories of colonialism, the lasting repercussions of which remain devastating to the life, liberty, and culture of the region and its ecology. It is more resenting since it is seen as emanating from a principal ally of the Israelis as well as a superpower that cannot readily be compelled to withdraw. A continuing policy of categorical support for the Israeli occupation, ambitions, and oppression of the Palestinian people, coupled with an overriding focus on controlling energy resources, opens a serious credibility gap between the American decision-makers and the Muslim and Arab peoples. Present concerted international measures [taken against Iraq] stand in clear contrast to actions taken against Israeli aggressions.[36]

The war would be a turning point in the history of Muslim American organizations, explains GhaneaBassiri. The Arab Gulf states, among them Saudi Arabia and Kuwait, major donors and supporters of Islamist organizations, were enthusiastic about the American-led war. They now asked American Muslim organizations also to endorse it. According to GhaneaBassiri, the only leader of a national Muslim American organization to endorse the war was W. D. Mohammed.[37]

Those who had refused to endorse Saudi Arabia's willingness to have non-Muslim troops stationed on its soil "saw the flow of petrodollars to their organizations dry up." The major issue discussed at an open meeting at the ISNA convention meeting of 1991 was the matter of ISNA's source of funding. "Members wanted to know," writes Ghanea-Bassiri, "whether or not ISNA was under the influence of Arab states in the Persian Gulf since it received funds from them. One attendee was reported to have said, 'Please make sure that you do not depend on those people because they are corrupted. We are more than happy to donate. Just organize yourself and ask for money. Believe me, you will get more than you need.'"

The major effect of this drying up of Gulf funds was that of pushing the organizations toward greater financial independence. Petrodollars, remarks GhaneaBassiri, had become "toxic assets." Even W. D. Mohammed would later declare that, as of the mid-nineties, he had ceased to accept funds from Saudi Arabia because "some strings" were attached.

As the war in Iraq ended in 1992 and sanctions were imposed on Iraq, Islamist Americans—in keeping with their long tradition of activism in support of those in need—began organizing a Humanitarian Fund to help Iraqi refugees and orphans. They also called on the U.S. government to end the sanctions against Iraq. The sanctions caused "undue hardship on the people," they said, "particularly the children of Iraq, without weakening the Saddam regime."

Charity booths were a prominent and lively element of the ISNA conventions when I first began attending these in the late 1990s. They lined the main lobby of the convention center and spilled over into the generally loud and colorful bazaar, with its stalls of books, music, and Quran-chanting, often all playing simultaneously, each growing louder or more muted as one moved along the stalls. Other stalls sold jewelry and clothes and carpets—and even fresh dates. The charity booths were typically bright with posters and running videotapes of the people for whom they were raising funds—Bosnians, Palestinians, Kashmiris, Iraqis, Guajaratis, wherever the distress and crisis of the day was. Their tables were laden also with books, fliers, and pamphlets.

It was at such booths that I first came across the work of Ramsey Clark, former U.S. attorney, including his *Impact of Sanctions on Iraq: The Children Are Dying* and *War Crimes: A Report on U.S. War Crimes Against Iraq*. I also encountered Paul Findley's books, among them *Silent*

No More: Confronting America's False Images of Islam and *They Dare to Speak Out: Confronting Israel's Lobby.* Findley, who also spoke at one of the early ISNA conventions I attended, was a former U.S. congressman from Illinois.

I formed the strong impression in the course of my several years of observation at ISNA that the majority of people attending the convention, who often came in large family groups, were there above all for personal reasons—to catch up with and socialize with family, friends, and other Muslims, and to search for matrimonial partners for themselves or their children. Still, the presence of these booths and conversations would doubtless have made ISNA conventiongoers more conscious as a group as to Muslim suffering in other parts of the world.

After 9/11 and the beginning of the U.S. "war on terror," the charity booths at ISNA, which had flourished in the late 1990s, would steadily dwindle to, by 2007, a handful of booths at the most. As part of the war on terror a number of Muslim charities were closed down by the U.S. government, and some Muslim Americans found themselves in trouble simply because they had, usually unknowingly, donated to charities that would come under suspicion as being fronts for terrorist organizations. Consequently, many Muslims were now fearful of making charitable donations, and so funds for charities had dried up. Many conscientious Muslims for whom making donations to charity was a religious obligation found themselves now in a quandary over how to fulfill this obligation.

This chapter, bringing us to the end of the 1990s and to the eve of the tragedy of 9/11, also brings Part I of this book—in which I have followed the rise of Islamism, along with the veil's resurgence from its appearance in Egypt in the 1970s to their establishment in America—to a close. The ensuing eventful first decade of the twenty-first century in America, and the turbulence around issues of Islam, Muslims, and women and Islam into which it plunged us, and the emergence of a new and dynamic Islamist feminism, form the subjects of Part II.

T•W•O

After 9/11

New Pathways in America

Prologue

As it proved, much of my research on Islam in America would be conducted in the context of one of the most eventful and volatile decades in modern history regarding relations between Islam and the West, as the 9/11 terrorist attack (followed by terrorist attacks by Muslims in Britain and in Spain) sparked new levels of fear and suspicion of Muslims in the Western world. In the wake of 9/11 the United States plunged into two wars, one after another, with two Muslim-majority countries, Afghanistan and Iraq, wars that are ongoing.

On the home front in America, 9/11 set in motion a variety of actions and responses that would directly touch many Muslim Americans —and similar actions and reactions emerged elsewhere in the West. In the United States initially, that is, in the days and weeks following 9/11, at the level of the citizenry there were eruptions of violence against Muslims, including several acts of murder committed against men believed to be Muslim. There was a rash of attacks too, some of them quite savage, on women in hijab.

The government took a clear stand against such violence, with President George W. Bush speaking out firmly against such acts. In addition, new laws would be enacted, among them the Patriot Act, subjecting Muslims to new levels of scrutiny, and new Immigration and Naturalization Service (INS) regulations would lead to the arrest of Muslims numbering in the thousands. Many Muslim charities were closed, and the homes of people associated with them were raided. In addition to the people whose lives were directly affected by these events, women as well as men, many American Muslims were indirectly affected, if only by virtue of their being aware—even if simply through hearing or reading the news—of what was happening to some other Muslim Americans.

In the arena of the public conversations on Islam there was now a new level of permissiveness as to the levels of open abuse that could be aired. A good proportion of these negative comments seemed to emanate from the Christian Right. Franklin Graham, for example, Billy Graham's son, called Islam a "very wicked, evil religion," and Jerry Falwell, another leader of the Christian Right, described the Prophet Muhammad as a terrorist. In similar vein, Ann Coulter, speaking of Muslims, said, "We should invade their countries, kill their leaders and convert them to Christianity."[1] Similar trends were under way in Europe, most memorably encapsulated in the publication in Denmark of cartoons of the Prophet Muhammad. The American media, mindful of the history of demeaning cartoons and representations of African Americans, refrained from republishing the cartoons.

This decade, inaugurated by the violence of 9/11, and threaded throughout with the intermittently rising and falling levels of violence of American-led wars in Muslim-majority countries, would be in these and many more ways an extraordinary and disturbing decade for many, Muslim and non-Muslim alike.

For those of us who had been working on the subject of women and Islam for many years in the pre-9/11 era, there was one feature of the new public conversation emerging in America and the West that was particularly startling. This was the way in which the subject of women in Islam, and in particular women's oppression and the emblems of that oppression, such as the veil and the burka, became recurring themes in the broad public conversation in America and elsewhere in the West.

Beginning soon after 9/11 and increasing steadily ever since, the subject would be repeatedly invoked by politicians and the media, including by people at the highest levels of government, often as if it were a matter of profound political import to the West and its democratic projects and commitments (including, for example, in relation to bringing democracy to Iraq), and as a matter that was pertinent even to American and Western national security. It was at this point, as I noted in the Introduction, that First Lady Laura Bush would declare in a radio address on November 17, 2001, that "civilized people throughout the world are speaking out in horror—not only because our hearts break for the women and children of Afghanistan, but also because in Afghanistan we see the world the terrorists would like to impose on the rest of us. . . . The fight against terrorism is also a fight for the rights and dignity of women."[2] And just two days later, as I noted, Cherie Blair would issue a similar statement in London. These views were echoed and disseminated in the media, which—with numerous images of and references to veils and burkas and the Taliban's horrifying treatment of women—portrayed the war as righteous by virtue of American and Western concern to save the women. As the British journalist Polly Toynbee wrote, the "burka" was now the "battle flag" and "shorthand moral justification" for the war in Afghanistan.[3]

Inaugurated in this way at the highest level of state as a subject of deep political import to the West and to "civilization," and as moral justification for war, the subject of women and Islam under one guise or another (often encapsulated by controversies around the hijab and burka) emerged as the flashpoint of conflicts and tensions around issues of "Islam and the West"—be it in relation to immigrant minorities or to wars abroad.

These tensions have remained high throughout this decade and concomitantly—repeating a pattern played out many times in history when women, Islam, and the veil emerged into the foreground as emblems of civilizational tensions (in the Cromer era in Egypt, for example, and in Iran after the revolution of 1979)—the topics of women, Islam, and the veil have remained through the decade in the stratosphere of political, media, and public interest in the West. Whereas once working on this subject had meant burying myself in libraries and reading obscure articles, now I followed the most significant events and publications on the topic by following the news. I learned first from newspapers and television and radio broadcasts what the latest debates and controversies were in the West about women and Islam, and about the events and the books and individuals who were sparking these. It is from the media also that I learn of the latest outbreaks of debates around veils or burkas and the call to ban one or the other, topics repeatedly flaring into the news in Western countries, where they often now figure as matters of import to the state. Of course, issues surrounding the veil have been matters of state in Muslim-majority countries for a long time—be it banning it, as in Turkey (and also in Egypt, as I described earlier) or enforcing it, as in Saudi Arabia and Iran. But now hijabs and burkas were emerging as matters of state also for Western nations.

In keeping with the suddenly intense media and public interest in the subject, a raft of books addressing the topic of women in Islam now appeared in quick succession and became instant best sellers. Among these most notably was Azar Nafisi's *Reading Lolita in Tehran* (2003), Irshad Manji's *Trouble with Islam* (2004), and Ayaan Hirsi Ali's *Caged Virgin* (2006). These and other such books, nearly all of them written by women of Muslim background whose relationship with Islam was at best ambiguous, both captured a huge readership in Europe and America and, simultaneously, triggered angry responses and sharply critical analyses from academics. Hamid Dabashi, for example, of Columbia University, declared that *Reading Lolita in Tehran* was in essence deploying concerns "about the plight of Muslim women" in the service "of U.S. ideological warmongering."[4] Others, too, as I discuss in Chapter 9, wrote of such books in similar vein.

Against this backdrop of intense national and international (and primarily Western) interest, the subject of women and Islam also took on now a new burst of liveliness among religiously committed Muslim American feminists, giving rise to a new level of Muslim feminist activism—a level unprecedented in my own lifetime in America. This activism was often followed and reported on in the national and international media. The story of Professor Aminah Wadud's woman-led congregational Friday prayer, for example, held in a rented chapel in New York, was covered by such major news organizations as the *New York Times* and the BBC (indeed, reporters at the event, as I saw, seemed almost to outnumber the congregation), and images of it were beamed across the world. Through this decade many women who were committed Muslims would emerge, as I describe in the following chapters, as activists and writers who were deeply committed too to pursuing the goal of women's rights.

Such is the lively, volatile, fraught, and complicated ground making up the subject of women, Islam, and the West, and specifically America, in this eventful first decade of the twenty-first century, and this therefore is the territory that I set out to describe in the following chapters. The core of my account is always the subject of women and Islam in the West in these times. But of course that subject is inextricably entangled in and formed by the broader context shaping the environment in relation to issues of Islam and Muslims and the West.

Having been drawn into researching this subject in the first place by the growing presence of the hijab in America, and by my desire to understand what its presence meant, along with that of Islamism, and what their trajectories might be in America and the West, it is Islamists in particular (and not secular or non-Islamist Muslims who actually make up the majority of American Muslims) who receive our primary attention.

I felt that it was essential to try to convey something of the complexity and packed eventfulness of these times with regard to Islam and Muslims in America, and in regard to the very issue of women and Islam as this topic surfaced and resurfaced in public discourse. It was important, for instance, to both take note of the public conversation on women and Islam with its concern over the oppression of Muslim women and register the fact that, even as these ideas were in common circulation in the public conversation, women in hijab were actually being attacked on the streets of America. These and other such details bearing at one level on the larger conversation on Muslim women in this country, and directly affecting on another level the daily lives of Muslim women in this same society—all of these together shape the environment in which Islamism has been evolving in this decade as regards Islam and women, and all therefore must be at least briefly taken note of in that they all have their part in affecting the broad environment and consequently the direction of Islam's development.

Chapter 9 takes as its starting point the first days and months after 9/11. My aim in this chapter was first to describe the impact and effects of that event on the social, political, and cultural environment in American society as regards Islam, and Islam and women, and the impact and consequences of these for Muslim women as well as men. Second, I was concerned to describe and analyze dominant themes and elements in the public conversation on women in Islam: obviously an important component shaping the cultural and political environment in which Muslim American women—and indeed all of us—live. In particular I am concerned to analyze and reflect on the ways in which this broad public conversation of proclaimed concern for the plight of Muslim women in fact plays out, intertwines and interacts with the actual lives of Muslim women, be this American Muslim women—such as Debbie Almontaser and Nadia Abu El-Haj—who live in the United States, or women who live abroad and whose lives are directly affected by American views and foreign policies.

In Chapter 10 I describe the impact of 9/11 on Muslim American organizations and in particular on ISNA. Drawing on my own observations of the evolving scene at their conventions through the post-9/11 years, I begin with a descriptive overview of the broad trends of development under way at these meetings. I focus in particular on developments affecting the subject of women and Islam, and I conclude with thumbnail sketches of the lives and activism of some notable ISNA women.

In Chapter 11, the book's final chapter, I set out to give an overview of the main trends of American Muslim women's activism today and through the first decade of the century. I conclude with reflections on and an overview and assessment of the broad direction in which Islamism appears to be evolving today as regards women within this Western, democratic, American context.

·9·

Backlash

The Veil, the Burka, and the Clamor of War

On September 18, 2001, President George W. Bush paid a visit to the mosque at the Islamic Center of Washington, D.C., from which he spoke, as the *Washington Post* reported, to "admonish the nation not to avenge last week's terrorist attacks on innocent American Arabs and Muslims."[1]

The president's visit had been prompted by a wave of hate crimes reported in the *Post.* Two men had been killed, one a Muslim Pakistani store owner who had been shot in Dallas on September 15, and the other the Sikh owner of a gas station in Mesa, Arizona, shot on the same day. Sikhs (the paper explained) are not Muslims, but because they wear beards and turbans the killer took the man for a Muslim. The FBI, the article also stated, had "initiated 40 hate crime investigations involving reported attacks on Arab American citizens and institutions." CAIR had also received reports "of more than 350 attacks against Arab Americans around the country, ranging from verbal abuse to physical assault. It also received reports of dozens of mosques being firebombed or vandalized." Among the reports the police were investigating was a case of "two Muslim girls" who were beaten at Moraine Valley College, in Palos Hills, Illinois.

President Bush's visit, which had "surprised and gratified Islamic leaders," the *Post* said, was one among a number of efforts on the part of the Bush administration to prevent hate crimes against the "nearly 10 million American Arabs and Muslims"—efforts, the paper noted, that had included inviting Muzzamil H. Siddiqui to the memorial service held at the national cathedral on September 14. Siddiqui, who had been president of ISNA (1997–2001), attended the service, reciting verses from the Quran as part of the ceremony.[2]

In addition to preventing an escalation in hate crimes, the president's visit to a mosque, as Deputy National Security Advisor Stephen Hadley explained, might help "convince would-be partners overseas that the U.S. effort is not anti-Arab or anti-Islam but anti-terrorist." The visit also "buttressed Bush's image as a 'compassionate conservative.'" Such goals were all "intertwined," a White House official had explained.

President Bush's address at the mosque included the remarks that the "face of terror is not the true face of Islam" and that "Islam is peace." In addition, the president made special mention of the attacks on Muslim women who wore hijab. "Women who cover their heads should not fear leaving their homes," he said. "That's not the America I know," he went on. "That should not and that will not stand in America."[3]

"The initial impact of 9/11 on the Muslim community," observed Yvonne Haddad, a longtime scholar of Islam in America, "was one of deep shock and fear of potential backlash."[4] Indeed, it was not only Muslims who were afraid and uncertain in these initial days as to what might transpire next and whether the early instances of violence were auguries of worse to come. One of my friends, a practicing Jew of European background, advised me to remove my name from the front door, as "one simply never knew" how things might go, and another, of Christian background, invited me to come stay until things were more settled. There were many anecdotal reports of such kindly advice and offers of help that Muslims all over the country reportedly received from friends and neighbors—advice and offers indicating that it was not only Muslims who feared a backlash.

Instances and reports of hate crimes and bias against Muslim and Arab Americans did rise dramatically immediately after 9/11, going up by 1,600 percent.[5] They included more of the kinds of attacks already mentioned—attacks on individuals, on women in hijab, and acts of arson and destruction against mosques and businesses, as well as several murders, among them the murder of an Egyptian American man of Coptic (Christian) background who was evidently assumed to be Muslim.

However, Muslims and people of Muslim background, individuals and organizations, also reported being the recipients of an extraordinary level of support. Sayyid M. Syeed, secretary general of ISNA, said that the "number of support calls and visits to Islamic centers to show solidarity by far outnumber the nasty phone-calls and attacks."[6] In a survey among Muslims conducted by CAIR in August 2002, about 80 percent said they had experienced "kindness or support from friends or colleagues of other faiths"—while 57 percent reported experiencing bias and discrimination.[7] After the Islamic center in San Diego was attacked, for instance, it received "bouquets of flower[s] and cards of support and sympathy from members of other faith groups—especially after reports of Muslim women being afraid to leave home." And when a store belonging to a Muslim was vandalized in San Francisco, the neighbors "tried to offer him money" toward its repair. One woman shopping with her two children reported that the manager gave her children little gifts of pencils and paper "to show support." And people of other faiths showed up at Friday prayers "to express solidarity."[8]

In addition to such expressions of support there was now an enormously increased interest in Islam and a desire to learn about it among the broader public. Books on Islam flew off the shelves, and when mosques began to hold open houses to offer information about Islam, inviting whoever wished to attend, such events were typically packed.[9] Those I attended in my own area were certainly crowded. At one such event mosque officials informed the audience that the rabbi of a nearby synagogue, who had opened the synagogue's parking lot to the mosque for the evening, had consistently been tremendously helpful as had the pastor of the neighborhood church.

As it happens, this particular mosque was the mosque where I had heard, a couple of years earlier, the sermon in praise of Hasan al-Banna, founder of the Muslim Brotherhood. At that time, as well as on subsequent visits, I had sat in the women's section in the basement—a dim, cramped, beige-carpeted, unaesthetic space, where the sermon and prayers came through to us on loudspeakers. Children played in a small room off the main basement room, occasionally running in to sit with their mothers or to clamber over them, or else join or play at joining in prayer. The open house was held upstairs in the men's space, a carpeted hall that was normally no doubt open but which now held rows of chairs. It was crowded; all the seats were taken, and people were sitting and standing along the walls and in the aisles.

The imam and a couple of other male mosque officers were present. After making some introductory comments, in part with the help of a translator, the task of giving a brief informative talk on Islam and responding to questions was handled by a young Euro-American woman, Andrea Useem. Useem, whom I had met as a non-hijabi student at Harvard, was a recent convert to Islam who now wore hijab. She was an extremely able and articulate speaker, as well as an amiable presence. The men also occasionally responded, usually with the help of a translator.

People asked questions and offered comments. One moment in particular in the evening's proceedings has remained with me. This was when a woman, perhaps in her forties, asked some question about Islam and followed this by saying that she wanted to explain why she was here at this open house. She was of Jewish background, she said, and was herself a nonbeliever who had dedicated her life to work in support of Native Americans. Not only was she a nonbeliever, she continued, she was also deeply critical of monotheisms. All of them, in her eyes, she said, were deeply patriarchal and oppressive toward women, as well as toward people who were not of their own group. She saw Islam as no different in this matter from Judaism and Christianity. However, her views on these points did not diminish (she said) her commitment to supporting Muslims in their right to be in this country and in their right to be treated with justice and without discrimination. This, she explained, was why she had come. She was politely heard, and one of the male mosque officers, as well as Useem, thanked her for her words and for coming.

Even as I listened I found myself thinking that this surely marked an unprecedented moment in the history of Islam—and a moment that could only happen in America and in the immediate aftermath of 9/11. In what other era or place was it even imaginable that an atheist woman of Jewish background (or a woman of any background, or even an atheist man) might come to a mosque to publicly state both her critique of monotheism, including Islam, for their chauvinism and patriarchy, as well as her support for the Muslim community members and their rights to pursue their lives and practice their faith as freely as other Americans?

Such a scene was unimaginable in any Muslim-majority country. Nor could it have unfolded in this particular way in Europe. The woman's speech (I will call her Judith—to my regret I did not get her name) was clearly steeped in ideals and assumptions that were quintessentially American: about individual rights, women's rights, and the rights of minorities. Along with these she conveyed, too—in referring to her work with Native Americans—an acute awareness of how flawed and incomplete was this deeply American project of realizing a society that was indeed one of equality for all.

That space had been created within a mosque in which such words could be spoken and courteously heard was also a matter that bore the distinct imprint of these particular times and country. The open house, a type of event that so far as I know had no precedent in American mosques in pre-9/11 times, was designed to inform people about Islam and to allow non-Muslims to get to know, ask questions of, and enter into conversations with their Muslim neighbors. Mosque authorities and Muslim organizations all across America had evidently decided it would be wise to hold such events. They feared a backlash against Islam and felt obliged to be open and to hear out the views of those who accepted their invitation.

Thus by force of circumstance and in consequence of their sense of precariousness and vulnerability as a minority, the mosque authorities were in effect compelled to listen, giving courteous reception to views that in ordinary times they would not have even permitted to have uttered in their mosques—views, moreover, articulated by people who ordinarily they would not even have allowed to enter into the sanctum of the upper level of the mosque, an area reserved exclusively for Muslim men.

As I was observing this scene I felt that I was present at a new moment in history—in the history of Islam as well as of America. It seemed an augury of the opening up of a new kind of space in which not only ordinary Muslims but also Muslim authorities were respectfully hearing out the views of those who spoke from completely different worldviews—among them people who spoke from a deeply American tradition of justice and indeed (like the Islamists themselves in their origins) from a tradition of activism in pursuit of justice.

In my own experience, Muslim religious authorities, by definition ensconced in power, do not listen. Rather they ignore, silence, or attempt to crush criticism of Islamic views and practices no matter how justified or ethically grounded. But we were now apparently in a new time in America, as new space seemed to be opening up for fruitful and collaborative exchanges between American Muslim religious authorities—now that Muslims found themselves an embattled minority needing the support of others—and people speaking from other American ethical traditions, religious and nonreligious.

Within days of the 9/11 attack, as the media began reporting incidents of attacks on Muslims, including attacks or harassments of Muslim women in hijab, there quickly surfaced reports of groups of non-Muslim women organizing events or actions in support of women in hijab, among them "headscarf days" and escort services for hijabi women.

Many of the reported incidents of harassment or attack took the form of schoolgirls being subject to insults and being spat on and having their hijabs pulled off as they were called "rag-heads" or told to "go home!"[10] One community worker reported that "after September 11 girls who wear hijab received lots of harassment on the bus, at school, and on the street. People tried to pull their hijab off, other students also might put their shirts over their heads saying 'we look like Osama's daughter, now. We look like you now.'"[11] One schoolgirl who had her headscarf pulled off was also kicked, and another teenager at a Baltimore airport experienced a distinct sense of menace when she was asked to remove her hijab when passing through security. When she asked why she should do so "and tried to explain that it was a religious symbol, she was surrounded by military personnel carrying rifles." She took it off.[12]

Not only schoolgirls found themselves subject to harassment and attack. The American-Arab Anti-Discrimination Committee (ADC) report, for example, notes that on September 16, 2001, a "Muslim woman dressed in traditional clothing was attacked while grocery shopping. Another woman began beating her while yelling, 'America is only for white people.' The victim was taken to the emergency room."[13]

Sometimes these assaults could be appallingly brutal. On September 26, for example, in Clarkson, Georgia, "three men attacked a woman as she was leaving her apartment building . . . One of them took off her hijab, another put his foot on her neck, while a third kicked her back." They continued to kick her "while cursing Arabs," then they "attempted to take off her clothes. She was dragged to a tree, screaming and pleading, while one of them held a knife to her two-year-old son." The attackers fled when they noticed cars approaching.[14] On September 30 the *San Diego Union Tribune* reported that "a car driven by a Sikh woman was idling at a red light when two men on a motorcycle pulled up beside her, yanked open her door and shouted 'This is what you get for what you've done to us!' and 'I'm going to slash your throat!' She raised her elbows to protect her neck and hunched over. She was slashed in the head at least twice before the men, hearing a car approach, sped off. She was treated in the emergency room and released that day."[15] And on October 12, in San Jose, California, a "pregnant Yemeni woman wearing a hijab and a long dress was beaten by a group of teenagers. She was hospitalized and remained in guarded condition until she delivered her baby."[16]

News of such incidents was reported widely in the media, which also reported that many Muslim women were now afraid to go out even to take their children to school or go shopping. Such incidents were also occurring on college campuses, where women began organizing campaigns against such assaults. At the University of Connecticut, Campus Safe, an organization dedicated to fighting relationship violence and sexual assault on the campus, set the headscarf campaign in motion. Ann D'Alleva, a professor of art history and women's studies who was involved, said the response to the action had been "very positive." "I think it's really important to speak out against any sort of crime," she explained to a journalist, "because who's going to be there for me. Any sort of act of hate is an act against me."[17] D'Alleva made a number of scarves from black cloth that she distributed, writing on each "Them equals Us."[18]

Such actions by women and feminists in support of women in hijab —from "headscarf days" to offers of escort and shopping services, and the holding of candlelight vigils in support of Muslim women—occurred in many communities across the nation. They were not confined to college settings, although college communities played a leading role.[19] Jennifer Schock, for example, a web designer and student in Washington, D.C., initiated the movement in her area on September 25. After posting her idea suggesting that non-Muslim women don the hijab for a day in support of Muslim women, Schock was "stunned by the firestorm of controversy it generated." She was criticized, among other things, she said, "for embracing a tradition that is viewed by many as a symbol of Islam's oppression of women." Her intention she said, had simply been to reach out to let Muslim women know that they were not alone. The gesture was at the same time, she thought, a "way to challenge our perceptions and foster some kind of dialogue . . . instead all of a sudden, I'm endorsing women's oppression. It made me realize how emotional this whole thing is."[20] Another woman, Ella Singer, a staff member on the campus of Wayne State University who had grown up in the South and who wanted to support Muslim women, also felt conflicted because "she had always refused to wear head scarves because she associated them with the oppression of slavery." Deciding to wear it nevertheless, and "pulling a scarf over her dreadlocks," she explained: "I'm wearing it because I understand how it marks you as an object for someone else's hatred. . . . It's still the same fight, but the symbol means something different."[21]

Schock subsequently established a global network called Scarves for Solidarity to "support the right of Muslim women to choose their headgear without fear of retaliation."[22] The Feminist Majority Foundation also issued the Scarves for Solidarity call to "action" for December 16–18, 2001, saying, "All women, regardless of faith, are wearing scarves covering their hair during Eid, Muslim celebratory days. . . . This simple gesture of solidarity is to communicate love and peace for women who wish to dress in a modest fashion. Our global days of solidarity speak volumes to women who have been afraid to wear traditional hijab since the horrific tragedy of September 11th."[23]

Similar campaigns in support of women in hijab were reported to have taken place across the globe, in Indonesia, for example, and in the United Kingdom and Australia.[24] For it was not of course only in America that 9/11 had precipitated such strong reactions against Muslims and a new level of suspicion and hostility toward them, including to women in hijab. Some of the negative responses would take the form, in Europe, of new government policies. In 2004, for example, France banned wearing the hijab in French public schools. In parts of Germany, public school teachers are banned from wearing hijabs at work.

The reactions to 9/11 and the dangers in which wearing hijab placed women would lead some Muslim women, as was widely reported at the time, to stop wearing this dress. (In response to the attacks, some Muslim authorities, among them Sheikh Ali Gomaa of Egypt, issued a fatwa allowing women to forgo hijab if wearing it placed them at risk.) Conversely, the attacks in fact spurred other women to take up hijab, as news stories from all over America as well as Europe and elsewhere reported. The interviews and reports of journalists, like the findings of the anthropologists in Cairo in an earlier time, are richly illuminating as to the reasons that Muslim women living in the West gave for taking up hijab at this historic moment.

A reporter in San Francisco interviewed Azadeh Zainab Sharif, a student at San Francisco State University, who decided to wear hijab after 9/11. For Sharif, the reporter (David Ian Miller) wrote, "putting the scarf on coincided with her spiritual awakening as a devout Muslim, but it was also a reaction to what she perceived to be a growing fear among Muslims in this country." Too many women, she said, "were afraid to wear one because they were worried about discrimination, and it hurt me to see that."[25]

Another reporter, in Austin, Texas, interviewed two women—one of whom had decided to stop wearing hijab while the other had chosen to embrace it. Khataw, who had stopped wearing it, had done so, she explained, in order to "protect herself," and because she felt that doing so would be "better for me and my family." Simultaneously the very conditions which led her to abandon it, and most particularly her son's being harassed at school for being Muslim, had also, she said, transformed her from "a shy and introverted" person into "an activist." She now threw herself into the task of educating people about Islam. She began speaking at churches and synagogues. Teaching people about Islam now became her "mission."[26]

Other Muslim women, this journalist also reported, similarly thought that after September 11, "wearing the veil is like stamping the scarlet letter on your chest." However, Annia Raja—a student at the University of Austin in Texas—had taken up the hijab after 9/11 precisely as a way of "negating" the widespread stereotypes about the hijab and Muslims. "It [wearing hijab] really made me more self-aware," Raja said, "as far as when I am in public I am representing Islam. And that I need to do all that I can to really show people what Islam really is. Through that [wearing hijab] people are more invited to ask me about it." Raja said that the veil had "liberated her and helped her create a strong Muslim American identity on campus."[27] Raja's use of the word "liberated" here is arresting: Raja felt "liberated," presumably by wearing hijab, from having to passively acquiescence in the face of negative stereotyping.

The same themes of affirmation of identity and community in the face of prejudice and of embracing the dress to counter false stereotypes and instruct people about Islam that emerge in these reports—including the account of the woman who stopped wearing hijab while simultaneously embarking on a new path of visibility as an activist Muslim—recur in many such reports. Emily Wax, for example, reporting for the *Washington Post* on the perceptible increase in 2002 of women wearing hijab, noted that Muslim student leaders and professors on a number of college campuses—Georgetown University, the University of Maryland, and the University of Virginia—had all noticed such an increase. Investigating why this was happening, Wax reported that Muslim women were saying that "by putting on the hijab, they are showing increased faith, their pride in being Muslims and their support for the Palestinian cause." One student said, "I wanted to show pride in being a Muslim. It gives me an identity and lets people know, here is this regular girl who does everything everyone else does and is also a Muslim. I also feel a sense of closeness to other Muslim sisters. And since I studied the religion before I made my choice, I also feel like I can explain Islam to other non-Muslims."[28]

Another woman who took up the hijab after 9/11 and who had a degree in engineering said, "I felt this is my culture and my heritage. This is something I have to represent." She continued, "I have changed so much after 9/11, and I think a lot of young Muslim women who felt we were being called terrorists really found ourselves researching our own religion and wanting to wear hijab." A third woman explained that the hijab was not about "just covering your hair." The "tragedy of 9/11 and the Palestinian cause," she said, "made me think about all the propaganda out there about Muslims. And I really thought about what my religion meant."[29]

Some of the professors Wax interviewed pointed out that in the past groups subjected to the "sting of prejudice" had reacted precisely by affirming that scorned identity. "Think of the expression 'Black is Beautiful' during the late 1960s."

Affirmations of identity and community, of pride in their religious heritage in the face of the "sting of prejudice" and of negative stereotyping, all elements threading these American Muslim responses, were similarly in evidence in responses that were articulated in Europe. Shiasta Aziz, for example, a British Muslim, explained on the BBC that while she had already been on a quest to deepen her knowledge of Islam, it was only after 9/11 and "when the Muslim community around the world and in the U.K. were under intense scrutiny by the politicians and the media" that she felt "that I wanted to be a visible Muslim." She wanted people to know, she said, "that I am a Muslim and that I am proud of my religion, heritage and culture." Wearing hijab was for her "an act of solidarity with Muslim women all around the world. Here I am an educated Muslim woman in the West, and even though I have no idea what it's like to be an Iraqi, Bosnian, Somalian, or Palestinian woman, I know that we share an identity through Islam and through the hijab." Wearing hijab had given her strength and had made her visible not only to the majority community but also to the handful of other women in hijab she saw on her way to work. "When I see another Muslim woman on the street we always smile, sometimes we nod at each other and other times we exchange greetings: Asalaam elekum Walikum Asalaam."[30]

The reasons the women offer in explanation for taking up hijab are obviously specific to the conditions in America and Europe. At the same time, these reasons and explanations are also clearly resonant in their underlying themes with those that women gave to enquiring anthropologists in the quite different context of Cairo, particularly in the 1970s and 1980s. This context was profoundly different in many ways, politically and socially, except for the fact that in those decades women in hijab made up at first only a minuscule number, and later still a small and distinctly marginal minority, as they do today in the West.

There are clear continuities in the meanings that wearers give in these quite different societies: as affirmation of identity and community, of pride in heritage, of rejection or resistance to, or even of protest against, mainstream society. In Cairo, it was resistance to mainstream society's perceived materialism and moral corruption, in America it was resistance to perceived discrimination and prejudice and to being seen as "terrorists." In these situations the hijab's capacity to signal resistance or protest against the views of the majority arises from and even depends on the fact that it is the dress of a minority. Similarly, in the West today, just as in Egypt in the 1970s and 1980s, wearing hijab makes visible to the dominant society the presence among them of a dissenting minority who are affirming their heritage and values and taking a stand in challenging the inequities and injustices of mainstream society: material and economic injustices in the case of Egypt, racial and religious in the West. Thus in both societies wearing hijab became sign and banner of a call for justice. In both contexts, wearing hijab enables this hijabi minority to recognize and silently signal support to each other in their difference.[31]

The community that Western Muslims typically affirms is implicitly and sometimes explicitly the global Muslim community. The list of Muslim women with whom Aziz in particular affirms a sense of connection and community—"Iraqi, Bosnian, Somalian, or Palestinian"—is telling too in that it is constituted of people perceived to have been the targets of violence fueled by Western prejudices against Muslims—the very prejudices that they themselves are attempting to resist by taking up hijab. On another plane, Aziz's words also bring home how successful the Islamist project had been—launched in the 1960s with Saudi funding and disseminated in the Middle East and across the world by the Muslim Brotherhood—in persuading Muslims to anchor their identity not in ethnicity or nation but in Islam alone and in the transnational Muslim community.

As some of the media accounts indicated, Palestine and solidarity with the Palestinians loomed large among the reasons given for donning the hijab. Wax reported that "support for the Palestinian cause" was one among three explanations that women typically gave in response to her enquiries as to why they had decided to wear hijab. As one respondent succinctly put it, "The tragedy of 9/11 and the Palestinian cause made me think about all the propaganda out there about Muslims."[32]

Solidarity with the Palestinians was among the meanings of wearing hijab that I encountered in interviews with hijabi women in 2002–3. One of the women I interviewed told me that she had starting wearing it "after I returned from a visit to my relatives in Palestine. I don't believe the Quran requires it," she said. "For me, wearing it is a way of affirming my community and identity, a way of saying that even as I enjoy the comforts we take for granted here and that people in Palestine totally lack, I will not forget the struggle for justice."

More surprising to me at the time had been the responses I received suggesting that the veil essentially often functioned as a way of signaling a call for justice in whatever aspect of it was in the foreground for the wearer. As I described in my introduction, one of my interviewees told me she wore it in the hope of raising people's consciousness about gender bias and injustice, while another said wearing hijab for her was a way of silently saying that Muslims, like other minorities, had the right to be treated equally. When I first received these responses, early in my research, I could not fathom by what process of transformation and reforging in the crucible of history the veil, widely viewed as the emblem of Islamic patriarchy and oppression, had come now to signal a call for gender justice (of all things) and a call for equality for minorities. It was only as I pursued my research on the veil and Islamism in Egypt and learned of the critical role of activism in the service of those in need in the Islamist movement, and the emphasis that the movement placed on social justice, that the veil's emergence as a call for justice no longer seemed so mysterious.

The meanings cited here that were offered by the hijab's wearers, whether in Cairo in the 1970s and 1980s or in European and American cities in the 21st century, are striking in that they are at once often highly specific and personal yet generically similar, often implicitly invoking a notion of justice and deliberately signaling differences from the majority. These are elements of its meanings that are notably persistent across both time and space in the post-1970s era.[33]

All of these meanings are distinctly post-1970s meanings, meanings, that is, that the veil began to have only following the rise and spread of Islamism. As this fact in itself implies, the veil's meanings are not fixed or static across histories and societies. The veil of the post-1970s era is distinctly not the veil of pre-colonial times, a veil which signaled both gender hierarchy and an understanding of society as necessarily and properly grounded in gender segregation. With colonial times and the rise of the Western world's interpretations of the world and its signs and meanings to global dominance, the veil would come to signify the Other to be subjugated and brought under the control of Europe, a project that was rhetorically cast in terms of the veil as emblem of Islam's civilizational inferiority and its "oppression of women."

In the era of struggle against colonialism and in the early post-colonial period, the veil was emphatically affirmed by the Muslim Brotherhood and other religiously grounded oppositional movements. It became an emblem of resistance to colonialism and of affirmation of indigenous values, a meaning that it retained in the initial years of the Islamic Resurgence.

Somehow with the rise of Islamism—and quite possibly because activist women and wearers of the hijab became directly involved in generating the meanings of the hijab—the hijab's meanings began to break loose from their older, historically bounded moorings. It was only after the veil had gone through that cycle of history that it would be unmoored, at least for its wearers, from its old meanings.

Today all of these meanings, old and new, are simultaneously freely in circulation in our societies, depending on which community the wearer or observer belongs to. Certainly for some it is still a powerful sign of the Otherness of Muslims, as the attacks that have occurred on women in hijab in America and elsewhere make clear. And for many it continues to be a sign of the oppression of women. For many of the hijab's wearers, on the other hand—or at least for many of its wearers who do not live in societies where the veil is required by law—the hijab does not, as their statements typically indicate, have this meaning. For its wearers, in societies where women are free to choose whether to wear it, the hijab can have any of the variety of meanings reviewed in these pages —and indeed, many, many more. For some women, surely wearing the hajib has the meaning that it very clearly had for Zainab al-Ghazali—that is, of obedience to God's commands as set forth, as they believe, in the Quran. And for others it may be an important personal expression of spiritual commitment. Noticeably, though, these are not reasons or explanations that women often offer—for whatever reason—to enquiring journalists or researchers.

Among the responses noted earlier were those indicating the veil's intended meanings of challenge to the sexism of the rules of dress in the dominant society and the meaning of the affirmation of the rights to equality of minorities in society. Clearly these are meanings that the hijab can come to have only in societies that declare themselves committed to gender equality and equality for minorities. They are not meanings that the hijab could possibly have in Cairo or Karachi or Riyadh or Tehran.

These are just some of the elements of meaning of the hijab emerging in this new cycle of history inaugurated by the rise and global spread of Islamism. There are many more ways that the issue of the hijab may be fruitfully explored: hijab as fashion statement, for instance, and hijab as an element (as all clothing is to some extent) in the construction, presentation, and performance of self and identity, judging by its title, the forthcoming *Visibly Muslim: Fashion, Politics, Faith* by Emma Tarlo promises to explore.[34]

Hate crimes and various forms of verbal and physical harassment of Muslims and Arabs and people perceived to be Muslim and Arab, as well as civil rights and discrimination offenses, have continued to rise since 9/11, as they had already begun to do in the late 1990s.

Analysts see many factors in the post-9/11 years as contributing to the rising numbers of such incidents, as well as of arson, violence, and physical and verbal attacks. Bakalian and Bozorgmehr note in their study *Backlash 9/11* that the way in which people's Muslim identity was foregrounded in media and public discourse as the one salient aspect of their identity had the effect of making that one element "trump" all other "distinguishing characteristics in the minds of the people among whom one lives." Very likely too, they argued, it would have had the "same effect on one's self. Other ways of identifying one's position in the world—occupational, national, some other—begin to pale in significance because of the sheer weight of the anti-Muslim hostility."[35]

In addition, "negative portrayals of Arabs and Muslims . . . in the mainstream media had the effect of continuously adding fuel to a raging fire," say Bakalian and Bozorgmehr, and these came to play, therefore, a "significant role in transmitting the discourse of fear and hatred." Media reports consequently, they found, were a major source of "anger and frustration" among Muslim and Arab Americans they interviewed. When these populations watch TV "or read the newspaper, they tend to find stereotypical assumptions, false interpretations and overall unfavorable representations" of Arabs and Muslims. They were generally "skeptical of journalists, who purport to report the 'truth.'" One respondent said, "If I want to know what is going on in America, I don't read the American media. I read the British media, I read the European. I read the Israeli media, for God's sake . . . the American media has become a mouthpiece for the government. Walter Cronkite the legend who is the godfather of the electronic media, said it, that it seemed like the American media rolled over and died."[36]

As the journalism professor Victor Navasky noted, post-9/11 journalism "in most mainstream media, including both reportage and analysis reflected a number of ideological assumptions." Among these was the assumption that "this was a time for rallying around the flag and that those who questioned national policy were giving aid and comfort to the enemy." Consequently, "any attempt to link the events of September 11 to America's previous role in the Middle East or elsewhere was unworthy of serious coverage or consideration and somehow smacked of apologetics."[37]

Other analysts have noted that media presentations often questioned Arab and Muslim Americans' "loyalty to the United States by questioning their stances on U.S. foreign policy." Many American Muslims now felt that their loyalties to America were automatically regarded as suspect, no matter what they said. American Muslims were also expected, observers reported, to repeatedly condemn and apologize for 9/11. And yet the "countless condemnations" of the attacks issued by mosques and Muslim American organizations typically also "received little media attention."[38]

Among the factors viewed by some as having seriously contributed to the rising incidents of prejudice and discrimination was the U.S. government's own discourse of the "war on terror," as well as such government actions as the profiling and singling out of Muslims at airports. Even more serious were the detentions, deportations, and the practice of "rendition" which occurred, as well as the raids on Muslim homes. These attitudes and actions would be reproduced, some scholars argue, in the public sphere—"in cases of harassment and hate crimes at school, work, on the bus, and in the streets."[39]

Arrests and detentions of Muslims appear to have occurred in waves, beginning immediately after 9/11, when new "anti-terrorist" legislation was introduced, including new INS regulations, followed by the Patriot Act, signed into law in October 2001. These arrests were "shrouded in mystery," wrote civil rights lawyer David Cole, with the government refusing to provide even the basic information of "how many people it had locked up." It is thought that around twelve hundred people were arrested immediately after 9/11 and more were arrested (Cole estimated a total of five thousand people) following Attorney General John Ashcroft's announcement of a "special call-in" registration program in June 2002.[40]

In June 2003 a "scathing" report was issued by the inspector general of the Department of Justice revealing that 738 foreign nationals had been detained, and that of these "not a single one was charged with any terrorist crime and virtually all were cleared of any connection with terrorism by the FBI." The report also noted that people had been arrested for the "flimsiest reasons," such as an anonymous tip that "too many Muslims worked at a convenience store, or that a Muslim neighbor kept odd hours."[41]

Many of these kinds of incidents were naturally well known to Muslim communities, and in particular to mosque-going Muslims, and they promoted anxiety and apprehension. Adding to the sense of uncertainty were reports that were circulating by 2002 of FBI agents enquiring about "mosque membership lists," and the counting of mosques. A Zogby Poll conducted in 2002 found that "66% of Muslim Americans worry about their future in this country, and 81% feel that their community is being profiled."[42]

Other incidents following from U.S. government action would also become well known as well as frightening to Muslims, and in particular to Muslims who were mosque-going and therefore regularly hearing these reports. Among these were the cases of Maher Arar and those of the Muslim homes that were raided by the FBI in Herndon, Virginia.

Arar was a Canadian citizen detained at John F. Kennedy airport in New York on his way back to Canada from a holiday in Tunisia. After holding him in solitary confinement for two weeks, the U.S. deported him not to Canada but to Syria, his country of origin. Here, Arar claimed, he was tortured and eventually released almost a year later. A Canadian Commission of enquiry confirmed Arar's story, including the claim that he had been tortured. The commission's work represented, according to the *Washington Post*, one of the first "public investigations into mistakes made as part of the United States' 'extraordinary rendition' program, which secretly spirited suspects to foreign countries for interrogation by often brutal methods."[43] The commission's findings cleared Arar of any link to terrorism, and the prime minister of Canada subsequently issued an apology and announced that Arar would receive $10.5 million in settlement for his ordeal. The U.S. throughout refused to cooperate with the Canadian Commission.[44]

U.S. government arrests and other actions directly affected, above all, Muslim men—although naturally the women and children in their families would be enormously affected. With respect to the FBI raids on homes in Virginia (in connection with the closing down of Muslim American charities on the grounds that they had links with such organizations as Hamas and Hezbollah), it was the experience of the women that would be most highlighted in accounts. One woman described men "breaking through her door and pointing a gun at her 19-year-old daughter as she tried to call 911." The two women were handcuffed for three hours as the men searched their house and took computers, passports, and bank information.[45]

Karamah, an organization of Muslim women lawyers for human rights based in Washington, D.C., together with the *Journal of Law and Religion,* organized a panel in January 2003 to look into "Reported Abuses of Muslim Civil Rights in America," including these cases in Virginia. One of those giving testimony was Meredith McEver, a clinical social worker who had counseled Muslim women who were victims of recent law enforcement raids. McEver explained that "all the women in this group exhibited symptoms of post-traumatic stress disorder" and that many "continue to cope with severe trauma and depression." Another woman, Mrs. Altomare, an employee of a school that was raided, said her experiences "brought to life the painful disruption caused to the school, her community and her own life by the raid," noting that the school at which she worked had not subsequently been charged of any crime. The school, however, "was left to cope with the damage to its infrastructure and decreased student enrollment resulting from the negative publicity."[46]

Besides government actions and perceived media bias, other factors, analysts note, contributed to the negatively charged atmosphere regarding Muslims and Arabs. These included the ongoing war in Iraq, as well as revelations involving the torture of suspects at Abu Ghraib and Guantanamo, and the images and stories that became widely known depicting the abuse and degradation of Muslims. These showed the shaming abuse and insults that Muslims and Arabs were subjected to, from physical torture to the destruction of items they held sacred, such as the text of their holy book reportedly thrown down toilets, and conveyed chilling messages as to the dehumanization of Muslims.

Other factors, analysts note, contributing to an atmosphere of permissiveness regarding expressions of hate toward Muslims included the expanded space that became available after 9/11 in American popular culture for "defamatory representation and vilification of Arabs, Arab culture and Islam."[47] Although a certain vein of hostility to Muslims and Arabs has long formed part of the fabric of European and American culture, as the ADC Report on the 9/11 backlash noted (a vein explored, as noted earlier, by Edward Said and others), hostile representations increased significantly and generally went uncensored in the wake of 9/11, often emanating from Christian evangelicals and the political Right.

Jerry Falwell, for instance, speaking on CBS's *60 Minutes* program, said that the Prophet Muhammad was a terrorist, and Franklin Graham, Billy Graham's son, called Islam "a very wicked, evil religion." And Ann Coulter, as noted earlier, also made remarks in similar vein. Paul M. Weyrich, a highly influential conservative political figure and cofounder of the Heritage Foundation (today one of the largest and best-funded conservative think tanks), coauthored a pamphlet entitled "Why Islam

Is a Threat to America and the West." The pamphlet stated, among other things, that "Islam is, quite simply, a religion of war. While there are lax Islamics [*sic*] there is no such thing as peaceful or tolerant Islam."[48]

The seemingly greater tolerance for the airing of open hostility toward Arabs and Muslims doubtless affected the experience of living in America for many Muslims. For some, however, the growing commonness of such negative stereotypes would not merely inflect and alter the ordinary and passing moments but would directly impact their lives.

Two women in particular were affected in this way—women whose cases would become well known. One of these women is Debbie Almontaser, and the other is Nadia Abu El-Haj. Their stories would be recounted by, respectively, the Pulitzer Prize–winning journalist Andrea Elliott in the *New York Times*, and the prominent journalist Jane Kramer in the *New Yorker*.

Almontaser, a Yemeni who came to the United States with her parents when she was three, had been approached to help create a new public school that would teach Arabic. The New York City Department of Education approved the school and announced that it would teach half its courses in Arabic. Soon after, Daniel Pipes (founder, as mentioned earlier, of the Middle East Forum and of Campus Watch) published an op-ed piece in the *New York Sun* disapproving of the project and describing the school as a "madrassa."[49] ("Madrassa" is the Arabic word for school. However, since 9/11 the term has often figured pejoratively in popular culture in the United States as implying institutions that inculcate the teachings of radical Islam.) A group calling itself the Stop the Madrassa Coalition was formed, and Pipes was on its advisory board. Almontaser, who had had a "longstanding reputation as a Muslim moderate," would find herself branded, in a number of "newspaper articles and Internet postings, [and] on television and talk radio," as "a 'radical,' a 'jihadist,' and a '9/11 denier.'" She was forced to resign.

This outcome, observed Elliott, was not the "result of a spontaneous outcry by concerned parents and neighborhood activists." Rather, she continued, "it was the work of a growing and organized movement to stop Muslim citizens who are seeking an expanded role in American public life." To those behind this movement, Elliott wrote, the fight against this school . . . was only an early skirmish in a broader national struggle." According to Pipes, who "helped lead the charge against Ms. Almontaser and the school," this was "a battle that's really just begun."[50]

The Abu El-Haj case related to Abu El-Haj's tenure review at Barnard College. Abu El-Haj (the American-born daughter of a Muslim Palestinian immigrant and his American "Long Island Episcopalian" wife) had published a book, *Facts on the Ground: Archeological Practice and Territorial Self-Fashioning in Israeli Society,* in 2001. The book, which examines the political role that archeology served in validating Jewish claims to the land of Israel, was very well received by academics in the field. Abu El-Haj's subsequent studies and teaching were positively evaluated by her colleagues at Barnard, and in early 2007 her tenure case was proceeding smoothly. At that point a petition entitled "Deny Nadia Abu El-Haj Tenure" was posted online. The petition described Abu El-Haj as a scholar of "inferior caliber" who denied "Israel's historical claims to the Holy Land." The petition quickly gathered signatures.[51]

Daniel Pipes was involved in this case, too, alongside those who wished to put a halt to Abu El-Haj's tenure effort, as Kramer describes in her account of the case, "The Petition: Israel, Palestine, and a Tenure Battle at Barnard." Also among those attempting to halt the case was Charles Jacobs, president of the David Project, and David Horowitz, who, Kramer wrote, regards the Left as an "enabler and abettor of the terrorist jihad." All three, along with their organizations, are described by Pipes (writes Kramer) as part of the "'general effort' to fight bias in the academy." Pipes's organization, the Middle East Forum, "does the research; Jacobs's David Project does the interventions; and Horowitz's Freedom Center does the 'left-right' issues. Their politics vary, but when it comes to defending Israel they agree."[52]

Judith Shapiro, an anthropologist who was president of Barnard at the time, issued a statement making clear that the tenure process entailed consultation with experts in the relevant field and that while she appreciated feedback she was wary of "letter writing campaigns" orchestrated by people "who may not be in the best position to judge the matter at hand."[53] Abu El-Haj was granted tenure in November 2007.

Abu El-Haj was one among a number of professors who had been targeted by a trend which, by 2001, had prompted the American Association of University Professors (AAUP) to appoint a committee to report on threats to academic freedom. Joan Wallach Scott, a professor at Princeton University's Institute for Advanced Study, had served on the AAUP's Committee A on Academic Freedom and Tenure since 1993 and she now chaired the committee.

Their report was issued in 2003. It noted that "new threats to academic freedom" were both a product of the 9/11 attacks and "of efforts by various groups on the right (many of them off campus) to impose controls on teachers and campus activities." It also noted in particular that "we have also been concerned about the impact of pro-Israeli lobbyists on pending federal legislation and on foundations. Conflating criticism of current Israeli policy with anti-Semitism, these groups have tried . . . to prevent speakers critical of Israel (among them left-wing Israelis) from coming to campuses." What was "worrisome" about such activities, the report noted, was "its inevitably chilling effect on classroom and campus expression."[54]

In subsequent articles, interviews, and statements, Scott also noted that the "assault on Middle East Studies scholars and programs," which had already been "well underway at the end of the 1990s," had made use of the 9/11 attack to identify Muslims with terrorism. The war in Iraq, she noted, had also undoubtedly contributed to the troubling situation in relation to Middle East studies programs. In the early period of the war in particular, wrote Scott, "any protests were considered not only unpatriotic, but threats to national security. Those who would offer critical perspectives were, if not silenced, intimidated." Scott mentioned Pipes's website Campus Watch (launched in 2002) and the various activities of David Horowitz, a neoconservative associated with Campus Watch and with Students for Academic Freedom, as significantly contributing to the new and "extraordinary pressures" being brought to bear on academic freedom, and that were creating a "climate of fear" leading to "caution, self-policing and a careful avoidance of controversy" on university campuses.[55] The costs of such silencing were dangerous for many, said Scott. Such groups were "equating criticism of Israel's policies with anti-Semitism and with opposition to the existence of the state of Israel." Such claims were both "irresponsible" and "dishonest," she said, and yet they seemed to "command a great deal of uncritical media attention."

Among the consequences of such actions was the erasure of the opposition to the Sharon government that existed among both Israelis and American Jews, "myself included."[56]

Horowitz would also launch the David Horowitz Freedom Center and FrontPage Magazine, as well as sponsor Islamo-Fascist Awareness Week, an event organized at many U.S. college campuses. Islamo-Fascist Awareness Week consisted of talks and teach-ins on Islamo-fascism, and it prominently featured the subject of the "oppression of women in Islam." As Horowitz explained, "Our theme will be the Oppression of Women in Islam and the threat posed by the Islamic crusade against the West."[57] Across "more than 100 college campuses," Horowitz and his supporters organized talks on "the oppression of women in Islam," as well as sit-ins targeting in particular Women's Studies departments "to protest the lack of concern for this oppression on the part of feminists."[58] Speakers at such events included Ann Coulter, Rick Santorum, Sean Hannity, and Ayaan Hirsi Ali (the Dutch Somali "ex-Muslim" author of *Caged Virgin* and *Infidel*, who was now a fellow at the conservative American Enterprise Institute).

Feminists such as Barbara Ehrenreich and Katha Pollitt would be surprised enough by this alignment of noted anti-feminists concerned purportedly about the oppression of women in Islam to cast a skeptical eye on the event. Ehrenreich, for example, noting that she had last seen Coulter on television "pining for the repeal of women's suffrage," commented that Coulter was far from the only speaker with a "credibility problem"; Senator Rick Santorum had blamed "radical feminism" for "destroying the American family."[59] Pollitt, listing the speakers, remarked that "these are people who have made careers out of attacking the mildest updates on American women's roles, whether it's working mothers, birth control or even, in the case of Coulter, the right to vote! In the zillions of words for which Horowitz is responsible . . . there is virtually no evidence of concern for the rights, liberties, opportunities or well-being of any women on earth, except for Muslims."[60]

Pollitt turned to Lila Abu Lughod of Columbia University for an explanation of this seemingly bizarre combination of anti-feminists displaying concern for the oppression of women in Islam. Abu Lughod responded that "the Islamofascist awareness people aren't at all interested in what's actually going on in the Muslim world." Rather, she continued, "they just use the woman question as an easy way to target Muslims."

Abu Lughod, a prominent scholar in the fields of anthropology and women's studies in relation to the Muslim world, is well acquainted with the history of British and French imperialism and its use of the issue of women to justify the occupation and political subjugation of Muslim countries. Similarly, she is well aware of the example of Lord Cromer, a fierce opponent (as we saw) of women's rights in England who claimed to be concerned about women's oppression in Islam, while simultaneously pursuing policies that held back Muslim women's education. For those of us familiar with the repeated use that anti-feminist imperialists have made of the issue of the "oppression" of women by men of Other societies, to justify imperial war and domination, there is nothing at all surprising about anti-feminists assuming a pose of concern for the oppression of Muslim women in the service of such ends. The replay of this ploy throughout history is all too familiar. In the preceding couple of decades feminist scholars had thoroughly examined and exposed the fraudulence of these ploys. Gayatri Spivak in particular had perfectly encapsulated the problematics of this history, coining the now famous phrase "white men saving brown women from brown men."

Yet in this post-9/11 era, as the United States launched wars on Afghanistan and Iraq, the reemergence of this theme and the extent to which these old, familiar imperial strategies were suddenly now resuscitated and replayed was startling. And even more shocking, given how in the feminist academic world these ploys had long ago been thoroughly exposed, was how persuasive they still were apparently among the wider public.

As the burka of Afghanistan became a pervasive image in the media, so also did the subject of women in Islam, and in particular the "oppression of women in Islam," emerge as a salient theme in relation to issues of war and the moral rightness of war and even in explanations of why America had been attacked. "They," as Chris Matthews said, "hated us" because "our culture teaches us to respect women."[61] Expressions of such views were widespread in the media and were voiced, as I noted earlier, even at the highest levels of the administration.

Soon after 9/11, as the United States prepared for war, the women of Afghanistan began to figure prominently in the administration's rhetoric. "The Bush Administration," as Yvonne Haddad wrote, now "launched an all out propaganda campaign to win the hearts and minds of the American public in support of its military campaign in Afghanistan. . . . The war propaganda cast American efforts to bring about regime change in Arab and Muslim nations as guided by noble and altruistic motives, aimed at bringing civilization to uncivilized Muslims and democracy to those living under autocratic regimes." This campaign now emphasized, continued Haddad, "the need to mobilize American armed forces to liberate the Muslim women of Afghanistan in particular from their degraded condition." Laura Bush, as Haddad also noted, gave a radio address describing the war against terrorism as a war also "for the rights and dignity of women." The American press, Haddad continues, "initially fell in lock step with the government propaganda effort."[62]

The media in general enthusiastically adopted and began to promote and disseminate the administration's rhetoric of the war on terror as being also a war to liberate Muslim women. For a while CNN for example repeatedly aired fictional films such as *Kandahar,* portraying the appalling brutalities to which Afghan women were subject under the Taliban, in the intervals between its newscasts on the progress of the war in Afghanistan.[63] Moreover, the idea that the war was being waged to liberate women from their oppression and their burkas often became part and parcel of the visual symbolism even of newscasts. As journalists reported that another town or village had been captured by American forces, the news would be accompanied by shots of women throwing off their burkas. Or, if they failed to do so, reporters would ask them why they had not. As the British reporter Polly Toynbee noted, for the West the burka had become the "battle flag" of the war. It was "shorthand moral justification," she wrote, for the war in Afghanistan.[64] In the United Kingdom, Cherie Blair made a speech about the oppression of the women of Afghanistan two days after Laura Bush delivered her speech.

Many academics, as I noted, were shocked at the blatant coopting of the issue of the "oppression of women in Islam" in the service of imperial wars and domination. For us it was an all too distressing instance of déjà vu all over again. Lila Abu Lughod quickly published an article addressing the matter. Citing Laura Bush's words, including her assertion that "the fight against terrorism is also a fight for the dignity of women," and referring to Cromer as well as to Spivak's famous phrase about white men saving brown women from brown men, Abu Lughod pointed out the "haunting resonances" that the theme of the oppression of women in other cultures had for anyone familiar with colonial history.

She noted also that she had been called by a reporter from PBS's *Newshour with Jim Lehrer* in connection with Laura Bush's address and asked such questions as "Do Muslim women believe 'x'? Are Muslim women 'y'? Does Islam allow 'z'?" Why, Abu Lughod asked, was the media focused on asking questions about Islam while ignoring what was crucial to what Afghan women were suffering: the "history of the development of repressive regimes in the region and the U.S. role in this history." Instead of "political and historical explanations," wrote Abu Lughod, "experts were being asked to give religious-cultural ones. Instead of questions that might lead to the exploration of global interconnections, we were offered ones that worked to artificially divide the world into separate spheres—recreating an imaginative geography of West versus East, us versus Muslims, cultures where First Ladies give speeches versus others where women shuffle around in burqas."[65]

Besides becoming a common topic in the media and in the national political conversation, "women's oppression in Islam" became a theme that was taken up in a raft of books that quickly became best sellers. These books were almost all, as Saba Mahmood, who wrote an essay analyzing them in some detail, has pointed out, in the genre of "native testimonials": autobiographical works in which the authors, all women, attested to their personal sufferings under Islam.[66]

The first of these to appear was Norma Khouri's *Forbidden Love: A Harrowing Story of Love and Revenge in Jordan* (2002). This book, which became a best seller, told the purportedly "true" story of the author's life in Jordan and her eye-witness account of the murder, in an "honor-crime," of her best friend by her Muslim father for her liaison with a Christian man. Soon, however, an investigative reporter revealed that Khouri had not lived in Jordan since she was three and that a Jordanian women's organization committed to fighting honor crimes had notified the publisher of numerous errors in the book. The publishers withdrew the book, and, in the debate that ensued over why publishers did not vet purportedly nonfiction books more carefully, one publishing executive pointed out that in the post-9/11 era there had been a strong demand for nonfiction books that "perpetuate negative stereotypes about Islamic men."[67]

Other books in this genre that Mahmood analyzes include Azar Nafisi's *Reading Lolita in Tehran,* Carmen bin Laden's *My Life in Saudi Arabia,* Irshad Manji's *Trouble with Islam,* and Ayaan Hirsi Ali's *Caged Virgin* and *Infidel.* All were among the "top-selling nonfiction books of the season" in America and Europe, notes Mahmood.[68] Nearly all, too, have been scathingly criticized by academics working in the field of Islam, including feminist academics such as Mahmood. Among the first and fiercest such critical reviews to appear was Hamid Dabashi's critique of *Reading Lolita in Tehran* in his article "Native Informers and the Making of the American Empire." Noting that a spate of such books had flooded the market since the commencement of the U.S. war on terrorism and as the U.S. had entered its "most belligerent period in recent . . . history," Dabashi observed that *Reading Lolita in Tehran* was notable for its "unfailing hatred for everything Iranian." Nafisi's book, Dabashi maintained, drew on "legitimate concerns about the plight of Muslim women" but deployed these concerns in the service of "U.S. ideological . . . global warmongering." In Nafisi's depiction, noted Dabashi, Islam was represented as "vile, violent and above all abusive of women—and thus fighting against Islamic terrorism, *ipso facto,* is also to save Muslim women from the evil of their men."[69]

Dabashi makes reference in his article to Nafisi's strong connections with well-known neoconservatives, and in her essay Mahmood systematically explores the neoconservative connections and politics of all of the writers mentioned above. Norma Khouri, for example, Mahmood notes, received support "from the highest offices in the Bush administration," including from Richard Cheney and his daughter Elizabeth. Nafisi, Mahmood asserts, had "deep links with leading neoconservative think tanks" and received endorsement from Bernard Lewis, the "Orientalist ideologue," writes Mahmood, whose views inspired the "current

U.S. imperial adventure in the Middle East." Furthermore, Mahmood observes, Nafisi's "support for the Bush agenda of regime change is well-known."[70]

Mahmood also points out similar connections that Irshad Manji and Ayaan Hirsi Ali have with neoconservatives and their agendas. Both writers, writes Mahmood, were supporters of the invasions of Afghanistan and Iraq and enjoyed the support of neoconservatives. Manji, for example, received high praise from Daniel Pipes, with whom she appeared at Israeli fundraising events. Hirsi Ali enjoyed the support of the right-wing People's Party in Holland. When the Dutch immigration services threatened to repeal her citizenship when it was discovered that she had fabricated her story of flight from the threat of an oppressive Muslim marriage in her immigration application, she was immediately offered a fellowship in the United States at the conservative think tank American Enterprise Institute. Hirsi Ali also was mentioned as appearing, as we saw earlier, alongside other luminaries such as Ann Coulter and Rick Santorum at the Islamo-Fascist Awareness Week organized by David Horowitz. Both Manji's and Hirsi Ali's works, as Mahmood and others have noted, are contemptuous and abusive of Muslims. Filled with "historical errors and willful inaccuracies about Islam," they generally depict Muslims as "unparalleled" in their "barbarity and misogyny."[71]

Such writers are invaluable to the neoconservatives, Mahmood argues, because they can deliver the message of women's oppression in Islam in "authentic Muslim women's voice," a message that fosters feelings of hostility toward Islam and Muslim men under the guise of concern for Muslim women, feelings that in turn translate into support for war in Muslim countries as legitimate and morally justified. Thus, argues Mahmood, while anti-Muslim feelings in Europe and America after 9/11 were "partly responsible" for the popularity of such books, the "arguments of these authors read like a blueprint for the neoconservative agenda for regime change in the Middle East." And, she maintains, "they would never have been able to achieve this success without the formidable support of the conservative political industry in Europe and the United States."[72]

Clearly Dabashi and Mahmood and others have a point that while the "oppression of women in Islam" theme appears to be centered on concern for Muslim women, its implicit message is that of reinforcing anti-Islamic stereotypes, and thus such works are useful in helping to "manufacture consent" in justifying attack on Muslim-majority countries. As Mahmood notes throughout her essay, stories in native voice recounting the personal sufferings of Muslim women can deliver this message particularly effectively. They can reach a far wider audience than, for example, David Horowitz or even Ann Coulter might.

The critiques of such writers as Dabashi and Mahmood bring out the important political dimensions which the theme of the "oppression of women in Islam" has in the West in our time. Similarly, these critiques also bring out how the tradition inaugurated by Cromer stretches in fact all the way from Cromer to Horowitz. Cromer was a well-known antifeminist in relation to English women, yet he presented himself as someone concerned about Islamic oppression of women.

Mahmood's findings also suggest that the tradition of the rearticulation in native voice of the imperialist theses about the inferiority of Islam, an inferiority showcased by Islam's "oppression" of women, a tradition that first clearly emerged in Amin's work, is also a tradition that continues to thrive.

Amin was by no means a feminist according to my understanding of feminism.[73] A fervent and uncritical admirer of European cultures and most particularly of European man, his book was to a large extent a tirade against the "backwardness" of Muslims. And it was also though an impassioned plea for change and improvement in Muslim society—a plea that was essentially a plea for the adoption of the ways of Europe. This is not to say that admiration of Europe and the West is not in many ways entirely warranted and that there are many Western institutions that certainly would be worthy of being adapted and adopted by others. But there is also much that is invaluable about the cultural and intellectual heritages and ways of living of other societies, including Muslim-majority societies.

Was Amin deliberately and consciously lending support through his work to the imperialist agenda of the day—or did he, rather, consider himself a reformer working, writing, and thinking out of a passion to improve the condition of Egypt and of his fellow Egyptians? I believe that despite the evident contempt in his work for Egyptians, and his lavish and uncritical admiration for all things European, including European-style patriarchy, Amin nevertheless considered himself to be a profeminist reformer. By the same token, it would be reasonable for us not to make any assumptions as to authorial intentions of contemporary writers. Rather, we should assume authorial intentions to be in the end inscrutable—even as, at the same time, we accept Mahmood's and Dabashi's analyses as enormously illuminating as to the conditions and forces, political and otherwise, that are at work in our times, affecting the reception of books such as those they discuss.

For indeed this phenomenon that Dabashi and Mahmood analyze —of the commercial success of works that apparently mobilize American readers' sympathies on behalf of Muslim women in the very period when the United States was engaging in ways unprecedented in its history in wars in Muslim-majority countries—is a phenomenon that distinctly calls for analysis and explanation. And it is unquestionably a phenomenon whose dynamics and implications need to be understood well beyond the academy.

For, as Mahmood pointed out, it was quite remarkable that in the midst of the searing destruction under way in Afghanistan and Iraq, destruction that brought enormous loss of life for women and children, such losses apparently "failed to arouse the same furor among most Euro-Americans" as did the "individualized accounts of women's suffering under Islam's tutelage."[74] Similarly, Abu Lughod asks in "The Active Social Life of 'Muslim Women's Rights'"—an essay written, as Abu Lughod notes, in the context of "violence against (Muslim) women inflicted in war and by militaries, not just in Afghanistan and Iraq, but also in Palestine, as in the Israeli attack on Gaza that was launched in December 2008"—"Where is the global feminist campaign against killing such significant numbers of (mostly) Muslim women? Or maiming them, traumatizing them, killing their children, sisters, mothers, husbands, fathers and brothers."[75]

For many of us, particularly those who have worked for years on issues of women's rights in Islam and in Muslim societies, these glaring disparities in our times between the notion of purported concern for the sufferings of Muslim women commonplace in our public conversation and the simultaneous seeming indifference and unconcern among many Americans and Europeans to the mounting death counts, maiming, and trauma suffered by mostly Muslim women and children was a sobering experience. Mahmood points out how the "discourses of feminism and democracy have been hijacked to serve an imperial project," then goes on to warn that "unless feminists rethink their complicity in this project . . . feminism runs the risk of becoming more of a handmaiden of empire in our age than a trenchant critic of the Euro-American will to power."[76]

Abu Lughod goes on to propose the fundamental rethinking of the very subject of "women in Islam" and of "Muslim Women's Rights" in light of the way in which the topic is being invoked and manipulated today in the service of political ends that, in reality, have nothing to do with improving Muslim women's rights or living conditions and that, indeed, may actually kill, maim, and traumatize many Muslim women.

I, too, have found myself wondering if the subject of the "oppression of women in Islam"—coming to us charged and loaded with the legacies of Cromer and his ilk, legacies that are capable evidently of taking on renewed life and force in the West in fraught political times in relation to Islam—is any longer a useful or even valid topic. Already in the late 1990s and thus even before our recent wars the palpably shifting climate in the West as regards Muslims and particularly Muslim minorities was giving both Aisha and myself pause as regards our work on women and Islam—as I described in the Introduction. Of course I continue to believe (as Abu Lughod and others evidently do too) that the rights and conditions of women in Muslim-majority societies often are acutely in need of improvement, as indeed they are in many other societies. But the question now is how we address such issues while not allowing our work and concerns to aid and abet imperialist projects, including war projects that mete out death and trauma to Muslim women under the guise and to the accompaniment of a rhetoric of saving them.

Over the course of this book I have described how and why the veiling revolution occurred, and what the appeal, methods, and driving force of the Islamist movement were, and then, also, as I follow in these chapters the impact of 9/11 on Muslim women in America and the ways in which Islamism is evolving in this country with respect to women, it is consistently clear that the subject of Muslim women, whether in relation to the veil or anything else, and whether in relation to Egypt and the Middle East or Europe and America, is inextricably entangled with the key political and social issues affecting society as a whole. Dress in Egypt was a political as well as a religious issue in the dynamics of power between the minority and the majority (a minority which in that instance became the majority), just as it is today in Europe and America an issue at times of religion and at others of attempts to negotiate power, to challenge, and to engage in conversation with the larger society, from the position of a minority and around issues in particular of social justice.

It would be impossible to understand the underlying dynamics of the veiling movement of the last four decades without reviewing the history of the Islamist movement and the political crises and conditions that gave rise to it—and how these affected men as well as women in society. There is no extricating the story of Muslim women from this larger story: to leave men and the broad political situation out of the picture would leave us with a history so full of gaps and silences that it would be quite unintelligible. This is the case with regard to trends affecting Muslim women in America: these trends also are inextricably part of the general and turbulent conditions and politics of our times affecting the larger society as well as specifically impacting Muslim American men as well as women in their diversity. Any attempt to follow out these trends too would make little sense if these general conditions were left out of the story.

This also means that today there is no intelligible overall subject of "women in Islam," any more than there is an intelligible overall subject of "women in Christianity" that might usefully describe or account for the conditions of Christian women in sub-Saharan Africa, Russia, Korea, South America, and the United States. Moreover, against the backdrop of the events and analyses reviewed here, it is evident that the very subject, in particular, of the "oppression of women in Islam" —the topic invoked now by Horowitz, Coulter, and others as it once was by Cromer—is above all a political construct conjured into being to serve particular political ends. As in British imperial days, the subject remains fraught and charged with the political agendas of war and domination.

The reality is that the conditions of Muslim women and what they are "oppressed" by varies enormously depending on the political conditions in specific moments of time in different countries—from France and Germany to America, Turkey, Iraq, Afghanistan, Saudi Arabia, Egypt, Nigeria, Iran, and many more. In each of these countries the nature and source of Muslim women's "oppression"—among them the forces in their variety that (to borrow Abu Lughod's words) are killing, traumatizing, and maiming them and their children—differ vastly from moment to moment. Overall it seems that it would be fair to say that the subjects of "women in Islam" and in particular of the "oppression of women in Islam" exist today essentially only as relics of an imperial past. They are relics that today are grounded in no contemporary reality, and their substance seems to be now entirely chimerical, rhetorical, and political.

These same general conditions, certainly causing anxiety and turmoil for many Muslim Americans, most particularly for those connected with mosque communities and with American Muslim organizations, would also have the effect of spurring the emergence of an unprecedented level of activism among American Muslim women around issues of Islam, women, and gender. I describe this decade of American Muslim women's activism in my final chapter, in which I assess the broad direction in which Islamism appears to be heading today as regards women and in the context of America's dynamic democracy.

But first, in the following chapter, I describe the impact that these post-9/11 events and circumstances had on the annual conventions of Muslim American organizations, and in particular on ISNA's conventions, as I continued to attend and observe these through the ensuing years. This chapter begins with a description of the broad themes and concerns emerging at these events, the types of speeches that were delivered there, and the kinds of overall conversations that were pursued. I then focus on changes in issues relating to women and gender that emerged at ISNA's conventions throughout those years, undoubtedly in response, in part, to the enormous attention that the "oppression of women in Islam" theme was getting in the media and broader public conversation in America. I conclude that chapter by conveying a general sense of women's roles and activism at ISNA, and with sketches of some of ISNA's most notable women.

· 10 ·

ISNA and the Women of ISNA

Almost every single one of the Muslim American conventions I attended in 2002 featured Zayed Yasin, a fresh-minted Harvard graduate, as one of its speakers. Although I did not know Yasin personally, he was familiar to me by name because of the fracas that had erupted around him at Harvard and that was quickly picked up by the national media, in connection with a speech he was due to deliver at the commencement events of June 2002. Yasin's proposed speech, in which he reflected on the tensions of being both American and Muslim, had been chosen from among the many entries received by the committee charged with selecting a graduating senior for the coveted honor of delivering the Senior English Address.[1]

Yasin's selection had been uncontroversial until the title of his speech, "My American Jihad," was announced. By Harvard tradition the actual speech is not made public until the day of the address, but on the basis of the title some people raised strenuous objections. They felt that a speech with such a title must undoubtedly be unpatriotic, and they began circulating a petition requesting the Harvard administration to release the text of the speech before commencement. Among those objecting was a Harvard professor who declared that the "speech was obviously an assault . . . primarily an assault on Jews, secondarily an assault on America."[2]

The controversy was picked up by the media, including the *New York Times,* and Yasin was interviewed on many of the major news channels. Chris Matthews on MSNBC described Yasin as a "supporter of terrorism" who had thrown a fundraiser for Hamas. In a prior year, in fact, Yasin, as president of the Islamic Society of Harvard, had thrown a fundraiser for the benefit of the Holy Land Foundation, a charity whose work in the service of refugees he had observed during a summer spent working for a health organization in the Balkans. After the fundraiser the Holy Land Foundation was charged with ties to Hamas and its assets frozen; the Harvard Islamic Society consequently donated the funds it had raised to the Red Crescent instead, an international organization affiliated with the Red Cross. The son of a Pakistani father and an Irish Catholic mother, Yasin had also been known during his presidency of the Islamic Society for his activism in promoting interfaith connections between the Islamic Society and Hillel, the Jewish Student Association, and the Catholic Students' Association.[3]

As commencement approached, Yasin received hate mail and death threats. Students opposed to his speech decided to distribute red, white, and blue ribbons that people could wear to show "that they were patriots and Yasin was not." Notably, Harvard Students for Israel dissociated themselves from this protest. Lawrence Summers, however, then president of Harvard, reportedly had been none too pleased with Yasin's selection for the commencement speech.[4]

Yasin did deliver his speech, and it proved to be entirely uncontroversial. Maintaining that the word "jihad" had been "corrupted and misinterpreted" by both Muslims and non-Muslims, Yasin said that the word's true meaning was the "determination to do right, to do justice even against your own interests." Both the Quran and the American Constitution, Yasin asserted, required of him the same thing: "As a Muslim and as an American I am commanded to stand up for the protection of life and liberty, to serve the poor and the weak, to celebrate the diversity of humankind."[5] Consequently, he concluded, there was no contradiction for him in being both Muslim and American. The speech was overwhelmingly well received—provoking, according to the *Crimson,* "loud applause in the audience—and even a partial standing ovation."[6]

Yasin's speech is interesting for how it seamlessly braids core American themes and values with those of Islam and indeed more specifically those of Islamism. The American notions of the protection of life and liberty for example are blended with the idea of the obligation to "serve the poor and the weak" that is specific to Islamism. For, as we saw earlier, it was Islamism rather than old-style Islam (with its focus on personal ethics rather than activism and service, and on personal rather than publicly enacted piety) that considered activism in the service of the poor and in pursuit of social justice to be integral to being Muslim. Similarly, drawing on Quranic language, Yasin brings together American ideals of racial, ethnic, and religious equality with Islamic teachings about honoring human diversity—as if indeed these elements in the two traditions quite naturally and self-evidently represented different ways of embodying the same ideals.

The particular Quranic verse (49:12) from which Yasin takes his language of honoring diversity is a verse that is very popular with Muslim American organizations. The verse reads, "O mankind! We created you from a single (pair) of a male and a female, and made you into nations and tribes that you may know one another. Verily the most honored of you in the sight of Allah is (he who is) the most righteous of you. And Allah has full knowledge and is well acquainted [with all things]." In fact this verse had been the theme of the preceding year's ISNA convention, entitled "Strength Through Diversity." Obviously for American Muslims, a minority themselves, the principle of honoring diversity is a very important one. In addition, internal Muslim diversity was emerging as an important issue for Muslim organizations to deal with and address in the context of America, where a greater variety of Muslim schools and sects coexists today than anywhere else on earth.

The easy blending of American and Islamist ideals of activism and ethical commitments that figure in Yasin's speech is in fact a common feature of the speeches and writings of American Muslims of Yasin's generation.

Doubtless, though, it was the attention Yasin received in the national media after the announcement merely of his title—before a single word of his speech was known—that had led to his being such a sought-after speaker at American Muslim conventions that year. In a time when even non-Muslims were liable to incur the charge of being unpatriotic should they criticize the administration's policies with regard to the "war on terror," whether abroad or at home, Yasin's case perfectly illustrated—as Yasin found himself the target of threats, anger, attempts to silence him in the name of patriotism—the difficulties with which even attempting to speak as an American Muslim were fraught.

The difficulties of speaking freely and forthrightly in these tense times, particularly for Muslims, were surely preoccupying issues for the convention organizers. Conventions, after all, are events at which speech constitutes the very heart of the proceedings. In addition, in this trying period a key responsibility for organizations was obviously that of providing members with information and analyses that accurately addressed and reflected American Muslim concerns and interests.

As I attended one convention after another, I noticed patterns and similarities in the speeches. These patterns, becoming particularly noticeable in 2002, would persist throughout the years that I continued to attend such conventions—that is, through 2007.

All of the conventions (as of 2002) typically featured speakers of both Muslim and non-Muslim background who presented information on what precisely was happening to Muslims in America in these times. For instance, panelists gave accounts of how many people had been arrested or deported, or noted that these figures had not as yet been disclosed and thus were uncertain. Other speakers, and sometimes entire panels, focused on describing the closure of Muslim charities and the raids on Muslim homes. They also discussed the impact of such events for Muslims on the religious requirement of donating funds to charity.

Another common feature and sign of the times at all the conventions that year was the passing out of fliers, along with the periodic announcements, offering pro bono legal services for people who, as a result of the 9/11 backlash, found themselves in need of legal assistance on "immigration issues and other matters." Such details brought home—as did the anxious looks on many people's faces at all of those conventions—that it was this segment of the Muslim American population most particularly (the people who typically attended mosques and Muslim American conventions) who, after 9/11, were coming under special scrutiny and feeling vulnerable to government suspicion. It would be this group who would feel most fearful and insecure at news of arrests and deportations of Muslims.

Invariably there would also be a U.S. government representative as speaker or publicly acknowledged visitor to the convention. Sometimes these were well-known figures—Robert S. Mueller III, for example, director at the time of the FBI, was the keynote speaker at one of these conventions in 2002, and in 2005, Karen Hughes, deputy Secretary of State at the time, came to the ISNA Convention to meet with the organization's leaders, as well as with other groups within ISNA, including "young people."[7] The importance of cooperating with government agencies in every way in matters of security was naturally a message that, in 2002 and subsequently, was repeatedly emphasized at all of the conventions—both by officials of the organization and by U.S. government speakers. The overt presence of government officials also demonstrated and made formally visible the organization's collaborative stance in relation to U.S. government agencies.

The speeches given by Muslims were generally distinct in themes and content from those delivered by non-Muslims. Muslims typically spoke more cautiously and less critically with respect to any American government action. The following synopsis and overview of some examples of such speeches conveys a sense of the general tenor and flavor of these conventions and their typical conversations.

*

Muslim Convention Speakers

"America, our home."[8]

> Firstly what happens to America happens to us. [Applause]
>
> Second, with regard to safety and security: we should support all efforts for this. No support of criminal behavior. We can have grievances and differences of opinion but criminal behavior is not to be tolerated.
>
> Third, with regard to civil rights: guilt by association, racial profiling, that is not acceptable.
>
> Fourthly, our duty is to inform about our faith. We must clearly say what is wrong. If a Muslim commits wrong we must say it is wrong.

> Fifth: American foreign policy must be based on justice. As Martin Luther King said, "Injustice in any place is a threat to justice in every place." This means that Muslims need to be politically active. [Applause]
>
> —Muzammil Siddiqui, former president of ISNA, 1997–2001, from his talk at the ICNA-MAS Annual Convention, July 5–7, 2002 (author's notes)

The phrase "America, our home" or some variant thereof was a recurrent phrase at all the conventions, as were statements such as "what happens to America happens to us." While such statements certainly emphasized a point that was rhetorically important, they were obviously also simply statements of fact.

Other predictably common and recurring themes among Muslim American speakers were expressions of the importance of showing "zero-tolerance for the fanatics and bigots among us," and of fully cooperating with the forces of law and order, remarks which were typically accompanied by forceful condemnations of terrorism. Other speeches reflected a new awareness of the extent to which American Muslims were indeed now American as well Muslim—even more fully perhaps than they had realized. As one speaker noted, it was quite clear now, in these difficult post-9/11 times, that Muslims were here to stay. There are no long lines, he pointed out (reiterating a point made by an earlier speaker), forming at airline counters of Muslim immigrants eager to return home. September 11 in fact had exploded the myth of return: "If you want to know if you're going home or not," he said, "just listen to the accent of your kids, then you'll know that you're not going anywhere." Whatever they had imagined when they came, the majority of immigrants now understood, he said, that America was in fact "home."[9]

Muslim Americans often represented their hopes and experiences and even their criticisms as integrally part of the American experience and of the ongoing *American* story. One speaker, for example, began by declaring that terrorism and the killing of innocent civilians was absolutely unacceptable: "no matter how just your cause," he stressed, "including the sufferings of the Palestinians." American Muslims had the privilege of being able to participate in the public debates and conversations under way in America, he continued, and they were in position to convey the concerns of Muslims to policy-makers. It was their responsibility to take up this task and in this way they would become bridge builders. "However imperfect this nation is," he said, "remember it is a nation built on certain ideals." No matter how hypocritical American foreign policy might be, the fact remains that America is built on a moral foundation. "The vision of Americans and that Americans have of themselves" is as a moral nation, he said. "The fact is, America would be nothing without its moral perspective." The Muslim community, he continued, "must contribute towards strengthening the moral foundation of this nation."[10]

Another speaker, touching in part on these same themes, noted that America was a "very young country." "Yesterday," he said—speaking on July 5, 2002—"we had the 4th of July. America will be a great force in world history if Muslims and other forces work together to make sure that America does not go the way of other civilizations. Every Muslim owes it to himself that the prophetic message is loud and clear in this country so that America will not be remembered in history as a technological giant but a moral pygmy. You have the responsibility," he concluded.[11] Another speaker, having begun his talk by labeling terrorism as intolerable criminal behavior and emphasizing the importance of an American foreign policy that was based on justice, brought home his point by invoking the words and leadership of the Reverend Martin Luther King, Jr.—thus invoking not the Islamist but the American tradition of struggle in the cause of justice.

Martin Luther King was a name frequently invoked at these post-9/11 conferences, as was the African-American experience and struggle generally. Often African Americans were referred to as models of resolve and activism for immigrant Muslim Americans. African American Muslims and non-Muslims were now also commonly featured speakers at the conventions. There had always been some African American presence among the speakers at ISNA conventions, even before 9/11, but after that date the presence of African American voices at ISNA, in particular Muslim voices, seemed to become entirely routine. When I was attending ISNA conventions from 1999 to 2001, some African American Muslims seemed to be regular speakers, among them Siraj Wahhaj, imam of al-Taqwa Mosque in New York and the first Muslim to offer an opening prayer at the U.S. House of Representatives (in 1991); Imam Zayid Shakir, scholar in residence and lecturer at Zaytuna Institute; and Sherman Jackson, professor of Islamic studies at the University of Michigan. On occasion, Warith D. Mohammed himself, who was on the ISNA board, also made an appearance.

Presenting their own narratives, American-born Caucasian as well as African American Muslims unambiguously foregrounded how their stories and perspectives as Muslims were integrally part of the story or stories of North America in a variety of ways. One of the more arresting speeches I heard embodying this perspective was that presented by Ingrid Mattson who was at the time—2002—the vice president of ISNA. Mattson, who was a Canadian Caucasian convert to Islam, took up the subject of terrorism and the importance of speaking out against terrorism (as many Muslim speakers clearly felt called upon to do) by telling the story of an African American slave who had fled slavery on the underground railroad and made his way to Canada. Asked how he had found the courage to undertake so desperate a journey, he had replied, Mattson recounted, that on one occasion, after a brutal beating by his master, he had found himself dreaming of burning down the master's house. The realization that in doing so he would also kill the master's wife and children had ceased to matter to him, he said. He simply could not get the thought out of his head. He knew then, said Mattson, that he would have to flee no matter how dangerous the journey and whatever the cost—he would have to leave in order to save his own soul.[12]

Besides implicitly underscoring the fact that America had not always lived up to its democratic ideals, Mattson's narrative obviously further contributed to the broad framing narrative that such stories were collectively bringing into being at these conferences: of American and Canadian Muslims as intrinsically and inextricably American and Canadian—not foreigners and aliens who embodied hostile, un-American perspectives. Mattson's narrative and the narratives of other Muslim speakers underscored how Muslim Americans, in their present struggles against discrimination, could find inspiration in Americans who had struggled under similar and indeed sometimes far worse conditions. For Muslim Americans now, this narrative emphasized, the struggle against discrimination on their own behalf was also a struggle to make America itself a better place, the society that it aspired and proclaimed itself to be.

Non-Muslim American Convention Speakers

> Every group and every generation must win liberty anew. There is no guarantee that liberty will be here if we don't fight for it.
>
> —Marcy Kaptur, congresswoman for Ohio, speaking at ISNA 2007[13]

Whether by strategy or coincidence, Muslim American organizations in 2002 seemed to have had more non-Muslim speakers at their conventions than they had had previously. Certainly there had been non-Muslim speakers at the ISNA conventions that I had attended prior to 9/11. I had heard Paul Findley for example, the former U.S. senator, speak against the sanctions in Iraq at one such convention in the late 1990s. But as of 2002 and through the ensuing years, non-Muslim speakers seemed distinctly more in evidence, and they were often featured on plenary sessions. In addition, in the case of one of these conventions, at least —that of ICNA—non-Muslim women speakers were, reportedly, featured for the very first time in 2002.[14]

Among the non-Muslims speakers at the 2002 conventions, for example, were Ralph Nader, who was running for U.S. president that year as the Green Party candidate. Others included James Zogby, founder of the Arab American Institute and senior analyst at the polling firm Zogby International; Hilary Shelton, vice president of the NAACP; David Bonior, congressman from Michigan and chief minority whip for the Democratic Party; Karen Armstrong, well-known writer on religion; Grayland Hagler, an African American preacher and activist; the Reverend Welton Gaddy, president of the Interfaith Alliance; Yvonne Haddad, professor and scholar of Islam in America at Georgetown University; and Stanley Cohen, a civil rights lawyer.[15]

As a rule, non-Muslim speakers were far more outspoken in their criticisms of the administration than were Muslim speakers. Nader, for example, was forthrightly critical of the administration's actions in relation to civil liberties, and he urged Muslims to take a stand against these erosions in civil rights and to "speak out against injustices." Haddad noted in her talk that Islam was a "religion of justice" and that Muslims did not necessarily "agree with a lot of the American government's foreign policy." Muslims, she said, were demanding justice and this was "their right as American citizens." But there had been an effort by some, said Haddad, "to silence Muslims and to say that if you're not supporting American foreign policy you're becoming un-American. And that's not acceptable, because the United States has freedom of speech and provides constitutional guarantees to disagree with American foreign policy."[16]

African American speakers were often among the most outspoken in their criticisms of the administration and of American history. Hagler, for example, a Christian preacher and activist, addressed the issue of terrorism by speaking about the activities of the Ku Klux Klan when he was growing up. "I don't feel safe in America," he said. "Never did. I am scared when I see a police car in the mirror, and what they're going to do to me." And he was afraid now, he went on, of what the consequences of 9/11 would be in terms of erosions of civil liberties. "I am an African American Christian," he said. "When we look around our families, we African Americans," he continued, "we see that they're Christian and Muslim." (Applause) "We are one," he went on. "I instruct deacons to bow down when they visit a Muslim mosque. Your struggle is my struggle." Hagler was similarly outspoken in his criticism of the administration's pro-Israeli policies and its neglect of the Palestinians.

The presence of non-Muslim speakers, including those who were prominent in their fields, grew more pronounced over the ensuing years. The list of non-Muslim speakers at ISNA alone over the following years, for example, included Amy Goodman of Democracy Now; David Cole, civil rights lawyer and author of *Enemy Aliens;* Robert Fisk, the well-known British journalist and author of *The Great War for Civilization;* the Reverend Richard Killmer, executive chair of the Religious Campaign Against Torture; and Jeanne Herrick-Stare, a Quaker who was also part of the Campaign Against Torture and lobbied on behalf of the Friends Committee against the extension of the Patriot Act.[17]

Howard Dean, former chair of the Democratic Party, also spoke at ISNA. Dean emphasized that "there is nothing more American and nothing more patriotic than speaking out." It was important, he said, to keep leadership accountable. "We need to restore American moral leadership in the world." Congresswoman Marcy Kaptur also spoke at ISNA, explaining that as a Polish American she deeply identified with the struggles of Muslim Americans. "Every group and every generation," she told the audience, "must win liberty anew." Jesse Jackson recalled how he had been jailed in 1960 for trying to use a public library. "In 1963, if you came from Texas to Florida you could not use a public toilet and could not buy ice cream." Today he said, Muslims were the targets of Islamophobia, and immigrants, including Mexicans, as well as blacks were the targets of racism. Blacks, Latinos, Muslims, gays—"We cannot survive alone," he said. "We need each other to survive."[18]

Another well-known American politician who spoke at ISNA was Keith Ellison, who is Muslim. Ellison spoke of the power of telling one's own story, and he urged Muslims to tell their stories as Muslim Americans. He also referred to the problems that the proposed Arabic-language school in New York had encountered (the school that Almontaser had been nominated to head), declaring that "we need more people to learn Arabic" and deploring what was happening to the proposed school.

Other prominent speakers included Rabbi Eric Yoffie, president of the Union of Reform Judaism and leader of more than a million American Jews. He addressed one of the plenary sessions. "How did it happen," he said, "that when a Muslim congressman takes his oath of office while holding the Koran, Dennis Prager suggests that the congressman is more dangerous to America than the terrorists of 9/11?" Even more important, he continued, "How did it happen that law-abiding Muslims in this country can find themselves condemned for dual loyalty and blamed for the crimes of the terrorists they abhor?" The time had come, Yoffie went on, "for Americans to learn how far removed Islam is from the perverse distortions of the terrorists who too often dominate the media, subverting Islam's image by professing to speak in its name. . . . The time has come to stand up to the opportunists in our midst—the media figures, religious leaders, and politicians who demonize Muslims and bash Islam, exploiting the fears of their fellow citizens for their own

purposes." Yoffie said, "I know that our sacred texts, including the Hebrew Bible, are filled with contradictory propositions, and these include passages that appear to promote violence and thus offend our ethical sensibilities. Such texts are to be found in all religions, including Christianity and Islam. The overwhelming majority of Jews reject violence by interpreting these texts in a constructive way . . . my Christian and Muslim friends tell me that precisely the same dynamic operates in their traditions. It is therefore," he concluded, "our collective task to strengthen and inspire one another as we fight the fanatics and work to promote the values of justice and love that are common to both our faiths."[19]

Another prominent speaker was Rabbi Arthur Waskow, a leading figure in the Jewish Renewal movement. Rabbi Waskow emphasized, as he would again in an essay he published a few weeks later, that it was important that "we brighten the threads of peace and justice and healing in *all* our traditions, while bleaching toward calm and caring the fiery blood-red threads of violence in all of them." Waskow's essay, in which he reflected warmly on his participation at the ISNA Convention, appeared in response to David Horowitz's launching of his Islamo-Fascist Awareness Week. Waskow characterized the Horowitz event as a "slap in the face of the Living God we claim to celebrate." Islamo-Fascist Awareness Week was also denounced by many interfaith groups.[20]

The presence over the years at ISNA conventions of such well-known figures as Howard Dean, Jesse Jackson, Ralph Nader, Marcy Kaptur, Amy Goodman, Rabbis Yoffie and Waskow, along with other non-Muslim activists, lawyers, academics, and public figures—David Cole, Richard Killmer, Jeanne Herrick-Stare, and many more—tremendously enriched the conversations under way at these conventions.

Their very presence there and the causes and concerns that many spoke out on—the Patriot Act, Abu Ghraib, Guantanamo, the war in Iraq, issues of torture and of law and civil rights, the role of the media—conveyed a clear message of support and solidarity with Muslim Americans and with their perspectives and concerns regarding the events of the day. These were *American* issues, their presence and words conveyed, and not just Muslim American ones.

The voices and perspectives of such people, whose concerns were strongly in resonance with and complemented each other, fostered an atmosphere at ISNA in which the trials and tribulations of Muslim Americans could be understood as representing not merely hardships to be endured but rather moments of extraordinary opportunity. Muslim Americans now had the chance to stand at the forefront of the struggle for equal rights, the struggle that other Americans had taken up before them and whose efforts had been vital to the country's progress toward a society of justice for all. Fighting for justice was the quintessential and defining American experience: Muslim Americans now had the opportunity, in taking up this struggle, to become fully and truly American.

Currents of Change

THE IMPACT OF THE "OPPRESSION OF WOMEN" THEME

> As American Muslims struggle to locate their place on a demographic map of this country, American Muslims now find themselves playing a historical role in reviving the principles upon which this country was founded. The greatest milestones of our history—the abolition movement, the suffrage movement, the civil rights movement, the peace movement—have been achieved only by the courage of a minority of our population who were willing to stand up and point out the inconsistencies and contradictions of our policies. Today American Muslims are playing that role by standing at the forefront of the movement to awaken America's collective conscience and to eliminate the violations and restore our role and credibility before the world.
>
> —Hadia Mubarak, first female and first American-born president of the MSA, 2004[21]

Ingrid Mattson had been elected vice president of ISNA at the 2001 convention, which took place over the weekend of August 31 to September 2—a few days, that is, prior to 9/11. Her election to this post therefore was obviously not a consequence of the 9/11 backlash. But 9/11 certainly did have a perceptible impact on women at Muslim American organizations, as well as on the subject of women at these organizations.

Indeed, as we saw in the previous chapter, 9/11 and its aftermath had had very direct impact on Muslim American women in general and on women who wore hijab in particular.

Both organizers and attendees at these conventions were obviously well aware that women who wore hijab—preponderantly women who belonged to those Muslim communities who habitually attended mosque and Muslim American annual conventions—were at risk or felt themselves to be at risk whenever they merely ventured outdoors. They were clearly well aware too of how the subject of the "oppression of Muslim women" was figuring in the media and in the administration's rhetoric of war. Speaking at one of the inaugural plenary sessions at the ICNA convention of 2002, Yvonne Haddad observed that the war in Afghanistan had "become a virtuous war because we were going to liberate Afghanistan and we were going to liberate the women of the Muslim world." It was more important than ever now, she stressed, for Muslim women in America to speak out on the subject and give voice to their own experiences and make clear "that no one is beating you up to make you wear a scarf."[22]

At all of the 2002 conventions it was clear that convention organizers also had seen the need to counter the theme of women's oppression. Beginning in that year it appeared that more women were featured as panelists and even as plenary speakers than previously, and that more women were listed as advisory board members and officers of the organizations. This does not mean that the presence of women serving in these capacities rose dramatically; nevertheless, the presence of just a couple of additional women on the podium when ISNA officers assembled palpably altered the experience of the convention, indicating new trends in ISNA's and other organizations' self-presentations.

There was also a distinct sense that new spaces were opening up at these conventions for direct criticism of the official stances and practices of the organizations—in relation specifically to women but also to other matters. These spaces seemed to have opened up as a consequence of Islam's being under attack in the larger society. Such organizations, representatives broadly of conservative Islam, were thus on the defensive, having to graciously accept or at least remain silent in the face of criticism —criticisms which in pre-9/11 days they might have dismissed or silenced. In the current climate, attempts by officials to dismiss criticisms regarding women's position would have left them distinctly vulnerable to criticism and attack.

The younger members attending these conventions seemed particularly eager to seize this opportunity to air their grievances. In 2002, for example, ISNA officers held a plenary session at the convention entitled "ISNA and You: Uniting the Muslim Community in North America," a session dedicated to receiving comments, questions, and suggestions from the floor.[23] Listening to these comments I formed the strong impression that people, and in particular the young, had been chafing for some time under the weight of the rules and conditions created by their immigrant elders. Among the comments I set down in my notes was one from a young woman who said she was pleased to see that ISNA now had a woman vice president, and pleased that there were now several women members of the advisory board. Ideally, however, she went on, ISNA leadership should be fifty/fifty women and men. When, she wanted to know, might this goal be realized?[24]

Although other issues came up, gender topics seemed to get the lion's share of attention. One young man suggested that all men over the age of fifty should resign to make room for women and younger people.[25] Another young man complained about the way that ISNA insisted on gender segregation, maintaining that such divisions were hypocritical. American Muslims lived their lives otherwise in a gender-integrated world, so it was absurd that at Muslim venues they had to observe these rules—rules that might have been relevant in their parents' home countries, he said, but were irrelevant here. Others complained about foreign policy issues, in particular that their parents seemed obsessed with political matters affecting their home countries. But these issues, one young man said, were simply not their issues as young Americans, and it was time to leave them behind.[26]

Already, even in 2002, there was a significantly more relaxed atmosphere with regard to veiling at ISNA's convention—a trend that would steadily grow over the ensuing years. When I first attended an ISNA convention I had found it impossibly uncomfortable, as I described, not to wear a scarf myself, since every other female head there seemingly was covered. But in 2002 and thereafter, there were always a few women who did not cover—and I personally never again felt the need to do so. My impression was not that women had changed their ordinary practice regarding dress, but rather that previously women who did not cover in their own lives, other than perhaps at their local mosques, had felt they had to do so while attending ISNA. After 2001 they seemed to feel free to be there simply as themselves. Even prior to 9/11 I had noticed that women whom I ran into at nearby restaurants often wore no veils, whereas inside the convention halls they appeared in their hijabs. In addition, several women I had spoken with at ISNA conventions prior to 2001 had told me that they did not normally wear hijabs and that they were irked by the hijab's increasingly coming to be viewed as mandatory at their local mosques in recent years.[27]

Even the observance of segregated seating, exits, and entryways, while nominally still in place, was now far more laxly observed. These changes did quite palpably alter the experience of being at an ISNA convention. Previously conventions, as spectacle and theater, had projected a sense of male dominance and of gender hierarchy as a foundational value that was ostentatiously and unapologetically asserted. Now this sense was eroding and being challenged.

The sense of new spaces opening up at ISNA for the airing of discontents and differences among its members seemed to gradually allow for the inclusion of speakers whose perspectives were different from the more conservative views typical of ISNA speakers, including views that at least implicitly challenged ISNA's notions of acceptable pieties. My impression that such a trend was under way was confirmed by Farid Esack's opening comments on a panel on which he spoke at the 2005 convention. Esack, a distinguished South African liberation theologian and activist well known for his work in relation, among other things, to HIV and AIDS, had been invited to speak at ISNA on a panel on the topic of "Islam, Activism, and Social Justice."

Esack began his talk by declaring that he had never imagined that he would ever be invited to speak at ISNA—but here he was at the invitation of a former student and colleague and member of ISNA. Esack's declaration drew a response from Mattson, who also was a speaker on the panel. Speaking in her capacity as vice president Mattson thanked Esack for his "courageous" voice and his presence and went on to say that ISNA belonged to its members and that ISNA's organizers welcomed proposals for parallel sessions. After Esack completed his talk—in which he addressed, among other things, the distortions of Islam that were being produced by the agendas of imperialism—Mattson spoke of her own history of activism. She had been active all her life, she said, on workers' issues, and had grown up "singing union songs in Canada." Women are not off the hook, she said. Gender oppression has to be dealt with, but women are also divided by class. "There are women who clean our mosques for below minimum wage and women who have to leave their children alone because they have to work ten-hour days."[28]

Others appearing on ISNA's panels were people whom I would previously have assumed would not have been among those that ISNA would feature. In 2004, for example, Asra Nomani, the former *Wall Street Journal* reporter, spoke at ISNA. Nomani was by then well known for the campaign she was conducting, extensively covered by the media, against her Morgantown, West Virginia, mosque for its discriminatory practices toward women, and in particular its relegation of women to the back of the mosque and its requirement that they use only the back door. In addition, Nomani had been an outspoken critic of conservative Islam generally, including of Islamic sexual rules and mores. She had also been very public—as a point of feminist politics—about her own unwed mother status.

Her speech, in which she declared that Islam "grants all people inalienable rights to respect, dignity, participation, leadership, voice, knowledge and worship," was reportedly well received, particularly by the young in the audience.[29] Sabreen Akhtar, for example, a writer for Muslim WakeUp! (a website founded by two young Muslims in 2003 to serve as a voice for "progressive Muslims," and whose contributors were mainly young people), described herself as "excited" to discover that the "revolutionary and inspiring activist, journalist and author Asra Nomani" had been allotted ten minutes on a panel. Akhtar also noted in her article that her own small Chicago-based Muslim group had had the privilege of previewing Nomani's presentation and that Nomani's "ideas and researches had been very warmly received."[30]

Nomani is a member of the generation of American Muslims who would come to maturity as professional adults in the shadow of 9/11—

an event that created an appalling, and for some an evidently nearly intolerable, mental association between Islam and terror, Islam and murderous violence. In Nomani's case that shadow of terror and its link with Islam was all the darker and sharper because of the horrific fate of Daniel Pearl, a fellow journalist and personal friend of Nomani's who was murdered by a terrorist group in Pakistan. It was this event, Nomani recounts, that had spurred her into activism against extremism and to pursue women's equal space in mosques.

In this post-9/11 climate, Nomani's activism appears to have quickly had a significant impact on ISNA and other Muslim American organizations as regards their publicly articulated position on women in mosques. Thus these organizations collectively issued a booklet in 2005 entitled "Women Friendly Mosques and Community Centers: Working Together to Reclaim Our Heritage."[31] The booklet recommends that "women and men, girls and boys should have equal access to and must feel equally welcome to participate in schools, the masjid [mosque] and other civic and cultural institutions." Noting that reports confirmed that many mosques relegated women to "small, dingy, secluded, airless and segregated quarters," the booklet declared that such practices were "unjust and degrading."[32] The booklet does not explicitly refer to Nomani or indicate that its publication was in any way a response to her activism, but, given the timing, it seems likely that it was.

Also at the 2005 convention, a film was shown on the topic of women's inadequate and unequal spaces in mosques. The filmmaker, Zarqa Nawas, does not indicate whether Nomani's campaign against her Morgantown mosque had in any way inspired or influenced her work. Nawas, who would go on to produce a successful series *Little Mosque on the Prairie* for Canadian television, retained a distinctly critical outlook in her film, but she handled her subject with playful humor rather than in Nomani's confrontational style. Nomani's sharp confrontations and run-ins with the mosque board and the community at her mosque (now depicted in a documentary that aired on PBS in July 2009, entitled the *Mosque at Morgantown*) convey the impression that she was intent on achieving her goals of front-door entry and acceptable and equal space for women regardless of how deeply she alienated the mosque community. In contrast, Nawas, who herself appears alongside her mother in her film *Me and the Mosque,* seems entirely at ease with her own mosque and with mosque communities more generally, even as she appears intent on bringing about change through the gentler work of persuasion. Even as she contests the separation of women and their unequal treatment, her work seems to be simultaneously an affirmation of community and of the value of conversation, inclusion, negotiation. Still, the combined activities of these two women and their supporters tell us that discontent and desire for change is brewing among young Americans regarding the issue of women and space in American mosques.

Overall, Nawas, like Yasin, appears to be entirely at home in both her American and Muslim heritages and communities. Nawas, like Yasin, also takes for granted the natural similarity and complementarity of the two ethical traditions. This is also the case with respect to another American Muslim of their generation, Hadia Mubarak—whose words I quoted above. She was elected in 2004 as the first female president of the Muslim Students' Association, and its first American-born president.

Mubarak grew up in Florida, where she began wearing hijab at the age of fourteen and where she was the only girl wearing it at her high school of over two thousand. This led her to become determined, she wrote, "to raise awareness about my faith and to break down the multiple barriers that exist." As her text makes clear, Mubarak takes for granted the fact that the American heritage of social struggle in the name of justice is a heritage that is rightfully her own. Abolition, suffrage, civil rights, and the peace movement, she maintains, are struggles for justice that to her are part of her own heritage and tradition as an American Muslim. This struggle for justice, as Mubarak presents it, is one that by force of circumstance now falls to Muslim Americans in particular to take up, it is they who must stand up and "awaken America's collective conscience." This way of understanding the role of American Muslims was, as already described, a commonly expressed view at ISNA conventions, conventions that Mubarak as a young MSA member would have regularly attended, as the MSA held its own panel sessions alongside those of ISNA.

Although grounded firmly in this speech in the American tradition of activism in the cause of justice, Mubarak shows herself to be just as firmly grounded in the Islamist tradition. Speaking of the hijab, for example, which Mubarak refers to as the "mandatory covering" for women —making use of a phrase that CAIR and other Muslim American organizations commonly use for this dress—Mubarak goes on to explain it in terms which entirely conform to Islamist rationalizations and explanations as offered by hijabis encountered in the preceding pages. Thus, though wearing hijab, Mubarak explains, is seen as a religious obligation by religious scholars, in fact, she continues (repeating an idea first reported, as we saw earlier, in relation to Cairo in the 1980s), "it is ultimately each woman's prerogative to decide whether or not she will cover her hair. No one—not a father, husband, or brother—can ever force a woman to cover against her will, for that in fact violates the Quranic spirit of 'let there be no compulsion in religion.'" She herself had made the decision to wear hijab, she informs her readers, and relished "the freedom the hijab gives me, the freedom from having my body exposed as a sex object or from being judged on a scale of 1–10 by strange men who have no right to know what my body or hair look like."[33] For Muslim women, Mubarak further explained, "the hijab is a form of modesty, security and protection, shifting the focus of attention from a woman's physical attraction, or lack thereof, to the personality that lies beneath. By forcing people to look beyond her physical realm, a woman is valued for her intellect, personality and merit."[34]

For Mubarak, just as for Yasin and Nawas and many others who live at the confluence of American and Islamic, and specifically Islamist, traditions, the ideas and worldviews of their dual heritages are naturally mutually reinforcing and complementary. These young people, growing up American and shaped by American schools and other socializing institutions, take for granted that the American heritage is naturally and rightfully their own. They have in common the key importance in their lives of the influence of Islamism—as distinct from the nonactivist and privately practiced tradition of Islam—with its commitments to activism in pursuit of justice, to serving the Muslim community, and to hijab. Besides being members of the Islamist-founded MSA, Mubarak and Yasin also served as presidents of the national and local organizations. Yasin—in a classic pattern of Islamist commitment and activism—served as a volunteer working with refugees in Bosnia. Their commitments to serving the community are evidenced even in their serving as presidents of their organizations—positions which place them at the hub of a network of the Muslim American extended community, and more exactly of the extended Islamist-influenced segment of the Muslim American community. In her film work too, Nawas, even as she gently criticizes some aspects of mosque life and practices, is similarly strongly affirming of this mosque-going and Islamist-influenced Canadian Muslim community with which she clearly identifies. And like Yasin and Mubarak, she is entirely at ease with her identity as both Canadian and as explicitly and self-affirmingly and visibly Muslim (for like Mubarak and many other young Islamist-influenced American Muslims, Nawas wears hijab).

Islamist influence is in fact a common feature in the lives of probably the overwhelming majority of the most prominent American Muslim activists of our day. The presence of this influence applies also—somewhat paradoxically, on the face of it—to American Muslims who are playing prominent activist roles today with respect to issues of women and gender, as I discuss in the following chapter.

American Muslims drawn from this Islamist-influenced segment of the population appear to be thoroughly at home in their identities as both Muslims and Americans. It is they who are most activist in social causes of import to American Muslims, and who commonly undertake their activism explicitly as self-identified, visibly *Muslim* Americans. They generally speak from positions that assume the natural similarity and complementarity of the two ethical traditions to which they are heir.

The fact that the majority of American Muslim activists today, even in relation to gender issues, appear to be drawn from this very specific and distinctive Islamist-influenced segment of the American Muslim population is in itself a remarkable and unexpected finding. It is all the more remarkable considering that this segment of Islamist-influenced Muslims —Muslims who attended mosques and/or Islamic schools and/or were members of the MSA and other American Muslim organizations and institutions—make up, according to the experts, no more than a minority of the American Muslim population.

The importance of creating and fostering a sense of community was clearly a critical aspect of the ISNA conventions' overall function and purpose. As I observed the greetings and the scenes of effusive reunions that were frequently in progress in the hallways, restaurants, and other public spaces, it became abundantly clear that reconnecting and socializing with family and friends living in far-flung towns and cities all over North America was an important dimension of the conference. In many cases this was probably the chief reason that people, coming from all over the United States and Canada, undertook the effort and expense of attending the ISNA conventions.

ISNA also offered matrimonial services. People could list themselves or their relatives as seeking spouses with ISNA's matrimonial department. Then, over the course of the convention, there would be several events dedicated to matrimonial get-togethers. These events, which I myself never attended, took place in huge ballrooms and drew enormous crowds.

The matrimonial lists (minus the individual names) were posted in a special room of the convention center where anyone could come to look through them. In browsing I saw that both men and women were listed, sometimes by family members, or by themselves. There seemed to be about equal numbers of each, and commonly those listed were in their twenties and thirties, or older. Women as well as men were generally professionally employed, and men as well as women often indicated that they were looking for professional spouses.[35]

Judging by the great numbers of people attending these get-togethers, such events seemed to be exceedingly important dimensions of the convention and important draws for attendees.

Organizations like ICNA likewise had matrimonial departments. Memorably, at ICNA's 2002 convention a middle-aged woman had angrily complained in an open question-and-answer session that she had found ICNA's matrimonial services most inadequate that year; since this was the chief reason that she and many others were ICNA members, she said (presumably to find spouses for their children), this was most disappointing. The ICNA official's response was no less telling: he said they were fully aware that this was among their most important functions for the community, and he was most apologetic regarding their shortcomings. It had been a difficult year, he said.

Other key features of the ISNA experience were the bazaar, already described, and, initially, the charity booths, with their videos and books and pamphlets. These booths, as I said earlier, steadily diminished in number over the years. The figures for ISNA attendance have been steadily rising, from about 25,000 in 1999 to 45,000 in 2005.

Reading Muslim WakeUp! I would discover that the changes that I had been pleased and surprised to see under way at ISNA after 9/11—the more relaxed atmosphere surrounding veiling and segregated seating, the presence of panelists representing more liberal positions than I associated with ISNA—were changes that, from the point of view of the younger membership of ISNA, were occurring all too slowly. One writer, for example, in Muslim WakeUp!—Ahmed Nassef, one of the cofounders of the site—reporting that Mike Knight, a young Muslim novelist, would be presenting his work at ISNA's 2004 convention, also noted that he had been pleased to see the previous year that ISNA organizers had permitted the screening of the film *Nazra* "despite the film's honest portrayal of gender and sexuality issues." He also was pleased to note that Asra Nomani also would be speaking. On the other hand, he continued, ISNA was still censoring speakers: they had refused to have Mohja Kahf, a professor, poet, and the editor of "Sex and the Umma," read her poetry in the main hall.[36]

Another writer for Muslim WakeUp! Umbreen Shah, reporting this time on ISNA's 2005 convention, declared that ISNA was "run mostly by first generation immigrant Muslims with cultural baggage from their homelands," and that consequently ISNA "management has been unable to relate to their American-born Muslim constituency which is the future of Islam in America." Shah also remarked that there was a tendency at ISNA "to enforce a particular religiously conservative philosophy without adapting to the people it serves." For example, Shah went on, "women presenters at ISNA have been routinely asked to wear hijab during presentation even though they don't normally wear the headscarf. This has promoted either hypocrisy or contention when presenters have refused to wear it."[37]

Whereas I had been pleased simply to see some relaxation of hijab observance at least among ISNA attendees, it had not occurred to me that ISNA would tolerate their own officials or even panelists appearing without it, given the Islamist roots of the organization. But clearly for some of the organization's younger and more restive members—people presumably who had grown up attending ISNA and possibly also had been members of the MSA—all of this should have been accomplished by now. As the young novelist and convert to Islam Michael Muhammad Knight would write in an essay in Muslim WakeUp! about the 2003 ISNA convention, "Maybe the 'old guard' still runs ISNA, and maybe the House of Saud still runs that old guard. But I saw a lot of young people there, and they are claiming their spots. The med-student who smoked weed, the NOFX kid, Farah the film-maker, Rima the poet, and even me, for whatever I am." Knight is a novelist of growing prominence who offers interesting glimpses into the lives of young American Muslims today, including glimpses into the lively and not always obediently chaste mores and practices of ISNA's more rebellious young. "My friend Sara," he wrote, "told me that while ISNA usually has cool programs, it can often become a big hookup place for horny young Muslims. 'I guess they're not all there for speeches and stuff,' she said."[38]

By way of conveying an overview of women's presence and activism at ISNA, as well as of suggesting something of the changes, evolutions, and continuities that are under way in women's roles and participation, I offer in the remaining pages of this chapter brief biographical sketches of a number of notable ISNA women. I selected these women (who make up a far from inclusive list) either because of their prominence in the organization, or because some facts and outlines regarding their personal journeys are available in published sources. Sometimes they have themselves penned their stories or they have been the subjects of biographical studies and interviews by others. I have, in addition, had the privilege of observing and often meeting almost all of the women mentioned here.

I begin with Ingrid Mattson. Mattson was in her late thirties when she was elected the first female president of ISNA, in 2006. Mattson's election represented a first not only with respect specifically to ISNA but also with respect to other Islamist organizations, such as the Muslim Brotherhood of Egypt (with branches in many more countries), organizations with which ISNA had once had important connections.

As we saw earlier, Zainab al-Ghazali had been a figure of major importance to the history of the Muslim Brotherhood, but she had never held any official position within the organization. To this day Islamist women who do important work for the organization in Egypt continue to find themselves marginalized and unrecognized.[39] Mattson's election represents a development that has so far occurred only in the American context.[40]

Raised a Catholic in Kitchener, Ontario, Mattson was a pious child until the age of about fifteen, when she found that she had "more and more questions," questions for which the nuns who taught her "had fewer answers." A priest "couldn't satisfy her either," and so "God disappeared." Spending her senior year of college in Paris, Mattson became friends with Senegalese Muslims whom she admired, and, eager to learn more about them, she began reading the Quran. Certain of its verses "gripped her," she wrote, "explaining God to her in new ways." This led her back to religious belief and to Islam.[41] (Mattson's sister is also a convert, in her case to Judaism.)

After graduating from college Mattson went to Pakistan in 1987 to work as a volunteer in a camp for Afghan refugees. There she met her husband, a fellow volunteer from Egypt and an engineer. Later Mattson came to the United States to attend the University of Chicago, where she obtained a doctorate in Islamic studies.[42] She currently teaches at the Hartford Seminary in Connecticut and is the author, most recently, of *The Story of the Quran* (2008), a book that captures a wealth of material regarding the Quran and its oral transmission, thereby offering a fresh and original perspective in English on the history of the Quran. Throughout her account she pays particular attention to the role of women in the history of the Quran's transmission, and she also follows the story of a young American girl called Reem who loved to study the Quran and who traveled to Syria to obtain an *ijaza,* or certificate in Quranic recitation.

Even prior to Mattson's election as vice president, female activists at ISNA had been pushing for women's inclusion in the formal structure of the organization. They had been pressing ISNA to recognize women's ongoing contributions, both to ISNA and at the local level of work to mosque and community.[43] Among the causes that some ISNA women had been committed to was that of domestic violence. Some women, most notably Bonita McGee and Sharifa Alkhateeb, had for some time been urging ISNA to take a strong public stand on the matter. As a result, in the summer of 2001 ISNA scheduled a conference for March 2002 that would focus on community issues, including domestic violence.

Persuading ISNA to agree to this had been uphill work, I learned from McGee and Alkhateeb. ISNA and other Muslim American organizations had resisted taking up the issue of domestic violence chiefly, the women thought, because their officials were reluctant to draw attention to a problem that could all too easily be used to fan prejudice against Muslim men in the larger society.

McGee, Alkhateeb, and others had had to repeatedly underscore that such abuse occurred across all religious, cultural, and class groups. They pointed out that the community's failure to address these issues, as well as to offer services and shelter for distressed Muslim women and their children, was extraordinarily costly to these women and children. McGee, a young African American whose mother had converted to Islam in the 1960s, was cofounder of Muslim Family Services, an organization serving Muslim communities in the greater Columbus, Ohio, area.[44] In one presentation McGee stressed that the problem of domestic violence was unambiguously present in the community: "It is there and it is real," she said. "We have to discuss what we can do about it starting today." Having worked at a domestic violence shelter, she said, she had seen "mothers and daughters, children who hate Islam because of what they've seen."[45]

Sherifa Alkhateeb was fifty-eight years old when she was awarded ISNA's Community Service Award at ISNA's 2004 convention. Alkhateeb, who died within weeks of receiving the award, was too ill to be present, so it was tearfully accepted on her behalf by her daughter, Maha. Born in Philadelphia, Alkhateeb was the daughter of a Yemeni father and a Czech mother. She began attending the University of Pennsylvania when she was sixteen, at which point she joined the MSA and began wearing the headscarf.[46] "In many ways," noted the *Washington Post* in its obituary, "Mrs. Alkhateeb lived a conventional Muslim life." The mother of three daughters, and a woman who prayed five times a day, Alkhateeb also managed, "within the bounds of her faith," the *Post* continued, "to forge a strong, independent voice for herself and for other Islamic women."[47] Typically wearing the headscarf along with "tailored pantsuits,"[48] Alkhateeb—as the *New York Times* noted in its obituary—"wrote and lectured extensively" in an effort "to challenge stereotypes of Muslims, and particularly of Muslim women."[49]

In 2000 Alkhateeb created the Peaceful Families Project, which studied and raised awareness about domestic violence. After 9/11, according to her daughter, Alkhateeb lived "in constant fear that someone would attack her."[50] Nevertheless, she became very active in the interfaith community, where she was greatly appreciated by fellow workers from other religions. Blu Greenberg, for instance, founder of the Jewish Orthodox Feminist Alliance, noted that when her own son J. J. died in Israel, Sharifa called "with the most tender and loving message, which I kept on my answering machine for a long, long time." Mary Hunt, co-director of the Women's Alliance for Theology, Ethics, and Ritual (WATER), attended Alkhateeb's funeral. Alkhateeb, who had died around midnight on Wednesday, was buried Thursday at 3 P.M. "on a grey, chilly, drizzly day" following prayers at her local mosque. There were about a hundred people at the cemetery, Hunt wrote, "including small children and many women with whom she had worked on countless projects. The body had been washed reverently and wrapped in a sheet. It was carried to the gravesite in an open wooden box with a beautiful black and yellow cloth over it. Several men, including her husband, climbed down into the grave to receive her body. . . . Then members of the family and close friends shoveled the dirt on top. We all watched as the cemetery workers finished the job. We gathered for a short prayer and then family members received condolences outside, as was the custom."[51]

Sharifa's daughter, Maha, continues her mother's work, editing a book on domestic violence published in 2007 as part of the Peaceful Families Project founded by her mother.[52]

Khadija Haffajee is another prominent ISNA woman. Haffajee was the first woman elected to sit on ISNA's Majlis Ash-Shura (Consultative Council) in 1997. Haffajee later recalled that as her name was read out in a packed Hilton auditorium—"the first woman to be elected to this bastion of males"—her heart was pounding so hard that she was unable to rise from her seat as she was supposed to do. She had traveled, she wrote "many lonely miles to be where I am today."[53]

Haffajee's account of her life, published in the collection *Muslim*

Women Activists in North America Speaking for Ourselves, is illuminating as to the path taken by one woman, a path that would lead her to a position of leadership at an organization such as ISNA. Haffajee was born to a conservative Muslim family in South Africa in the late 1930s. While the older daughters in the family received no education, Haffajee was able to attend school with the help of her sisters.

Haffajee's father, who died when she was very young, had been determined, wrote Haffajee, to educate his daughters. He was a *hafiz*—someone who had mastered the recitation of the Quran and whose voice, chanting it, formed one of her important childhood memories. Haffajee sees herself in her desire for knowledge and education as very much her father's heir and as following in his footsteps.

She won a scholarship to attend college, and after graduating she went on to teach at a girls' high school. This was the apartheid era. Nonwhites (such as Haffajee) were not allowed to use the "Whites Only" facilities in the main building, and Haffajee was given a key to the outhouse. "Nonwhites in South Africa had to find ways to improve the condition of their people," she wrote, "so activism became a way of life. We raised funds and awarded scholarships for them, and we provided facilities for extracurricular activities, such as monies for tennis courts. Social injustices were a way of life in South Africa."

Haffajee made her way to Canada, and here she was taken by a friend to attend an MSA meeting in 1968. "Wow!" she would write of this event, "the images are still fresh thirty-six years later. For the first time in my life I heard individuals speak so eloquently about Islam, affirming its relevance in the twentieth century." She was invited a few years later to address an MSA annual convention. She stipulated that she would speak only if she could address a mixed-gender audience. When she rose to speak men tried to shout her down, and some then staged a walkout. She continued "unfazed," she wrote.

After going to Mecca for ʻumra (the "lesser pilgrimage") in 1979, she starting wearing hijab—the first woman to do so at the school in Canada where she taught. Haffajee was always open about her beliefs and fully explained them to her students. She never encountered hostility from anyone, she wrote, about her hijab. On the contrary, she said, she received only friendliness and gifts—baked goodies and scarves—

from students and parents alike. Through the seventies and early eighties Haffajee spent her vacations in a supervisory role in summer camps for Muslim girls.

Her life in this way was filled with firsts, Haffajee wrote. Among such firsts were her travels with another Muslim woman activist to Zimbabwe and Malawi, to address Muslims in a tour sponsored by the Islamic Federation of Students' Organizations. She felt a deep kinship with her fellow-lecturer, whom she had never met. They were "Muslim sisters," she wrote, both "shaped by the Quran." Among her most cherished memories of this trip was of their speaking at a mosque, after which a "very old man, a man who needed help to stand, got up, tears streaming down his face, and told us he was so happy to see two women from so far away speak to a mixed gathering in the mosque!"

Haffajee went on to take on challenge after challenge. During the Soviet war in Afghanistan she grew concerned about the plight of women in Afghanistan, and she traveled to that country in 1987 to work with local women's organizations in refugee camps. She returned armed with many photographs, with which she traveled and lectured in Canada to raise donations for refugee women and children. In 1995 she attended the U.N. women's conference at Beijing and subsequently became active in interfaith work. Haffajee did not marry until she was about fifty, becoming, as she put it, "wife, stepmother, and grandmother, all in one year!"

Haffajee (like other ISNA women mentioned here) does not use the term "feminism," a term belonging to other discursive worlds and one that is perhaps not necessarily very meaningful in relation to the struggles in which Haffajee herself was most enmeshed. Her commitments and actions in pursuit of her own education and in the service of other nonwhites in South Africa, and her later struggles and endeavors in Canada—always fired to be sure by her faith as a Muslim and her own passion for justice—seem nevertheless to directly parallel the motivations and commitments of many other women in the larger societies of America and Canada—motivations and commitments typically labeled "feminist."

Other prominent women in the ISNA gallery of characters include Maha Elgenaidi, Nimat Hafez Barazangi, and Ekram Beshir. Elgenaidi, a woman perhaps in her mid-thirties in the early 2000s, was founder and president of Islamic Networks Group, an educational and outreach organization with affiliates now in twenty U.S. states, as well as in Canada and the United Kingdom. Growing up in America with an interest in mathematics, Elgenaidi was sent by her parents to study engineering in Egypt (their home country) to help her to "reconnect with my Arab heritage." In the end she attended the American University in Cairo, where she obtained degrees in political science and economics. She then returned to graduate school in the United States, after which she began work as a marketing analyst manager.[54]

In the ensuing years the first Arab Gulf war and the sanctions imposed on Iraq, as well as the "dehumanizing, automated existence of the corporate world," brought Elgenaidi to crisis, and she began reading the scriptures of her Christian, Buddhist, and Jewish friends. Then she decided to read the Quran, "which had an immediate profound impact on my life." She began to pray and "to dress more modestly": Elgenaidi, like all the ISNA women mentioned above other than Alkhateeb (who wore a headscarf)—Mattson, McGee, Haffajee—wears the strictly concealing hijab as well as the loose, flowing robes of conservative Islamic women.

Growing up Elgenaidi had kept her distance from Islam because, she said, she herself had so completely absorbed and internalized the negative views of Islam and in particular those notions of its "oppressive" treatment of women that are commonplace in American culture. Her own former prejudices with regard to Islam would prove useful to her, she believed, in her work as president of the Islamic Networks Group (ING), an outreach agency working to provide institutions such as schools and the police with accurate information about Islam, with a view to addressing and correcting prevailing false stereotypes and misperceptions of Islam and Muslims.

Elgenaidi's greatest challenges in the course of her career, she observed, had been those encountered in working with Muslims who thought women's roles should be confined to sitting on women's committees and staying home to raise the children. "Here I was a young corporate manager being told to take notes in all male meetings . . . so I had to learn very fast about women's rights and roles in Islam to be able to fight back and hold my ground, while continuing to manifest my faith in the way I was inspired to by God." In pursuing the educational goals of ING, Elgenaidi encourages and promotes interfaith work, drawing inspiration from "the civil rights movement where groups across different sectors in society joined together successfully to gain their rights and freedoms."

Nimat Barazangi, who, in the 1980s, would become the first woman invited to serve on the ISNA Education Committee, arrived in the U.S. from Syria in the late 1960s. At that point, in rebellion against her mother, she wrote, who wore only a headscarf, Barazangi herself chose to wear a jilbab and khimar: a "heavy coat" and "heavy headcover" in her words. Over the ensuing years, studying, getting degrees, becoming involved as researcher and practitioner in Muslim education in America, Barazangi would undergo a number of sartorial transformations—abandoning hijab altogether, then adopting a headscarf, then changing again to a more conservative head covering—transformations accompanied by a number of intellectual revolutions that she describes in her biographical account "Silent Revolution of a Muslim Arab American Scholar-Activist."

Core and consistent elements in Barazangi's ongoing revolutionary commitments, as she describes these, included "revolution against the social systems that abuse and stereotype Muslim Arab women—be it the Muslim, the Arab or the American system," and a commitment to Islam, which she understood as a "belief system and worldview" whose main objective was that of bringing about "social change and, in particular, enhancing gender justice." At ISNA she worked with some of the women mentioned above, including Haffajee, who chaired one of the committees that Barazangi served on, and Alkhateeb, whom she describes as a very good friend. Barazangi, along with Alkhateeb, attended a White House Eid celebration in 1998 at the invitation of First Lady Hillary Rodham Clinton.[55]

Ekram Beshir, described as a frequent speaker at ISNA and ICNA and other American Muslim organizations, and a leader (along with her husband, Mohamed Rida Beshir) of workshops on Muslim parenting and education across North America, Europe, and South Africa, is a founder of Rahma and Abraar, Islamic schools in Ottawa, Canada.

Beshir, the only woman figuring on this list whom I have never personally met, appeared earlier in these pages as the young college student in Alexandria, Egypt, who in the early 1970s was among the first wave of young women to embrace hijab and the activist Islam of the Islamic Resurgence. Concerned to find a husband no less dedicated than she was to serving and spreading Islam, and who, just as importantly, understood that her commitments to serving Islam took precedence over providing him with a "freshly cooked meal every day" or keeping a "spotless house," she met and married Mohamed Rida Beshir and immigrated with him to Canada, where they settled in 1975. There her husband became "heavily involved" in founding the first MSA chapter at Carleton University in Ottawa, and Beshir, who had, like her husband, qualified as a doctor, decided to involve herself as a volunteer in the activities of her own children, as well as other children. In this way she "became aware of the pressures her children faced in the North American school system."[56]

For Beshir, in true Islamist tradition, Islam above all entailed activism. "I believe it's everyone's job to promote Islam and do *da'wa* (spreading the news about Islam)," she wrote, "in whatever form they are capable of." Beshir would involve herself in Islamic education, pioneering the field in North America: founding two Islamic schools and writing several books with her husband on parenting Muslim children in the West.[58] As the biographical information offered on the cover of several of her books notes, in 2000, Beshir received the Ottawa-Carlton District School Board award for her contributions as "best educator."

·11·

American Muslim Women's Activism in the Twenty-First Century

Tayyibah Taylor, founder of *Azizah* magazine, was born in Trinidad and raised in Canada. Taught by her parents always to "behave perfectly, speak eloquently, and dress impressively, so that, as a person of color, others would deem me acceptable," Taylor recalled her first encounter with *Ebony* magazine as marking a particularly important moment. For the first time, she wrote, she saw "media images of people of color that were positive." The experience began for her the process of undercutting an "internalized sense of inferiority" that had begun to seep into her with her move to Canada at the age of seven.[1]

On a visit to Barbados during her college years in Toronto, Taylor embraced Islam as her "spiritual path." Subsequently she lived for a time in Saudi Arabia, then in Seattle, where she helped to found an Islamic school at which she also taught. Thereafter she set about pursuing her dream of launching *Azizah,* a magazine "for the woman who doesn't apologize for being a Muslim and doesn't apologize for being a woman." The magazine deliberately avoids focusing on any particular ethnic group, and does not affiliate itself with any particular a school of thought or organization. "Instead," Taylor wrote, "it reflects all Muslim women in their diversity, thus speaking to the polycentric nature of Islam." The name Azizah, Taylor further explains, a name found "in any Muslim country," means "dear, strong, noble. So, we defined the *Azizah* woman as the one who is dear to herself and others, with noble strength and dignity, boldly reclaiming our attribute of strength."

Azizah, which features the fabrics, colors, and dress styles of the Muslim world in its transcontinental diversity, is known for the elegance of the fashions that fill its pages, including its stylish hijabs—a garment that Taylor herself elegantly sports. The magazine, which Taylor describes as a "catalyst for empowerment," is also known for its coverage of issues, activities, and books of importance to Muslim American women. In 2007, for example, *Azizah* published a discussion of a newly published translation of the Quran, along with an interview with the translator, Laleh Bakhtiar.[2]

Bakhtiar's translation, *The Sublime Quran,* the first English translation by a Muslim American woman, created a stir because of Bakhtiar's translation of one particular verse in the Quran, a verse of critical importance with regard to the treatment of women—verse 4:34.

Bakhtiar herself anticipated controversy over her unconventional rendering of this verse. In her Preface and Introduction to the translation she describes her research methods and sources, explaining how she established the exact meanings of words and where her translation differed from other English translations. Bakhtiar observes that one underlying difference between her own and other translations is that in prior translations "little attention had been given to the woman's point of view."[3]

"The absence of a woman's point of view for over 1440 years since the revelation" was clearly, Bakhtiar observes, a situation that needed to be changed. Convinced that "the intention of the Quran is to see man and woman as complements of one another, not as superior-inferior," and acutely aware of the widespread criticisms that were made of Islam "with regard to the inferiority of women," Bakhtiar now paid particular attention to the one key verse on which the notion of the inferiority of women might be said to hinge. This, she says, is verse 4:34, which is typically interpreted to mean that a husband may beat his wife "after two stages of trying to discipline her."[4]

Her research, Bakhtiar explains, led her to challenge conventional readings of a key word in this verse—the word *daraba.* Conventional readings understand the word as being derived from the root verb "to beat" or "to hit." Consequently, the verse is commonly understood and translated as specifically permitting men (in the words of various other prior translators) to "beat," "hit," or "spank" their wives, if the first two recommended stages—of first "admonishing" the wife and then leaving her "alone in bed"—failed to tame the woman's resistance.[5]

Bakhtiar found that the root verb "daraba" had a number of possible root meanings besides "to beat," including "to go away." In addition, Bakhtiar points out, the Prophet Muhammad was never known to have beaten any of his wives and thus had never himself put into practice a method of controlling wives that the Quran purportedly recommended. Furthermore, taking account of the fact that the interpretation of the word "daraba" as "to beat" is internally inconsistent with the broad, general tenor of Quranic statements and recommendations regarding relations between men and women, Bakhtiar concluded that the correct interpretation of this word could not possibly be "to beat": rather, she concluded that in this context it must mean "go away from." The verse thus basically instructs men, as Bakhtiar interprets it, to leave—divorce—women who persist in challenging or resisting them. Given that the Quran also explicitly instructs men to grant divorce to women who do not wish to remain in a marriage, this reading and translation of the verse, Bakhtiar maintains, was in every way internally consistent with the Quran's other specific teachings, as well as its broad, general teachings.

Raised in the United States by her American Christian mother, a single parent, Bakhtiar describes herself as "schooled in Sufism" and as someone who is on the Sufi path. Now in her sixties, Bakhtiar has been a longtime student of Islam and is deeply familiar, she explains, with the dominant Muslim schools of thought, both Shi'i and Sunni. On her own initiative, as a child of eight, Bakhtiar had converted to Catholicism—not her mother's faith. When she traveled to Iran with her Iranian husband at the age of twenty-four she found herself drawn to Islam. At this time Bakhtiar got to know her father, an Iranian who was "not religious, but spiritual, devoting his life as a physician to help to heal the suffering of people."

When Bakhtiar's translation was first published, Mohammad Ashraf, ISNA's secretary general in Canada, declared that "this woman-friendly translation will be out of line and will not fly too far." Maintaining that "women have been given a very good place in Islam," Ashraf also said that he would not permit the translation to be sold in ISNA's bookstore. "Our bookstore would not allow this kind of translation," he said. "I will consider banning it."[6]

His remarks drew a stern response from Ingrid Mattson, the president of ISNA. Calling on the secretary general to retract his comments about banning the translation from their bookstore, Mattson (herself a noted scholar of the Quran) went on to declare in a statement that ISNA was an organization that strove to represent the "diversity of North American Islam." Affirming the "validity of different schools of Islamic thought," ISNA also did not recognize, Mattson's statement continued, that "any particular scholar, school of thought or institution," was "necessarily authoritative for all Muslims." Pointing out that an Islamic scholar had in fact advanced a similar thesis to Bakhtiar's regarding verse 4:34 in the pages of ISNA's own magazine, *Islamic Horizons,* in 2003, Mattson's statement also declared ISNA's support for all "scholarly enquiry and intellectual discussion on issues related to Islam," and its support and encouragement of "honest debate and scholarship on issues affecting the Muslim community. In particular, we have long been concerned with the misuse of Islam to justify injustice towards women." ISNA "expects its administrators," her statement concludes, "to promote ISNA's values and mission." Although she takes a clear position on freedom of thought and speech, Mattson notably does not take a position as to the accuracy or religious acceptability of Bakhtiar's translation.[7]

ISNA, like other American Muslim organizations, has been undergoing palpable changes in the post-9/11 era, as I described in Chapter 10, regarding dress and speech, and the group has exhibited signs of generational change. The Ashraf-Mattson exchange symbolically captures key and telling elements of the processes of transition as a new, American-born generation begins to take the reins.

Ashraf's comments reflect a worldview that is confidently grounded in a sense of the absolute rightness of male dominance and of readings of the Quran that embody that view. Clearly they are grounded too in the assumption that banning dissenting views from circulation, at least in

ISNA-sponsored bookshops, is a perfectly acceptable way of dealing with divergent opinions. Such notions, entirely normative in most Muslim-majority societies, are obviously not notions that would necessarily have much purchase in America or Europe.

As Mohammed Ayoob has pointed out in his study *The Many Faces of Political Islam,* Islamist organizations in different countries, even when they are branches of the same mother organization, commonly evolve in profoundly different ways in response to the local situation.[8] ISNA, with its Islamist Middle Eastern and South Asian heritage, is evidently developing along lines shaped by its American context, lines that distinctly bear the imprint of that context: it is becoming, that is, an *American*-Muslim organization. The Mattson-Ashraf exchange, taking place some twenty-five years after the founding of ISNA, can be seen as one clear sign of this evolution. As I mentioned earlier, even the fact that ISNA has a female president may not have been something that ISNA's founders had ever envisioned. At any rate, no Islamist organization in the home countries is headed by a woman.[9]

Andrea Useem, the young Anglo-American convert to Islam we encountered earlier as the spokesperson and interpreter at the open house meeting at a Boston mosque in the weeks after 9/11, now a working journalist, interviewed Bakhtiar about her translation of the Quran and in particular her rendering of verse 4:34. Useem also interviewed Bonita McGee, the community activist also mentioned earlier who worked with ISNA on domestic violence, as well as Hadia Mubarak, the former president of the MSA, regarding this verse, inviting them to reflect on the significance of Bakhtiar's translation from their own professional and personal perspectives.

What impact, Useem asked McGee, might this new translation have on the community that she served, and did she think that this verse as conventionally translated had "actually result[ed] in abuse." McGee said she did not believe that the verse caused domestic violence. "Abusers abuse because it works for them," she said. "If you had a perfect translation of the Quran, guess what? Abusers would still abuse and find justification for it. It's a behavior choice." McGee did, however, go on to say that in its conventional rendering the "verse can create a serious crisis of faith for women who are hurting and don't know how to accept it in their hearts."[10]

Mubarak, whose statements as president and then as former president of the MSA had been notable for how they interwove elements from both her American and her Islamist ethical heritages, again displays these same attitudes and assumptions in her responses to Useem. Thus, noting in her reply that other scholars of Arabic besides Bakhtiar had also interpreted the verses as not endorsing the beating of women, Mubarak goes on to express her gratitude to Bakhtiar "for putting this interpretation into an English translation." The verse had posed a "personal dilemma" for her, she said, when she was growing up. It had been difficult to "reconcile this verse, 'to beat them,' with my own notions of Islam's egalitarianism." She explained further, "You read the Quran and see the basic gender paradigm that ordains mercy and justice between men and women. Then you come to this one verse that seems to contradict everything you believe Islam stands for, and it just doesn't fit. I never accepted that this verse actually instructed men to beat their wives. That to me is an absolute contradiction to the way God describes Himself, as absolutely just."[11]

Even prior to the publication of Bakhtiar's translation, Mubarak's personal uneasiness with this verse had spurred her to write an article about it in which she had drawn attention to the multiple meanings of the word "daraba," including its meaning "to leave," and she had also speculated as to the misogynist societies whose assumptions may have informed earlier interpretations. Mubarak carefully remains within the accepted bounds of orthodox belief—as indeed Bakhtiar does in her translation: that is, they challenge interpretations of the Quran but never so much as gesture toward questioning the divine origins of the word or words themselves. This is the one inviolable stricture, the one inviolable line that cannot be crossed by anyone who wishes to be viewed as a Muslim by orthodox Muslims.[12]

It is clear from Mubarak's responses to Useem that she understands Islamic justice as unambiguously including gender justice: if Islamic justice does not include gender justice, her reply implies, then it would not be justice. The same assumptions are reflected in her article. "As God's justness is unarguably a basic principle in Islamic theology, then God would not permit or promote acts that inflict *zulm* (injustice) upon any human being. No one can disagree that misogyny is a form of *zulm* by justifying women's degradation as well as violating her rights."[13]

Given that Mubarak was president of the MSA it seems reasonable to assume that her views fall within the range of the views considered acceptable for a member and representative of the MSA (and they do remain fully within the bounds of orthodoxy and of acceptable dissent) and even that they probably reflect those of many other MSA members and college students. Indeed, Mubarak goes on to say in her response to Useem that "a lot of educated young women" she knew felt just as she did with regard to this verse, feeling that it "seemed to contradict everything you believe Islam stands for."[14] Doubtless, too, though, there are probably a range of differing opinions around such issues among young Muslims. Dalia Mogahed, for example, another prominent young American-Muslim hijabi, coauthor of *Who Speaks for Islam* and a recent Obama appointee to the White House Advisory Council (on Faith-Based and Neighborhood Partnerships), seems to speak a language of complementarity rather than of equality with regard to men's and women's roles. Often such language also implies accepting legal inequalities as reflecting the complementarity of gender roles. Such a position would seem to be essentially different from that implied by Mubarak's notion of "Islam's egalitarianism."[15]

Published in 2007, Bakhtiar's translation of the Quran, with its important recasting of orthodox patriarchal readings, was part of a post-9/11 trend of outspoken criticism and challenge by Muslim women of established Islamic teachings and practices as regards women.

Already, as we saw, the young scholar Mubarak had published an article on the issue in 2004; in 2005, a couple of years before Bakhtiar's translation appeared, a group of young academics (Ayesha Siddiqua Chaudhry, Kecia Ali, Laury Silvers, and Karen Bauer) presented a joint panel at the American Academy of Religion in which they focused entirely on verse 4:34, analyzing its inherent problematics and exploring the different readings of it offered by different interpreters over the course of history. Like Mubarak and Bakhtiar herself—and like many of the activists and critics of conservative Islam of this post-9/11 era—these critics spoke for the most part as committed Muslims, albeit Muslims who were troubled by and found themselves questioning the dominant, conservative interpretations of Islam.[16]

Similarly, Amina Wadud, who had in her earlier work, *Quran and Woman* (1992), addressed herself to the subject of verse 4:34, now returned to the subject. And in this post-9/11 era she arrived at a far more categorically critical conclusion than she had previously. Quoting the verse she wrote: "There is no getting around this one, even though I have tried through different methods for two decades. I simply do not and cannot condone permission for a man to 'scourge' or apply any kind of strike to a woman." Consequently, Wadud continued—explaining now (as Bakhtiar had done) the scholarly and intellectual grounds for her position—"I have finally come to say 'no' outright to the literal implementation of this passage." Saying an "outright no" to a verse from the Quran represented a quite dramatic shift from Wadud's earlier position. The book in which Wadud put forth these views, *Gender Jihad,* was published in 2006.

Like Bakhtiar, Wadud was already a well-known scholar in the field of women and Islam prior to 9/11. And, like Bakhtiar, Wadud is a convert to Islam. She writes that she began to cover her head and wear long clothes even before formally converting to Islam. "As a descendant of African slave women," she explained, "I have carried the awareness that my ancestors were not given any choice to determine how much of their bodies would be exposed on the auction block or in their living conditions. So I chose intentionally to cover my body as a means of reflecting my historical identity, personal dignity, and sexual integrity." The mosque at which Wadud made her *shahadah* (her declaration of faith—the declaration that "there is no God but God and Muhammad is his Prophet," which seals the conversion) at the age of twenty, a mosque conveniently located near where she lived, was "heavily influenced" by Maulana Mawdudi (founder of the Jamaat-i Islami). All the women associated with the mosque, Wadud wrote, were "dressed in face veil as well."[17]

Furthermore, in this post-9/11 era Wadud, along with a group of four other women, would join to support Nomani in her activism regarding women's space at the Morgantown, West Virginia, mosque. On

June 4, 2004, this group, consisting of five women, marched together on the mosque in Morgantown, declaring that they were creating a "national organization," the Daughters of Hajar, "dedicated to reclaiming Muslim women's rights from the mosque to the bedroom."[18]

Given the salience in the national public conversation in these times of the subject of Islam and women, the media not surprisingly widely reported on these women's activism. In the context of the lively national interest that this subject now commanded, the mayor of Morgantown now formally welcomed their initiative, declaring that Morgantown was "honored to host this historical meeting of Muslim women. The women," he continued, "are courageous pioneers and leaders. We are at a crossroads in creating communities of tolerance and inclusion. Morgantown is proud to serve as a shining example of what can be accomplished through the active and vocal participation of women."[19]

The mayor's words reflected in part the women's own sense that these were historic times and that they were making history, taking part in actions that could transform Islam for Muslim women across the world. Wadud asserted, according to one report, that the group's march on the mosque "would have a historic impact and help us rescript the current history of the face of Islam."

And indeed this was a moment—extending through the entire post-9/11 era in America thus far—of unprecedented opportunity for Muslim feminists, liberals, and progressives—and even liberal conservatives. The climate of the day was fiercely critical of radical and even of strongly conservative Islam (such as Wahhabism), and it was a climate that was in general strongly supportive of critics of Islam from whatever perspective they spoke, including most particularly of Muslims speaking as feminists or liberals. In addition these were years when the issue of women in Islam had been squarely placed on the table as a matter of national interest to Americans in the public conversation on Islam. People speaking out against Islam in the name of feminism and women's rights could almost count in these times (far more than in the past) on the likelihood that their words and activism would capture national media attention. Consequently, their messages and activism, amplified by media attention, could come to have important and even, as Wadud asserted, historic consequences. The *New York Times*, among other national papers, intermittently reported on the developments regarding Nomani and the Morgantown mosque. An article in that paper in July 2004 quoted Nomani as declaring that "this is part of the war within Islam for how it's defined in the world." Since 9/11, Nomani said, "I've seen that if we don't assert ourselves, we're relinquishing our religion to be defined by those who speak the loudest and act the toughest."[20]

Nomani and Wadud continued to try to seize the moment to put forward their definition of Islam and their particular understanding of the religion. In March 2005, for example, in an event timed to coincide with the publication of Nomani's book, *Standing Alone in Mecca: An American Woman's Struggle for the Soul of Islam,* Nomani and Wadud resumed their activism by staging a mixed-gender congregational prayer to be led by a woman—Amina Wadud. In doing this they were explicitly challenging conventional orthodox teachings as to the acceptability of women leading mixed-gender prayers, as well as with regard to observing separation between men and women during prayers. The event was held in the Synod House at the Cathedral of St. John the Divine, which had been rented for the occasion.

This mixed-gender prayer was cosponsored by another self-defined "progressive" Muslim organization, which had also come into being in this moment of opportunity, the group that had founded the Muslim WakeUp! website in 2003. Attended by "more than a hundred men and women," and drawing a handful of protestors outside the cathedral, the event was covered by national and international media, including the *New York Times* and BBC television.[21]

Like the women who formed the Daughters of Hajar and the individuals who established Muslim WakeUp! other liberal Muslims seized the moment and formed groups and associations. Among other such organizations to emerge at this time was al-Fatiha, for example, a gay, lesbian, bisexual, and transgender Muslim organization, and also the Progressive Muslim Union. Al-Fatiha had been founded in the late 1990s by Feisal Alam, an American Muslim of South Asian background. Prior to 9/11 the organization had kept a very low profile for fear of becoming the target of violence from extremists. They had operated in the shadows, organizing conventions through semi-secret arrangements and revealing their location to attendees at the last moment for fear of violence.

After 9/11 and the tremendously heightened scrutiny by the U.S. government, al-Fatiha emerged from the shadows, holding its conventions relatively openly and listing the names of its board and founders.

The Progressive Muslim Union was founded in November 2004 by Omid Safi, a professor at the time at Colgate University, along with a group of other younger generation American Muslims, most of whom were academics or academics in the making. In an introduction to an edited book entitled *Progressive Muslims: On Justice, Gender, and Pluralism,* Safi wrote that an "important part of being a progressive Muslim is the determination to hold Muslim societies accountable for justice and pluralism. It means openly and purposefully resisting, challenging and overthrowing structures of tyranny and injustice in these societies. At a general level, it means contesting injustices of gender apartheid (practiced by groups such as the Taliban) as well as the persecution of religious and ethnic minorities. . . . More specifically it means embracing and implementing a different vision of Islam than that offered by Wahhabi and neo-Wahhabi groups."[22] Safi also liberally invoked the name not only of Martin Luther King, Jr. (as ISNA speakers also had often done), but also of Bob Dylan. Such names clearly signaled the American as well as the Muslim roots of the "progressive" form of Islam that the Progressive Muslims were proclaiming.

The book included several essays by Muslim feminists, as well an essay addressing the question of homosexuality in Islam by Scott Siraj al-Haqq Kugle. It included essays by a number of the most prominent younger Muslim male academics who identified as "progressive" or as "moderate" Muslims. These included (besides Omid Safi) Khaled Abou El Fadl, Farid Esack, and Ebrahim Moosa. One of the notable facts about these post-9/11 times and this rising generation of male Muslim academics is that issues of women and gender are now routinely among the issues they address. Indeed, it seems that anyone aspiring to leadership today in the religious-cum-academic community among Western Muslims, American or European, must give some generally liberally inclined attention at least to issues of women and gender.[23]

Overall, the individuals making up these groups generally speak as committed Muslims. No matter how critical they are of conservative (as well as, of course, of militant) Islam, their common base position is that the dominant conservative forms of Islam represent not, as they claim, some "true" and foundational Islam but rather particular ways of reading and interpreting Islam's foundational texts and of translating them into law.

Most of those progressive and gender-conscious Islamic organizations founded in the early to mid-2000s such as those just mentioned—Daughters of Hajar, Muslim WakeUp! and Progressive Muslim Union—proved ephemeral. Even al-Fatiha, founded a few years before 9/11 but emerging publicly after that date, disappeared from the web, although it has since reappeared. A Ramadan dinner, for example, hosted by President Obama on September 2, 2009, included on its guest list Mina Trudeau, "Executive Director of al-Fatiha Foundation." Also among the guests was Ingrid Mattson, president of ISNA.[24]

Other organizations emerging in this post-9/11 moment have proved more enduring—particularly, for example, the American Society for Muslim Advancement—ASMA. Founded in 1997 by Imam Feisal Rauf, author of *What's Right with Islam: A New Vision for Muslims and the West* (2004), and by Imam Rauf's wife, Daisy Khan, who is executive director of ASMA Society, the society surged to new levels of activism, prominence, and visibility in the post-9/11 era. Supported by an impressive list of U.S. foundations—among them the Carnegie Corporation of New York, the Ford Foundation, and the Rockefeller Brothers—ASMA describes its mission as being to "elevate the discourse on Islam and foster environments in which Muslims thrive. We are dedicated," the ASMA mission statement continues, "to strengthening an authentic expression of Islam based on cultural and religious harmony through interfaith collaboration, youth and women's empowerment, and arts and cultural exchange."[25] ASMA has hosted a number of conventions bringing together "more than a hundred Muslim women activists, thinkers and writers from across world." One such conference, the "Women's Islamic Initiative in Spirituality and Equity Conference" (WISE), was held in New York in 2006, and another, entitled "Muslim Women: Building Institutions, Creating Change," was held in Kuala Lumpur in July 2009. Among the topics discussed were domestic violence and ways of establishing grass-roots initiatives to support Muslim women worldwide.[26]

Though several organizations proved to be quite ephemeral, they were nevertheless important for the ideas they generated and put into the public domain—ideas that now form part of the repertoire of possibilities of thought and activism in relation to issues of women, feminism, and sexuality, and, in general, issues of progressive and liberal contestations of conservative forms of Islam. Moreover, the scholars who were associated with these organizations—among them Sa'diyya Sheikh, Marcia Hermensen, Abou El Fadl, Esack, Safi, Moosa, Wadud, and Kecia Ali (author of *Gender and Sexuality in Islam*)—continue to be productive, pioneering scholars in relation to work on women, gender, feminism, and other areas pertaining to progressive, liberal, or moderate forms of Islam.

Furthermore, another generation of young academics is already pressing forward. Like the generation just ahead of them, this generation includes many scholars who identify as committed Muslims. Often they are people for whom Islamic justice must, by definition, include gender justice, even if, as they see it, past androcentric generations failed to interpret the Quran as entailing gender justice. By definition Islamic justice must—in the eyes of this new generation of committed American Muslims—self-evidently and rationally include gender justice if it is to be counted as, indeed, justice.

Among such younger academics is Asifa Quraishi. Quraishi, a former hijabi, is a specialist in Islamic law and legal theory. Currently based at the University of Wisconsin, she has been actively working for women's rights in various capacities. Quraishi was a founding member of the National Association of Muslim Lawyers, in which capacity she drafted, in 2001, "a clemency appeal brief in the case of Bariya Ibrahim Magazu, who was sentenced to flogging in Nigeria."[27] Quraishi was also president for a time of Karamah, an organization which describes itself as an organization of Muslim Women Lawyers for Human Rights founded by Aziza al-Hibri and based in Washington, D.C. Established in the 1990s, Karamah, like the ASMA Society, was able to garner new support and to considerably expand its reach and services in the post-9/11 era.

Altogether, the study of the Islamic textual and legal heritage as regards women is livelier and more dynamic today than at any other time in my own lifetime—and indeed livelier than at any other moment in the history of feminism and Islam. I personally know, for example, as many as four Muslim women at Harvard University alone who are currently pursuing advanced degrees in areas pertinent to the legal and scriptural heritage of Islam in relation to women. Moreover, all of them—Havva Guney-Ruebenacker (hijabi), Yousra Fazli (former hijabi), Sara Omar (former hijabi), and Sarah Eltantawi—are women who bring to their work a passion for women's rights and a familiarity with women's studies scholarship as well as, in most cases, a religious commitment to Islam. Remarkably, many of this cohort of young scholars bring new skills and knowledge to the table. Often, young scholars who have obtained B.A.'s at American academic institutions then follow this up with studies at traditional Islamic universities and other sites of Islamic learning in the Muslim world—in Damascus or Cairo, for example. Then they return to pursue their graduate work at American universities, bringing these skills in Islamic traditional scholarship and learning to their work. We have never yet had academic work in the field of the study of women in Islam that draws fully on the intellectual and scholarly resources of both the Islamic world and the West. These are unprecedented times that promise to bring into being a new kind of scholarship.

In terms of the level of intellectual liveliness, ferment, and activism, the era we are in today seems to be one that most directly parallels and resembles, in relation now to Muslim American women, the era of extraordinarily dynamic activism and cultural and intellectual productivity which American feminism more broadly—Christian, Jewish, secular, and to some extent Muslim—underwent when second wave feminism vigorously emerged in the 1960s and 1970s.

Nor is it only in relation to legal and scriptural texts that the field of the study of women in Islam is a dynamically expanding field of knowledge and scholarship. Year by year the number of American Muslim female voices in the academic world is steadily growing. Books that have appeared since 2008 include a study by Jamillah Karim, author of *American Muslim Women* and a hijabi professor at Spellman College; another by Jasmine Zine, a former hijabi and author of *Canadian Islamic Schools* and professor at Wilfrid Laurier University; and a third by Sherene Razack, author of *Casting Out the Eviction of Muslims from Western Law and Politics,* a professor at the University of Toronto.

From the 1970s to the 1990s, when feminist scholarship in relation to the Euro-American heritage and to Christianity and Judaism came into its own on American campuses, the study of women in Islam and in particular in relation to the Middle East also expanded, albeit not quite as extensively, alongside other areas of feminist study. Through that era a good proportion of these studies were undertaken by non-Muslim academics. Some also were done by women of Muslim background, very few of whom self-identified as believing Muslims. But that was an era, perhaps now passing, when secularism seemed de rigueur in the academy and open commitment to any religious belief rare. Today a shift seems to be distinctly under way as regards American Muslim women. Often self-identified as committed Muslims, such women are increasingly now coming to make up the majority of those studying Islam and women.

Notably too, it was typically Christian women, and sometimes women of Christian background, who studied women in Christianity. And similarly it was Jewish women or women of Jewish background who studied women in Judaism. Today's trend of increasing numbers of Muslim women studying women in Islam thus appears to be bringing the study of women in Islam into balance with what has been the norm in academia (in recent decades, anyway) in relation to women in Christianity and Judaism.

Activist commitments today by American Muslim women to issues of gender and women's rights are by no means confined to the academic arena but are emerging in a variety of other fields too, among them fiction, documentaries, and television series and plays. One notable collection, *Living Islam Out Loud,* brings together the voices of a number of American Muslim women, all of whom share a commitment to women's rights—though "feminist" is not a term that women of this generation willingly apply to themselves. All share a commitment to Islam typically as faith and certainly in any case as identity. Among them—as was the case among Islamists most evidently in the Resurgence of the 1970s to the 1990s in Cairo—Islamic identity is typically not merely an ascribed and passively accepted identity, but rather it is actively embraced. It is the identity they speak from and which they enact and make visible, sometimes through the adoption of hijab. This is an identity (again as with Islamists) that often entails ethical commitments—including commitments to women's rights. This collection of stories, bringing together the personal narratives of sixteen such women from a range of professions, offers an overview of the interests and perspectives of this rising generation of American Muslim women in their diversity.

All of the contributors to *Living Islam Out Loud* are under forty, and all are also women who "do not remember a time when they weren't both American and Muslim," and who come from a variety of ethnic backgrounds. "We are the children of immigrants from Pakistan, Egypt, Senegal," writes the editor, Saleemah Abdul Ghafur, and "we are the distant descendants of African slaves brought to the Americas as well as the children of American men and women who accepted Islam in adulthood."[28]

They see themselves, as the editor writes, as a generation breaking new ground in the ongoing story of Islam in the world. For the first time in history, Abdul Ghafur writes, "we have a critical mass of women under forty raised as Muslims in the United States by parents who themselves struggled to reconcile their American and Muslim identities." Consequently they are "the first true generation of American Muslim women." Braiding in their own lives new combinations of identities and histories, this cohort understand themselves as pioneers, forging a way forward for other Muslims across the world. "I believe," she writes, "that Islam is in the midst of global transformation." This transformation, she continues, is being led "largely by Muslims in the West: because we have certain academic freedoms along with freedom of speech and freedom to worship. These civil liberties are largely unknown in Muslim-majority countries. Those of us leading this transformation are confident in claiming Islam for ourselves."[29]

The conditions Abdul Ghafur lists—freedom of speech, of worship, and so forth, which American and European Muslims enjoy and which many other Muslims across the world lack—are real enough. It is certainly plausible and even likely that American Muslims, like American Catholics and American Jews before them, will come to be an important force in global Islam. It is also possible that—as is the case with Catholicism and Judaism—Muslims in other parts of the world will not necessarily easily cede authority in matters Islamic to Western Muslims.

In any case, the book brings together the personal stories of a range of young Muslim professionals—a CEO, a woman working at MTV networks, and a member of the board of al-Fatiha, as well as several writers, including poets and novelists. Among their number are four of the women who made up the Daughters of Hajar. The women's stories illuminate the ways in which their multiple heritages as Muslim Americans are affecting their lives as women and often in relation, specifically, to issues of sexuality. For sexuality and problems around sexuality are unmistakably among the core themes in many of the women's stories.

Samina Ali, for example, a novelist born in Hyderabad, India, who arrived in Minnesota with her immigrant parents at the age of one, offers an intimate account of growing up attending the Urdu-speaking Islamic Center of Minnesota, and a childhood and an adolescence that were followed by an arranged marriage to a man from the home country who proved to be gay and who divorced her as soon as he got his green card. Falling in love subsequently with a man who was "white and atheist," she decided to marry him despite the rift that it would cause in her family. Subsequently journeying through atheism herself and rejecting much of what she had been taught was Islam, she finds life without God a "vast emptiness." After immersing herself in studying Buddhism and surviving some harrowing experiences, she finds her way to Sufism.[30]

A contributor of Iranian background tells the story of her struggles as a Muslim lesbian. Writing under a pen name "for safety reasons," Khalida Saed describes wearing hijab and starting up a Muslim Student Association chapter at her high school. After meeting her first girlfriend and experiencing her mother's hostility to her sexuality when she came out to her, Saed rejected Islam. "I equated all things Iranian and Muslim with being anti-gay, and therefore anti-me, and those messages were reinforced by the mainstream LGBTQ movement."[31]

Discovering al-Fatiha at college, Saed joined the organization and through it found her way back to Islam. Al-Fatiha included women in its leadership, she tells us, provided inclusive prayer space, and encouraged women to lead prayers. "This was the Islam every woman dreams about,"

Saed wrote, explaining that "progressive" Islam "operates under the belief that anything that sanctions discrimination against anyone is un-Islamic." This "branch of Islam," Saed explains, is grounded in the belief "that working towards social justice is an integral part of the religion." Strikingly—but not, after all, surprisingly in a young woman who was a founding member of her local MSA—Saed's words here directly echo the Islamist understanding of Islam as centered on the quest for social justice and the activist commitment to working to bring this about. Saed goes on to explain that according to this "distinctly American" understanding of Islam, "patriarchy and sexism are not necessarily Islamic traits but are actually cultural traits."[32]

And indeed, Saed is right to emphasize that these latter concerns are "distinctly American." The Islamist core commitment to activism in pursuit of social justice becomes, in the American context, for Saed as for others of her generation living at the confluence of the two traditions, a quest also for equal rights for women and minorities, among them, in Saed's view, for gays. For, today in America, equal rights for women and gays are constitutive elements of what many in this society mean by "justice."

Other contributors to *Living Islam Out Loud* similarly illuminate the complex and evidently often richly productive braiding of culture and history and of Islamist and American ethics under way in our time in the lives and thought of this rising generation. Precious Muhammad, for example, explains that her parents had been followers of Elijah Muhammad at a time when "Islam, as freedom, justice, and equality, offered sorely needed structural solutions to combat the terror of American racism." Later her parents followed W. D. Mohammed into Sunni Islam. Thus, Muhammad tells us, "I was not born into the Nation of Islam but rather into true Islam as revealed to the Prophet Muhammad 1400 years ago."[33]

From childhood on, growing up among "strong Muslim women," Muhammad never doubted that Islam "gives recognition to women's independent existence." Like many Muslim American writers of her generation concerned about women's issues, Muhammad is acutely aware of the multiple fronts on which she must fight as woman, African American, and Muslim.[34] As a Muslim feminist website succinctly put it, "As Muslim feminists we aim to locate and critique misogyny, sexism, patriarchy, Islamophobia, racism and xenophobia as they affect Muslim women."[35]

Another contributor to the volume, Mohja Kahf, similarly makes clear her commitment to fighting on several fronts: as an impressive line of American minority feminists and women of color (Audre Lorde, Gloria Anzaldua, Cherie Moraga, bell hooks, Alice Walker, and many more) had done before them. Deeply critical of what she considers to be sexist interpretations of Islam, Kahf at the same time considers herself committed to Islam, a religion she understands as being intrinsically just and nonsexist. Consequently, critical of Islamic patriarchy, Kahf is also deeply critical of "Muslim-bashers" who manipulate the issue of the oppression of women in Islam for their own purposes. "Spare me the sermon on Muslim women," she wrote in an article published in the *Washington Post.* Going on to describe, in the same article, the pleasure she takes in choosing which hijab to wear, Kahf observes that even as she protests against Muslim-bashers and rebuts and exposes the inaccuracies of people's perceptions about women in Islam she continues, she notes, to "put in my time struggling for a more woman-affirming interpretation of Islam and in criticizing Muslim misogyny." Like most contributors to the volume, Kahf also mentions details that indicate her early exposure to Islamism. In Kahf's case she grew up, we learn, enjoying the apples "on the ISNA farm in Indiana." This detail presumably indicates that her family had been active in founding or in running ISNA.[36]

As Abdul Ghafur observes in her Introduction, the issue of the hijab was one of two themes that almost every contributor chose to address in relation to her own life and practice. Women wear hijab for many reasons, Ghafur explains, some "because they believe it is mandated by God, others to demonstrate solidarity or resistance, and still others to follow familial and community mores." She then goes on to note that "there are many reasons a woman does not wear hijab. Some don't because they don't want to distinguish themselves in Western society; others don't believe that Islam requires hijab of its female followers, believing that modesty is required of all Muslims." Above all, Abdul Ghafur continues, "most of us are exhausted with the hijab debate and envision a future where we move beyond the judgments of women with and sans hijab."[37]

The very fact that the subject of wearing hijab is a salient issue for many of the contributors is in itself indication of the shaping influence that an Islamist understanding of Islam has had on this first explicitly Muslim-identified and numerically significant generation of American-born and/or American-raised Muslims. A number of contributors to the volume (Abdul Ghafur, Yousra Fazli, and Saed, for example) note they had once worn hijab and had then ceased to do so for various reasons —Fazli because she became convinced in the course of her research that hijab was not an Islamic requirement after all.[38] Similarly, a number of academic Muslim-American women, including women mentioned above, once wore hijab but subsequently ceased to do so. Typically these women continue, despite removing their hijab, to consider themselves to be committed Muslims.

The decision to "dehijabize" (or "de-jab," as another former hijabi called it) while remaining a committed Muslim seems to be a growing trend among this generation of professional Muslim Americans.[39] A number of women, both academics and journalists, have written about and have begun to track this emergent trend. Among those writing on the subject is Andrea Useem, who writes about her own decision to cast aside her hijab. Converting to Islam while abroad in Harare, Zimbabwe, Useem says that she had never thought of changing her dress or of taking up hijab until she returned to America and saw educated Muslim women her own age wearing hijab.

Gradually, and after checking with the "de facto Muslim chaplain at Harvard," where she was studying (a chaplain whose wife, Useem observes, wore full, black Islamic robes and a face veil, and who confirmed to her that all four schools of Sunni law agreed that covering was required), Useem, after reading and praying about the subject, became convinced that God required her to dress this way. Various subsequent experiences, however, including a sojourn in Muscat, Oman, where hijab was the norm, led Useem to increasingly question this form of dress. Eventually, thinking about the "medieval scholars who had decreed covering from head to toe to be mandatory for women," Useem arrived at the understanding that "I did not convert to Islam to follow their lead: I had little if any allegiance to them."[40]

For Useem as for others mentioned in these pages, aspects of Islam and even of the Quran that violate their own sense of the meaning of justice as, by definition, inclusive of justice for women, are elements that in the end come to be for them irreducibly troubling. Thus Useem, for example, finds herself compelled in good conscience to dissociate herself from interpretations and even Quranic verses that do not conform to her understanding of justice. As she wrote, "I am uncomfortable with aspects of the Quran and classical Islamic law that allow polygamy, or unilateral male divorce, or make a woman's legal testimony worth less than a man's. In my mind, now, the scarf is of one cloth with these ideas, and I needed to separate myself, at least symbolically, from them."[41]

Over all, these committed and activist American Muslims share a number of noteworthy traits. Among these is the fact that as a cohort they make up the first numerically significant generation of American-born (or raised) Muslims—or they are converts to the faith. Ranging in age from twenty-five to forty-five (as the ASMA Society identified American Muslim activists of this generation in a conference it organized in 2004 for "Muslim Leaders of Tomorrow"), these activists are typically also "ethnically diverse and as well affiliated with different sects of Islam." They share too a "demonstrated commitment" (as ASMA described it) to the Muslim community, "not only in America but throughout the umma," evidenced in the various activities they pursue, be this "in the area of political engagement, interfaith work, social work, community service, religious service, academia, journalism, or a slew of other professions and interests."[42]

Markedly for this generation of American Muslims who pursue their work and activism within the framework of Islam, their identity as Muslim Americans clearly trumps and supersedes their sense of identity and community as grounded in either ethnicity or national origins. In the foreground of their work is their identity as Muslim Americans: a trait which sharply distinguishes them from many other Americans of Muslim heritage from backgrounds that were not influenced by Islamism and who did not attend mosques or Islamic schools and thus were not exposed to Islamist thought via those institutions. For this latter group, who in fact probably make up the majority of American Muslims, Islam, whether as faith or as identity, is not generally ground either of action or self-presentation. In contrast to that larger group, this younger generation of American Muslims who are grounded in Islam as faith and/or identity seem to see themselves first of all as part of a multiethnic Muslim American generation whose bonds of commonality as Muslim Americans are stronger and more important—in contrast to the perceptions and sense of identity of their parents' generation—than are other national or ethnically based identities.

Consequently they work collaboratively as Muslim Americans, and their activism and writings are intensely in conversation with each other. Abdul Ghafur's collection is a perfect example of the culturally and intellectually multiethnic American reading of Islam beginning to come into flower in our times. While there are indeed frictions occurring at mosques and at ground level between different Muslim American ethnicities and communities, on the cultural and intellectual plane, at least among people for whom issues of women and gender are primary areas of concern, their work collectively and their multiple histories and perspectives are drawn on not in rivalry but in collaboration. They bring into being a complex and richly variegated exploration of the Islamic religious heritage in its intersections with the twenty-first-century American Muslim experience in its diversity. This trend, distinctly in evidence in activists whose focuses are issues of women and gender, also appears to be more broadly a feature of American Muslim intellectual and cultural production in our times.

Finally, another distinguishing mark these American Muslim women and gender activists share is (as I have implicitly suggested) the fact that nearly all were directly touched and influenced by Islamism at some point in their lives. This is obviously the case with the people associated with ISNA or the MSA. But it is also the case with respect to many of the liberals and even the radicals who often also had connections with the MSA or ISNA, and/or grew up assuming that the hijab was a basic requirement for Muslim women—itself a sign of the shaping presence of Islamist influence. Or they are people like Wadud, who at some point in their lives (and in Wadud's case this was in the critical time of her conversion) frequented mosques influenced by Islamists such as Mawdudi.

Even non-Sunnis were affected by such influence: Samina Ali, for example, of Shi'i background, grew up attending a Sunni-dominated Islamic center because (as must have often been the case in many towns) this was the only available Islamic center in the neighborhood. Islamic centers, like most institutional forms of Islam in this country, as already noted, tended to be dominated by Islamist perspectives. To be sure not all the activists mentioned here appear to have been influenced by Islamism: Laleh Bakhtiar, for example, and Omid Safi seem not to have been so influenced. But they appear to be the exceptions.[43]

This Islamist heritage is in many ways implicit in some of the traits which characterize this generation of activists. It is after all Islamism specifically that valorized activism and activism explicitly undertaken as committed and visible Muslims in the cause of social justice as a fundamental religious obligation. These goals and obligations of activism as committed Muslims formed no part of the old-style, quietist, inward-looking, and private rather than overtly enacted forms of Islam that were commonplace in the Middle East and elsewhere prior to the Islamic Resurgence. Similarly it is Islamism that emphasizes the primary character of Islam and the Muslim umma as the true and proper ground of identity and community for Muslims.

Indeed, the Muslim World League founded by Saudi Arabia in the 1960s specifically set out, in its initial confrontation with Nasserism and Arab nationalism, to promote Muslim identity and loyalty to the Muslim umma—rather than ethnicity—as the only true grounds of identity and community for Muslims. This is possibly one element contributing to the sea-change that Arab Christian as well as Muslim identities have been undergoing in the last couple of decades as Arabness, formerly the bond holding together Muslim and Christian Arabs, steadily fades almost into insignificance and Muslim identity takes its place (thus loosening the bonds between Muslim and Christian Arabs) as ground of identity, meaning, and community. Similarly, to the American majority and most particularly to the forces of security, it is no longer now, as it was until the 1990s, Arab identity that triggers alarms but rather more specifically today Muslim identity, whether Arab or not. Naturally, though, there are many forces, including forces internal to America, that have their part in shaping contemporary American Muslim identities.[44]

*

> The Jews. It's the other question [the first being the "woman question"] that perturbed me during my madressa years because the Jews came in for a regular tarring. Mr. Khaki taught us with a straight face that Jews worship moolah not Allah, and that their idolatry would pollute my piety if I hung out with them. (Irshad Manji, *The Trouble with Islam*)

This influence of Islamism is present even among American Muslim feminists who take a radically critical stance vis-à-vis Islam and women (and indeed often vis-à-vis Islam more generally), such as Nomani and Manji. In Nomani's case there appear to be distinct traces of Islamism in her early life. For example, she mentions that when her father first came to America in 1962 he became involved with "Muslim students who had met earlier in the year and formed a national organization they called the Muslim Students' Association."[45] After a visit to India her father returned to America and became involved in New Jersey in coordinating prayers and Sunday school with the local Islamic community organization, work which laid the ground for what would become the Islamic Center of Central New Jersey. These activities would seem to suggest that if not an Islamist himself, Nomani's father shared in some of their goals as regards instituting Muslim spaces. At the same time, the positions that Nomani describes her father as consistently taking—including his unwavering support for her as an unwed mother—seem to suggest that, if he was an Islamist, he was certainly a flexible and open-minded one. Nomani's descriptions of her mother suggest that her way of practicing Islam was distinctly more in line with old-world, traditional forms of Islamic practice rather than with Islamism. Islam for her mother, for example, Nomani tells us, was "a private act of faith." Going on to observe also that her mother did not perform the regular prayers, Nomani further writes that for her mother "prayer doesn't know a time clock or prostration. Life is prayer."[46]

Nevertheless, once Nomani began to be actively engaged with

working and wrestling with Islam her activism would in important ways remain within the Islamist framework—even as she vigorously took on the task of contesting and protesting against Islamic and Islamist sexism. It was not until early 2002, she tells us—in the wake of the murder of her friend Daniel Pearl and of her own difficult experiences in Pakistan in January 2002—that Nomani found herself precipitated into wrestling with and in general plunged into deep involvement with Islam. Previously, in addition to working as a Wall Street journalist, Nomani had written *Tantrica: Traveling the Road of Divine Love,* a book which appeared in 2003. The shock and horror of Pearl's murder and her own difficult personal experiences with the father of her child led her to feel "very much at odds with my religion." Now, "instead of turning away from Islam, I decided to find out more about my faith." Thus Nomani decided to make the hajj, or pilgrimage, setting forth on the journey that would also lead to her feminist activism in relation to Islam.

Her work as an activist has centered on creating equal space for women in mosques. At no point does Nomani ask—as did many radical feminists of the sixties and seventies among them most notably Mary Daly—whether creating equal space for women within a patriarchal institution is necessarily a worthwhile goal for feminists. Mosques obviously—along with churches and other religious spaces—may be seen as places where audiences can be collectively inculcated with the run-of-the-mill patriarchal views that have typically pervaded and formed the staples of monotheistic religious teachings. It was the Islamic Resurgence, after all, which brought women back into mosques after centuries of exclusion—exclusion which, from a feminist perspective, might plausibly be regarded as having perhaps been in fact a boon rather than a deprivation. Naturally mosques today in America serve complex purposes, and it is easy to see that equal space and roles in mosques for women might indeed be desirable. But some acknowledgment along the way, from Nomani and others seeking improved or equal space in mosques, of the inherent ambiguities of the situation from the feminist point of view, would have added a valuable layer of complexity to the subject.

In Manji's case the issue of her early exposure to Islamist ideas is unambiguous. In *The Trouble with Islam,* Manji writes of her ongoing distress and unhappiness at having to attend Islamic school as a child.

This school, or "madressa," as she calls it, was located in the local mosque where "men and women entered the mosque from different doors and planted themselves on the correct sides of an immovable wall." Attending this school, which Manji continued to do for five years, entailed wearing "a white polyester chador," a garment which Manji describes as "a condom over my head" intended to protect her from "unsafe intellectual activity." Manji was critical from early on of the school's position on gender issues—such as girls not being allowed to lead prayers—and her attendance at the school ended when she was dismissed for objecting to her teacher's derogatory references to Jews.[47]

Both Nomani and Manji share with other Islamist-influenced Muslims of their generation their explicit self-identification as religiously committed Muslims as well as their commitment to activism in the service of Islam: in the service specifically of reforming Islam, a project and objective shared in one form or another by most other American Muslim "feminists." (The influence of Islamism is even more starkly present in the life of Hirsi Ali, another fierce critic of Islam who now describes herself as an ex-Muslim. Hirsi Ali moved as a child of six with her parents from her native Somalia to Saudi Arabia, where she remained for a number of years living in the Saudi environment of Wahhabism, a form of Islam to which her mother was strongly drawn. Her subsequent critiques of Islam following her immigration to Holland took shape in the context of the politically fraught debates around immigration issues in Holland and they have been extensively discussed in relation to their context in numerous reviews and books.)[48]

Nomani and Manji also differ from most other such activists in that their relation to Islam and the broad Muslim community seems to be above all adversarial. In contrast to other such activists, neither views either their local mosque-going community or the global umma or Muslim community as communities to which they naturally and properly belong. Both depict their experience of the American versus the Islamic ethos as tantamount to—as Manji put it (borrowing obviously on Bernard Lewis's phrase)—"my own personal clash of civilizations." And both present themselves as intrepid and lonely reformers striving to change a benighted and in many ways profoundly repugnant religious heritage.[49] Nomani, for example, writes of the "fear and loathing" she felt "in my heart" for Islam in response to the atrocities committed in its name.[50] And Manji, as Mahmood pointed out, commonly expresses deep contempt for Muslims.

Neither Nomani nor Manji display much awareness of the well-established tradition as regards minority feminism of the need to simultaneously fight on two fronts: the fronts of gender bigotry and also of racial or religious bigotry. But as a result, Nomani's and Manji's works have the virtues of vividly exposing the entrenched bias and prejudice around gender and other matters that are doubtless endemic to the everyday practices and ideas informing some strains of Islam and Islamism in America. Nomani's experiences, as recounted in her book and even more vividly as captured in the PBS documentary *Mosque at Morgantown*, make sharply clear the entrenched patriarchal and misogynist assumptions that sometimes inform the attitudes of mosque officials. Similarly, Manji's account vividly brings to the fore the dogmatic and prejudiced views of women and others, that no doubt too are to be found sometimes among mosque teachers: a subject certainly deserving further research.[51]

Clearly in the wake of 9/11 we have entered an era of exuberant and highly visible American Muslim "feminist" activism: an era of creative challenge to patriarchal norms that is reminiscent in its liveliness and creativity of American feminism in the sixties and seventies. In this era, this exuberant efflorescence seems to be occurring specifically and uniquely in relation to women in Islam. This is a "feminism" too, we should note, that, for all its resemblance in its goals and ideals to the familiar feminism of the last decades, nevertheless also often refuses to be identified by the brand name and label of "feminism."

As in past eras of American feminist activism, the views and positions that are finding expression span the gamut from radical and liberal to conservative. At the conservative end are ISNA and MSA women such as Mattson, McGee, Alkhateeb, Haffajee, Mubarak, Elgenaidi, Barazangi, and Beshir. At the liberal and radical end are Kahf, Wadud, Saed, Nomani, Manji, and others. Some at the liberal and radical end of the spectrum are skilled too at courting and making use of media attention to convey their messages. There are differences, to be sure, distinguishing the conservatives. Most notably, perhaps, is the fact that liberals and radicals take up issues of sexuality, while conservatives typically eschew the subject. Noticeably, however, conservative "feminists" do not explicitly speak out against liberal positions on sexuality. Similarly, conservative women generally do not, unlike liberals and radicals, overtly challenge the validity of Quranic verses and/or their classical interpretations, although they may indeed express, as Mubarak did, uneasiness about them. Commonly they express their conservatism in their dress: liberal women may or may not be hijabis, whereas ISNA and MSA women are consistently hijabis who, moreover, commonly wear long, loose Islamic robes and strictly concealing headdress.

Rooted originally in the gender-conservative Islamist movement and deeply influenced by the Muslim Brotherhood and the Jamaati, ISNA and the MSA naturally and by definition represent the conservative end of the spectrum. Such movements in their home countries, far from challenging the patriarchal rules that are endemic to the world's dominant forms of Islam, in fact typically emphatically reaffirmed them. Besides insisting on the hijab and gender separation as foundational requirements of Islam, Islamists in the home countries certainly did not include as part of their agenda any discussion of the idea of women's equal rights or of justice for women in the American sense of equal justice—the very ideas that today inform the thought and perspectives of a number of prominent MSA and ISNA women mentioned in these pages. Such ideas were not even broached within the Islamist framework in the context of the Middle East. Although al-Ghazali and other Islamists in the Egyptian context developed lines of argument that permitted women's activism in the cause of Islam to take precedence over their duties as wives and mothers, these measures were understood to be essentially exceptional and temporary measures to be resorted to only in times of crisis for the community.

Furthermore, the radical Islamist Sayyid Qutb explicitly endorsed men's permanent dominion over women as part of the Quranic vision of the ideal Muslim society. Qutb excluded women from among those who were to be considered autonomous human subjects subservient to no one and entitled to equal justice in the ideal Islamic state that was to be ruled by sharia. This was the state that Islamists were dedicated to realizing through ongoing struggle. To this day in the Middle East there are no cases of religious or Islamist women heading major Islamic organizations consisting of both men and women. There have been no cases, that is, of women seeking, let alone attaining, the positions that conservative American Muslim women have already attained in America—in the person, for example, of Ingrid Mattson. Even Zainab al-Ghazali, the "unsung mother" of the Muslim Brotherhood, as we saw earlier, never held an official position in the Brotherhood. Similarly, although Nadia Yassine today in Morocco is the very visible and public spokeswoman for the Justice and Spirituality Party founded by her father, she does not officially hold a position of leadership in the party other than as the leader of the women's division.[52]

Needless to say, there have been no cases in the Middle East of women leading or even seeking to lead mixed-gender prayers. These, as well as other "feminist" claims and projects described here, represent specifically American Muslim developments—developments in which Americans are forging the way forward even in relation to trends under way in Europe. For instance, women-led prayer events were held in Oxford in the United Kingdom in 2008 and 2010, but in both instances the women brought in to lead them—Amina Wadud and Raheel Raza—were North American (U.S. and Canadian) Muslims.

Many forces played a part in creating the conditions that brought about the rise of the second wave of American feminism in the 1960s, among them most notably the struggle for African American civil rights. Similarly, a variety of factors and conditions coming together today appear to be contributing to the sudden emergence in the post-9/11 era of the extraordinarily dynamic Islamic "feminist" activism we are witnessing. Among these are the coming of age of a new cohort of a numerically significant generation of American-born (or raised) American Muslims, along with converts also of their generation—a generation conscious of themselves as pioneers of the American Muslim experience. Another factor is the opening up of new space for criticism of Islam in the post-9/11 era, including in relation to women. The very prominence now of the topic of the "oppression of women in Islam" in the national conversation in this country itself clearly put the issue on the table for American Muslims.

Another important factor contributing to this ferment and activism is—paradoxically—the very presence now not only of Islam but also and more specifically of Islamism in the fabric of America. For while feminism and the idea of rights and justice for women formed no part of the original Islamist agenda, activism in the cause of justice most emphatically *was* a foundational requirement and obligation of Islamism.

Translated to American society in the late twentieth and early twenty-first centuries, the Islamist obligation to pursue activist work in the cause of social justice easily came to mean, for many of those who grew up imbibing both American and Islamic and specifically Islamist values, a commitment to working for justice as understood by Americans at this moment in history.

For of course the particular moment we are in right now in the history of America and American notions of justice has been crucially decisive in producing the lively activism of this decade among American Muslims on matters of women and gender. It would be a very different story if this were America of a hundred years ago, when women did not have the right to vote, let alone the many other rights they have won since. It would be very different, too, if this were America of some fifty years ago, when it was legal to exclude blacks from "whites only" restaurants, hotels, latrines, drinking fountains, libraries, and so on, as it would also be very different if this were America even of the 1980s in relation to gays.

In both traditions, Islamic and American, at different moments in their shifting histories both women and minorities were not among the groups included as entitled to equal justice. The emergence of this wave of Islamic activism in relation to issues of women and gender is thus the product of the convergence of key elements in the teachings of Islamism with the ideals and understanding of justice in America in these very specific decades. Today evidently for a significant group among Islamist-influenced American Muslims who are living their lives at the confluence of those traditions—a group spanning the spectrum from Mattson to Kahf, Useem, Wadud, and Nomani—the justice they are working for is inclusive of women and minorities.

This group includes people based in ISNA and the MSA, and people therefore who are by definition at the conservative end of the spectrum of Islamic practice. Still, it would probably be accurate to describe

ISNA- and MSA-based women concerned implicitly or explicitly with issues of justice for women as most distinctly at the liberal end of the conservative spectrum: for concern for equal justice for women does indeed represent a departure from the Islamist blueprint where gender issues are seen as necessarily and properly grounded in gender separation and also typically in a notion of gender hierarchy.

Consequently, it is important to note that it is not only in relation to gender issues that some Islamist-based American Muslims have revised and expanded their understanding of the meaning of justice in light of the American understanding of justice. In the home countries Islamists did not (and do not) espouse a notion of the equal rights of minorities any more than they espoused the notion of equal rights for women. But today in America, where Muslims are themselves a minority, Islamists do emphatically embrace and support the idea of equal justice for minorities. This is clearly the case with CAIR, a Muslim American organization with roots in Islamism that is playing a prominent role in supporting and defending the civil rights of Muslims. By definition and by virtue of its activities in defense of civil rights and equal rights for Muslim Americans, CAIR now, in a clear departure from Islamist views in the home countries, grounds itself and its activism and its very raison-d'être in the American definition of justice as inclusive of justice for minorities as fully equal citizens.

In the confluence of histories that is unfolding now in America—a confluence signaled among other things by the growing commonness of the hijab, the phenomenon that I set out in the first place to explore—it is clearly the Islamist understanding of Islam which has not only come to gain institutional and public dominance but which also, ironically, with its commitments to activism in the service of the poor and in pursuit of social justice, is now most easily and naturally merging with the American tradition of activism in the cause of justice and social change. This tradition arguably is the signature American tradition: rooted in the idea of America as a work-in-progress, a society always striving forward, in struggle after struggle, toward an ever fuller and greater realization of the goal of social justice for all, through the commitment of its activist citizens—from the founding fathers on through abolition, suffrage, workers' rights, civil rights, women's rights, rights for gays and other minorities. There is nothing more American, Howard Dean had said at ISNA, than protest, and every generation, as Marcy Kaptur said at that same venue, must win liberty anew.

And so we have now the deeply ironic and paradoxical situation in which it is Islamists and those touched and influenced in some way by Islamism who, in their lives, writings, and activism, are joining and becoming part of this signature American tradition of speaking out and taking stands in the cause of justice, joining their voices with those of other socially committed and activist non-Muslim Americans—writers, politicians, media figures, and others.

It is not, by and large, secular American Muslims nor American Muslims for whom religion is a private matter but rather the children of Islamists who are notably present in and at the forefront of the activist American and American Muslim struggles of our times: be it against torture, erosions of civil rights, racial profiling, the wars in Iraq and Afghanistan and other foreign policy issues, and also in the cause of women's rights and gay rights in relation to Islam. Voices in support of nearly all of these causes, non-Muslim as well as Muslim, were part of the tapestry of voices I heard at ISNA conventions. Ingrid Mattson, Bonita McGee, Khadijah Haffajee, Maha Elgenaidi, Howard Dean, Marcy Kaptur, Eric Yoffie, Arnold Waskow, Keith Ellison, Amy Goodman—all seemed to be speaking from within a recognizably similar understanding of what the project of America was and should be, and a largely shared understanding of the meaning of justice. True, voices in support of gay rights and those fundamentally challenging Quranic readings on women were not among the spectrum of voices speaking out at ISNA. But it is the case too that such voices are no less contested, marginalized, and excluded within other mainstream American religious traditions.

This then is the conclusion that I find myself arriving at in light of the evidence surveyed through the preceding pages—a conclusion that represents in fact a complete reversal of my initial expectations: that it is, after all, Islamists and the children of Islamists and not secular or privately religious Muslims who are most fully and actively integrating into this core and definingly American tradition of social and political activism and protest in pursuit of justice. It is they, after all—they and not us, the secular or privately religious Muslims—who are now in the forefront of the struggle in relation to gender issues in Islam, as well as with respect to other human rights issues of importance to Muslims in America today—and implicitly of importance in the long term to other Americans too.

This fact is all the more remarkable in that, as scholars of Islam in America unanimously assert, Muslims who attend mosques or associate with American Muslim organizations—the venues typically influenced by Islamism—in fact still constitute only a minority of American Muslims. The estimated percentages of those attending such institutions in America is gradually rising, according to these experts, from an estimated 5 or 10 percent into the late 1990s to perhaps 30 or 40 percent today: a rising percentage that nevertheless still leaves them as making up the minority of American Muslims. Thus Islamists and their heirs and children are for the present no more than a minority of a minority. However, controlling most American Muslim institutions, they constitute the most influential and most publicly visible segment of this minority. And they are also quite visibly and publicly the most socially and politically committed and activist segment of the Muslim community.

*

> I'm not the woman president of Harvard, I'm the president of Harvard.
>
> —Drew Faust, 2007[53]

Shirin Neshat and Lalla el-Sayyedi are today prominent American artists of Muslim background. Both make ample use in their work of the visual resources of their Islamic heritage, often incorporating, for example, the Arabic script in their art, as well as images of women in hijabs and chadors. Neither artist is herself a hijabi or appears to have been at any point influenced by Islamism. On the basis of her art and films and also of her statements in lectures and interviews, Neshat evidently draws on this heritage as a committed secularist, though she at times gestures too toward some unspecified notion of mysticism. El-Sayyedi's art in this matter is perhaps even more inscrutable and ambiguous: neither her art nor her statements rule out the possibility that Islam may be for her also a spiritual resource.

Many American Muslims, the majority, according to most statistics, are pursuing lives in which, in accordance with another well-established American tradition for ethnic and religious minorities, they are doing their best to blend and meld as unobtrusively as possible into the fabric of America as they pursue their lives. As one writer, Tariq Ahmad, a doctor at Brigham and Women's Hospital in Boston, put it in an op-ed column in the *New York Times,* "We are trying to succeed in life, trying to be effective doctors, lawyers, business people, artists and other kinds of professionals."[54]

Some no doubt define themselves, as does the author of these words, simply as secular. However, it is possible—in light of the recent Pew Report indicating that many younger Americans do not belong to religious institutions but nevertheless believe in God, life after death, and the existence of "heaven, hell and miracles" at about the same rate as older generations—that some Muslims are believers who are at the same time non-mosquegoing Muslims.[55]

Studying what the term "secular" means exactly when applied to Muslims and Muslim histories in their diversity, as well as exploring shifts in meanings of that word over time, in different locales, and as it crossed borders, is a matter that unquestionably calls for further investigation and more precise understanding of the subject than we currently have. Similarly tracing the word's specific histories in English when applied to Muslims and Muslim-majority societies, and the origins and provenance of such English usage, is a no less essential task. Notably, the meaning of "secular" implied by the op-ed author just cited, Dr. Ahmad, itself opens up some questions. Describing himself and many other Muslims as secular, he writes, "We do not pray five times a day, do not read the Koran and have not spent much time inside a mosque. We only turn to Islam when a child is born, someone gets married or someone dies." This description, it should be noted, focusing as it does on the *mazhar*—the external and outward dimensions of religion as measures of commitment to religious belief—in fact describes the norms of practice prior to the rise of Islamism of many believing Muslims (in Egypt at any rate, as we saw) who nevertheless considered themselves to be faithful Muslims according to the *jawhar* or inner and "essential" meanings and rules of living Islam as ground of faith.

Also, as we saw earlier, "secular" in the Middle Eastern context was a term that was applied pejoratively early on in the rise of Islamism to

Muslims who were not Islamists and who did not practice Islam as Islamists did: to women, for example, who did not wear hijab even though many such women were, in their own eyes, believing Muslims. And as we also saw, the definitions of Islamists as to what "true" Islam was and what forms of dress and practices were "mandated" by Islam began to gain power in the Middle East in the 1970s and in America too by the 1990s. Today it is above all Islamists and Islamist-grounded institutions who are the authorities defining and determining the beliefs and practices of Islam in this country.

So powerful and effective have Islamist definitions of Islam become today in America and the West (and elsewhere), that even Muslims who grew up thinking they were believing Muslims and for whom Islam was above all a spiritual and ethical resource might well come to doubt their own sense and understanding of Islam. Finding themselves alienated by and feeling no empathy with the views and practices of this now dominant form of Islam—from its obligatory hijab to its activist social and political agendas—they perhaps begin to wonder if they are in fact Muslim after all: if *this* is Islam. I recall being told by an American Muslim friend that her twelve-year-old niece who attended Islamic school on weekends came home one day to inform her Sufi-practicing grandmother that the way she was practicing Islam was "wrong" and "not Islam." Although this is merely a personal anecdote, it would not surprise me if future researchers were to find that similar scenes of Islamist-influenced youngsters challenging their families' form of Islam were being played out in these years all across America.

Not uncommonly in our times this larger group of American and Western Muslims, whether secular or non-Islamist, feel—much as their non-Islamist Muslim predecessors did in Cairo as Islamism was gaining power—a degree of suspicion and even hostility toward the Western Islamists whose institutions and definitions of Islam now dominate the West's landscape.

Many, for example, are thoroughly irked at the way that Islamists have "hijacked the mike," as Kabbani had put it. And they are put off by its activist commitments to causes that non-Islamists see as essentially political. Altogether they often seem to feel a deep antipathy toward this Islamist form of Islam now so widely proclaimed and accepted in the West as Islam *tout court.*

Ahmad succinctly articulates many of these specific peeves in his column. He complains, for example, that on those few occasions when he attended meetings at Islamic centers there were invariably speeches "about the Palestine conflict, the Kashmir conflict, the Chechnya conflict, the Bosnian conflict," issues which, he writes, "secular" Muslims such as himself who make up (he notes) the majority of Muslims in America, are in fact quite "dispassionate" about. "We certainly have no interest," he explains, "in civilizational battles." Moreover, he continues, "we are loathed" by this dominant Muslim minority who now loudly speak for Islam and Muslims. Despite constituting the majority, he continues, "we have no clear voice, no representation and no one in the Western world appears to be aware of our existence." And indeed this is surely an extraordinary situation: a situation in which one form of Islam —a form that just four or five decades ago was marginal in most Muslim-majority countries and which at that point constituted just one strand within the multiple strands of Islam—is today globally dominant in the West as elsewhere.

Other non-Islamist Western Muslims also sometimes give vent to their dislike for Islamism. The prominent British journalist Yasmin Alibhai-Brown, for example, wrote, "I am but Muslim lite, a non-conformist believer who will not be told what and how by sanctimonious religious sentinels for whom religion is a long list of rules to be obeyed by bovine followers."[56] Alibhai-Brown differs from Ahmad in that she is by no means "dispassionate"—as her work and the positions she takes make clear—about political issues, including those affecting Muslims and other minorities, whether at home or abroad. Appointed to the Order of the British Empire (MBE) in 2001, Alibhai-Brown returned the award in 2003 in protest in part against the Labour government's conduct with respect to the Iraq war. All the same, though, as her words here (and most obviously, of course, "bovine") make clear, she too evidently feels a distinct antipathy toward Islamists.

And indeed a dislike for and even a fear of Islamists and a strong sense that they loathed "us" certainly described my own feelings about Islamists when I began the research whose findings I present in these pages. As I described, Aisha and I had no doubt that "they" hated us and all that we and other feminists, liberals and progressives, stood for. Nor was this perception mistaken. As we saw earlier, feminism along with communism and Zionism was ranked among the most hated enemies of Islamism through the 1970s and onward, and feminists were defined as people who were "un-Islamic and culturally westernized." This no doubt continues to be a view that flourishes among some Islamists. Quite likely, too, some level of anti-feminism and even of deep-seated opposition to the idea of justice as extending fully and equally to women is still alive and well among many ordinary Islamists in Muslim-majority countries. And as regards non-Islamist Muslims generally, as we saw, Islamists typically viewed such Muslims as, at best, suitable targets for da'wa and conversion to their own uniquely "true" form of Islam.

But these may be the traits mainly of an older home-country Islamism and of the Islamism, in this country, of an older and generally immigrant generation. Already there are significant changes under way as another and rising generation of American-born and/or American-raised Muslims shaped to some degree by Islamism begins to emerge into the foreground of Islamic activism and to take over the reins of power. Obviously, for example, these old Islamist traits of hostility to the idea of equal justice for women are not characteristic of that segment of the American Muslim and Islamist-influenced population committed to women's rights and activism that I was observing—the group, making up a segment of the broader Islamist population, who are at the forefront of this study *because* of their concern and activism in relation to issues of women and gender.

This means, too, as it is important to acknowledge and underscore here, that these positive elements regarding issues of women and gender that are emerging today in America are elements that are characteristic only of a particular segment of the Islamist-influenced American Muslim population—specifically of the most liberal and progressive segment. Certainly one cannot assume that such views and attitudes are typical of the entire Islamist-influenced American Muslim population. Similarly, this means that had I focused not on activism in relation to women and gender but on observing and following out other forms of activism and views on other themes and concerns in circulation among the American Islamist population—had I set out to study, for example, the prevalence among them of ideas as to a God-given gender hierarchy and God-given male prerogative—I would no doubt have accumulated quite different kinds of evidence and found myself writing a very different kind of book, and one in which I might well have arrived at a far bleaker and more disheartening conclusion.

It is important, therefore, to underscore that these positive traits and views related to issues of women and gender emerging among the Islamist-influenced American Muslim population represent the traits and views of those making up the distinctly liberal end of American Islamist-influenced thought. Moreover, this liberal end of Islamist thought is itself constituted of a spectrum of positions ranging from the conservative pro-feminist views emerging among ISNA and MSA women, to those making up the more radical and progressive ends of the spectrum. And just as was the case with the American feminist movement, such views obviously are by no means necessarily generalizable to the broader population of which they are part.

While it is American Islamists and the children of Islamists today who are most visibly in the lead as activists and who are most distinctively assimilating into the American tradition of protest and activism in the cause of justice, others of Muslim heritage who are secular or simply non-Islamist are clearly also contributing in other and no less time-honored American ways to their society. The route of hard work and professional achievement is obviously one such route. And sometimes, and quite possibly frequently (this is a matter yet to be studied), such work involves, as the example of Alibhai-Brown suggests, taking up issues of rights of minorities, including Muslims, in varieties of ways. Thus the defining differences between this reportedly larger proportion of the American Muslim population on the one hand and the Islamist-influenced American Muslims we have been focusing on in these last chapters on the other, may in fact prove to be above all that often the former, in distinct contrast to the latter, do not explicitly ground themselves and their life goals and actions in Islam as religious commitment and as proclaimed and visible ground of action and identity.

Being Muslim by heritage, secular or not, seems to have a place in this larger group's professional and public lives that is perhaps comparable to the place which, as Drew Faust's above-quoted words suggest, being woman has in Faust's public and professional life.[57] Following out how non-Islamist people of Muslim heritage are relating to their Islamic heritage as they become part of the fabric of North America is a whole other field of enquiry and one that awaits exploration. In this book I set out to understand the significance of the appearance of Islamism and the veiling trend in the United States and how these currents would evolve in the context of a Western democratic nation.

Following out this story and focusing in particular in the last chapters on American Muslim women's activism in relation to gender and women's rights has brought me to the astonishing conclusion that it is after all Islamists and the children of Islamists—the very people whose presence in this country had initially alarmed me—who were now in the vanguard of those who were most fully and rapidly assimilating into the distinctively American tradition of activism in pursuit of justice and who now essentially made up the vanguard of those who are struggling for women's rights in Islam.

The conclusion that I find myself arriving at is clearly a far happier and more optimistic one than I had ever imagined I would find myself arriving at. Still, optimistic though my overall conclusion is, as I just suggested it would be a mistake to imagine that Islamists and Muslim Americans who are staunch believers in God-given gender hierarchy are now perhaps a vanishing species. Just as it would be a mistake for researchers focused, for example, on following out the story of American feminism in the 1960s and 1970s to conclude, as they chronicle the extraordinary successes and liveliness of that movement in that era, that American women and men who believed in or practiced notions of male dominance must now be a vanishing species.

As it turned out, this first decade of the twenty-first century has proved to be one of tremendous liveliness and activism among American Muslim women in relation to issues of women and gender. It is this activism that occupies the foreground of the last chapters of this book, just as, were this a book about American feminism in the 1960s, it would be the ideas and activism of those feminists that the book would be following out—and not the positions and perspectives of members of the broader society whose views the feminists were challenging and resisting. It would be quite untrue, for example, if I were to claim that I never heard androcentric and patriarchal views expressed, say, at ISNA. Such elements were certainly present in the background to the women's activism and the women-affirming themes and concerns that I was focused on observing.

It is important, too, to take note of a number of features and characteristics of our times pertinent to and affecting the developments that have occupied the forefront of my attention. Thus in the first place it is important to emphatically underscore the fact that the very conditions of our post-9/11 era, which favor the emergence of voices critical of conservative Islam, were conditions which conversely would have no doubt caused conservative, firmly patriarchal voices to retreat into silence. In a time when the "oppression of women in Islam" was on the front burner in the broad American conversation and when conservative as well as militant Islam was on the defensive in American public space, Muslim supporters of gender hierarchy and male precedence were surely unlikely to openly air their views. When even speeches as innocuous as Yasin's were capable of stirring intense hostility and suspicion and even of provoking death threats, as well as of precipitating a public grilling in the media, it was surely unlikely that people who believed in a God-given gender hierarchy or, say, in men's inviolable Quranic right to beat wives would come out and say so. And as we saw, the suggestion by an ISNA official that the Bakhtiar translation of the Quran should be banned from ISNA's bookstores—a suggestion that quite possibly might have won support at ISNA in the climate of a few years earlier—now drew swift rebuke from the organization's president.

It may be that there are entrenched American Muslim patriarchs who are quietly biding their time and planning, perhaps, in private meetings, for a time when they will institute rules at ISNA forbidding women from serving as presidents, and when they will ban translations such as Bakhtiar's from the stalls of ISNA and other Muslim American organizations, and exclude voices such as Nomani's from such gatherings. But if such meetings and plans are under way they are occurring behind the scenes. The story I tell in these pages is based entirely on publicly available materials and information. It is based on published books and articles, and on activism carried out in the public domain and reported on in the media. And it is based on my own observations and on speeches delivered at American Muslim conventions that are open to journalists and other observers.

It may well be that there are Islamists here (and even more probably back in the home countries of Islamism) who respond with rage and revulsion to the emergence of the hated spectacle of feminism (or of the demand, at any rate, for justice for women) among Islamist women in America and Western countries, and even among young Islamist men —as well as to the emergence of supporters of equal rights for gays.

It may well be that there are Islamists in America and around the globe who are now ruing the day when the Islamist movement and male leadership expanded the sweep of their recruitment and activism to reach out to, draw in, and include women as activists and leaders (even if not formally). For above all, perhaps, the story of the activist involvement of women in Islamism that I have followed out in these pages, from its beginnings in the early 1970s in Egypt to America in the post-9/11 world, is the story also of the expansion of the understanding and interpretation of religious texts that occurs, and similarly of the rethinking and transformation of the notion of justice that begins to take place when the work of interpretation is democratized and women are able to enter and participate in the broad arenas of social and religious movements and of public life as activists, teachers, and leaders, and as people proactively engaged in defining the public good and the meaning of justice and the meanings also of sacred scriptures.

I can certainly imagine that the findings that I put forward here and that are for me grounds for optimism might well cause some Islamists to feel outrage at what is happening to Islam in America and cause them to desperately begin to seek to figure out a way to, some day, put the genie back in the bottle.

Some fifty or more years ago Albert Hourani, surveying the trends under way in that era, confidently predicted that the veil would soon be a thing of the past. And in fact, the evidence of the day incontrovertibly pointed to the steady ascendancy of the unveiling trend among the dominant classes across most of the Arab and Muslim world, and his predictions therefore were entirely well grounded. Today we live in a world where it is the veiling trend, steadily gaining ground across the globe, that is now no less incontrovertibly in the ascendant.

The quest for women's equality is not a new quest in relation to women in Islam, and the activism of today among American Muslim women represents the most recent and now, for the first time, distinctly Western and specifically American turn in a history of struggle for women's rights in Islam—a struggle that stretches back for more than a century. In many Muslim-majority countries women have already attained considerable achievements. Women have had the right to vote in many Muslim countries for more than half a century (Turkey 1930, Pakistan 1947, Indonesia 1947, Iraq and Syria 1948, Egypt 1956, Afghanistan 1963—in the subsequent turbulent history of Afghanistan women also lost that right for a time). Several Muslim countries too have had women heads of state —among them Turkey, Pakistan, and Indonesia—something we have yet to achieve in America.

There are particular features in the "feminist" currents emerging today that seem to mark them as specifically American. Among these most particularly is the forthright challenge to core scriptural and interpretative texts being pursued here today by religiously committed Muslims. Challenge to core religious texts is not in itself new for Muslim women—for secular Muslim women, and most notably among them Nawal el-Saadawi, have issued such challenges going back to the 1960s. What is new in this moment in America is that these challenges are coming now from committed, believing Muslims. Second, another new move specific to America today is the emergence of the demand for equal space physically within Muslim religious institutions, and the beginnings of a demand for equal rights to leadership in religious institutions.

These represent the first stirrings of a new era in the history of Islam in the West, and most particularly in America. The history and prehistory of the present that I have described in these pages attest to the extraordinary transformations that religions—in this case Islam—undergo as to the ways that they are lived, practiced, understood, and interpreted, as one era gives way to another and one strain of belief and practice gains ascendancy while another (to the astonishment and near-disbelief of contemporaries caught up in the throes of such turbulence) is thrust aside or falls into abeyance. This history attests to the ways in which religious movements can evolve as they cross frontiers and take root in environments where new social and political conditions open up new possibilities of belief, practice, and interpretation for the rising generations.

We stand poised to observe the newest turns in these evolving stories: the newest turns in the stories of Islam and of America and the West.

Notes

Introduction

1. Jane I. Smith, *Islam in America* (New York: Columbia University Press, 1999), 46, 169.

2. These are and continue to be very lively questions often asked most sharply in relation to Europe. See, for example, Christopher Caldwell, *Reflections on the Revolution in Europe: Immigration, Islam and the West* (New York: Doubleday, 2009). Other works addressing this topic, often more extreme and sensational, include Oriana Fallaci's *The Rage and the Pride* (New York: Rizzoli, 2002); Bruce Bawer, *While Europe Slept: How Radical Islam Destroyed the West from Within* (New York: Doubleday, 2006); Brigitte Gabriel, *They Must Be Stopped: Why We Must Defeat Radical Islam and How We Can Do It* (New York: St. Martin's, 2008); and Mark Steyn, *America Alone: The End of the World as We Know It* (Washington, D.C.: Regnery, 2006). For a discussion of some of these and other such works see Laila Lalami, "The New Inquisition," *Nation*, November 24, 2009, and John R. Bowen, "Nothing to Fear Misreading Muslim Immigration in Europe," *Boston Review*, January–February 2010. See also on this general subject Bowen's *Can Islam Be French? Pluralism and Pragmatism in a Secular State* (Princeton, N.J.: Princeton University Press, 2010).

3. Their views seemed consonant with those I had heard conservative women of other religious traditions (for example, Blu Greenberg, co-founder of the Jewish Orthodox Feminist Alliance) express at the Pluralism Project conferences, hosted by Professor Diana Eck, which I attended at Harvard University—among them, for instance, the conference on "Women, Religion and Social Change" held at Harvard in April–May 2003; and "Harvard University Consultation on Women's Networks in Multi-Religious America," held at Harvard April 27–29, 2002.

4. My notes of interviews conducted 2002–3.

5. Fawaz A. Gerges, *The Far Enemy: Why Jihad Went Global* (New York: Cambridge University Press, 2005), 2. See also John L. Esposito, *The Islamic Threat: Myth or Reality?* (New York: Oxford University Press, 1995), where the author notes the key role of the Muslim Brotherhood, along with the Jamaat-i Islami of Pakistan, in spurring the spread of the Islamic Resurgence (128–29).

6. See Azza Karam, ed., *Transnational Political Islam: Religion, Ideology and Power,* foreword by John Esposito (London: Pluto, 2004), 5–7. See also "Islamism," William E. Shepard, François Burgat, James Piscatori, and Armando Salvatore, in *The Oxford Encyclopedia of the Islamic World,* Oxford Islamic Studies Online. http://www.oxfordislamicstudies.com/article/opr/t236/e0888. Accessed November 14, 2009.

7. Karam, *Transnational Political Islam,* 5–6.

8. Roxanne L. Euben and Muhammad Qasim Zaman, eds., *Princeton Readings in Islamist Thought: Texts and Contexts from al-Banna to Bin Laden* (Princeton, N.J.: Princeton University Press, 2009), 275.

9. See Nilufer Gole, *The Forbidden Modern Civilization and Veiling* (Ann Arbor: University of Michigan Press, 1996); Jenny B. White, *Islamic Mobilization in Turkey: A Study in Vernacular Politics,* Studies in Modernity and National Identity (Seattle: University of Washington Press, 2002). Other important works analyzing the veil, in particular in relation to France and the internal politics of France, include Joan Wallach Scott, *The Politics of the Veil* (Princeton, N.J.: Princeton University Press, 2007), and John R. Bowen, *Why the French Don't Like Headscarves: Islam, the State, and Public Space* (Princeton, N.J.: Princeton University Press, 2006).

10. Gerges, *Far Enemy,* 3.

11. This is the question at the heart of several books on Islam in the West—such as those cited in note 2.

12. "Brutality Against Women and Children," Radio Address by Laura Bush, November 17, 2001. George Bush White House Archives, georgewbush-whitehouse.archives.gov/. Accessed April 10, 2010.

13. Scoop, Independent News, "Cherie Blair Press Conference on Taliban and Women," November 20, 2001, press release, U.K. Government. http://www.scoop.co.nz/stories/WO0111/S00149.htm. Accessed April 10, 2010.

14. Polly Toynbee, "Was It Worth It?" *Guardian,* November 13, 2002.

Chapter 1. Unveiling

1. This quotation and those in the following two paragraphs are from Albert Hourani, "The Vanishing Veil a Challenge to the Old Order," *UNESCO Courier,* January 1956, 35–37.

2. This quotation and those from Amin's work in the following two paragraphs are cited in Leila Ahmed, *Women and Gender in Islam: Historical Roots of a Modern Debate* (New Haven: Yale University Press, 1992), 155–56, 160–61.

3. Gayatri Chakravorty Spivak, "Can the Subaltern Speak?" in *Marxism and the Interpretation of Culture,* ed. Cary Nelson and Lawrence Grossberg (Urbana: University of Illinois Press, 1988), 296.

4. See Joseph A. Massad, *Desiring Arabs* (Chicago: University of Chicago Press, 2007), 56.

5. Roger Owen cites General Sir Francis Grenfell as observing that Nazli was a "champion of female emancipation." Owen, *Lord Cromer: Victorian Imperialist, Edwardian Proconsul* (New York: Oxford University Press, 2004), 254.

6. Margot Badran, *Feminists, Islam, and Nation* (Princeton, N.J.: Princeton University Press, 1995), 7, 18.

7. Owen, *Lord Cromer,* 254.

8. Nancy Micklewright, "Women's Dress in Nineteenth-Century Istanbul: Mirror of a Changing Society (Ottoman Costume, Westernization, Turkey)," Ph.D. diss., University of Pennsylvania, 1986.

9. Cited in Ahmed, *Women and Gender,* 42.

10. Afaf Lutfi al-Sayyid Marsot, *A Short History of Modern Egypt* (Cambridge: Cambridge University Press, 1985), 75.

11. Owen, *Lord Cromer,* 243–46.

12. Evelyn Baring, Earl of Cromer, *Modern Egypt* (London: Macmillan, 1908), 2: 539–40.

13. Cromer, *Modern Egypt,* 2, 540.

14. Owen, *Lord Cromer,* 315.

15. Owen, *Lord Cromer,* 328–52. See also Jamal Mohammed Ahmed, *The Intellectual Origins of Egyptian Nationalism* (London: Oxford University Press, 1960), 63; and Salama Musa, *The Education of Salama Musa,* trans. L. O. Schuman (Leiden: Brill, 1961), 32.

16. Cromer, *Modern Egypt,* 2, 144–48. Owen notes in *Lord Cromer* that Lord Northbrook was Cromer's cousin (66).

17. Owen, *Lord Cromer,* 355. In this era, which had witnessed the rapid expansion of Europe's empires into the non-European world, ideas and beliefs about Europe's inherent racial and civilizational superiority, Owen suggests, were now politically useful. Such views enabled the European powers to justify the "despotic form of rule" that they exercised in their foreign territories and to represent it as a civilizing "mission" and as the "white man's burden."

18. Owen, *Lord Cromer,* 362.

19. Cromer, *Modern Egypt,* 2, 155–57.

20. Owen, *Lord Cromer,* 374–75.

21. Cromer, *Modern Egypt,* 2, 156, 539.

22. Owen, *Lord Cromer,* 359.

23. Ahmed, *Women and Gender,* 153.

24. Cromer, *Modern Egypt,* 2, 180–81 note 1.

25. Oliver Scharbrodt, *Islam and the Bahai Faith: A Comparative Study of Muhammad 'Abduh and 'Abdul-Baha 'Abbas* (London: Routledge, 2008), 133.

26. Cromer, *Modern Egypt,* 2, 179–80.

27. Cromer, *Modern Egypt,* 2, 180, 180–81 note 1. Of course the accuracy of Cromer's views regarding Abduh, as well as Cromer's motivation in writing this passage, probably should not be taken entirely at face value.

28. See, for instance, Scharbrodt, *Islam and the Bahai Faith*, and Nikki Keddie, *Sayyid Jamal ad-din al-Afghani: A Political Biography* (Berkeley: University of California Press, 1972).

29. Ahmed, *Women and Gender*, 159.

30. Ahmed, *Women and Gender*, 162–63; Owen, *Cromer*, 251.

31. Ahmed, *Women and Gender*, chapters 8 and 9; Beth Baron, *Egypt as a Woman: Nationalism, Gender, and Politics* (Berkeley: University of California Press, 2005), 33.

32. Badran, *Feminism, Islam, and Nation*, 33; Roxanne L. Euben and Muhammad Qasim Zaman, eds., *Princeton Readings in Islamist Thought: Texts and Contexts from al-Banna to Bin Laden* (Princeton, N.J.: Princeton University Press, 2009), 276.

33. Beth Baron mentions that Amin, in his book *al-Mar'a al-Jadida* (The New Woman), notes that Jewish and Christian women had unveiled. Baron, "Unveiling in Early Twentieth Century Egypt: Practical and Symbolic Considerations," *Middle Eastern Studies* 25, no. 3 (July 1989): 370–86; 379.

34. Musa, *Education of Salama Musa*, 15.

35. Quotations in this and the following three paragraphs are from Baron, "Unveiling," 374–81.

36. Baron, "Unveiling," 381, and Baron, *Egypt as a Woman*, 67–68.

37. Badran, *Feminists, Islam, and Nation*, 42.

38. Quotations in this and the following paragraph are from Badran, *Feminists, Islam, and Nation*, 43–44. Nabawiya Musa described in some detail Dunlop's attempt to prevent her from sitting for this exam in a journal article she wrote, cited by Badran in her detailed account of Musa's life in *Feminism, Islam, and Nation*. The story of Musa's encounter with Dunlop appears to have been familiar to contemporaries: Salama Musa, for example (no relation to Nabawiya), refers to it: *Education of Salama Musa*, 50. See also Muhammad Abu al-Is'ad, *Nabawiya Musa wa-Dawruha fi al-Hayah al-Misriya (1886–1951)* (Cairo: Al-Hay'ah al-Misriyah al-'Ammah lil-Kitab, 1994).

39. Anwar al-Jindi, *Adab al-Mar'ah al-'Arabiyah. Al-Qissa al-'Arabiyah al-Mu'asirah, Abidin*, 3 vols. (Cairo: Matba'at al-Risalah, n.d.), 1: 71.

40. Baron, "Unveiling," 380–81.

41. Baron, *Egypt as a Woman*, 33–35.

42. Quotations in this and the following paragraph are from Baron, "Unveiling," 380–81.

43. Quotations in this and the following two paragraphs are from al-Sayyid Marsot, *Short History*, 80–81.

44. Hourani, "Vanishing Veil," 36.

45. Cited in Ahmed, *Women and Gender*, 164.

Chapter 2. The Veil's Vanishing Past

1. Brynjar Lia, *The Society of the Muslim Brothers in Egypt: The Rise of an Islamic Mass Movement, 1928–42* (Reading: Garner, 1998), 74.

2. Lia, *Society of the Muslim Brothers*, 67.

3. Richard P. Mitchell, *The Society of the Muslim Brothers* (New York: Oxford University Press, 1993; originally published 1969), 7.

4. Mitchell, *Society,* 8.

5. Arthur Goldschmidt, Jr., *A Brief History of Egypt* (New York: Checkmark, 2007), 136.

6. Afaf Lutfi al-Sayyid Marsot, *A Short History of Modern Egypt* (Cambridge: Cambridge University Press, 1985), 101–2.

7. Quotations in this and the following paragraph are from Lia, *Society,* 79–80.

8. Lia noted that "these extremists were, however, expelled from the Society . . . and this expulsion firmly established the principle that the society's message should be spread by persuasion, not force" (*Society,* 85).

9. The material in this and in the following four paragraphs is from Lia, *Society,* 69, 83–86.

10. Lia, *Society,* cites Mitchell's view that their attitudes nurtured self-righteousness and arrogance (85).

11. Al-Sayyid Marsot, *Short History,* 100.

12. Goldschmidt, *Brief History,* 134–36; Al-Sayyid Marsot, *Short History,* 102.

13. Mitchell, *Society,* 63–67.

14. Al-Sayyid Marsot, *Short History,* 103; Goldschmidt, *Brief History,* 138–39.

15. Goldschmidt, *Brief History,* 144; Derek Hopwood, *Egypt Politics and Society, 1945–90* (London: Routledge, 1991), 36.

16. Al-Sayyid Marsot, *Short History,* 109.

17. Roxanne L. Euben and Muhammad Qasim Zaman, eds., *Princeton Readings in Islamist Thought: Texts and Contexts from al-Banna to Bin Laden* (Princeton, N.J.: Princeton University Press, 2009), 275.

18. Al-Sayyid Marsot, *Short History,* 112–16.

19. See Hopwood, *Egypt Politics and Society,* 95–97; and Ann Alexander, *Nasser* (London: Haus, 2005), 93.

20. Hopwood, *Egypt Politics and Society;* 97. See also Tamir Moustapha, "Conflict and Cooperation Between the State and Religious Institutions in Contemporary Egypt," *International Journal of Middle East Studies* 32 (2000): 3–22. See also Malika Zeghal, "Religion and Politics in Egypt: The Ulema of the Al-Azhar, Radical Islam and the State (1952–94)," *International Journal of Middle East Studies* 31 (1999): 371–99.

21. Yvonne Yazbeck Haddad, "Arab-Israeli Wars, Nasserism, and Islamic Identity," in John L. Esposito, ed., *Islam and Development: Religion and Socio-Political Change* (Syracuse: Syracuse University Press, 1980), 116–19.

22. Malcolm H. Kerr, *Arab Cold War: Gamal 'Abd al-Nasir and His Rivals, 1958–70* (London: Oxford University Press, 1971, issued under the auspices of the Royal Institute of International Affairs).

23. Reinhard Schulze and Gabriele Tecchiato, "Muslim World League," in *The Oxford Encyclopedia of the Islamic World,* Oxford Islamic Studies Online. Accessed December 24, 2009.

24. Schulze and Tecchiato, "Muslim World League."

25. John L. Esposito, "Contemporary Islam: Reform or Revolution?" in *Oxford History of Islam,* ed. John L. Esposito (New York: Oxford University Press, 1999), 655. See also Gilles Kepel, *Jihad: The Trail of Political Islam,* trans. Anthony F. Roberts (Cambridge, Mass.: Belknap Press of Harvard University Press, 2000), 69.

26. Goldschmidt, in *Brief History,* says that at its height, in the forties, the Muslim Brotherhood's membership was about half a million (138). See also Nazih N. Ayubi et al., "The Muslim Brotherhood," in *The Oxford Encyclopedia of the Islamic World,* Oxford Islamic Studies Online. Accessed July 4, 2010. The total population of Egypt in 1947 was estimated at 19 million. Helen Chapin Metz, ed., *Egypt: A Country Study* (Washington, D.C.: GPO for the Library of Congress, 1990). http://countrystudies.us/egypt/55.htm. Accessed August 6, 2010.

27. Ghada Hashem Talhami, *The Mobilization of Muslim Women in Egypt* (Gainesville: University Press of Florida, 1996), 19.

28. Al-Sayyid Marsot, *Short History,* mentions 12,000 men (124).

29. Peter Bergen, *The Osama bin Laden I Know: An Oral History of the al-Qaeda Leader* (New York: Free Press, 2006), 6.

30. Fadwa El Guindi, "Religious Revival and Islamic Survival in Egypt," *International Insight* 1, no. 2 (May–June 1980): 7.

31. Al-Sayyid Marsot, *Short History,* 126.

32. Haddad, "Arab-Israeli Wars," 119.

33. Kepel, *Jihad,* 63.

34. Hopwood, *Egypt,* 97.

Chapter 3. The 1970s

1. See Derek Hopwood, *Egypt: Politics and Society, 1945–90* (London: Routledge, 1991), 117–18; and Afaf Lutfi al-Sayyid Marsot, *A Short History of Modern Egypt* (New York: Cambridge University Press, 1985), 137–38.

2. John L. Esposito, "Contemporary Islam: Reform or Revolution?" in *Oxford History of Islam,* ed. John L. Esposito (New York: Oxford University Press, 1999), 657. See also Gilles Kepel, *Muslim Extremism in Egypt: The Prophet and Pharaoh,* trans. Jon Rothschild, With a New Preface for 2003 (Berkeley: University of California Press, 2003), 137–38.

3. Joel Beinin and Joe Stork, eds., *Political Islam: Essays from Middle East Report* (Berkeley: University of California Press, 1997), 9–11.

4. See Ghada Hashem Talhami, *The Mobilization of Muslim Women in Egypt* (Gainesville: University Press of Florida, 1996), 63. Esposito wrote, "From Egypt to Indonesia, Islamic movements and organizations created alternative educational, medical, legal and social services (schools, clinics, hospitals, youth centers, and legal aid societies, for example), publishing houses, and financial institutions" ("Contemporary Islam," 667).

5. Saad Eddin Ibrahim, "Egypt's Islamic Activism in the 1980s," *Third World Quarterly* 10, no. 2 (April 1988): 644. See also Fawaz A. Gerges, *The Far Enemy: Why Jihad Went Global* (Cambridge: Cambridge University Press, 2005), 2–3.

6. Ibrahim, "Egypt's Islamic Activism," 644.

7. See Yvonne Y. Haddad, "Sayyid Qutb: Ideologue of the Islamic Revival," in John L. Esposito, ed., *Voices of Resurgent Islam* (New York: Oxford University Press, 1983), 85.

8. Haddad, "Sayyid Qutb," 85.

9. Cited in Haddad, "Sayyid Qutb," 85. See also the discussion of Qutb and jahiliyya in Kepel, *Muslim Extremism*, 12–13, 61–63.

10. Sayed Qutb, *Milestones* (Cedar Rapids, Iowa: Unity, n.d.), 20.

11. Quotations in this and the following paragraph are from Haddad, "Sayyid Qutb," 70, 87–89.

12. Adnan A. Musallam, *From Secularism to Jihad: Sayyid Qutb and the Foundations of Radical Islamism* (Westport, Conn.: Praeger, 2005), 179–80.

13. See Barbara H. E. Zollner, *The Muslim Brotherhood: Hasan al-Hudaybi and Ideology* (London: Routledge, 2009), 3. See also Kepel, *Muslim Extremism*, 61–63.

14. Talhami, *Mobilization*, 63.

15. Gerges, *Far Enemy*, 2–3.

16. Zainab al-Ghazali, *Return of the Pharaoh: Memoir in Nasir's Prison*, trans. Mokrane Guezzou (Leicester: Islamic Foundation, 1994/1415 AH), 40. This is the translation I cite throughout. I give throughout, too, page references to the Arabic text. Zainab al-Ghazali, *Ayam min Hayati, Dar al-Shuruq*, 10th ed. (Cairo, 1988), 38. According to Kepel, *Muslim Extremism*, al-Ghazali stood at the other extreme from the young advocates of violence to overthrow the Nasser regime, arguing that the best they could do would be to establish "educational programmes" (31).

17. Al-Ghazali, *Return of the Pharaoh*, 41; *Ayam min Hayati*, 39–40.

18. Carrie Rosefsky Wickham, *Mobilizing Islam: Religion, Activism, and Political Change in Egypt* (New York: Columbia University Press, 2002), 127.

19. Kepel, *Muslim Extremism*, 29–31.

20. Talhami, *Mobilization*, 63–64.

21. Ibrahim, "Egypt's Islamic Activism," 642–43. See also Esposito, "Contemporary Islam," 667.

22. Esposito, "Contemporary Islam," 667.

23. See al-Sayyid Marsot, *Short History*, 134–36; and John Waterbury, *Egypt: Burdens of the Past, Options for the Future* (Bloomington: Indiana University Press in association with the American Universities Field Staff, 1978), 151. See also Saad Eddin Ibrahim, *The New Arab Social Order: A Study of the Social Impact of Oil Wealth* (Boulder, Colo.: Westview; London: Croom Helm, 1982), 18.

24. Ahmed, *Women and Gender*, 219.

25. Fadwa El Guindi, "Veiling Infitah with Muslim Ethic: Egypt's Contemporary Islamic Movement," *Social Problems* 28, no. 4 (April 1981): 476.

26. Known collectively as *al-Gamaa al-Islamiyya*. Wickham, *Mobilizing Islam*, 96; Esposito, "Contemporary Islam," 657.

27. Wickham, *Mobilizing Islam*, 116

28. El Guindi, "Veiling Infitah," 479–80.

29. Ahmed, *Women and Gender*, 219.

30. Gilles Kepel, *Jihad: The Trail of Political Islam*, trans. Anthony F. Roberts (Cambridge, Mass.: Belknap Press of Harvard University Press, 2000), 63.

31. Esposito, "Contemporary Islam," 657.

32. Fadwa El Guindi, "The Emerging Islamic Order: The Case of Egypt's Contemporary Islamic Movement," *Journal of Arab Affairs* 1, no. 2 (1982): 253.

33. El Guindi sets forth much of this material in three articles in particular: "Veiling Infitah" and "The Emerging Islamic Order," both mentioned above, and "Religious Revival and Islamic Survival in Egypt," *International Insight* 1, no. 2 (1980): 6–10.

34. El Guindi, "Religious Revival," 8.

35. Talhami, *Mobilization,* 48.

36. El Guindi, "Veiling Infitah," 475.

37. Talhami, *Mobilization,* 59–60; Kepel, *Jihad,* 84–85.

38. El Guindi, "Emerging Islamic Order," 256.

39. Material in this and the following paragraph is from El Guindi, "Veiling Infitah," 376, 474–75.

40. El Guindi, "Emerging Islamic Order," 253–54.

41. Fadwa El Guindi, *Veil: Modesty, Privacy, and Resistance* (New York: Berg, Oxford International, 1999), 161.

42. El Guindi, *Veil,* 168, and "Veiling Infitah," 470.

43. Material in this and the following paragraph are from Talhami, *Mobilization,* 43–44, 54.

44. John Alden Williams, "Return of the Veil in Egypt," *Middle East Review* 11 (Spring 1979): 53; Sherifa Zuhur, *Revealing Reveiling: Islamic Gender Ideology in Contemporary Egypt* (Albany: State University of New York Press, 1992), 77, 104.

45. Quotations in this and the following four paragraphs are from Williams, "Return of the Veil,"49–53.

46. Williams, "Return of the Veil," 50–51; John Alden Williams, "Veiling in Egypt as a Political and Social Phenomenon," in John L. Esposito, ed., *Islam and Development Religion and Sociopolitical Change* (Syracuse: Syracuse University Press, 1980), 75.

47. This and the following quotation are from El Guindi, "Veiling Infitah," 383, 481.

48. Quotations in this and the following five paragraphs are from Williams, "Return of the Veil,"53–54.

49. Zainab Abdel Mejid Radwan, *Thahirat al-Hijab bayn al-Jam'iyyat* (Cairo: Al-Markaz al-Qawmi lil-Buhuth al-Ijtima'iyya, 1982), 92. See also *Thahirat al-Hijab bayn al-Jam'iyyat, al-Taqrir al-Thani* (Cairo: Al-Markaz al-Qawmi lil-Buhuth al-Ijtima'iyah, Wahdat al-Buhuth al-Diniyah wa al-Mu'taqadat, 1984.

50. Ekram Beshir, "Allah Doesn't Change the Condition of People Until They Change Themselves," in Katherine Bullock, ed., *Muslim Women Activists in North America: Speaking for Ourselves* (Austin: University of Texas Press, 2005), 24. All quotations in the ensuing paragraphs of this chapter are from this text, pp. 22–26.

Chapter 4. The New Veil

1. Gilles Kepel, *Jihad: The Trail of Political Islam,* trans. Anthony F. Roberts (Cambridge, Mass.: Belknap Press of Harvard University Press, 2000), 69.

2. Natana J. Delong-Bas, *Wahhabi Islam: From Revival and Reform to Global Jihad* (New York: Oxford University Press, 2004), 24–26.

3. Kepel, *Jihad*, 70–73.

4. Kepel, *Jihad*, 72.

5. Gilles Kepel, *The War for Muslim Minds: Islam and the West*, trans. Pascale Ghazaleh (Cambridge, Mass.: Belknap Press of Harvard University Press, 2004), 173.

6. See Olivier Roy, *The Failure of Political Islam*, trans. by Carol Volk (Cambridge, Mass.: Harvard University Press, 1994; 5th printing, 2001), 117; Brynjar Lia, *The Society of the Muslim Brothers in Egypt* (Reading: Garner, 1998), 25, 59–60.

7. Material cited in this and the following two paragraphs is from Lia, *Society*, 76, 86, 286.

8. Roy, *Failure*, 36, and 208n4.

9. Roy, *Failure*, 21.

10. Carrie Rosefsky Wickham, *Mobilizing Islam: Religion, Activism, and Political Change in Egypt* (New York: Columbia University Press, 2002), 96.

11. Kepel, *Jihad*, 71.

12. "Egyptians in the Gulf countries experienced a cultural transformation and began to associate the new abundance and wealth with Islamic practices and even with the Islamic outer dress." Ghada Hashem Talhami, *The Mobilization of Muslim Women in Egypt* (Gainesville: University Press of Florida, 1996), 40–41.

13. Wickham, *Mobilizing Islam*, 98.

14. Gilles Kepel, *Muslim Extremism in Egypt: The Prophet and Pharaoh*, trans. Jon Rothschild, With a New Preface for 2003 (Berkeley: University of California Press, 2003), 139; Kepel, *Jihad*, 81.

15. Kepel, *Jihad*, 73.

16. See Fauzi M. Najjar, "The Debate on Islam and Secularism in Egypt," *Arab Studies Quarterly* 18, no. 2 (Spring 1996).

17. Material cited in this and the following three paragraphs is from Kepel, *Muslim Extremism*, 149–50, 192–93, 210–14.

18. Quoted in Adnan A. Musallam, *From Secularism to Jihad: Sayyid Qutb and the Foundations of Radical Islamism* (Westport, Conn.: Praeger, 2005), 167.

19. Sayed Qutb, *Milestones* (Cedar Rapids, Iowa: Unity, n.d), 7–9.

20. Musallam, *From Secularism*, 155.

21. Roxanne L. Euben and Muhammad Qasim Zaman, eds., *Princeton Readings in Islamist Thought: Texts and Contexts from al-Banna to Bin Laden* (Princeton, N.J.: Princeton University Press, 2009), 275, 129.

22. Yvonne Y. Haddad, "Sayyid Qutb: Ideologue of the Islamic Revival," in John L. Esposito, ed., *Voices of Resurgent Islam* (New York: Oxford University Press, 1983), 81, 68.

23. J. Brugman, *An Introduction to the History of Modern Arabic Literature in Egypt* (Leiden: Brill, 1984), 126.

24. Haddad, "Qutb," 69.

25. Musallam, *From Secularism*, 86.

26. Sayyid Qutb, *A Child from the Village*, ed., trans., and introduced by John

Calvert and William Shepard (Syracuse: Syracuse University Press, 2004), xviii–xix. See also Euben and Zaman, *Princeton Readings,* 130.

27. Quotations in this and the following paragraph are from Musallam, *From Secularism,* 97, 122–29.

28. Roxanne L. Euben, *Enemy in the Mirror: Islamic Fundamentalism and the Limits of Modern Rationalism* (Princeton, N.J.: Princeton University Press, 1999), 65.

29. Quotations in this and the following paragraph are from Lamia Rustum Shehadeh, *The Idea of Women in Fundamentalist Islam* (Gainesville: University Press of Florida, 2003), 68–70.

30. Kepel, *War for Muslim Minds,* 174–75.

31. Quotations in this and the following two paragraphs are from Euben and Zaman, *Princeton Readings,* 276, 283–290.

32. This organization, the Association of Muslim Youth (Jam'iyyat Shubban al-Muslimin), commonly called the YMMA, was founded in 1927. Thought of as the "Muslim answer to the YMCA," it was "more militant in its orientation than its constitution professed." Euben and Zaman, *Princeton Readings,* 289n14.

33. Material in this and the following three paragraphs is from Euben and Zaman, *Princeton Readings,* 289–92.

34. Talhami, *Mobilization,* 51; Zainab al-Ghazali, *Return of the Pharaoh: Memoir in Nasir's Prison,* trans. Mokrane Guezzou Leicester, Islamic Foundation, 1994/1415 AH), 39–40; Zainab al-Ghazali, *Ayam min Hayati,* 10th ed. (Cairo: Dar al-Shuruq, 1988), 39.

35. Euben and Zaman, *Princeton Readings,* 297.

36. Valerie J. Hoffman-Ladd, "Ghazali, Zaynab al-," *The Oxford Encyclopedia of the Islamic World,* Oxford Islamic Studies Online, http://www.oxfordislamicstudies.com/article/opr/t236/e273. Accessed July 3, 2010.

37. Euben and Zaman, *Princeton Readings,* 277. The material cited in the following paragraph also is from this book (280–81).

38. Quotations in this and the following two paragraphs are from Kristin Helmore, "Islam and Women: An Egyptian Speaks Out," *Christian Science Monitor,* November 26, 1985.

39. Leila Ahmed, *Women and Gender in Islam: Historical Roots of a Modern Debate* (New Haven: Yale University Press, 1992), 200; Euben and Zaman, *Princeton Readings,* 280.

40. Al-Ghazali, *Return of the Pharaoh,* 38; *Ayam,* 35.

41. Al-Ghazali, *Return of the Pharaoh,* 134; *Ayam,* 144.

42. Euben and Zaman, *Princeton Readings,* 280.

43. As Talhami noted, al-Ghazali refers to herself in her memoir as part of the vanguard. Talhami, *Mobilization,* 70. See also al-Ghazali, *Return of the Pharaoh,* 133–4; *Ayam,* 143–44.

44. This and the quotation below are from Hoffman-Ladd, "Ghazali, Zaynab al-."

45. See Janet Afary and Kevin B. Anderson, *Foucault and the Iranian Revolution: Gender and the Seductions of Islamism* (Chicago: University of Chicago Press, 2005).

Chapter 5. The 1980s

1. Ghada Hashem Talhami, *The Mobilization of Muslim Women in Egypt* (Gainesville: University Press of Florida, 1996), 61.

2. See, for example, Nawal el-Saadawi, "An Unholy Alliance," *Al-Ahram Weekly Online,* no. 674, January 22–28, 2004.

3. Quotations and references in this and the following five paragraphs are from Arlene Elowe Macleod, *Accommodating Protest: Working Women, the New Veiling, and Change in Cairo* (New York: Columbia University Press, 1991), 40, 109–13, 119–21.

4. Quotations and references in this and the following five paragraphs are to Macleod, *Accommodating Protest,* 38–39, 110–15, 119–23.

5. Quotations and references in this and the following seven paragraphs are from Macleod, *Accommodating Protest,* 40–41, 108–9, 113–15, 121, 154–55.

6. Sherifa Zuhur, *Revealing Reveiling: Islamic Gender Ideology in Contemporary Egypt* (Albany: State University of New York Press, 1992), 76.

7. Zuhur, *Revealing Reveiling,* 116.

8. Zuhur, *Revealing Reveiling,* 1, 9, 15, 116.

9. Quotations and references in this and the following paragraph are from Zuhur, *Revealing Reveiling,* 71, 77, 104, 117–120.

10. Zuhur, *Revealing Reveiling,* 12, 20, 73, 116.

11. Quotations in this and the following paragraph are from Zuhur, *Revealing Reveiling,* 74, 120.

12. Zuhur, *Revealing Reveiling,* 5, 8.

13. Laura Deeb's study of women of the Hezbollah during the 1990s vividly documents a similar process under way in Lebanon. *An Enchanted Modern: Gender and Public Piety in Shi'i Lebanon* (Princeton, N.J.: Princeton University Press), 2006.

Chapter 6. Islamist Connections

1. Gilles Kepel, *Muslim Extremism in Egypt: The Prophet and Pharaoh,* trans. Jon Rothschild, With a New Preface for 2003 (Berkeley: University of California Press, 2003), 142–43. See also Ghada Hashem Talhami, *The Mobilization of Muslim Women in Egypt* (Gainesville: University Press of Florida, 1996), 53.

2. Kepel, *Extremism,* 142–43.

3. Gilles Kepel, *Jihad: The Trail of Political Islam,* trans. Anthony F. Roberts (Cambridge, Mass.: Belknap Press of Harvard University Press, 2000), 82.

4. Talhami, in *Mobilization,* says, regarding the bus service and the separate seating, that "female students . . . welcomed the Islamist assistance" (53).

5. Kepel, *Extremism,* 144.

6. Material cited in this and the following three paragraphs is from Kepel, *Extremism,* 145–46, 152–53.

7. Sherifa Zuhur, *Revealing Reveiling: Islamic Gender Ideology in Contemporary Egypt* (Albany: State University of New York Press, 1992), 127.

8. Quotations in this and the following paragraph are from Talhami, *Mobilization,* 47–48, 52.

9. Talhami, *Mobilization,* 49, 52. See also Carnegie Papers, *Women in Islamist Movements: Towards an Islamist Model of Women's Activism,* Omayma Abdellatif [*sic*] and Marina Ottaway, Carnegie Middle East Center, no. 2, June 2007; Carnegie Papers, *In the Shadow of the Brothers the Women of the Egyptian Muslim Brotherhood,* Omayma Abdel-Latif [*sic*], Carnegie Middle East Center, no. 13, October 2008.

10. Talhami, *Mobilization,* 132–33, 67.

11. Talhami, *Mobilization,* 128, 66.

12. Raymond William Baker, *Islam Without Fear: Egypt and the New Islamists* (Cambridge, Mass.: Harvard University Press, 2003), 96–97.

13. Material cited in this and the following four paragraphs is from Talhami, *Mobilization,* 65, 70–3, 134, 145.

14. Material cited in this and the following three paragraphs is from Talhami, *Mobilization,* 55, 125, 134, 138.

15. Linda Herrera, "Islamization and Education in Egypt: Between Politics, Culture, and the Market," in *Modernizing Islam: Religion in the Public Sphere in Europe and the Middle East,* ed. John L. Esposito and François Burgat (New Brunswick, N.J.: Rutgers University Press, 2003), 167–88. Herrara notes that schools for the middle and upper classes also increased religious teaching.

16. Herrera, "Islamization and Education," 172.

17. Carrie Rosefsky Wickham, *Mobilizing Islam: Religion, Activism, and Political Change in Egypt* (New York: Columbia University Press, 2002), 110; Herrera, "Islamization and Education," 172.

18. Kepel, *Jihad,* 276–78.

19. Wickham, *Mobilizing Islam,* 155.

20. Fauzi Najjar writes that "Foda considered himself a true Muslim." Najjar in "The Debate on Islam and Secularism in Egypt," *Arab Studies Quarterly* 18, no. 2 (Spring 1996).

21. Baker, *Islam Without Fear,* 83–84, 53.

22. Douglas Jehl, "Mohammed al-Ghazali, 78, an Egyptian Cleric and Scholar," *New York Times,* March 14, 1996.

23. Najjar, "Debate on Islam and Secularism in Egypt." See also Gregory Starrett, *Putting Islam to Work: Education, Politics, and Religious Transformation in Egypt* (Berkeley: University of California Press, 1998), 210–11; and Baker, *Islam Without Fear,* 190–91. Baker portrays al-Ghazali more favorably, claiming that his testimony was distorted by others. However, al-Ghazali does bear partial responsibility, Baker argues, "because he failed to elaborate his views" (190–91).

24. In fact, in a book entitled *Bitter Harvest: The Muslim Brotherhood in Sixty Years,* Ayman al-Zawahiri would launch a fierce attack on the Brotherhood, accusing its leaders of blasphemy on the grounds that they "substituted the democracy of the dark ages to God's rule and gave up on jihad." Such Islamists, he argued, had "sold out their faith to the corrupt secular regimes in return for . . . participation in the socio-political process." Cited in Fawaz A. Gerges, *The Far Enemy: Why Jihad Went Global* (New York: Cambridge University Press, 2005), 111.

25. Kepel, *Jihad,* 289. See also Azza Karam, ed., *Transnational Political Islam: Religion, Ideology, and Power,* foreword by John Esposito (London: Pluto, 2004), 7.

26. Quotations in this and the following paragraph are from Wickham, *Mobilizing Islam,* 103, 122.

27. The article reads more fully: "From inside the private mosque, the light of re-

ligious extremism beams forth . . . after the militant groups dominate the mosques, they plan inside them to assassinate prominent people and publish propaganda, execute terrorist activities, and store weapons." "From Here Extremism Begins: The Independent Mosques," *Akhir Sa'a,* December 2, 1992, 12–13, cited in Wickham, *Mobilizing Islam,* 103, 154–55.

28. Quotations in this and the following seven paragraphs are from Herrera, "Islamization and Education," 173–80.

29. Starrett, *Putting Islam to Work,* 90.

30. Quotations in this and the following three paragraphs are from Wickham, *Mobilizing Islam,* 2–3, 15, 26.

31. John L. Esposito, *Unholy War: Terror in the Name of Islam* (New York: Oxford University Press, 2002), 92–93.

32. Quotations in this and the following three paragraphs are from Wickham, *Mobilizing Islam,* 15, 125–27.

33. Quotations in this and the following two paragraphs are from Wickham, *Mobilizing Islam,* 132–33, 153, 170.

34. Wickham, *Mobilizing Islam,* 130.

35. Quotations in this and the following three paragraphs are from Wickham, *Mobilizing Islam,* 128, 131, 155, 171.

36. Material in this and the following two paragraphs is from Wickham, *Mobilizing Islam,* x–xi, 171.

37. Wickham, *Mobilizing Islam,* 172. One former jihadist who had been in prison would articulate these views particularly succinctly. Kamal Habib explained that he had married a woman he met at university and that they lived simply: "We need very little, live life simply, don't need fancy cars and apartments and all that. . . . We live very simply, but we don't feel poor. Society imposes shackles on people; it pressures them to worry about clothes and apartments and money"(168). Habib's prediction was that "the future is with us . . . the neighborhoods, because they did not change when the upper classes began to imitate the west . . . American society is in decline. All societies pass through phases, they rise and fall. Now is a period of transition. Soon Islam will be resurgent" (171).

38. This and the following quotation are from Wickham, *Mobilizing Islam,* 172–73.

39. An even more recent book based on research on Islamic women in Egypt is Saba Mahmood's *Politics of Piety: The Islamic Revival and the Feminist Subject (*Princeton, N.J.: Princeton University Press, 2005). As Cynthia Nelson observed in her review, this is a book which engages throughout its five chapters in "a running argument with and against key analytic concepts in liberal thought as these concepts have come to inform various strands of feminist theory," and it is to this field that the book makes its most significant contributions. Cynthia Nelson, "'The Politics of Piety: The Islamic Revival and the Feminist Subject,' by Saba Mahmood," *Middle East Journal* 59, no. 3 (Summer 2005): 507–10. With these issues in the foreground, Mahmood seems distinctly less interested in exploring the historical, social, political and religious currents and fierce

internal struggles shaping the local Egyptian scene. See Samah Selim, "Book Review: 'The Politics of Piety: The Islamic Revival and the Feminist Subject.'" Jadaliyya, October 2010: http://www.jadaliyya.com/pages/index/235.

Chapter 7. Migrations

1. Material in this and the following paragraph is from Kambiz GhaneaBassiri, *A History of Islam in America: From the New World to the New World Order* (New York: Cambridge University Press, 2010), chapter 6.

2. Karen Isaksen Leonard, *Muslims in the United States: The State of Research* (New York: Sage Foundation, 2003), 9.

3. These are the figures that Sherman A. Jackson, for instance, gives in *Islam and the Blackamerican: Looking Toward the Third Resurrection* (New York: Oxford University Press, 2005), 23. Estimates vary, but overall the relative proportions remain similar, with African Americans and Asian Americans in the lead.

4. I have heard Sulayman Nyang—a Muslim academic and community leader—among others make a point of emphasizing this fact in speeches he has given at Islamic conferences, among them, for example, at the ICNA-MAS Annual Convention 2002: "Islam in North America Challenges, Hopes and Responsibilities," July 5–7, 2002, Baltimore.

5. GhaneaBassiri, *History,* chapter 6. GhaneaBassiri writes also, "Of the 181,036 immigrants who came to the United States from Muslim-majority countries between 1966 and 1982, for example, 20 percent came under the category professional and technical workers and 56 percent came as the dependents of these individuals."

6. See GhaneaBassiri, *History,* chapter 6. Also, writing on Islam in America and describing Islamism and the Islamist activist agenda, Larry Poston writes, "At the same time, even a casual acquaintance with indigenous Muslim communities is enough to convince the unbiased observer that no more than a tiny minority perceives an activist mission as being a religious duty at all." Larry Poston, *Islamic Da'wah in the West: Muslim Missionary Activity and the Dynamics of Conversion to Islam* (New York: Oxford University Press, 1992), 4.

7. Beshir Adam Rehma, "How to Establish an Islamic Center: A Step-by-Step Approach," in *Let Us Learn: Issues of Your Concern,* ed. Abdel-Hadi Omer (Beloit, Wis.: By the Editor, 1987); cited in Poston, *Islamic Da'wah,* 79, 206.

8. Gutbi Mahdi Ahmed, "Muslim Organizations in the United States," in *The Muslims of America,* ed. Yvonne Yazbeck Haddad (New York: Oxford University Press, 1991), 14.

9. Poston, *Islamic Da'wah,* 79.

10. Ahmed, "Muslim Organizations," 14.

11. Ahmed, "Muslim Organizations," 14.

12. GhaneaBassiri, *History,* chapter 5, also makes this point, citing Yvonne Y. Haddad, "Arab Muslims and Islamic Institutions in America: Adaptation and Reform," in *Arabs in the New World,* ed. Sameer Y. Abraham and Nabeel Abraham (Detroit: Wayne

State University Press, 1983), 70. Poston similarly notes that the MSA was "undoubtedly the most activist of the da'wa organizations in America. Many of the founding members of this agency were members of or had connections to one or the other of two organizations in question and it was through these persons that the ideologies of al-Banna and Maududi were integrated into the goals and philosophies of the organization." Poston, "Da'wa in the West," in *The Muslims of America,* ed. Yvonne Yazbeck Haddad (New York: Oxford University Press, 1991), 129.

13. Ahmed, "Muslim Organizations," 14.

14. GhaneaBassiri, *History,* chapter 5.

15. GhaneaBassiri, *History,* chapter 5.

16. Poston, *Islamic Da'wah,* 79, 193. Poston is here citing Yvonne Yazbeck Haddad and Adair T. Lummis, *Islamic Values in the United States: A Comparative Study* (New York: Oxford University Press, 1984). He also cites Ihsan Bagby as stating that ISNA "has always sought inspiration and guidance from the intellectual leaders of the modern Islamic movement (Maududi, Sayyid Qutb, Hasan al-Banna, etc.)"; see "Is ISNA an Islamic Movement?" *Islamic Horizons* (ISNA's magazine), March 1986, 4.

17. Robert Dannin says that El-Hajj Wali Akram founded the "First Cleveland Mosque in 1932, which is now the oldest continuously running Muslim institution in America." Akram was an African American born in Texas who was converted to Islam —by Ahmadiyyas—in 1925. He subsequently turned to orthodoxy. Robert Dannin, *Black Pilgrimage to Islam* (New York: Oxford University Press, 2002), 5, 37, 102–3.

18. GhaneaBassiri, *History,* chapter 4.

19. Ahmed, "Muslim Organizations," 15.

20. Poston, *Islamic Da'wah,* 104.

21. Poston, *Islamic Da'wah,* 105, 127.

22. Material in this and the following paragraph is from GhaneaBassiri, *History,* chapter 5.

23. Material in this and the following paragraph is from Hamid Algar, *Wahhabism: A Critical Essay* (Oneonta, N.Y.: Islamic Publications, 2002), 51–52.

24. Poston "Da'wa in the West,"131.

25. Ahmed, "Muslim Organizations," 15–16.

26. Ahmed, "Muslim Organizations," 15.

27. Steve A. Johnson, "Political Activity of Muslims in America," in *The Muslims of America,* ed. Yvonne Yazbeck Haddad (New York: Oxford University Press, 1991), 119. Bagby gives 962 as the number of mosques in America in 1994, in *The Mosque in America: A National Portrait,* a report from the Mosque Study Project, Ihsan Bagby, Paul M. Perl, and Bryan T. Froehle (Washington, D.C.: Council on American-Islamic Relations, April 26, 2001), 3.

28. Poston, "Da'wa in the West," 129.

29. Poston, *Islamic Da'wah,* 106.

30. Johnson, "Political Activity," 111–12.

31. Leonard, *Muslims in the United States,* 88.

32. GhaneaBassiri notes that ICNA is not an exclusively South Asian organization but that it is still dominated by South Asians and generally conducts its meetings in Urdu. *History,* chapter 5.

33. Johnson, "Political Activity," 112.

34. Hassan Hathout, Fathi Osman, and Maher Hathout, *In Fraternity: A Message to Muslims in America* (Los Angeles: Minaret, 1989), 3–4, 13–15.

35. Karen Isaksen Leonard, *Muslims in the United States: The State of Research* (New York: Sage Foundation, 2003), 102.

36. GhaneaBassiri, *History,* chapter 6.

37. Pew Report, "Muslim Americans: Middle Class and Mostly Mainstream," May 22, 2007, 8 and 23–25.

38. See, for instance, Bagby and Froehle, *Mosque in America.*

39. GhaneaBassiri, *History,* chapter 6.

40. This quotation and those in the following paragraph are from GhaneaBassiri, *History,* chapter 6.

41. Edward E. Curtis IV, "Islamism and Its African American Muslim Critics: Black Muslims in the Era of the Arab Cold War," in *American Quarterly* 59, no. 3 (September 2007): 683–709; 690.

42. Curtis, "Islamism," 692. See also Jackson, *Islam and the Blackamerican,* 49.

43. Quotations in this and the following 2 paragraphs are from Curtis, "Islamism," 692–94.

44. Curtis, "Islamism," 693.

45. Malcolm X with Alex Haley, *The Autobiography of Malcolm X* (New York: Ballantine, 1999), 346–47.

46. Curtis, "Islamism," 694–95. In an interview on *Democracy Now,* Tariq Ramadan, the European Muslim intellectual and son of Said Ramadan, noted that after going on hajj Malcolm X came back through Geneva and met with his father. Ramadan also says that the last letter Malcolm X was writing—the paper that was on his typewriter—was to his father, and that in it he had written, "'They are going to kill me,' because he knew this was going to happen, 'because I came back to the true Islam.' And in his mind, true Islam meant it's not black against white. It's all the people of principles against all the oppressors and colonizers. And at that point, he became very dangerous." http://democracynow.org/2010/4/9/once_banned_muslim_scholar_tariq_ramadan. Accessed May 15, 2010.

47. Curtis, "Islamism," 695.

48. Dannin, *Black Pilgrimage,* 58–61, 68–69.

49. GhaneaBassiri, *History,* chapter 6.

50. Jackson, *Islam and the Blackamerican,* 49.

51. Curtis, "Islamism," 702–3.

52. Quotations in this and the following paragraph are from GhaneaBassiri, *History,* chapter 6.

53. Jocelyne Cesari, *When Islam and Democracy Meet: Muslims in Europe and in the United States* (New York: Palgrave Macmillan, 2004), 188–90.

Chapter 8. The 1990s

1. Gilles Kepel, *The War for Muslim Minds,* trans. Pascale Ghazaleh (Cambridge, Mass.: Belknap Press of Harvard University Press, 2004), 154.

2. Gilles Kepel, *The Roots of Radical Islam,* trans. Jon Rothschild (London: Saqi, 2005), With a New Preface trans. Pascale Ghazaleh, 14.

3. Kepel, *War,* 156.

4. Lawrence Wright, *The Looming Tower: Al-Qaeda and the Road to 9/11* (New York: Knopf, 2006), 179.

5. Wright, *Looming Tower,* 179; Kepel, *War,* 156.

6. Kepel, *War,* 156.

7. Poston, "Da'wa in the West," in *The Muslims of America,* ed. Yvonne Yazbeck Haddad (New York: Oxford University Press, 1991), 129–30.

8. Fawaz A. Gerges, *The Far Enemy: Why Jihad Went Global* (New York: Cambridge University Press, 2005), 73.

9. Esposito, *Unholy War: Terror in the Name of Islam* (New York: Oxford University Press, 2002), 91.

10. Kepel, *Roots of Radical Islam,* 14.

11. Esposito, *Unholy War,* 90.

12. Wright, *Looming Tower,* 56–57.

13. Kepel writes: "In 1986, two years after his release from prison, the blind Sheik . . . obtained his first American visa through the CIA, which he used to attend conferences of Islamic students in the United States. Next he visited Pakistan, where he preached at Peshawar, lunched at the Saudi embassy in Islamabad, and was lionized at receptions heavily attended by Americans. The sheik was a leading figure in the campaign to recruit fighters who were ready to face martyrdom for the chance to enter paradise—and in the process bring about the fall of the Soviet system for the greater benefit of Washington, D.C." Kepel, *Jihad: The Trail of Political Islam,* trans. Anthony F. Roberts (Cambridge, Mass.: Belknap Press of Harvard University Press, 2000), 300–301.

14. Kepel, *War,* 89.

15. Kepel, *Jihad,* 301.

16. Kepel, *War,* 89.

17. Colin Miner, "Sources Claim CIA Aid Fueled Trade Center Blast," in *Boston Herald,* January 24, 1994, 4, cited in Kambiz GhaneaBassiri, *A History of Islam in America: From the New World to the New World Order* (Cambridge: Cambridge University Press, 2010), chapter 7.

18. Chalmers Johnson, *Blowback: The Costs and Consequences of American Empire* (New York: Henry Holt, 2001), 8. Cited in Azza Karam, ed., *Transnational Political Islam: Religion, Ideology, and Power,* foreword by John Esposito (London: Pluto, 2004), 12. See also Mahmood Mamdani, *Good Muslim, Bad Muslim: America, the Cold War, and the Roots of Terror* (New York: Three Leaves, 2005).

19. As discussed in Chapter 6. See also, for instance, Esposito, *Unholy War,* 92–93, and Carrie Rosefsky Wickham, *Mobilizing Islam: Religion, Activism, and Political Change in Egypt* (New York: Columbia University Press, 2002), 153.

20. Zachary Lockman, *Contending Visions of the Middle East: The History and Politics of Orientalism* (Cambridge: Cambridge University Press, 2004), 233. See in particular chapter 7, for Lockman's analysis of this thesis; see also GhaneaBassiri, *History,* chapter 7.

21. Lockman, *Contending Visions,* 233–34.

22. Samuel Huntington, "Clash of Civilizations," *Foreign Affairs* 72 (1993): 22–49; Lockman, *Contending Visions,* 234.

23. Saad Eddin Ibrahim, "Islamic Activism and the Western Search for a New Enemy," *Egypt, Islam, and Democracy: Critical Essays* (Cairo: American University in Cairo Press, 2002); Roy Mottahedeh, "The Clash of Civilizations: An Islamicist's Critique," *Harvard Middle Eastern and Islamic Review* 2 (1996): 1–26. See also Lockman, *Contending Visions,* 235–36.

24. The quotation in this and the following paragraph are from GhaneaBassiri, *History,* chapter 7.

25. Lockman, *Contending Visions,* 254–55.

26. GhaneaBassiri, *History,* chapter 7.

27. Quotations in this and the following paragraph are from Lockman, *Contending Visions,* 255–57.

28. E.g., the George Polk Award for best TV documentary.

29. This and the quotation in the following paragraph are from Robert I. Friedman, "One Man's Jihad," *Nation,* May 15, 1995, 655–58.

30. This and the quotation in the following paragraph are from Carla Hinton, "Murrah Building Bombing Shaped Muslim Organization," *Oklahoman,* May 3, 2008.

31. Leonard, *Muslims in the United States,* 26.

32. Khaled Abou El Fadl, *The Great Theft: Wrestling Islam from the Extremists* (New York: HarperSanFranciso, 2005), 5.

33. This as well as the quotation in the following paragraph are from *Islamic Extremism: A Viable Threat to U.S. National Security,* an Open Forum at the U.S. Department of State, January 7, 1999. Transcript of presentation by Sheikh Muhammad Hisham Kabbani (updated). The Islamic Supreme Council of America: http://web.archive.org/web/20060929175628/http://www.islamicsupremecouncil.org/bin/site/wrappers/extremism_inamerica_unveiling010799.html. Accessed April 21, 2010.

Kabbani also said that "extremist ideology" was spreading "very quickly into the universities through the national organizations, associations and clubs that they are establishing around the universities. Most of these clubs—and they are Muslim clubs and the biggest is the national one—are being run mostly by the extremist ideology."

34. Richard H. Curtiss, "Dispute Between U.S. Muslim Groups Goes Public," *Washington Report on Middle East Affairs,* April–May 1999, 71, 101. See also "Major Muslim Organizations Condemn Kabbani's Statements; American Muslim Leaders Demand Retraction and Apology," MSA-News, February 25, 1999. http://www.geocities.com/CapitolHill/Senate/8841/cair.text. Accessed March 13, 2008.

35. Laurie Goodstein, "A Nation Challenged: The Cleric, Muslim Leader Who Was Once Labeled an Alarmist, Is Suddenly a Sage," *New York Times,* October 28, 2001.

36. "A Statement on the Recent Conflict in the Middle East," *Islamic Horizons,* July–August 1990, 8–9. Cited in GhaneaBassiri, *History,* chapter 7.

37. This and the following quotations in the remaining paragraphs of this chapter are all from GhaneaBassiri, *History,* chapter 7.

Prologue to Part Two

1. Ann Coulter, "This Is War," *National Review Online,* September 13, 2001. Accessed August 8, 2010.

2. "Brutality Against Women and Children," Radio Address by Laura Bush, November 17, 2001. George Bush White House archives.gov. Accessed April 10, 2010.

3. Polly Toynbee, "Was It Worth It?" *Guardian,* November 13, 2002.

4. Hamid Dabashi, "Native Informers and the Making of the American Empire," *Al-Ahram Weekly,* Online, June 1–7, 2006, issue 797. http://weekly.ahram.org.eg/2006. Accessed February 20, 2010.

Chapter 9. Backlash

1. Dana Milbank and Emily Wax, "Bush Visits Mosque to Forestall Hate Crimes; President Condemns an Increase in Violence Aimed at Arab Americans," *Washington Post,* September 18, 2001.

2. Teresa Novelino, "Leaders Pray at National Cathedral," *ABC News,* September 14, 2001. Accessed April 10, 2008.

3. Milbank and Wax, "Bush Visits Mosque to Forestall Hate Crimes."

4. Yvonne Yazbeck Haddad, *Not Quite American? The Shaping of Arab and Muslim Identity in the United States* (Waco, Texas: Baylor University Press, 2004), 41.

5. Nadine Naber, "Look, Mohammed the Terrorist Is Coming!" in *Race and Arab Americans Before and After 9/11: From Invisible Citizens to Visible Subjects,* ed. Amaney Jamal and Nadine Naber (Syracuse: Syracuse University Press, 2008), 289–90.

6. Milbank and Wax, "Bush Visits Mosque to Forestall Hate Crimes."

7. Council on American-Islamic Relations (CAIR), *American Muslims, One Year After 9–11* (Washington, D.C.: CAIR, 2002), 16–17.

8. CAIR, *American Muslims,* 16–17.

9. CAIR, *American Muslims,* 12–13.

10. See, for example, CAIR, *American Muslims.* See also *The Status of Muslim Civil Rights in the United States, 2002: Stereotypes and Civil Liberties* (Washington, D.C.: Council on American-Islamic Relations, CAIR Research Center, 2002); *The Status of Muslim Civil Rights in the United States, 2003: Guilt by Association* (Washington, D.C.: Council on American-Islamic Relations, CAIR Research Center, 2003); Anny Bakalian and Mehdi Bozorgmehr, *Backlash 9/11: Middle Eastern and Muslim Americans Respond* (Berkeley: University of California Press, 2009), 144.

11. Naber, "Look, Mohammed the Terrorist Is Coming!" 294.

12. Bakalian and Bozorgmehr, *Backlash,* 145–46.

13. *Report on Hate Crimes and Discrimination Against Arab Americans: The Post-September 11 Backlash: September 11, 2001 to October 11, 2002,* Hussein Ibish, editor, Ann Steward, principal researcher (Washington, D.C.: American-Arab Anti-Discrimination Committee Research Institute, 2003), 64. Attacks also occurred on college campuses, including at Harvard, where a student was attacked in Harvard Square. See Juliet J. Chung, "Harvard Grad Student Assaulted in Alleged Hate Crime," *Harvard Crimson,* October 1, 2001. Other attacks on college students are mentioned in the following pages.

14. CAIR, *One Year After,* 28.

15. *Report on Hate Crimes,*66.

16. *Report on Hate Crimes,* 67.

17. Courtney Hickson, "Women Show Solidarity Wearing Hijab," *Daily Campus,* University of Connecticut, Storrs, October 2, 2001.

18. *Report on Hate Crimes,* 135.

19. *Report on Hate Crimes,* 136.

20. Sandy Banks, "Donning Scarves in Solidarity," *Los Angeles Times,* September 25, 2001. See also CAIR, *One Year After,* 16.

21. Alexa Capeloto, "Women Don Scarfs in Solidarity with Female Muslims; Event at Wayne State Is Like Ones Elsewhere," *Detroit Free Press,* October 18, 2001.

22. CAIR, *One Year After,* 16.

23. Feminist Majority Foundation, "Feminist Calendar Event Description—12/16/01: Scarves for Solidarity," http://www.feminist.org/calendar/cal_details.asp?idSchedule=958. Accessed June 10, 2006.

24. Capeloto, "Women Don Scarfs in Solidarity."

25. David Ian Miller, "Finding My Religion: After 9/11 Azadeh Zainab Sharif Started Wearing the Hijab," March 21, 2005, http://articles.sfgate.com/2005–03–21/news/17362464_1_muslim-student-muslim-women-hijab-or-scarf. Accessed April 24, 2010.

26. Jiltin Hingorani, "Islam Post 9/11: Islamophobia in Austin," News 8 Austin, www.news8austin.com, updated November 30, 2004.

27. Hingorani, "Islamophobia in Austin."

28. Emily Wax, "The Fabric of Their Faith; Since Sept. 11, Head Scarf More Meaningful for Many Muslim Women," *Washington Post,* May 19, 2002.

29. Wax, "Fabric of Their Faith."

30. Shiasta Aziz, "Viewpoint: Why I Decided To Wear the Veil," London, BBC News 24, updated September 12, 2003.

31. Aziz, "Viewpoint."

32. Wax, "Fabric of Their Faith."

33. The explanation for wearing hijab offered by the noted feminist academic Amina Wadud, for example, seems to clearly fall within these parameters. "As a descendent of African slave women," she wrote, "I have carried the awareness that my ancestors were not given any choice to determine how much of their bodies would be exposed at the auction block or in their living conditions. So I chose intentionally to cover my body as a means of reflecting my historical identity, personal dignity, and sexual in-

tegrity." Amina Wadud, *Inside the Gender Jihad: Women's Reform in Islam* (Oxford: Oneworld, 2006), 221.

34. Feminist critiques of the veil also continue to appear. Among the more substantive of these is Marnia Lazreg, *Questioning the Veil: Open Letters to Muslim Women* (Princeton, N.J.: Princeton University Press, 2009).

35. Bakalian and Bozorgmehr, *Backlash,* 149. See also Louise Cainkar, *Homeland Insecurity: The Arab and Muslim American Experience After 9/11* (New York: Sage Foundation, 2009); and Jocelyne Cesari, ed., *The Muslims in the West After 9/11: Religion, Politics, and Law* (London: Routledge, 2010).

36. Bakalian and Bozorgmehr, *Backlash,* 150–51.

37. Barbie Zelizer and Stuart Allan, eds., *Journalism After September 11* (London: Routledge, 2002), Foreword by Victor Navasky, xiii.

38. Suad Joseph and Benjamin D'Harlingue, "Arab Americans and Muslim Americans in the New York Times, Before and After 9/11," in Jamal and Naber, *Race and Arab Americans Before and After 9/11,* 242; and Amaney Jamal, "Civil Liberties and the Otherization of Arab and Muslim Americans," also in Jamal and Naber, 120.

39. Naber, "Look, Mohammed the Terrorist Is Coming!" 278.

40. David Cole, *Enemy Aliens: Double Standards, and Constitutional Freedoms in the War on Terrorism* (New York: New Press, 2003), 25.

41. Cole, *Enemy Aliens,* 30.

42. Jamal, "Civil Liberties and the Otherization of Arab and Muslim Americans," 115.

43. Doug Struck, "Canadian Was Falsely Accused, Panel Says," *Washington Post Foreign Service,* September 19, 2006.

44. Ian Austen, "Harper's Apology 'Means the World': Arar," *CBC News,* January 26, 2007. "Canadians Fault U.S. for Its Role in Torture Case," *New York Times,* September 19, 2006.

45. Nancy Murray, "Profiled: Arabs, Muslims, and the Post-9/11 Hunt for the 'Enemy Within,'" in *Civil Rights in Peril: The Targeting of Arabs and Muslims,* ed. Elaine C. Hagopian (Chicago: Haymarket, and London: Pluto, 2004), 40–41.

46. "Panel discussion on the Reported Abuses of Muslim Civil Rights in America," Karamah, Muslim Women Lawyers for Human Rights, http://www.karamah.org/news_panel_discussion.htm n.d. Accessed May 16, 2008. The article notes that "on January 2003 Karamah joined the Journal of Law and Religion in sponsoring a panel discussion on the overall status of the civil rights of Muslims in the U.S. with emphasis on the recent registration requirements announced by the Immigration and Naturalization Service [INS] and the subsequent mass detentions in Los Angeles."

47. *Report on Hate Crimes,* 119.

48. *Report on Hate Crimes,* 120–24.

49. Andrea Elliott, "Battle in Brooklyn, a Principal's Rise and Fall; Critics Cost Muslim Educator Her Dream School," *New York Times,* April 28, 2008.

50. Elliott, "Battle in Brooklyn." See also Andrea Elliott, "Federal Panel Finds Bias in Ouster of Principal," *New York Times,* March 12, 2010, in which Elliott reported that

a "federal commission—the United States Equal Opportunity Commission," acting on a complaint filed by Debbie Almontaser, found that New York City's Department of Education "discriminated" against Almontaser when they forced her to resign in 2007. The commission found that the Department "succumbed to the very bias the creation of the school was intended to dispel and a small segment of the public succeeded in imposing its prejudices on D.O.E. as an employer."

51. Jane Kramer, "The Petition: Israel, Palestine, and a Tenure Battle at Barnard," *New Yorker,* April 14, 2008, 53, 50.

52. Kramer, "Petition," 56–57.

53. A Message to Alumnae from President Judith Shapiro, November 11, 2006. Barnard Alumnae Affairs, Barnard College, New York.

54. American Association of University Professors (AAUP) 2003–04 Committee A Report, Chair, Joan Wallach Scott. http://www.aaup.org/AAUP/comm/rep/A/2003–04-CommAreport.htm. Accessed April 23, 2010.

55. Joan W. Scott, "Middle East Studies Under Siege," *Americans for Middle East Understanding* 30, no. 1 (January–March 2006). http://www.ameu.org/printer.asp?iid=265&aid=575. Accessed April 23, 2010.

56. American Association of University Professors, "Joan Wallach Scott on Threats to Academic Freedom," interview in *Academe Online* 2005. http://www.aaup.org/AAUP/pubsres/academe/2005/SO/Feat/scot.htm?PF=1. Accessed June 24, 2008. See also "Princeton Panelists Share Cautionary Tales of Dangers to Academic Freedom," *Washington Report on Middle East Affairs,* December 2005, 46–48.

57. "The Horowitz Corner," August 28, 2007. www.frontpagemag.com. Accessed January 6, 2010.

58. "Islamo-Fascism Awareness Week," Terrorism Awareness Project, information sheet. http://www.terrorismawareness.org/islamo-fascism-awareness-week/. Accessed July 26, 2009.

59. Barbara Ehrenreich, "It's Islamo-Fascism Awareness Week!" *Nation,* October 22, 2007.

60. This and the quotation in the following paragraph are from Katha Pollitt, "David Horowitz, Feminist?" *Nation,* November 1, 2007.

61. Cited in Yvonne Haddad, "The Post-9/11 Hijab as Icon," *Sociology of Religion* 68, no. 33 (2007): 253–67, 255.

62. Haddad, "Post-9/11 Hijab as Icon," 255.

63. As Paula Zahn noted when she interviewed Nelofer Pazira, the star of *Kandahar,* when the film debuted the previous year it had been "largely ignored," and now "the war in Afghanistan had stirred new interest." Paula Zahn and Nelofer Pazira, "'Kandahar' Mirrors Real Life Experience of Female Star," CNN Transcripts, April 23, 2010.

For an interesting analysis of *Return to Kandahar,* see Usamah Ansari, "Should I Go and Pull Her Burqa Off?" in *Critical Studies in Media Communication* 25, no. 1 (March 2008): 48–67.

64. Polly Toynbee, "Was it Worth It?" *Guardian,* November 13, 2002.

65. Lila Abu Lughod, "Do Muslim Women Really Need Saving? Anthropological

Reflections on Cultural Relativism and Its Others," *American Anthropologist* 104, no. 3 (2002).

66. Saba Mahmood, "Feminism, Democracy, and Empire: Islam and the War on Terror," in *Women's Studies on the Edge,* ed. Joan Wallach Scott (Durham, N.C.: Duke University Press, 2008).

67. Kate Legge, "Hoaxer So Hard to Read," *Weekend Australian,* July 31, 2004.

68. Mahmood, "Feminism, Democracy, and Empire," 83.

69. Hamid Dabashi, "Native Informers and the Making of the American Empire," *Al-Ahram Weekly,* June 1–7, 2006, no. 797. http://weekly.ahram,org.eg/2006. Accessed February 20, 2010.

70. Mahmood, "Feminism, Democracy, and Empire," 85, 93, 98.

71. Mahmood, "Feminism, Democracy, and Empire," 86–87. See also, for instance, Lila Abu Lughod, "The Active Social Life of 'Muslim Women's Rights': A Plea for Ethnography, Not Polemic, with Cases from Egypt and Palestine," *Journal of Middle Eastern Women's Studies* 6, no, 1 (Winter 2010).

72. Mahmood, "Feminism, Democracy, and Empire," 88–89.

73. See my *Women and Gender in Islam: Historical Roots of a Modern Debate* (New Haven: Yale University Press, 1992), chapter 8.

74. Mahmood, "Feminism, Democracy, and Empire," 100.

75. Abu Lughod, "Active Social Life of 'Muslim Women's Rights,'" 17.

76. Mahmood, "Feminism, Democracy, and Empire," 82.

Chapter 10. ISNA and the Women of ISNA

1. I attended several Islamic conventions in 2002, the first post-9/11 year, eager to observe how Muslim American organizations would respond to the times. These included the 11th annual convention of the American Muslim Council (AMC—an organization that is now defunct), "American Muslims: Part of America," June 27–30, Alexandria, Virginia; the convention held jointly by the Islamic Circle of North America (ICNA) and the Muslim American Society (MAS), "Islam in North America: Challenges, Hopes, and Responsibilities," July 5–7, Baltimore; and ISNA's 39th annual convention, "Islam: A Call for Peace and Justice," August 30–September 2, Washington, D.C. Only one of the Islamic conferences I attended that year, held in March—and thus before the Yasin controversy had erupted —had not included him on its program. This conference was ISNA's "Community Development Conference," which included the discussion "Muslims Against Domestic Violence: Conflict Resolution Training Program, Marriage Counseling Training Seminar, Islamic Perspectives on Counseling, Imam Training Program," March 29–31, Chicago.

2. Richard Bradley, *Harvard Rules: The Struggle for the Soul of the World's Most Powerful University* (New York: HarperCollins, 2005), 162.

3. Bradley, *Harvard Rules,* 158–63.

4. Quotations and material in this paragraph are, in order, from Bradley, *Harvard Rules,* 164; Ann H. Kofol, "Yasin Delivers Heavily Debated 'Jihad' Speech," *Harvard Crimson,* June 28, 2002; and Bradley, *Harvard Rules,* 163.

5. Zayed Yasin, "Of Faith and Citizenship," Senior English Address, 2002. Reprinted from *Harvard Magazine*, July–August 2002; Harvard Archives, General Information on Harvard Commencement and Class Day in 2002 (Commencement Box 2002).

6. Kofol, "Yasin Delivers Heavily Debated 'Jihad' Speech."

7. Robert S. Mueller gave the Friday Luncheon Address at AMC's Convention. See Program, "AMC's 11th National Convention, American Muslims: Part of America," June 27–30, 2002. See also *AMC Report* 11, no. 2 (Summer 2002): 1. Karen Hughes's visit was reported in the press; see, for instance, Laurie Goodstein, "From State Dept., Advice for Muslim Convention," *New York Times*, September 3, 2005. Hughes's presence was also widely announced during the 2005 ISNA convention.

8. Versions of this phrase occurred numerous times in the course of these conferences. It figured too, for example, in the "Message from the Convention Chair," of the ICNA-MAS Convention that year, printed on the inside page of the program. "During the current times of tests and tribulations," the message from Naeem Saroya, chairperson, read, "we Muslims have to play an important role in removing the oppression, the corruption and the other evil elements from our society and our home, America, to make it a better and a safer place for many generations to come." ICNA-MSA Program Guide, July 5–7, 2002.

9. Sulayman Nyang, speaking at the ICNA-MAS Annual Convention 2002, my notes.

10. Mumtaz Ahmed, speaking at the ICNA-MAS Annual Convention 2002, my notes.

11. Nyang, conclusion of his talk at ICNA-MAS Annual Convention 2002, cited above.

12. ISNA Annual Convention 2002, my notes.

13. ISNA Annual Convention 2007, my notes.

14. An article reporting on the conference noted that "for the first time two non-Muslim women were invited as the guest speakers, which is something of a new tradition for conservative groups such as ICNA and MAS." "ICNA and MAS: Moving Kinship Closer," *Islamic Horizons*, September–October 1423/2002, 16.

15. The programs of the conventions list Stanley Cohen and Karen Armstrong at the AMC's Annual Convention, 2002, Grayland Hagler, Welton Gaddy, Yvonne Haddad, and Ralph Nader at the ICNA-MAS Annual Convention, 2002, and James Zogby, Hilary Shelton, and David Bonior at ISNA's Annual Convention, 2002.

16. Material in this and the following paragraph are from "ICNA and MAS: Moving Kinship Closer" and from my notes of this conference.

17. Amy Goodman and Robert Fisk were at the ISNA Convention of 2006, and Richard Killmer, Herrick-Stare, and Cole were at the ISNA Annual Convention of 2007. See programs. See also Tom Curry, "Two Faith-Based Lobbyists Work the Capitol, a Quaker Urges Patriot Act Limits; a Conservative Christian Works for Restrictions on Abortion," msnbc.com, March 24, 2005. Accessed July 25, 2009.

18. Quotations in this and the following paragraph are from my notes of the ISNA Convention 2007.

19. "Remarks to Islamic Society of North America," 44th Annual Convention, Chicago, August 31, 2007, by Rabbi Eric H. Yoffie, president, Union of Reform Judaism. From a copy of his speech forwarded to me by Debra Eichenbaum, Program Associate for the Commission of Religious Affairs, Religious Action Center of Reform Judaism.

20. Arthur Waskow, "Judeo-Christo-Fascism Awareness Week Comes to American Campuses!" October, 10, 2007, Shalom Center. http://www.theshalomcenter.org/node/1305. Accessed April 24, 2010. See also, for instance, "Widespread Denunciation of 'Islamo-Fascism Awareness Week,'" in Jews on First! http://jewsonfirst.org/07c/islamo_fascism.html. Accessed July 26, 2009.

21. House Judiciary Committee Hearing, "Muslim American Civil Rights: Citizens' Hearing on the Status of Civil Rights and Liberties After the September 11 Attacks," C-Span, October 13, 2004. http://www.cspanarchives.org/library/index.php?main_page=product_video_info&products_id=183921–1&showVid=true. Accessed August 2, 2009.

22. From Haddad's talk at ICNA Annual Convention 2002, my notes.

23. See ISNA Convention Program 2002, 55.

24. ISNA Annual Convention 2002, my notes.

25. I heard this comment at ISNA's "Community Development Conference, Muslims Against Domestic Violence: Conflict Resolution Training Program, Marriage Counseling Training Seminar, Islamic Perspectives on Counseling, Imam Training Program," March 29–31, 2002, Chicago, my notes.

26. ISNA Annual Convention 2002, my notes.

27. A report issued in 2001, for example, noted that in 2001, 66 percent of mosques had women praying behind a curtain or partition or in another room. In 1994, only 52 percent of mosques had maintained such separation, and thus the "practice of having women pray behind a curtain or in another room is becoming more widespread," the report noted. Ihsan Bagby, Paul M. Perl, and Bryan T. Froehle, *The Mosque in America: A National Portrait,* Mosque Study Project (Washington, D.C.: Council on American-Islamic Relations, 2001), 11.

28. "Islam, Activism, and Social Justice," Panel, ISNA Annual Convention 2005, my notes. See also podcast of this panel at http://ihsan-net.blogspot.com/2005/09/islam-and-social-justice.html.

29. Asra Q. Nomani, "Time for Muslim Organizations to Campaign for Women's Rights in Mosques," Muslim WakeUp! September 8, 2004. A statement at the end of article notes: "This article was adapted from a presentation given by Ms. Nomani on September 4, 2004, at the Annual Convention of the Islamic Society of North America (ISNA)." www.muslimwakeup.com/mainarchive/2004. Accessed July 13, 2008.

30. Sabreen Akhtar, "An Example to Live By: Asra Nomani at the ISNA Convention," *Muslim Wakeup!* September 8, 2004. http://www.muslimwakeup.com/mainarchive/2004. Accessed July 13, 2008.

31. "Women Friendly Mosques and Community Centers: Working Together to

Reclaim Our Heritage" (n.d.). The booklet lists the following organizations as supporting it: Council on American Islamic relations—Canada; Islamic Circle of North America; Islamic Society of North America; Muslim Alliance in North America; Muslim Association of Canada; MSA-National. http://www.islamawareness.net/Mosque/WomenAndMosquesBooklet.pdf. Accessed April 26, 2010. I first received an email announcement of its distribution in June 2005.

32. "Women Friendly Mosques," 3–4.

33. Hadia Mubarak, "My Hijab Is for Me and for God," Newsweek.washingtonpost.com: "On Faith: A Conversation on Religion with Jon Meacham and Sally Quinn." Posted July 27, 2007. http://newsweek.washingtonpost.com/onfaith/panelists/hadia_mubarak/2007/07/women_are_more_than_just_mens.html? Accessed April 26, 2010.

34. Mubarak, "My Hijab Is for Me and for God."

35. "ISNA online matrimonial service is a web-based matrimonial service that provides networking opportunities for Muslims seeking a spouse. This site includes a rich database of members with detailed profiles and communication platform. By becoming a member you can create profiles and communicate with other members of this program. A number of different membership options are available based on your special needs." From ISNA website, "ISNA Matrimonials," http://www.isna.net/Matrimonial/pages/Matrimonial.aspx. Accessed January 16, 2010.

36. Ahmed Nassef, "Mike Knight Speaking at ISNA!" Muslim WakeUp! September 4, 2004. http://web.archive.org/web/20040909100829/www.muslimwakeup.com/archives/00184. Accessed July 13, 2008.

37. Umbreen Shah, "ISNA Thugs," Muslim WakeUp! September 7, 2005. Accessed July 13, 2008.

38. Michael Muhammad Knight, "Wresting with Muzzamil: The 2003 ISNA Convention," Muslim WakeUp! September 6, 2003. http://www.muslimwakeup.com/mainarchive/000195.html. Accessed June 6, 2008.

39. See Carnegie Papers, "Women in Islamist Movements: Towards an Islamist Model of Women's Activism," Omayma Abdellatif [*sic*] and Marina Ottaway, Carnegie Middle East Center, no. 2, June 2007. See also Carnegie Papers, "In the Shadow of the Brothers the Women of the Egyptian Muslim Brotherhood," Omayma Abdel-Latif [*sic*], Carnegie Middle East Center, no. 13, October 2008.

40. In Morocco, Nadia Yassine is the very visible spokeswoman for the Justice and Spirituality Party founded by her father. Nevertheless, she holds no position of official leadership in the party other than as leader of the women's division. See Euben and Zaman, *Princeton Readings,* 303. Yassine's prominence exemplifies another pattern by which women have risen to power in Islamic societies: as the wives or daughters of prominent men. Such was the path followed by Benazir Bhutto, daughter of Zulfikar Ali Bhutto, former prime minister of Pakistan, who herself became prime minister, and by Megawati Sukarnoputri, daughter of President Sukarno of Indonesia and later president of the country herself. Evidently then, within secular political parties, in contrast to Islamist organizations (in the Sunni world at any rate), women were able to formally take on positions of leadership.

41. Matthai Chakko Kuruvila, "Woman Leads a Wave of Change for U.S. Muslims," *San Francisco Chronicle,* November 24, 2006. http://articles.sfgate.com/2006–11–24/news/17319351_1_ingrid-mattson-american-muslims-muslim-chaplains/2. Accessed April 26, 2010.

42. Kuruvila, "Woman Leads a Wave of Change."

43. Personal conversations with women at ISNA conventions in 1999 and 2001. Also personal observations at the ISNA March 2002 conference on domestic violence. Also, for women serving as volunteers and their serving on boards, see Bagby et al., *Mosque in America.*

44. John Perry Barlow, "Africa Rising," *Wired,* January 1, 1998. http://www.wired.com. Accessed June 4, 2008. Andrea Useem describes McGee as "co-founder of Muslim Family Services, a social service organization serving the Muslim community in the greater Columbus, Ohio, area. She has worked with domestic violence survivors for many years and has advised the Islamic Society of North America on the issue." Useem, "Does the Qur'an Tolerate Domestic Abuse?" Beliefnet.com. http://www.beliefnet.com/Faiths/Islam/2007/07/Does-The-Quran-Tolerate-Domestic-Abuse.aspx. Accessed June 2, 2008.

45. Bonita McGee, Presentation, Islamic Society of North America Community Development Conference, March 29–31, 2002, Chicago, my notes.

46. Delinda C. Hanley, "In Memoriam: Dr. Sharifa Alkhateeb (1946–2004)," *Washington Report on Middle East Affairs,* December 2004, 51. http://washington-report.org/archives/December_2004/0412051.html. Accessed March 25, 2008.

47. Matt Schudel, "Sharifa Alkhateeb Dies; U.S. Muslim Scholar," *Washington Post,* October 27, 2004. http://www.washingtonpost.com/ac2/wp-dyn/A766–2004Oct26?language=printer. Accessed April 26, 2010.

48. Suzannah Evans, "Sharifa Alkhateeb, Muslim Activist, Dies; Ashburn Resident Had Educated Americans about Muslim Life for Decades," *Ashburn Connection,* November 5, 2004. http://www.connectionnewspapers.com/article.asp?article=245938&paper=67&cat=104. Accessed April 26, 2010.

49. Jennifer Bayot, "Sharifa Alkhateeb, Feminist Within Islam, Dies at 58," *New York Times,* November 4, 2004.

50. Schudel, "Sharifa Alkhateeb Dies."

51. "Remembering Sharifa Alkhateeb: A Tribute Page from the Pluralism Project," Pluralism Project at Harvard University. http://www.pluralism.org/wn/sharifa. Accessed June 6, 2008.

52. Maha B. Alkhateeb and Salma Elkadi Abugideiri, *Diverse Perspectives on Domestic Violence in Muslim Communities* (N.p.: Peaceful Families Project, 2007).

53. Khadija Haffajee, "Rawahil," in *Muslim Women Activists in North America Speaking for Ourselves,* ed. Katherine Bullock (Austin: University of Texas Press, 2005), 79. Quotations in the following seven paragraphs are all from this text (79–87).

54. Quotations in this and the following three paragraphs are from Shereen Khan, "Transcending Immediate Comfort Zones: The Making of an Interfaith Movement and Need for Religious Literacy in a Post 9/11 World," *Illume,* no. 9 (n.d.): 116–17.

55. Nimat Hafez Barazangi, "Silent Revolution of a Muslim Arab American Scholar-Activist," in Bullock, *Muslim Women Activists,* 1–2, 10, 13–14.

56. Ekram Beshir, "Allah Doesn't Change the Condition of People Until They Change Themselves," in Bullock, *Muslim Women Activists,* 25–26, 204.

57. Beshir, "Allah Doesn't Change," 23.

Chapter 11. American Muslim Women's Activism in the Twenty-First Century

1. Quotations in this and the following paragraph are from Tayyibah Taylor, "Undoing Internalized Inferiority," in *Muslim Women Activists in North America Speaking for Ourselves,* ed. Katherine Bullock (Austin: University of Texas Press, 2005), 193–95.

2. Taylor, "Undoing Internalized Inferiority," 196; Tayyibah Taylor, "Lost in Translation," *Azizah* 4, no. 4 (June 2007): 39.

3. Laleh Bakhtiar, *The Sublime Quran* (Islamicworld.com; Chicago: Kazi, 2007), xliii.

4. Bakhtiar, *Sublime Quran,* xliii.

5. Material in this and the following two paragraphs is from Bakhtiar, *Sublime Quran,* lii–lv.

6. Leslie Scrivener, "Furor over a Five-Letter Word," *Toronto Star,* October 21, 2007.

7. Ingrid Mattson, "Re: Statements Made by ISNA Canada Secretary General Regarding Laleh Bakhtiar's Quran Translation," October 24, 2007. http://www.isna.net/articles/Press-Releases/PUBLIC-STATEMENT.aspx. Accessed April 28, 2010.

8. Mohammed Ayoob, *The Many Faces of Political Islam: Religion and Politics in the Muslim World* (Ann Arbor: University of Michigan Press, 2008).

9. Nadia Yassine, the prominent spokesperson for the Justice and Spirituality Party of Morocco, officially holds the position only of leader of the women's division. Roxanne L. Euben and Muhammad Qasim Zaman, eds., *Princeton Readings in Islamist Thought: Texts and Contexts from al-Banna to Bin Laden* (Princeton, N.J.: Princeton University Press, 2009), 303.

10. Andrea Useem, "Does the Quran Tolerate Domestic Abuse?" Beliefnet.com (n.d.). http://www.beliefnet.com/Faiths/Islam/2007/07/Does-The-Quran-Tolerate-Domestic-Abuse.aspx. Accessed June 2, 2008.

11. Useem, "Does the Quran Tolerate Domestic Abuse?"

12. Mubarak openly acknowledges in her article that she deliberately chose to write her paper while remaining within an "Islamic framework." Academics, she explains, "have a moral responsibility to engage the society in which they live in a purposeful and meaningful way," and she goes on to quote another Muslim interpreter, Asma Barlas, to reinforce her point: "It is safe to say that no meaningful change can occur in those societies that does not derive its legitimacy from the Quran's teachings, a lesson secular Muslims everywhere are having to learn to their detriment." Hadia Mubarak, "Breaking the Interpretative Monopoly: A Re-Examination of Verse 4:34," *Hawwa* 2, no. 3 (2004): 261–89; 264.

However, the problem with the position that Mubarak takes as regards scholars' responsibilities to engage with the "society in which they live" and remain within an "Islamic framework"—a position which she bolsters with Barlas's pragmatic view that anchoring debate in Quranic teachings is essential since otherwise the arguments advanced will lack legitimacy and thus be ineffective—is that such commitments may seriously interfere with another fundamental scholarly commitment: that of engaging forthrightly and without compromise with the issues at hand. Although it may be (or may appear to be) pragmatically a more effective strategy to remain within the preset bounds of acceptable thought, how persuasive in the end is the work of a scholar who explicitly and for whatever reasons, pragmatic or otherwise, commits herself or himself a priori to thinking only within the preset boundaries? What of the scholarly obligation to explore the commitments and assertions of communities as to the meanings and implications of words and ideas they hold to be sacred? (Mattson, for example, asked "more and more questions" of the nuns and priests of her Catholic faith and eventually left that faith because those she spoke with had no acceptable answers.) Similarly, what of the scholar's obligation to articulate the issues and concerns—as she or he sees them—that inhere in particular views or positions their communities affirm, regardless of whether their explorations and findings are likely to find acceptance?

13. Mubarak, "Breaking the Interpretative Monopoly," 263–64.

14. Useem, "Does the Quran Tolerate Domestic Abuse?"

15. See, for example, John L. Esposito and Dahlia Mogahed, *Who Speaks for Islam* (New York: Gallup, 2007), chapter 4, 118–19. See also Dahlia Mogahed and Irshad Manji, "Who Speaks for Islam?" a conversation between the two authors hosted by Aspen Institute, July 1, 2008.

16. Karen Bauer, "'Traditional' Exegeses of 4:34"; Kecia Ali, "'The Best of You Will Not Strike': Al-Shafi'i on Qur'an, Sunnah, and Wife-Beating"; Ayesha Siddiqua Chaudhry, "The Problems of Conscience and Hermeneutics: A Few Contemporary Approaches"; Laury Silvers, "In the Book We Have Left Out Nothing: The Ethical Problem of the Existence of Verse 4:34 in the Qur'an," all in *Comparative Islamic Studies* 2, no. 2 (2006).

17. Amina Wadud, *Inside the Gender Jihad: Women's Reform in Islam* (Oxford: Oneworld, 2006), 221.

18. Muslim Women's League, "Muslim Women Meet in Morgantown, [West Virginia,] to Create Historic New Women's Rights Group," n.d. http://www.mwlusa.org/news/muslim_women_meet_in_morgantown.htm. Accessed April 30, 2010. The Muslim Women's League, based in Los Angeles, describes itself as a "nonprofit American Muslim organization working to implement the values of Islam and thereby reclaim the status of women as free, equal and vital contributors to society." Core members of the Daughters of Hajar group included Asra Nomani, Amina Wadud, Saleemah Abdul-Ghafur, Sarah Eltantawi, and Samina Ali.

19. Quotations in this and the following paragraph are from "WVU Women's Studies to Co-Sponsor Literary Reading by Renowned Muslim Women," *West Virginia Today*, June 6, 2004. http://wvutoday.wvu.edu/n/2004/6/6/3934. Accessed April 30, 2010.

20. Laurie Goodstein, "Women's Mosque Protest Brings Furor in the U.S.," *New York Times*, July 22, 2004.

21. Andrea Elliott, "Woman Leads Muslim Prayer Service in New York," *New York Times,* March 19, 2005.

22. Omid Safi, ed., *Progressive Muslims: On Justice, Gender, and Pluralism* (Oxford: Oneworld, 2003), 2.

23. In Europe, for example, Tariq Ramadan takes up the issue in several of his books, including *Western Muslims and the Future of Islam* (New York: Oxford University Press, 2004).

24. The White House, Office of the Press Secretary, September 1, 2009. "Below is the list of some of the expected attendees at tonight's White House dinner celebrating Ramadan." http://www.whitehouse.gov/the_press_office/Expected-attendees-at-tonights-White-House-dinner-celebrating-Ramadan/. Accessed September 3, 2009.

25. All information in this paragraph taken from the ASMA Society website. http://www.asmasociety.org. Accessed April 30, 2010. As of early September 2010 (and since the completion of this manuscript), Imam Rauf and Daisy Khan have become widely known nationally as a result of the controversy that erupted around Park 51, the Islamic Community Center which Imam Rauf and others proposed building two blocks from Ground Zero.

26. Rasha Elass, "Guiding Light for Gender Progress." *National* [Abu Dhabi], United Arab Emirates, updated July 17, 2009. Posted on ASMA Society website, http://www.asmasociety.org, under "What's New . . . Press Releases." Accessed April 30, 2010.

27. Asifa Quraishi, University of Wisconsin Law School website.

28. Saleemah Abdul-Ghafur, Introduction, in *Living Islam Out Loud: American Muslim Women Speak,* ed. Saleemah Abdul-Ghafur (Boston: Beacon, 2005), 1.

29. Abdul-Ghafur, *Living Islam Out Loud,* 3–4.

30. Samina Ali, "How I Met God," in Abdul-Ghafur, *Living Islam Out Loud,* 30–31.

31. Khalida Saed, "On the Edge of Belonging," in Abdul-Ghafur, *Living Islam Out Loud,* 208, 90.

32. Saed, "On the Edge of Belonging," 92.

33. Precious Rasheeda Muhammad, "To Be Young, Gifted, Black, American, Muslim and Woman," in Abdul-Ghafur, *Living Islam Out Loud,* 37, 40.

34. Muhammad, "To be Young," 45.

35. Muslim Media Watch, http://www.muslimahmediawatch.org. Accessed April 30, 2010.

36. Mohja Kahf, "Spare Me the Sermon on Muslim Women," *Washington Post,* October 5, 2008; Kahf, "The Muslim in the Mirror," *Living Islam Out Loud,* 131, 207.

37. Abdul-Ghafur, *Living Islam Out Loud,* 4–5.

38. Yousra Y. Fazli, "Fumbling Toward Ecstasy," in Abdul-Ghafur, *Living Islam Out Loud,* 76.

39. I am grateful to my former student Amina Chaudary, who first drew my attention to this trend in a research paper she wrote: "De-Veiling: The American Muslim Woman's Experience," Spring 2009. Chaudary is preparing this paper for publication

and presenting a portion of it at the American Academy of Religion meeting, November 2010.

40. Andrea Useem, "Taking Off My Hijab," Beliefnet.com, no date. http://www.beliefnet.com/Faiths/Islam/2008/08/Taking-Off-My-Hijab.aspx. Accessed May 1, 2010. See also Useem, "Loving and Leaving the Head Scarf," Slate.com, May 12, 2008. http://www.slate.com/toolbar.aspx?action=print&id=2191103. Accessed May 1, 2010. See also Darah Rateb, "The Dehijabization Phenomenon," Altmuslim, March 30, 2009. http://www.altmuslim.com/a/a/a/2999/. Accessed May 1, 2010.

41. Useem, "Taking Off My Hijab."

42. "Muslim Leaders of Tomorrow," ASMA Society webpage. http://www.asmasociety.org/religion/mlt_04retreat.html. Accessed May 1, 2010.

43. A number of studies cast interesting light on Islamic schooling, hijab, and feminism: among these most notably are Jasmine Zine, *Canadian Islamic Schools* (Toronto: University of Toronto Press, 2008); K. Haw, "Why Muslim Girls Are More Feminist in Muslim Schools," in M. Griffiths and B. Troyna, eds., *Antiracism, Culture, and Social Justice in Education* (Stoke-on-Trent, U.K.: Trentham, 1997); and M. Parker-Jenkins and K. Haw, "Equality Within Islam, Not Without It: The Perspective of Muslim Girls in a Muslim School in Britain," *Muslim Educational Quarterly* 3, no. 3 (1996): 17–34.

44. See Mahmood Mamdani, *Good Muslim, Bad Muslim: America, the Cold War, and the Roots of Terror* (New York: Pantheon, 2004), capitalized as given here.

45. Asra Q. Nomani, *Standing Alone in Mecca: An American Woman's Struggle for the Soul of Islam* (San Francisco: HarperSan Francisco, 2005), 103.

46. Nomani, *Standing Alone,* 103, 30.

47. Irshad Manji, *The Trouble with Islam: A Muslim's Call for Reform in Her Faith* (New York: St. Martin's, 2004), 10–11.

48. Hirsi Ali writes that her mother "flourished in a country with such a strict religious climate." Ayaan Hirsi Ali, *The Caged Virgin: An Emancipation Proclamation for Women and Islam* (New York: Free Press, 2006), 71. For discussions and reviews of Hirsi Ali's work see among others Deborah Scroggins, "The Dutch-Muslim Culture War," *Nation,* June 27, 2005; and Ian Buruma, *Taming of the Gods: Religion and Democracy on Three Continents* (Princeton, N.J.: Princeton University Press, 2010).

49. Manji, *Trouble with Islam,* 11.

50. Nomani, *Standing Alone,* 22.

51. Some preliminary research has been done specifically on the topic of the representation of Jews and women in the textbooks available at some mosques. Freedom House, for example, published a report entitled *Saudi Publications on Hate Ideology Invade American Mosques* (2005).

The findings of this report, however, were disputed by a reviewer who pointed out a number of flaws to the study, though he also goes on to acknowledge that the report "highlights an ugly undercurrent in modern Islamic discourse" which American-Muslims need to confront. Junaid M. Affeef, "Are American Muslim Mosques Promoting Hate Ideology?" Altmuslim, February 4, 2005. http://www.altmuslim.com/a/a/a/2178/. Accessed May 1, 2010. Another work exploring textbooks in the Middle East further complicates the picture, pointing out that representations of Jews in Arab textbooks are often "in dialogue with Israeli textbooks," which "similarly represent Arabs pejoratively." Eleanor Abdella Doumato and Gregory Starrett, *Teaching Islam: Textbooks and Religion in the Middle East* (Boulder: Lynne Rienner, 2008).

52. Euben and Zaman, *Princeton Readings,* 303.

53. Aditi Banga, "Before Faust, Women Make Their Move," *Harvard Crimson,* June 4, 2007. Cited in Tori Moi, "'I Am Not a Woman Writer!': About Women, Literature, and Feminist Theory Today," Eurozine.com, published June 12, 2009. http://www.eurozine.com/articles/2009–06–12-moi-en.html. Accessed February 13, 2010.

54. Tariq Ahmad, "The Price of Being Born Muslim," *New York Times,* December 5, 2009.

55. *Religion Among the Millennials: Less Religiously Active Than Older Americans, But Fairly Traditional in Other Ways,* Pew Research Center Publications, February 17, 2010.

56. Yasmin Alibhai-Brown, "British Muslims Are Running Out of Friends," *Independent,* March 8, 2010.

57. The problematics of identity in which American Muslims, like other minorities, are caught up in America are not unlike—as Tori Moi illuminatingly explores in her essay "'I Am Not a Woman Writer!'"—those in which women may find themselves caught up in this country even to this day, as Drew Faust's implicitly corrective remarks (cited above), made as recently as 2007, themselves indicate.

Index